Nonviolence in America

THE AMERICAN HERITAGE SERIES

THE

American Heritage

Series

UNDER THE GENERAL EDITORSHIP OF

LEONARD W. LEVY AND ALFRED YOUNG

Nonviolence in America:

A DOCUMENTARY HISTORY

EDITED BY

STAUGHTON LYND

Yale University

THE BOBBS-MERRILL COMPANY, INC.

A Subsidiary of Howard W. Sams & Co., Inc.

PUBLISHERS • INDIANAPOLIS • NEW YORK • KANSAS CITY

Foreword

It is not surprising that this first collection of materials on the American tradition of nonviolence should appear in the 1960's when the disciples of Martin Luther King, Jr. and A. J. Muste have had so dramatic an impact on contemporary American life. Scholars, too, are inspired by movements around them and in the case of this anthology, it should be readily apparent that the influence of "the present" in the search for "the past" has been fruitful.

The emphasis on Mohandas Gandhi and Leo Tolstoy as the intellectual forerunners of contemporary nonviolence has obscured a fact that Staughton Lynd has amply documented: America "has more often been the teacher than the student of the nonviolent idea." From the Quakers of colonial America, through the abolitionists and peace crusaders of pre-Civil War years, the anarchists of the industrial era, and the pacifist progressives of the early twentieth century, down through the sit-down strikes of the 1930's and the conscientious objectors of two world wars, there has been an indigenous American tradition of nonviolent resistance to social evil.

The idea was expressed in many ways, as the variety of materials assembled in itself suggests. Here are the philosophic essays of Henry David Thoreau, William James, and Reinhold Neibuhr, seminal in importance; here are the philosophic manifestos of the Reverends King and Muste and Bayard Rustin, ideologues of the recent movements. Here, too, are documents of the experiences of the many little-known crusaders who expressed themselves by their deeds. For the 1960's the throbbing, vivid accounts of the Negro and white civil rights activists provide the documentation for which historians of later years will search.

Staughton Lynd is a citizen-historian who recalls in some ways the tradition of a Carl Becker or Charles Beard. Director of the "Freedom Schools" for the Council of Federated Organizations in Mississippi in the summer of 1964, he is an advocate of the nonviolent idea. He employs his talents as a historian in essential tasks of analysis: to distinguish the different forms of nonviolence (pacifism, direct action, civil disobedience), nonviolence as a "tactic" and as a "way of life"; to explore the relationship of movements of nonviolence with other methods of social change (political action, class conflict); and to probe the similarities and differences of the present movement with those of the past, their failures as well as their "successes." His Introduction is the first effort by a scholar to piece together the many strands of the nonviolent tradition in the United States. Like the book as a whole it beckons scholars to tread the paths he has opened, at the same time that it invites those who are dedicated to the goals of social justice and racial equality in a world at peace to clarify the means of reaching those goals.

This book is one of a series the aim of which is to provide the essential primary sources of the American experience, especially of American thought. The series, when completed, will constitute a documentary library of American history, filling a need long felt among scholars, students, libraries, and general readers for authoritative collections of original materials. Some volumes will illuminate the thought of significant individuals, such as James Madison or Louis Brandeis; some will deal with movements, organized around special themes, such as Puritan political thought, or American Catholic thought on social questions. Many volumes will take up the large number of subjects traditionally studied in American history for which, surprisingly, there are no documentary anthologies; others will pioneer in introducing contemporary subjects of increasing importance to scholars. The series aspires to maintain the high standards demanded of contemporary editing, providing authentic texts, intelligently and unobtrusively edited. It will also have the distinction of presenting pieces of substantial length that give the full character and flavor of the original. The series will be the most comprehensive and authoritative of its kind.

ALFRED YOUNG
LEONARD W. LEVY

Contents

PART III

Anarchists

PART IV

Progressives

PART V

Conscientious Objectors, World War I

PART VI

Trade Unionists

PART VII

Conscientious Objectors, World War II

PART VIII

Direct Action for Peace, Post-World War II

PART IX

Direct Action for Civil Rights, Post-World War II

PART X

Nonviolent Revolution

Introduction

This book attempts to present the history of the idea of nonviolence in America. While there are several good anthologies of writings on nonviolence currently in print, these do not provide a consecutive account of the American tradition of nonviolence. Moreover, there is no volume where one can find the full text of the key American essays on nonviolence—Thoreau's "Civil Disobedience," William James' "The Moral Equivalent of War," and Martin Luther King, Jr.'s "Pilgrimage to Non-violence"—brought together between two covers.

It is often supposed that nonviolence is a philosophy conceived by Gandhi and Tolstoy, and recently imported into the United States by Martin Luther King, Jr. The fact is that a distinctive American tradition of nonviolence runs back to the seventeenth century. Thoreau's influence on Gandhi is well-known. Tolstoy, too, was indebted to American predecessors. In "A Message to the American People," written in 1901, Tolstoy stated that "Garrison, Parker, Emerson, Ballou, and Thoreau . . . specially influenced me."[1] Three years later Tolstoy wrote that "Garrison was the first to proclaim this principle [of nonresistance to evil] as a rule for the organization of

---

[1] Quoted from the *North American Review* (April 1901) in Lev N. Tolstoy, *Miscellaneous Letters and Essays, The Complete Works of Count Tolstoy*, ed. Leo Wiener, XXIII (Boston: Dana Estes & Co., 1905), 462. See Ernest J. Simmons, *Leo Tolstoy* (Boston: Little, Brown and Co., 1946), p. 436, for Tolstoy's appreciation of Ballou.

man's life."[2] There is good ground for arguing that the Christian pacifism of the radical Reformation was kept alive from about 1650 to 1850 primarily by Americans; and that, in view of the cumulative impact of Penn and Woolman, Garrison and Thoreau, William James and Jane Addams, and now Martin Luther King, Jr., America has more often been teacher than student in the history of the nonviolent idea.

That idea has itself changed in the course of its application in America. Before the Revolution, nonviolence was the conviction of some of the members of a few small Christian sects. They understood nonviolence as literal obedience to the teaching of Jesus concerning nonresistance to evil. In its name they sought reconciliation with the Indians, appealed for the abolition of slavery, and on occasion broke the law rather than disobey conscience. The major development since the Revolution has been a tendency to secularization as masses of men have employed nonviolent tactics for social, political, or economic reasons. An advantage of the historical approach employed in this volume is that it enables the reader to watch the unfolding of nonviolent philosophy as it was brought to bear in a series of specific contexts. William James, for example, introduced a new concern with the psychological roots of nonviolence, emphasizing the need for a positive, constructive expression of the idea. On the other hand, Martin Luther King, Jr., while retaining an emphasis on personal action, has sought

---

[2] "Introduction to a Short Biography of William Lloyd Garrison," *The Kingdom of God and Peace Essays*, trans. Aylmer Maude, in *The Works of Leo Tolstoy*, Tolstoy Centenary Edition, XX (London: Oxford University Press for the Tolstoy Society, 1935), 581. Tolstoy made the following comment elsewhere in the same brief essay (p. 578): "Formerly the question was how to free the negroes from the violence of slaveholders; now it is how to free the negroes from the violence of the whites and the whites from the violence of the blacks.

"The solution of this problem in its new form can certainly not be accomplished by lynching negroes, nor by any skilful and liberal measures of American politicians, but only by the application to life of the principle Garrison proclaimed half a century ago."

to restore the older vision that the springs of nonviolence are ultimately religious.

The following documents have been selected on the assumption that the understanding of a tradition that has involved both direct action and sophisticated personal philosophy means including samples of both. This is particularly true when attempting to convey some sense of nonviolent actions on behalf of peace and civil rights since World War II. Much of this recent experience has not yet been articulated, except in the fugitive form of broadsides and pamphlets. It is history, nonetheless, and must be apprehended in whatever form it can be found.

This experimental emphasis cautions against rigid definition. Nevertheless, it may help the reader to view the term "nonviolence" as including the following overlapping but distinct elements: (1) refusal to retaliate ("pacifism," "nonresistance"); (2) deliberate lawbreaking for conscience's sake ("civil disobedience"); (3) acting-out of conviction by demonstrative action ("direct action"). Beyond this, in this volume "nonviolence" itself means all these things and something more: the vision of love as an agent for fundamental social change.

QUAKERS

The practice of nonviolent civil disobedience in American history began with the struggle for freedom of conscience. It is no accident that most of the pre-twentieth-century authors in this volume were Pennsylvanians or New Englanders. These were the two principal theaters for the early nonviolent movement: Pennsylvania, uniquely tolerant to dissenters but after 1750 no longer pacifist in its Indian policy; Massachusetts, intolerant mother of a long line of rebels, including Garrison and Thoreau.

Before the American Revolution, nonviolence was peculiarly identified with Quakers. There were other pacifist sects, of course: John Woolman recorded in his *Journal* the case of a

Mennonite who slept in the woods rather than receive hospitality from a slaveholder. But the Quakers were more numerous, and as Englishmen they were more in touch with the English majority in the colonies than Continental pietists could hope to be. The Quakers, moreover, insisted stubbornly on defying what Roger Williams called "that body-killing, soule-killing, and State-killing doctrine of not permitting, but persecuting all other consciences and wayes of worship. . . ."[3]

There was nothing respectable or middle-class about Quakerism then. In 1660 an act of Virginia referred to the Friends as an

. . . unreasonable and turbulent sort of people . . . teaching and publishing, lies, miracles, false visions, prophecies and doctrines, which have influence upon the communities of men both ecclesiasticall and civil endeavouring and attemp[t]ing thereby to destroy religion, lawes, comunities and all bonds of civil societie, leaveing it arbitrarie to everie vaine and vitious person whether men shall be safe, lawes established, offenders punished, and Governours rule, hereby disturbing the publique peace and just interest. . . .[4]

While this was being said in Virginia, Quakers were mounting a nonviolent invasion of Massachusetts Bay.[5] In July, 1656 Mary Fisher and Ann Austin arrived in Boston. They were de-

---

[3] Roger Williams, "Mr. Cottons Letter Examined and Answered," *Publications of the Narragansett Club*, First Series, I (Providence: Providence Press Co., 1866), 328.

[4] William W. Hening, ed., *The Statutes at Large*, I (New York: R. & W. & G. Bartow, 1823), 532–533.

[5] This description of the Quaker encounter with Massachusetts Bay is drawn from George Lakey, *Nonviolent Action: How It Works*, Pendle Hill Pamphlet No. 129 (Wallingford, Pa.: Pendle Hill, 1963), pp. 11–12. Permission to reprint was granted by Pendle Hill, Wallingford, Pa. Lakey cites Harvey Joseph Daniel Seifert, "The Use by American Quakers of Nonviolent Resistance as a Method of Social Change" (unpublished Ph.D. dissertation, Boston University, 1940).

ported, but two days after their ship sailed out eight more Friends sailed in. As described by George Lakey:

These formidable zealots carried the battle to the Puritans, avoiding devious means of spreading their message. They attempted to speak after the sermon in church, made speeches during trials and from jail windows during imprisonments, issued pamphlets and tracts, held illegal public meetings, refused to pay fines, and refused to work in prison even though it meant going without food.

Again and again Quakers returned to the Bay Colony, despite whippings and executions. "While William Leddra was being considered for the death penalty, Wenlock Christison, who had already been banished on pain of death, calmly walked into the courtroom. And while Christison was being tried, Edward Wharton, who also had been ordered to leave the colony or lose his life, wrote to the authorities from his home that he was still there."

This early experiment in nonviolence, to use Gandhi's phrase, was successful.

The jailer's fees were often paid by sympathetic citizens and food was brought to the prisoners through the jail window at night. A number of colonists were converted to Quakerism by witnessing the suffering. For example, Edward Wanton, an officer of the guard at the execution of Robinson and Stephenson, was so impressed that he came home saying, "Alas, mother! we have been murdering the Lord's people."

When Hored Gardner prayed for her persecutors after her whipping, a woman spectator was so affected that she said, "Surely if she had not the support of the Lord she could not do this thing."

Governor Endicott was not so easily moved. When Catherine Scott indicated her willingness to die for her faith, the Governor replied, "And we shall be as ready to take away your lives, as ye shall be to lay them down." But the protest against the treatment of the Quakers continued to grow.

After William Brend had been so cruelly beaten that he seemed about to die, even Governor Endicott became so alarmed at the attitude of the people that he announced that the jailer would be prosecuted. The later execution of a woman, Mary Dyer, added to the discontent, and even the General Court began to weaken. Virtual abolition of the death penalty followed; there were problems in getting the constables to enforce laws which became ever milder.

"By 1675," Lakey's account concludes, "Quakers were regularly meeting undisturbed in Boston."

Shortly thereafter, in the early 1680's, William Penn experimented with another form of nonviolence in his treaty with the Delaware Indians. No reliable account of the treaty exists. It may be that there were several treaties which were remembered as one event. According to Indian tradition, which carefully preserved the memory of the treaty as a bright chain to be kept free of rust, the principal points of the agreement included: (1) that all paths should be open and free to both Christians and Indians; (2) that the doors of the Christians' houses should be open to the Indians and the houses of the Indians open to the Christians, and they should make each other welcome as friends; (3) that the Christians should not believe any false rumors or reports of the Indians, nor the Indians believe any such rumors or reports of the Christians, but should first come as brethren to inquire of each other.

There were prudential as well as idealistic motives in Penn's approach to the Delaware Indians. He wrote to the commissioners who went out to Pennsylvania ahead of him: "Be tender of offending the Indians, and hearken by honest spies, if you can hear that any body inveigles them not to sell, or to stand off, and raise the value upon you."[6] Yet the policy appears to have worked. Not only did it keep the peace in Pennsylvania for two generations; it seems to be true also that

---

6 William Penn to William Crispin, John Bezar, and Nathaniel Allen, September 30, 1681, quoted in Samuel M. Janney, *The Life of William Penn; With Selections from his Correspondence and Autobiography* (Philadelphia: Hogan, Perkins & Co., 1852), p. 168.

when, in the mid-eighteenth century, warfare between the colony and the Indians began, Quaker families were spared. The influential English Quaker of the early nineteenth century, Jonathan Dymond, passed on to abolitionist readers the tradition that Friends who refused to arm themselves or to retire to garrisons were left unharmed by the Indians.[7]

Pennsylvania's decision to arm against the Indians prompted another form of nonviolent action: the refusal to pay taxes for military purposes. The issue pitted John Woolman and Anthony Benezet, the best remembered American Quakers of the eighteenth century, against Benjamin Franklin, who led the non-Quakers of Pennsylvania in insisting on military preparations.

John Woolman found the decision to refuse payment of taxes a difficult one. His problem sprang from the very concept of religious tolerance. He was fully convinced that the Catholic Thomas à Kempis and the Protestant John Huss were both acceptable Christians in the sight of God. And if it was "true Charity . . . to sincerely Labour for their good, whose belief in all points, doth not agree with ours," how could one be so self-righteous as "to refuse the active payment of a Tax which our Society [of Friends] generally paid"? Woolman was the more perplexed because, while his conscience was clearly uneasy about paying the tax, "Scrupling to pay a tax on account of the application hath seldom been heard of heretofore."[8]

His solution was interesting. Tax refusal was appropriate for American Friends, Woolman argued, precisely because their

---

[7] Jonathan Dymond, *Essays on the Principles of Morality, and on the Private and Political Rights and Obligations of Mankind* (New York: Collins, Brother & Co., 1845), pp. 558–559. In 1849 Charles Sumner cited Dymond as the exemplar of absolute pacifism in the "War System of the Commonwealth of Nations," *Charles Sumner; his complete works,* II (Boston: Lee and Shepard, 1900), 335.

[8] These quotations are from *The Journal and Essays of John Woolman,* ed. Amelia Mott Gummere (New York: The Macmillan Co., 1922), pp. 205–207; see Document 2.

religion was so tolerated and secure. In England, where Quakers had no share in civil government, the danger of uniting with their rulers "in things inconsistent with the purity of Truth" had been slight. American Quakers, "tryed with favour and prosperity," were in a different position. Woolman urged his coreligionists to consider tax refusal as a protection against "a Carnal mind," and also against the danger that Quakers in public office might "quench the tender movings of the Holy Spirit in their minds" if they saw Quakers out of office united in paying war taxes.

Woolman died on the eve of the Revolution, but Franklin and Benezet, antagonists over the French and Indian War, differed once more about the War for Independence. Franklin spoke for the majority when he made his well-known proposal for a seal of the United States: Moses lifting up his wand and dividing the Red Sea, Pharaoh in his chariot overwhelmed with the waters, and the motto, "Rebellion to tyrants is obedience to God." Benezet, drawing on the New Testament rather than the Old, expressed the feelings of the pacifist minority in a letter of 1779 to the President of the Continental Congress, John Jay. Benezet asked Jay "to distinguish between such who are active in opposition [to the war], and those who have been restrained from an apprehension of duty, and a persuasion that our common beneficent Father who has the hearts of all men in his power, and has in former times so eminently displayed his goodness in favour of these countries, if properly sought unto, would in his love and mercy have averted the evil effects of any attempt which might have been made to impede our real welfare."[9]

Symbolized by the confrontation of these leaders was the conflict between Quaker nonviolence and the dominant philosophy of Locke. Locke was contemptuous of those whose

[9] Anthony Benezet to John Jay, February 7, 1779, quoted in George S. Brookes, *Friend Anthony Benezet* (Philadelphia: University of Pennsylvania Press, 1937), pp. 330–331. See Document 4.

scruples over violence permitted tyranny to reign unchecked. Thus in his *Second Treatise of Government* Locke declared:

If the innocent honest Man must quietly quit all he has for Peace sake, to him who will lay violent hands upon it, I desire it may be consider'd, what a kind of Peace there will be in the World, which consists only in Violence and Rapine; and which is to be maintain'd only for the benefit of Robbers and Oppressors. Who would not think it an admirable Peace betwixt the Mighty and the Mean, when the Lamb, without resistance, yielded his Throat to be torn by the imperious Wolf?[10]

Probably at no other time in American history was nonviolence so alien to the mainstream of American social thought as in the Revolutionary generation. Even in the nineteenth century only a few pacifists, such as the South Carolina abolitionist Thomas Grimké, were prepared to say flatly that the violence of the Revolution had been wrong.

ABOLITIONISTS

The Lockean Franklin and his Quaker antagonists were united, however, in their concern to abolish slavery. Woolman made

---

[10] John Locke, *Two Treatises of Government,* ed. Peter Laslett (Cambridge, England: Cambridge University Press, 1960), p. 435. The attitude of radical Whigs toward nonviolence in the era of the American Revolution is suggested by the following examples: John Adams called it "the most mischievous of all doctrines"; John Cartwright spoke of "the dark regions of passive-obedience and non-resistance"; while Richard Price referred to "the odious doctrines of passive obedience, non-resistance, and the divine right of kings" ("A Dissertation On The Canon And Feudal Law," *The Political Writings of John Adams: Representative Selections,* ed. George A. Peek, Jr. [New York: The Bobbs-Merrill Company Inc., The Liberal Arts Press, 1954], p. 10; John Cartwright, *The Legislative Right Of The Commonalty Vindicated; Or, Take Your Choice!* [London, 1777], p. xxvi; Richard Price, *A Discourse On The Love Of Our Country* [London, 1790], p. 35). For nonviolence as a favorite theme of American Tories, see Leonard Labaree, *Conservatism In Early American History* (New York City: New York University Press, 1948), pp. 74–75, 126–130.

long journeys through the South admonishing Quaker slave-holders, and refused to use the products of slave labor. Benezet founded a school for the instruction of free Negroes. In 1790 the aged Franklin set his name at the head of a petition against slavery to the new United States Congress. Southern Congressmen responded by extended reference to the pacifism of Quakers during the Revolution, insisting that the "self-constituted" Society of Friends not be permitted to disturb sectional harmony. ". . . The Northern States adopted us with our slaves," declared Representative William Smith of South Carolina, "and we adopted them with their Quakers."[11] The clash between the Founding Fathers' pragmatic acceptance of slavery and the "fanatical" objections of the Quakers was to reappear writ large in the decades after 1830.

Abolitionism, as it developed in the context of religious revivalism, was at first committed to nonviolence. Nathaniel Macon, Congressman from North Carolina, wrote to a friend in 1818: "We have abolition, colonization, bible and peace societies. . . . The character and spirit of one may without injustice be considered that of all. . . ."[12] In 1815–1860, as in the years since World War II, peace movements and civil rights organizations attracted the same people. Samuel May and William Ellery Channing were advocates of peace before they became abolitionists. Antislavery stalwarts Henry C. Wright, Edmund Quincy, Maria W. Chapman, Lucretia Mott, and Lydia Maria Child joined William Lloyd Garrison in launching the New England Non-Resistance Society. Frederick Douglass denounced "the whole naval system" and capital punishment. Charles Sumner made his political debut by condemning war

---

[11] "On Slavery," Speech of March 17, 1790, *The Debates and Proceedings in the Congress of the United States*, ed. Joseph Gales, Senior, II (Washington: Gales and Seaton, 1834), 1508.

[12] Nathaniel Macon to Bartlett Yancey, March 8, 1818, quoted in William E. Dodd, *The Life of Nathaniel Macon* (Raleigh, N. C.: Edwards & Broughton, 1903), p. 313.

before a Fourth of July audience on the Boston Common, and in 1849, in a speech called "War System of the Commonwealth of Nations," produced the most comprehensive indictment of war by any American in the nineteenth century. William Jay, Lewis Tappan, and Theodore Parker were others prominent in both the peace and antislavery movements.[13]

The manifesto of the American Antislavery Society in 1833 espoused nonviolence in almost the same language as the declaration of the New England Non-Resistance Society in 1838: a natural outcome, since Garrison wrote both. Nor was this nineteenth century nonviolent movement confined to words. Direct action against railroad segregation began almost coincidentally with railroads themselves, in New England, New York, and Pennsylvania.[14] Assisting fugitive slaves was "constructive work" in the best Gandhian sense.

But Garrisonian nonviolence in 1840, like Quaker pacifism in 1776, was open to the charge that it salved the conscience of the individual yet failed to change the structure of power. Garrison disavowed the French Revolution: "We advocate no jacobinical doctrines. The spirit of jacobinism is the spirit of retaliation, violence and murder." The American Antislavery Society asked not only its members but also the slaves of the South to forego the use of violence. Its declaration said that "[we reject and] entreat the oppressed to reject, the use of all carnal weapons for deliverance from bondage; relying solely

---

[13] *The Life and Writings of Frederick Douglass,* ed. Philip S. Foner (New York: International Publishers, 1950), II, 13–14; Sumner . . . *works,* I (1889), 5–132 and II, 323–429; *William Lloyd Garrison, 1805–1879: The Story of His Life Told by His Children* (New York: The Century Co., 1885–1889), II, 221–242, 326–328; Merle E. Curti, *The American Peace Crusade, 1815–1860* (Durham: Duke University Press, 1929), pp. 64, 80–82 *et passim.*

[14] Leon Litwack, "Non-Violence in Negro Rights Movements of the Ante-Bellum North" and Louis Filler, "Non-Violence and Abolition," papers presented to a conference on nonviolence at Hobart and William Smith College, May 1962.

upon those which are spiritual, and mighty through God to the pulling down of strongholds."[15] As the years passed and the strongholds remained, as the war with Mexico of 1846–1848 was followed by the Fugitive Slave Law of 1850, many abolitionists began to wonder if nonviolence was enough.

One of these was Garrison's lieutenant, Wendell Phillips. In his first public speech, on the murder of abolitionist editor Elijah Lovejoy in 1837, Phillips had disassociated himself from "what are called Peace principles" and justified Lovejoy's use of arms to protect his press. After the Fugitive Slave Law he went further: ". . . It seems to me that the man who is not conscientiously a non-resistant, is not only entitled, he is bound, to use every means that he has or can get to resist arrest in the last resort." Yet while justifying violence in defense of individuals, Phillips continued to believe in nonviolent abolition of slavery as an institution until the Civil War began. Then he abandoned pacifism completely. "I think," Phillips told a cheering audience in 1861, "the South is all wrong, and the administration [of Abraham Lincoln] is all right."[16]

A more dramatic conversion to violence was the case of Frederick Douglass. As late as September 1849 Douglass could say: "I am willing at all times to be known as a Garrisonian abolitionist." But earlier that same year Douglass had thrown Faneuil Hall into an uproar by declaring that he would welcome the news of a slave insurrection in the South. In 1854, his attitude hardened by the Fugitive Slave Law, Douglass posed the question, "Is It Right and Wise to Kill a Kidnapper?," and answered, Yes. In 1856 Douglass said of the slave

---

15 The first quotation is from the "Declaration of Sentiments adopted by the [American] Peace Convention . . . 1838," *Selections from the Writings and Speeches of William Lloyd Garrison* (Boston: R. F. Wallcutt, 1852), p. 75 (see Document 5); for the second, see *William Lloyd Garrison, 1805–1879*, I, 409.

16 "The Murder of Lovejoy," in Wendell Phillips, *Speeches, Lectures, and Letters* (Boston: James Redpath, 1863), p. 7; "Sims Anniversary," *ibid.*, p. 89; "Under the Flag," *ibid.*, p. 400.

system, "its peaceful annihilation is almost hopeless." In June 1860 the former slave came full circle, stating:

I have little hope of the freedom of the slave by peaceful means. A long course of peaceful slaveholding has placed the slaveholders beyond the reach of moral and humane considerations. . . . The only penetrable point of a tyrant is the *fear of death.*[17]

Henry Thoreau's emphasis, even in "Civil Disobedience," was on lawbreaking, not on pacifism. Conscious of writing near Concord Bridge, Thoreau asked, in effect: If violence was justified against a tax on tea, how much more would it be justified to emancipate the slaves? The essay is, in fact, a subtle and ambiguous synthesis of the previously disparate Quaker and Lockean traditions. Thoreau, like Roger Williams or William Penn, affirms the peril of coercion in spiritual matters: he refused to pay a tax for the established church several years before his more celebrated refusal of the Massachusetts poll tax. At the same time Thoreau breaks with Garrison's disavowal of jacobinism, and flatly declares that "all men recognize the right of revolution" and that "it is not too soon for honest men to rebel and revolutionize." Thoreau's condemnation of all government can be misleading here. Tom Paine's *Common Sense* also began with the conception that "Society in every state is a blessing, but government, even in its best state, is but a necessary evil. . . ." This belief did not prevent Paine from advocating a political revolution; and Thoreau himself tells us that, speaking practically, what he wants is not *no* government, but a better government at once.[18]

In "Civil Disobedience" Thoreau presented individual non-

---

[17] *Life and Writings of Frederick Douglass,* II, 49–51, 284–289.

[18] Henry Thoreau, "Civil Disobedience," in *A Yankee in Canada, with Anti-Slavery and Reform Papers* (Boston: Ticknor and Fields, 1866), pp. 127, 124 (see Document 7); *The Complete Writings of Thomas Paine,* ed. Philip S. Foner, I (New York: The Citadel Press, 1945), 4.

cooperation with the state as "the definition of a peaceable revolution, if any such is possible." By 1854, under the hammer of the Fugitive Slave Law, Thoreau was prepared to say: "Show me a free state, and a court truly of justice, and I will fight for them, if need be." In 1859, speaking on the death of John Brown, Thoreau said: "I do not wish to kill nor to be killed, but I can foresee circumstances in which both these things would be by me unavoidable." He squarely supported Brown's violent raid:

It was his [Brown's] peculiar doctrine that a man has a perfect right to interfere by force with the slaveholder, in order to rescue the slave. I agree with him. . . . I shall not be forward to think him mistaken in his method who quickest succeeds to liberate the slave. I speak for the slave when I say, that I prefer the philanthropy of Captain Brown to that philanthropy which neither shoots me nor liberates me.[19]

The collapse of Garrisonian nonviolence is the most striking failure of nonviolence in American history to date. One can argue endlessly whether it might have been otherwise. Should Garrison have gone into the South, like Woolman, and tried to reason with slaveholders face-to-face rather than condemn them at a distance? It is idle to ask. The great and unavoidable fact is that the abolitionist movement, virtually unanimous in adhering to nonviolence in the 1830's, was almost equally united in supporting Lincoln when the war came.

Garrison's unctuous explanations for his own change of position hardly help. "Oh, Mr. President," Garrison declared at a July Fourth picnic in the first year of the Civil War,

. . . how it delights my heart when I think that the worst thing we propose to do for the South is the very best thing that God or men can do! . . . Yes, we will make it possible for them to be a happy

---

19 "Civil Disobedience," in *A Yankee in Canada,* p. 137; "Slavery in Massachusetts," *ibid.,* p. 112; "A Plea for Captain John Brown," *ibid.,* pp. 175, 174–175.

and prosperous people, as they have never been, and never can be, with slavery. We will make it possible for them to have free schools, and free presses, and free institutions, as we do at the North. . . . Let us return them good for evil, by seizing this opportunity to deliver them from their deadliest curse—that is Christian.

To Quakers distressed that their sons had joined the Union Army, Garrison said: "They had imagined they were on the plane of the Sermon on the Mount, and they found they were only up to the level of Lexington and Bunker Hill. . . ."[20] Clearly Garrison had reconsidered the American Revolution, and found it good.

Perhaps the most significant contribution to the nonviolent tradition between the Revolution and the Civil War was the thinking of Elihu Burritt, one of the few abolitionists to oppose the Civil War on pacifist grounds. Burritt was imaginative in devising techniques of peace agitation. In 1846, when England and the United States came to the brink of war over Oregon, Burritt urged workingmen and merchants to send "friendly addresses" to their English counterparts. In the same year Burritt founded in England the League of Universal Brotherhood, members of which took the following pledge:

Believing all war to be inconsistent with the spirit of Christianity, and destructive to the best interests of mankind, I do hereby pledge myself never to enlist or enter into any army or navy, or to yield any voluntary support or sanction to the preparation for or prosecution of any war, by whomsoever, for whatsoever proposed, declared or waged. And I do hereby associate myself with all persons, of whatever country, condition, or colour, who have signed, or shall hereafter sign this pledge, in a "League of Universal Brotherhood"; whose object shall be, to employ all legitimate and moral means for the abolition of all war, and all spirit, and all manifestation of war,

---

[20] *William Lloyd Garrison, 1805–1879,* IV, 31–32, 37.

throughout the world; for the abolition of all restrictions upon international correspondence and friendly intercourse, and of whatever else tends to make enemies of nations, or prevents their fusion into one peaceful brotherhood; for the abolition of all institutions and customs which do not recognize the image of God and a human brother in every man of whatever clime, colour, or condition of humanity.[21]

Finally, Burritt's proposal for a general strike of workingmen against war foreshadowed the mass (as opposed to individual) nonviolence of trade unionists and Negroes in the twentieth century.

ANARCHISTS AND PROGRESSIVES

Nonviolence was quiescent for a generation after 1861, just as it had been after 1776. A few of the prewar reformers, such as Adin Ballou and Henry C. Wright, joined with Alfred Henry Love to form the Universal Peace Union shortly after the war. Its membership was never more than about 10,000.

Anarchism formed an important connecting link between nineteenth- and twentieth-century nonviolence in America. Its alien character has been exaggerated. The bitter tone of anarchist writing during the industrial wars of the 1870's and 1880's echoed such prewar antistatists as John Humphrey Noyes, founder of Perfectionism and the Oneida Community, who wrote to his close friend William Lloyd Garrison in March 1837:

When I wish to form a conception of the government of the United States (using a personified representation), I picture to myself a bloated, swaggering libertine, trampling on the Bible—its own Constitution—its treaties with the Indians—the petitions of its citizens; with one hand whipping a negro tied to a liberty-pole, and with the other dashing an emaciated Indian to the ground. . . . The question

---

[21] Quoted in Curti, *The American Peace Crusade,* p. 145.

urges itself upon me—"What Have I, as a Christian, to do with such a villain?"

"My hope of the millennium," Noyes asserted, "begins where Dr. Beecher's expires—viz., AT THE OVERTHROW OF THIS NATION."[22]

The ultimate goal of all anarchists was a society that would function nonviolently without need of the aggressive state. Some also believed in nonviolence as a means. *The Alarm,* founded by Haymarket anarchist Albert Parsons, printed in 1888 a piece by Gertrude Kelly called: "Passive Resistance. Robbery of the People Based on Force Cannot be Remedied by Force." It contrasted the effect upon the public mind of passive resistance, which causes "the capitalist to stand forth unmasked before the world as the enemy of mankind," and violence, which casts "ourselves [instead of the capitalists] before the world in the light of criminals." A rent strike in tenements owned by the Trinity Church would therefore be better advised than blowing up the Church. Besides, "we must never fail to remember that it is upon an improvement in the moral tone of the people that true progress depends, that, therefore, our means as our ends must be pure." The gentle anarchist concluded by recommending to her readers Parker Pillsbury's *Acts of the Anti-Slavery Apostles.*[23]

American anarchism wavered between an individualist and a communal vision of the good society. Josiah Warren, editor of *The Peaceable Revolutionist,* lived for a time at Robert Owen's New Harmony colony before developing the atomistic doctrine that he passed on to his disciple, Benjamin Tucker. But the Haymarket anarchists were trade-unionists; and Emma Goldman was influenced by the idealization of the peasant vil-

---

[22] John Humphrey Noyes to W. L. Garrison, March 22, 1837, in *William Lloyd Garrison 1805–1879,* II, 145–148.

[23] *The Alarm* (Chicago), July 14, 1888. I owe this reference to the kindness of Professor Herbert Gutman of the University of Buffalo.

lage common among the Narodnik revolutionaries with whom she worked in Russia before emigrating to the United States.

Russia also influenced America through Tolstoy, who, finding his own Christian pacifism expressed by Garrison and other Americans, transmitted the Garrisonian doctrine of nonviolence to a new generation of American reformers. Clarence Darrow, William Jennings Bryan, and Jane Addams made the pilgrimage to Tolstoy's home at Yasnaya Polyana to sit at the great man's feet. Hamlin Garland has recorded the influence of Tolstoy upon American reformers at the close of the century. From 1888 to 1890, Garland wrote, they received "utterances of such apostolic austerity that they read like encyclicals from the head of a great church—the church of humanity. . . . We quoted Ibsen to reform the drama and Tolstoy to reform society. We made use of every available argument his letters offered."[24] Later, Darrow would help to revolutionize the treatment of criminals with *Resist Not Evil* (1903), and Bryan would resign as Secretary of State in protest against America's drift toward war in 1915.

Another powerful influence on prewar nonviolence, but of a quite different character, was the thinking of William James. James, a physiologist and psychologist as well as a philosopher, broke away from the traditional Christian conception that killing and loving service are completely contradictory kinds of action. In his famous essay, "The Moral Equivalent of War," he asserted that war and constructive labor are varying expressions of an impulse to heroic self-sacrifice. Thus war is not all bad. It is "the great preserver of our ideals of hardihood," "the supreme theatre of human strenuousness," the approved social mechanism for calling forth "strenuous honor and disinterestedness." These qualities of military service help to explain

---

[24] Hamlin Garland, "The Reformer Tolstoy," Introduction to *Recollections and Essays*, by Leo Tolstoy, in *The Works of Leo Tolstoy*, vii–viii.

why "war-taxes are the only ones men never hesitate to pay."
Jane Addams' *Newer Ideals of Peace* (1907) blended the
teachings of Tolstoy and James. Toward the close of the book
Miss Addams told again one of the Russian master's famous
anecdotes:

The Doukhobors are a religious sect in Russia whose creed emphasizes the teaching of non-resistance. A story is told of one of their
young men who, because of his refusal to enter the Russian army,
was brought for trial before a judge, who reasoned with him concerning the folly of his course and in return received a homily upon
the teachings of Jesus. "Quite right you are," answered the judge,
"from the point of abstract virtue, but the time has not yet come
to put into practise the literal sayings of Christ." "The time may not
have come for you, your Honor," was the reply, "but the time has
come for us."[25]

In America, such conscientious objection to military service
is for the most part a twentieth-century phenomenon because
conscription itself is a modern practice. During the Civil War
both North and South provided for compulsory military service, but it was possible to hire a substitute under the Union
law, and to secure exemption by a $500 payment under its Confederate counterpart. During the Spanish-American War there
was no conscription law. Hence it was World War I which for
the first time brought the objector and the state into unavoidable frontal conflict.

While most prewar pacifists followed John Dewey in supporting President Wilson, others held fast to Wilson's own
"peace without victory" doctrine of January 1917. One such
was Randolph Bourne, who indignantly struck off the phrase,
"War is essentially the health of the State."[26] Another was Jane
Addams herself. Compelled to watch immigrants whom she had

---

[25] Jane Addams, *Newer Ideals of Peace* (New York: The Macmillan Co., 1907), p. 230.

[26] Randolph S. Bourne, *War and the Intellectuals: Collected Essays, 1915–1919*, ed. Carl Resek (New York: Harper & Row, 1964), p. 69.

helped to become citizens resentfully submit to conscription, Jane Addams decided it was necessary that "at least a small number of us should be forced into an unequivocal position."[27] In this belief she supported Henry Ford's Peace Ship, took part in the Women's Congress at the Hague in 1915, and became the first president of the Women's International League for Peace and Freedom.

The WILPF was one among many peace organizations founded during World War I. The Fellowship of Reconciliation grew out of a pledge between the Kaiser's chaplain, Friedrich Siegmund-Schultze, and an English Quaker, Henry Hodgkin, on the day before the war began, to "keep the bonds of Christian love unbroken across the frontier." Organized in England late in 1914, the FOR set up an American branch in November 1915. The American Civil Liberties Union originated in 1916 as the American Union Against Militarism. The American Friends Service Committee came into being three weeks after America's entry into the war under the leadership of Rufus Jones. The AFSC, prototype of the later Civilian Conservation Corps and Peace Corps, was a practical expression of the philosophy of William James' "The Moral Equivalent of War."

The conscription law of May 1917 provided that members of "well recognized" religious groups "whose existing creed or principles" forbade their members "to participate in war in any form" might be assigned to noncombatant service within the armed forces. According to War Department figures, 64,693 claims for noncombatant status under the law were made. Of these, 56,830 claims were accepted by local draft boards; however, only 20,873 of these applicants were actually inducted, and just 3,989 of that number persisted in their position after reaching camp because of the extraordinary harshness with which objectors were treated.

---

[27] Jane Addams, "Personal Reactions During War," *Peace and Bread in Time of War* (Boston: G. K. Hall, 1960), p. 133; see Document 17.

If the war stimulated nonviolence in the form of conscientious objection, it also witnessed spectacular direct action by the women's suffrage movement. Only slightly less radical than their sisters in England, one of whom threw herself under the hooves of the King's horse in the Grand National, Alice Paul and her American associates refused to work and eat in jail when they were denied the status of political prisoners. The suffragette represented Progressivism's nearest approach to the tradition of civil disobedience and direct action.

TOWARD NONVIOLENT REVOLUTION

Between the two world wars, antiwar sentiment took its tone not from the essentially religious outlook of Jane Addams, but from the political pacifism of Eugene Debs. As Garrison had placed on the masthead of *The Liberator* the motto of Tom Paine, "Our country is the world, our countrymen are all mankind," so at the outbreak of World War I Debs said: "I have no country to fight for; my country is the earth, and I am a citizen of the world." Debs was sentenced to ten years in the Atlanta Penitentiary at the age of sixty-five. He responded with "My Prison Creed":

> While there is a lower class I am in it;
> While there is a criminal element I am of it;
> While there's a soul in prison I am not free.[28]

While Debs was in Atlanta Penitentiary, however, the Unitarian minister John Haynes Holmes began to popularize in America the teaching of Gandhi. One expression of the resulting dialogue between pacifism and socialism was Reinhold Niebuhr's brilliant and still unsurpassed inquiry into the meaning of terms such as "violence," "nonviolence," "coercion," and

---

[28] These words will be found at the beginning of Deb's account of his prison experiences, *Walls and Bars* (Chicago: Socialist Party, 1927), p. 11.

"force" in *Moral Man and Immoral Society,* published in 1932. In this book, the most influential American theologian of the twentieth century was in transition between his early, socialist and pacifist phase (Niebuhr was at one time national chairman of the Fellowship of Reconciliation), and the later, "neo-orthodox" phase for which he is better known. Demanding that the Christian confront the realities of class struggle, Niebuhr condemned any teaching of nonviolence that permitted the comfortable to make peace with oppression. When used to change society, Niebuhr argued, nonviolence inevitably involves coercion. "Once the principle of coercion and resistance has been accepted as necessary to the social struggle, and pure pacifism has thus been abandoned," Niebuhr continued, "the differences between violence and nonviolence lose some of their significance though they remain important."[29]

Moral Man and Immoral Society also contained a startling prophecy. Writing a generation before Montgomery in the bitter era of the Scottsboro case, Niebuhr declared:

It is hopeless for the Negro to expect complete emancipation from the menial social and economic position into which the white man has forced him, merely by trusting in the moral sense of the white race. It is equally hopeless to attempt emancipation through violent rebellion.[30]

The alternative was nonviolent mass action. "It will, if persisted in with the same patience and discipline attained by Mr. Gandhi and his followers, achieve a degree of justice which neither pure moral suasion nor violence could gain." The Negro, Niebuhr concluded, "would need only to fuse the aggressiveness of the new and young Negro with the patience and forebearance of the old Negro, to rob the former of its

---

[29] Reinhold Niebuhr, "Is Peace or Justice the Goal?" *The World Tomorrow,* XV, September 21, 1932, 277.

[30] Reinhold Niebuhr, *Moral Man and Immoral Society* (New York: Charles Scribner's Sons, 1932), p. 252. See Document 40.

vindictiveness and the latter of its lethargy."[31] This must surely be one of the most remarkable anticipations in the history of American social thought.

Class conflict influenced the practice as well as the theory of nonviolence. No organization in American history has been so wholeheartedly dedicated to direct action as the syndicalist Industrial Workers of the World, or "Wobblies." They were hardly nonviolent. But they believed that labor laws would remain dead letters unless direct action created pressure for enforcement; that the way to fight violations of free speech was to fill the jails; that the means for destroying capitalism was not politics, but the general strike. The Wobblies' vision of industrial self-government has much in common with the idea of "participatory democracy" that attracts civil rights activists in the 1960's.

The nonviolent movement since World War II is in many ways the direct descendant of the labor movement of the 1930's. Many leaders, such as A. J. Muste and James Peck, were labor-union organizers during the Depression. The theme song of Negro sit-inners, "We Shall Overcome," was previously sung by striking Appalachian textile workers. And the sit-in technique was unquestionably influenced by the sit-down strikes of the previous generation. Mrs. Rosa Parks acted spontaneously when she refused to move to the back of a bus in Montgomery, Alabama in December 1955; yet it is also true that she had just returned from a leadership seminar at the Highlander Folk School in Tennessee, the South's principal training center for union organizers. During World War II, sit-ins were employed against racial segregation both by the newly-formed Congress Of Racial Equality and, within federal prisons, by incarcerated conscientious objectors.

World War II also produced a resurgence of religious pacifism. As Niebuhr moved away from nonviolence, the imminence of war in the late 1930's drove others back to it. One of

[31] *Ibid.*, p. 254.

these was A. J. Muste, whose thought and action over the last fifty years form an instructive counterpoint to the development of Reinhold Niebuhr. A Christian minister, Muste resigned his pastorate during World War I because of pacifist convictions. He then turned to the organization of labor; for a time during the Depression he abandoned Christianity and became a leader of the American Trotskyist movement. While in Paris in 1936 he was reconverted to Christian pacifism. He described the experience in a moving letter to Cara Cook:

War is the central problem for us all today. . . . International war and coercion at home will continue to exist for just so long as people regard these things as suitable, as even conceivable, instruments of policy. . . . The Christian position does not mean to justify or condone the capitalist system. Quite the contrary. It provides the one measure by which the capitalist system stands thoroughly and effectively condemned. It stands condemned because it makes the Christian relation in its full sense, the relation of brotherhood between human beings, impossible. . . . So long, however, as the matter remains on the plane of economics and self-interest, no one is in a position to condemn another. When we feel indignation, as we do even in spite of ourselves, we then enter the realm of standards and values, the realm in which moral judgment is pronounced, the realm in which ethical and spiritual appeals are made . . . the realm of morality and religion.[32]

In World War II, under a draft law more liberal than that of World War I, there were more than 15,000 conscientious objectors (this figure does not include persons who served as noncombatants in the armed forces). Two-thirds of these performed alternative service in government camps, whereas about 5,000 went to prison, either because they refused to register or because their objection was based on political grounds inadmissible under the law. Approximately half of the American conscientious objectors in World War II were members of the

---

[32] Quoted in Nat Hentoff, *Peace Agitator: The Story of A. J. Muste* (New York: The Macmillan Co., 1963), pp. 99–100.

Brethren, Mennonite, and Jehovah's Witness denominations, testimony to the essentially religious character of their protest. Pacifism persisted and grew stronger after World War II because of the way the war ended. Early in the morning of August 6, 1945, a United States Air Force pilot named Claude Eatherly flew his B-29 bomber, the *Straight Flush*, over Hiroshima, Japan. "The weather seemed ideal" for dropping the first atomic bomb, the reconnaissance plane reported. A few hours later four-fifths of Hiroshima's population of 245,000 were dead or seriously wounded. Eatherly spoke for many others when he wrote, subsequently, that the bombing of Hiroshima convinced him "that cruelty, hatred, violence and injustice never can and never will be able to create a mental, moral and material millennium. The only road to it is the all giving creative love, trust and brotherhood, not only preached but consistently practised."[33]

There emerged after World War II a group of men who had joined in the labor organizing drive of the 1930's; who had been conscientious objectors, often the organizers of prison strikes, while the war was in progress; and who threw themselves into nonviolent direct action for peace and racial equality when the war ended. Among these postwar leaders of nonviolence were Bayard Rustin and David Dellinger, who joined with Muste to edit the pacifist magazine *Liberation*. The Congress Of Racial Equality (1943), Peacemakers (1948), and the Committee for Nonviolent Action (1957) provided organizational channels for this new nonviolent movement.

James Peck later recalled that the first nonviolent direct action against nuclear tests occurred in the summer of 1946, when he and forty others led around New York City's Times Square a stuffed goat mounted on roller-skate wheels with a

---

[33] "Claude Eatherly to the Reverend N.," August 8, 1960, *Burning Conscience. The case of the Hiroshima pilot, Claude Eatherly, told in his letters to Gunther Anders with a postscript for American readers by Anders* (New York: Monthly Review Press, 1962), p. 82.

placard around its neck saying "Today me—Tomorrow you."
(The Bikini hydrogen bomb tests, then being conducted, involved the use of goats and other animals for experimental
purposes.) The odds against the demonstrators were great.
Nevertheless, an informal moratorium on testing and, after this
proved inadequate, a Soviet-American treaty banning atmospheric and underwater tests, were finally achieved.

With the Montgomery bus boycott of 1955–1956 and still
more with the student sit-ins of 1960, nonviolence became a
more significant social force than at any earlier period in American history. Bus service in Montgomery was a daily humiliation for the city's 50,000 Negroes. Often they were required to
get off the bus and reboard at the rear after paying their fare
in front. If there were not enough seats in the section reserved
for whites to accommodate the white passengers, then the
Negroes had to move further back to other seats, or stand. On
December 1, 1955 the city's Negro community began to boycott the buses in protest against these conditions. The boycott
continued until November 13, 1956, when the United States
Supreme Court declared bus segregation in Montgomery illegal. The combination of nonviolent direct action with legal
pressure, successful in Montgomery, provided a model for subsequent agitation in the areas of public accommodations and
the right to vote.

The genesis of the 1960 sit-ins has been described by Martin
Oppenheimer. "On Aug. 9, 1958, the NAACP Youth Council
in Oklahoma City began the first formal sit-in by predomi-
nantly Negro students." During the next year and a half there
were several sporadic and unpublicized sit-ins in other border
states. Then:

Among the students at North Carolina Agricultural and Technical
College in Greensboro, in the Fall of 1959, were four who were in
the habit of getting together in the campus rooms of two of them
for "bull-sessions." They assigned each other books to read—Frederick Douglass, Langston Hughes, Gandhi, among others. They

watched a T-V documentary on Gandhi that semester. In January, 1960, one of the boys read Robert E. Davis' *The American Negro's Dilemma*, which complains of the Negro's apathy and failure to "do something on his own to alleviate his burdens, . . ." All of the boys were, or at some time had been, members of an NAACP Youth Council, but were not in contact with the NAACP at this point. Some months earlier they had asked for advice on how to run a direct action project, but had not heard from the National Office by the time action was decided on. At 4:30 P.M. on Feb. 1, 1960, the four went into the F. W. Woolworth store in downtown Greensboro, sat down, and waited for service.[34]

By December 31, 1960 sit-in demonstrations had occurred in over one hundred communities. Meantime, in April 1960 more than two hundred delegates, representing fifty-two colleges and high schools in thirty-seven communities in thirteen different states, met in Raleigh, North Carolina, and formed the Student Nonviolent Coordinating Committee (SNCC). It was SNCC that during the next five years led the effort to register unfranchised Negroes in the Deep South.

This nonviolent movement since World War II resembles in many ways the Garrisonian movement of the 1830's. In one as in the other, peace and civil rights are closely intertwined. Channing and Burritt have their twentieth-century counterparts in a Bayard Rustin, who organized both a direct-action protest against French atomic testing in the Sahara Desert and the 1963 civil rights March on Washington, or a James Peck, one of four men to sail a small boat into the Pacific testing area in 1958 and also a participant in the 1961 Freedom Rides.

---

[34] Martin Oppenheimer, "The Southern Student Movement: Year I," *The Journal of Negro Education* (Fall 1964), pp. 396–398, summarizing his "The Genesis of the Southern Negro Student Movement (Sit-In Movement): A Study in Contemporary Negro Protest" (unpublished Ph.D. dissertation, University of Pennsylvania, 1963). See also the account of Izell Blair, one of the Greensboro four, in Robert Penn Warren, *Who Speaks For The Negro?* (New York: Random House, 1965), pp. 358–361.

When a Nashville-to-Washington peace walk in 1962 left Nashville it walked right past a sit-in demonstration. By the time the group reached Washington, moved and heartened by its reception at Negro churches along the way, the group had decided there was one issue, not two. Members of the Quebec-to-Guantanamo peace walk two years later spent two months hunger-striking in Albany, Georgia, for the right to walk through the white business district where civil rights demonstrations had been forbidden.

The older and newer movements are similar, too, in their underlying philosophies. Garrison could have written the declaration of the Student Nonviolent Coordinating Committee at its founding conference in 1960; John Woolman would have affirmed the rules for action of the Congress Of Racial Equality (see Document 31). From Penn to Burritt, the Quaker and abolitionist forerunners of twentieth-century American nonviolence were in sympathy with the spirit behind the "discipline" of the Quebec-to-Guantanamo peace walk of 1963–1964 (see Document 28A) or the writings of Dr. King.

These very similarities between the old and the new nonviolent movements raise the question: Will nonviolence now, as then, prove only a passing phase of a movement ending in force and bloodshed? There are some indications that this is so. The distinctions by which Phillips and Thoreau moved in the early 1850's toward a full acceptance of violence can be paralleled from Martin Luther King, Jr.'s "Letter from Birmingham City Jail." As Phillips justified violence first for individual self-defense, then for the transformation of society, so in the middle of the 1960's civil rights workers in the ghettoes of the North and in the hard-core areas of the South begin to arm for self-protection and to look to Africa for models.

The civil rights turmoil of the middle 1960's can, however, be diagnosed in a different way: as a turning toward more fundamental social change, inevitable when masses of men, not just solitary intellectuals, become involved in action. Thoreau had defined individual civil disobedience as the method of peaceable revolution, if such a revolution were possible. The Civil War came, seeming to disprove this possibility; but a generation later Gandhi discovered in South Africa how masses of men—without which no genuine revolution can occur—could use nonviolent action. In the 1930's, the American labor movement coupled the strike, itself an essentially nonviolent technique, with the deliberate civil disobedience of the sit-down. Like the labor movement, and unlike abolitionism, the Negro protest movement involves (and increasingly so as time goes on) thousands of poor, uneducated people. They ask from nonviolence tangible results: they want jobs as well as freedom. The violence encountered in 1963–1964 signified that the direction of nonviolent action was shifting from public accommodations to the twin levers of power in our society, the vote and the job. Because the objectives were more basic, resistance was more bitter and tenacious. Violence increased as the target of the protest became "the system" and "the power structure." Nonviolent action tended to become nonviolent revolution.

In this modern civil rights struggle, nonviolence has been referred to both as a "tactic" and as a "way of life." Both are long-standing and essential components of the American tradition of nonviolence. In a nonviolent mass movement, such as the organizing strikes of the 1930's or the civil rights actions of the 1950's and 1960's, most participants have been nonviolent because they were outnumbered and outgunned, and because their refusal to retaliate when attacked won them necessary sympathizers. Yet throughout our history there have always been a few who chose nonviolence because it answered a personal need to live in harmony with universal forces of life and love. For them, nature and nature's God required, not violent revolution, but surrender of self to service of their fellow man.

What distinguishes this absolutist strain in the nonviolent tradition is a reluctance to accept a stereotyped image of "the enemy," a refusal to relinquish the conception that the antagonist is human. Yet the best of this group feel also compelled to confront the full reality of violence and murder as practiced, for example, in the American South. If there is a way out of the dilemma, it cannot be found in history. It will be found only in the action of persons who refuse to choose between justice and love, and seek a way forward that includes both.

This book went to press at a time of mingled success and tragedy for nonviolence in America. On the one hand there were victories: the Soviet-American treaty banning nuclear tests in the atmosphere (summer 1963), the civil rights bill (summer 1964), the voting bill (summer 1965). But in Alabama and Mississippi, these years brought death to William Moore, walking from Baltimore to Jackson, Mississippi on behalf of civil rights; to Medgar Evers, shot in the back in Jackson; to four children bombed in a Birmingham, Alabama church; to Michael Schwerner, James Chaney, and Andrew Goodman, murdered on the first day of the 1964 Mississippi Summer Project; to Willie Jackson, James Reeb, and Viola Liuzzo in Selma, Alabama.

Speaking at a memorial service for Schwerner, Chaney and Goodman, Robert Moses, director of the Summer Project, observed that on the day their bodies were discovered the President of the United States ordered a bombing raid of a foreign country. The lesson of the deaths, Moses said, was that man simply had to stop killing. Martin Luther King also stressed the connection between nonviolence at home and abroad, in a book on the Birmingham demonstrations of 1963:

In measuring the full implications of the civil-rights revolution, the greatest contribution may be in the area of world peace. The concept of nonviolence has spread on a mass scale in the United States as an instrument of change in the field of race relations. To date, only a few practitioners of nonviolent direct action have been committed to its philosophy. The great mass have used it pragmatically as a tactical weapon, without being ready to live it.

More and more people, however, have begun to conceive of this powerful ethic as a necessary way of life in a world where the wildly accelerated development of nuclear power has brought into being weapons that can annihilate all humanity. . . .

King summed up: "'Nonviolence, the answer to the Negroes' need, may become the answer to the most desperate need of all humanity."[35]

[35] Martin Luther King, Jr., *Why We Can't Wait* (New York: Harper & Row, 1964), pp. 168–169.

Selected Bibliography

COLLATERAL READING

In such an unconventional scholarly subject, available literature is inevitably heterogeneous. There are two good, recent anthologies of writings on nonviolence from all over the world: Mulford Q. Sibley, *The Quiet Battle: Writings on the Theory and Practice of Non-violent Resistance* (Garden City, New York: Doubleday and Company, 1963) and Arthur and Lila Weinberg eds., *Instead of Violence: Writings by the great advocates of peace and nonviolence throughout history* (New York: Grossman Publishers, 1963). Merle Curti and Mulford Sibley have written helpful studies of the American peace movement: see Curti, *The American Peace Crusade, 1815–1860* (Durham: Duke University Press, 1929) and *Peace or War— The American Struggle, 1636–1936* (New York: W. W. Norton, 1936); and Mulford Q. Sibley and Philip E. Jacob, *Conscription of Conscience* (Ithaca: Cornell University Press, 1952). The best book on the post-World War II civil rights movement is Howard Zinn, *SNCC: The New Abolitionists* (Boston: Beacon Press, 1964). Nat Hentoff's *Peace Agitator: The Story of A. J. Muste* (New York: The Macmillan Company, 1964) is, like its subject, an encyclopedia of the twentieth-century peace and labor movements.

American studies of the general theory of nonviolence which merit the attention of every student are Richard Gregg, *The Power of Nonviolence* (second revised edition; Nyack, N. Y.: Fellowship Publications, 1959); Joan V. Bondurant, *Conquest of Violence: The Gandhian Philosophy of Conflict* (Princeton: Princeton University Press, 1958); revised paperback edition (Berkeley and Los Angeles: University of California Press, 1965); William Robert Miller, *Nonviolence: A Christian Interpretation* (New York: Association Press, 1964); and Harvey Seifert, *Conquest By Suffering. The Process and Prospects of Nonviolent Resistance* (Philadelphia: The Westminster Press, 1965).

As to the older nonviolent movement, Peter Brock of Columbia University has completed the first draft of a book on American pacifism up to World War I which promises to be the long-needed standard work on this subject.

ORIGINAL SOURCES

In addition to sources cited in the footnotes, mention may be made of two books which contain much of the recent history of the peace and civil rights movements: Albert Bigelow, *The Voyage of the Golden Rule: An Experiment with Truth* (Garden City: Doubleday and Company, 1959) and James Peck, *Freedom Ride* (New York: Simon and Schuster, 1961). Thoreau's essays on social problems are conveniently available for the first time in almost a hundred years, in Henry David Thoreau, *Anti-Slavery and Reform Papers* (paperback edition; Montreal: Harvest House, 1963).

The inadequacy with which the modern nonviolent movement is being chronicled and documented is a disgrace to American social science. If this book directs attention to the subject as one worthy of serious scholarly concern, it will have more than served its purpose.

Editor's Note and Acknowledgments

Original spelling and punctuation have been retained in the documents except for the correction of obvious typographical errors. Brackets indicate a change, addition, or doubt on the part of the editor, except in the case of John Woolman's works where brackets were provided by its editor, Amelia Mott Cummere, to indicate variations in the manuscripts. Whenever possible the earliest text of each document has been selected: thus Martin Luther King, Jr.'s *Letter From Birmingham City Jail* appears here as first published by the American Friends Service Committee, rather than in the slightly revised form in which Dr. King included it in his *Why We Can't Wait*. Footnotes throughout the documents occur in the original text, except where placed in brackets and marked "Ed."

It is a pleasure to acknowledge the assistance of the following persons who have helped in locating material for this volume: Ruby Doris Smith Robinson, of the Student Nonviolent Coordinating Committee; Marvin Rich, of the Congress Of Racial Equality; Neil Haworth, Robert Swann and David Dellinger, of the Committee for Nonviolent Action; David McReynolds, of the War Resisters League; Rev. Maurice McCrackin of the Community Church of Cincinnati; Vincent Harding, of the Mennonite Central Committee; John Yungblut, director of Quaker House in Atlanta; Paul Lauter, of the American Friends Service Committee; and Jane Stembridge of the Council of Federated Organizations. None of these persons, all honorably active in good causes, have any responsibility for errors of fact or interpretation in the editing of documents they kindly made available.

I would also like to thank the members of the Social Science Honors Seminar at Spelman College for many good hours of discussion about the themes of this book. The patience and craftsmanship of Alfred Young have, as always, been invaluable. My wife, Alice Lynd, finished the editorial work on the volume with sensitivity and skill, thus making it possible for me to spend a summer attempting to practice nonviolence in Mississippi.

Staughton Lynd

Jackson, Mississippi
August 1964
New Haven, Connecticut
January 1966

Nonviolence in America

PART I

Quakers

---

1. William Penn,
First Letter to the Delaware Indians

William Penn (1644–1718), son of an English admiral, came in contact with Quakers while he was a student at Oxford University. After joining the Friends, he was arrested and jailed several times under Restoration laws that restricted nonconformity. (One of these cases, in 1670, settled the legal precedent that a jury's verdict of "not guilty" shall prevail despite a contrary instruction from the judge.) His radicalism notwithstanding, in 1681 Penn was given Pennsylvania as a proprietary province.

Document 1 is a letter of October 18, 1681, which Penn gave the commissioners who preceded him to Pennsylvania to read to the Indians on their arrival. The result was the famous treaty or treaties of peace between Penn and the Delaware Indians.

"William Penn's First Letter to the Indians," *Annals of Pennsylvania, from the Discovery of the Delaware, 1609–1682*, ed. Samuel Hazard (Philadelphia: Hazard and Mitchell, 1850), pp. 532–533.

London, 18th of 8th Month, 1681

MY FRIENDS–There is one great God and power that hath made the world and all things therein, to whom you and I, and all people owe their being and well-being, and to whom you and I must one day give an account for all that we do in the world; this great God hath written his law in our hearts, by which we are taught and commanded to love and help, and do good to one another, and not to do harm and mischief one to another. Now this great God hath been pleased to make me concerned in your parts of the world, and the king of the country where I live hath given unto me a great province, but I desire to enjoy it with your love and consent, that we may always live together as neighbours and friends, else what would the great God say to us, who hath made us not to devour and destroy one another, but live soberly and kindly together in the world? Now I would have you well observe, that I am very sensible of the unkindness and injustice that hath been too much exercised towards you by the people of these parts of the world, who sought themselves, and to make great advantages by you, rather than be examples of justice and goodness unto you, which I hear hath been matter of trouble to you, and caused great grudgings and animosities, sometimes to the shedding of blood, which hath made the great God angry; but I am not such a man, as is well known in my own country; I have great love and regard towards you, and I desire to win and gain your love and friendship, by a kind, just, and peaceable life, and the people I send are of the same mind, and shall in all things behave themselves accordingly; and if in any thing any shall offend you or your people, you shall have a full and speedy satisfaction for the same, by an equal number of just men on both sides, that by no means you may have just occasion of being offended against them. I shall shortly come to you myself, at what time we may more largely and freely confer and discourse of these matters. In the mean time, I have sent my

commissioners to treat with you about land, and a firm league of peace. Let me desire you to be kind to them and the people, and receive these presents and tokens which I have sent to you, as a testimony of my good will to you, and my resolution to live justly, peaceably, and friendly with you.
I am your loving friend,

WILLIAM PENN.

2. John Woolman,

Journal

The most significant figure in the early history of nonviolence in America is John Woolman (1720 1722). A Quaker, his thought belonged to the tradition of the radical Reformation, with its insistence on pacifism, civil disobedience, and community of goods, and its mystical intuition of the oneness of creation.

Woolman's best-known work, his *Journal* (first published in 1774), tells the story of his life. Unlike the aristocratic William Penn, but like William Lloyd Garrison and Elihu Burritt, Woolman belonged to the class of self-educated craftsmen and small shopkeepers then known as "mechanics and tradesmen." A keen sense of social concern drove him to leave his New Jersey home for long trips to admonish Quaker slaveholders in the South, to visit the

---

"The Journal of John Woolman," *The Journal and Essays of John Woolman*, edited from the original manuscripts with a biographical introduction by Amelia Mott Gummere (New York: The Macmillan Company, 1922), pp. 160–162, 187–190, 204–207, 248–249, 254–256. The slavery excerpts were written in 1743 and 1757; tax refusal in 1757; treatment of Indians in 1763. Bracketed material in the text, but not the subheadings, were supplied by Mrs. Gummere. Reprinted with the permission of Richard M. Gummere for the Estate of F. B. Gummere.

Indians, and finally to England, where he died shortly before the American Revolution.

These excerpts from the *Journal* illustrate the development of Woolman's thought in response to encounters in daily life. Thus, his objection to slavery sprang from occasions on which neighbors asked him to write legal documents relating to their human chattels. The French and Indian War led Woolman as well as Anthony Benezet and other Quakers to refuse to pay taxes in support of war. Woolman's account of his tax refusal reveals how new a practice it was, even among Friends. Believing that "conduct is more convincing than language," Woolman also refused free hospitality from slaveholders and gave up the use of commodities, such as cotton, cloth and sugar, which were made with slave labor.

[*Slavery*]

About the twenty third year of my age I had many fresh and heavenly openings, in respect to the care and providence of the Almighty over his creatures in general, and over man as the most noble amongst those which are visible, and Being clearly convinced in my Judgmt that to place my whole trust in God was best for me, I felt renewed engagements that in all things I might act on an inward principle of Virtue, and pursue worldly business no further than as Truth open'd my way therein. . . .

. . . My Employer having a Negro woman sold her, and directed me to write a bill of Sale, The man being waiting who had bought her. The thing was Sudden, and though the thoughts of writing an Instrument of Slavery for one of my fellow creatures felt uneasie, yet I remembered I was hired by the year; that it was my master who [directed] me to do it, and that it was an Elderly man, a member of our society who bought her, so through weakness I gave way, and wrote it, but at the Executing it I was so Afflicted in my mind, that I said before my Master and the friend, that I believed Slavekeeping to be a practice inconsistent with the Christian Religion: this in some degree abated my uneasiness, yet as often as I reflected seriously upon it I thought I should have been clearer, if I had desired to be Excused from it, as a thing against my conscience, for such it was. [And] some time after this a young man of our Society, spake to me to write [an instrument of Slavery], he having lately taken a Negro into his house. I told him I was not easie to write it, for though many [people] kept slaves in our society as in others, I still believed the practice was not right, and desired to be excused from doing the writing. I spoke to him in good will, and he told me, that keeping slaves was not altogether agreable to his mind, but that the slave being a gift made to his wife, he had accepted of her. . . .

. . . Feeling an exercise in relation to a visit to the Southern parts to increase upon me, I acquainted our monthly meeting therewith, and Obtained their Certificate. . . .

As the people in this and the southern provinces, live much on the labour of Slaves, many of whom are used hardly, my concern was, that I might attend with singleness of heart to the Voice of the True Shepherd, and be so supported as to remain unmoved at the faces of men.

As it is common for Friends on a visit to have Entertainment free cost, a difficulty arose in my mind with respect to saveing my own money by kindness received, which to me appeared to be the gain of Opression.

Receiving a gift, considered as a gift, brings the receiver under Obligations to the Benefactor, and has a natural tendency to draw the Obliged into a party with the giver. To prevent difficulties of this kind, and to preserve the minds of Judges from any byas, was that Divine Prohibition "Thou shalt not receive any gift, for a gift blindeth the wise, and perverteth the words of the Righteous." Exod. xxiii. 8. As the Disciples were sent forth without any Provision for their Journey, and our Lord said, the workman is worthy of his meat, Their labour in the Gospel was considered as a reward for their Entertainment, and therefore not received as a gift: yet in re-

gard to my present Journey I could not see my way clear in
that respect—the odds appeared thus: The entertainment the
disciples met with, was from such whose hearts God had
opened to receive them, from a Love to them, and the Truth
which they published: But we, considered as members of the
same society, look upon it as a piece of Civility to receive each
other in such visits, and Such reception, at times, is partly in
regard to reputation, and not from an inward Unity of heart
and Spirit.

Conduct is more convincing than language; and where people by their actions manifest that the Slave trade is not so disagreeable to their principles but that it may be encouraged,
there is not a Sound uniting with some Friends who Visit
them.

The prospect of so weighty a work & being so distinguished
from many whom I Esteemed before myself, brought me verry
low, & Such were the conflicts of my Soul, that I had a near
sympathy with the profet in the time of his weakness, when
he said "If thou deal thus with me, kill me, I pray thee out of
hand if I have found favour in thy Sight," but I soon saw that
this proceeded from the want of a full resignation to Him.
Many were the afflictions which attended me and in great
Abasement, with many tears, my Cries were to the Almighty
for his Gracious and Fatherly assistance, and then, after a
Time of Deep Tryals I was favoured to understand the state
mentioned by the psalmist more clearly than ever I had before,
to wit: "My Soul is even as a weaned child."

Being thus helped to sink down into Resignation I felt a
deliverance from that Tempest in which I had been sorely Exercised, and in Calmness of mind went forward Trusting that
the Lord Jesus Christ, as I faithfully attended to Him, would be
a Councellor to me in all Difficulties, and that by his Strength I
should be enabled even to leave money with the members of
Society where I had Entertainment, when I found that omiting
of it would Obstruct that work to which I believed he had

called me. And as I copy this after my return [from that Journey] I may here add, that oftentimes I did so, Under a sense of duty. The Manner in which I did it was thus: when I expected soon to leave a Friend's house where I had Entertainment, if I believed that I should not keep clear from the gain of Oppression without leaving some money, I spoke to One of the heads of the Family privately, and desired them to accept of them pieces of Silver, and give them to such of their Negroes as they believ'd would make the best use of them; And at other times, I gave them to the Negroes myself, [according] as the way looked clearest to me. As I expected this before I came out, I had provided a large number of small pieces [of silver] and thus offering them to Some who appeared to be wealthy people was a tryal both to me and them· But the [Exercise of my mind was Such and the] fear of the Lord so covered me at times, that way was made easier than I expected, and few, if any, manifested any resentment at the offer, and most of them, after some [little] talk, accepted of them. . . .

[*Tax Refusal*]

A few years past, money being made current in our province for carrying on wars, and to be sunk by Taxes laid on the Inhabitants, my mind was often affected with the thoughts of paying such Taxes, and I believe it right for me to preserve a memorandum concerning it.

I was told that Friends in England frequently paid Taxes when the money was applied to such purposes. I had [conference] with several Noted Friends on the subject, who all favoured the payment of such taxes, Some of whom I preferred before myself, and this made me easier for a time: yet there was in the deeps of my mind, a scruple which I never could get over; and, at certain times, I was greatly distressed on that account.

I all along believed that there were some upright-hearted

men who paid such taxes, but could not see that their Example was a Sufficient Reason for me to do so, while I believed that the Spirit of Truth required of me as an individual to suffer patiently the distress of goods, rather than pay actively.

I have been informed that Thomas à Kempis lived & died in the profession of the Roman Catholick Religion, and in reading his writings, I have believed him to be a man of a true Christian spirit, as fully so as many who died Martyrs because they could not join with some superstitions in that Church.

All true Christians are of [one and] the same spirit, but their gifts are diverse; [Jesus] Christ appointing to each one their peculiar Office, agreeable to his Infinite Wisdom.

John Huss Contended against the Errors crept into the Church, in oposition to the Council of Constance, which the historian reports to have consisted of many thousand persons. He modestly vindicated the cause which he believed was right, and though his language and Conduct toward his Judges appear to have been respectfull, yet he never could be moved from the principles settled in his mind. To use his own words: "This I most humbly require and desire of you all, even for His sake who is the God of us all, that I be not compelled to the thing which my Conscience doth repugn or strive against." And again in his answer to the emperor "I refuse nothing, most noble Emperor whatsoever the council shall decree or determine upon me, this only one thing I except, that I do not offend God and my Conscience." At length rather than act contrary to that which he believed the Lord required of Him, he chose to Suffer death by fire. Thomas à Kempis, without disputing against the Articles then generally agreed to, appears to have laboured, by a Pious Example as well as by Preaching & writing to promote Virtue and the Inward Spiritual Religion, and I believe they were both sincere-hearted followers of Christ. [To me it looks likely that they were both in their proper places.]

True Charity is an excellent Virtue, and to sincerely Labour for their good, whose belief in all points, doth not agree with ours, is a happy case. To refuse the active payment of a Tax which our Society generally paid, was exceeding disagreeable; but to do a thing contrary to my Conscience appeared yet more dreadfull. When this exercise came upon me I knew of none under the like difficulty, and in my distress I besought the Lord to enable me to give up all, that so I might follow him wheresoever he was pleased to lead me, and under this Exercise I went to our Yearly Meeting at Philada, in 1755, at which a Committee was appointed, some from each Quarter to Correspond with the meeting for Sufferings in London, and another to Visit our Monthly and Quarterly meetings, and after their appointment before the last Adjournment of the meeting, it was agreed on in the meeting that these two Committees should meet together in Friends School House in the Citty, at a time [when the Meeting stood adjourned] to consider some [cases] in which the cause of Truth was concerned: and these Committees meeting together had a weighty conferrence in the fear of the Lord, at which time I perceived there were many Friends under a Scruple like that before mentioned.

As Scrupling to pay a tax on account of the application[1] hath seldom been heard of heretofore, even amongst men of Integrity, who have Steadily born their testimony against outward wars in their time, I may here note some things which have opened on my mind, as I have been inwardly Exercised on that account.

From the Steady oposition which Faithfull Friends in early times made to wrong things then approved of, they were hated and persecuted by men living in the Spirit of this world, & Suffering with firmness, they were made a Blessing to the Church, & the work prospered. It equaly concerns men in every age to take heed to their own Spirit: & in comparing their Situ-

---

[1] Christians refused to pay taxes to support Heathen Temples. See Cave's Primitive Christianity, part iii, page 327. [Note by Woolman. Ed.]

ation with ours, it looks to me there was less danger of their being infected with the Spirit of this world in paying their taxes, than there is of us now. They had little or no Share in Civil Government, neither Legislative nor Executive & many of them declared they were through the power of God separated from the Spirit in which wars were, and being Afflicted by the Rulers on account of their Testimony, there was less likelyhood of uniting in Spirit with them in things inconsistent with the purity of Truth. We, from the first settlement of this Land have known little or no troubles of that sort. The profession, which for a time was accounted reproachfull, at length the uprightness of our predecessors being understood by the Rulers, & their Innocent Sufferings moving them, our way of Worship was tolerated, and many of our members in these colonies became active in Civil Government. Being thus tryed with favour and prosperity, this world hath appeared inviteing; our minds have been turned to the Improvement of our Country, to Merchandize and Sciences, amongst which are many things usefull, being followed in pure wisdom, but in our present condition that a Carnal mind is gaining upon us I believe will not be denied.

Some of our members who are Officers in Civil Government are in one case or other called upon in their respective Stations to Assist in things relative to the wars, Such being in doubt whether to act or crave to be excused from their Office, Seeing their Brethren united in the payment of a Tax to carry on the said wars, might think their case [nearly like theirs, &] so quench the tender movings of the Holy Spirit in their minds, and thus by small degrees there might be an approach toward that of Fighting, till we came so near it, as that the distinction would be little else but the name of a peaceible people.

It requires great self-denial and Resignation of ourselves to God to attain that state wherein we can freely cease from fighting when wrongfully Invaded, if by our Fighting there were a probability of overcoming the invaders. Whoever rightly attains to it, does in some degree feel that Spirit in which our Redeemer gave his life for us, and, through Divine goodness many of our predecessors, and many now living, have learned this blessed lesson, but many others having their Religion chiefly by Education, & not being enough acquainted with that Cross which Crucifies to the world, do manifest a Temper distinguishable from that of an Entire trust in God.

In calmly considering these things it hath not appeared strange to me, that an exercise hath now fallen upon some, which as to the outward means of it is different from what was known to many of those who went before us. . . .

[*Treatment of Indians*]

Having many years felt Love in my heart towards the Natives of this Land, who dwell far back in the Wilderness, whose Ancestors were the owners and possessors of the [Country] where we dwell, and who for a very small consideration Assigned their Inheritance to us . . . I felt inward drawings toward a Visit to that place. . . .

. . . And as I rode over the barren Hills my meditations were on the Alterations of the Circumstances of the Natives of this land since the coming in of the English. The Lands near the Sea are Conveniently scituated for fishing. The lands near the Rivers where the tides flow, and some above, are in many places fertile, and not mountainous; while the Runing of the Tides makes passing up and down easie with any kind of Traffick. Those natives have in some places for [small] considerations sold their Inheritance so favourably Scituated and in other places been driven back by superior force. So that in many places as their way of Clothing themselves is now altered from what it was, and they far remote from us have to pass over Mountains, Swamps, and Barran deserts, where Traveling is very troublesome, in bringing their furs & skins to trade with us.

By the Extending of English Settlements and partly by English Hunters, those wild Beasts they chiefly depend on for a subsistence are not so plenty as they were. And people too often for the Sake of gain open a Door for them to waste their Skins & furs, in purchasing a Liquor which tends to the ruin of y^m [them] & their Families.

My own will and desire being now very much broken, and my heart with much earnestness turned to the Lord, to whom alone I looked for help in the dangers before me, I had a prospect of the English along the Coast for upwards of nine hundred miles where I have traveled. And the favourable Situation of the English, and the difficulties attending the natives [and the Slaves amongst us,] were open before me, and a weighty and Heavenly care came over my mind, and love filled my heart toward all mankind, in which I felt a Strong Engagement that we might be [faithful] to the Lord while His mercies [are yet extended] to us, and so attend to pure Universal Righteousness as to give no just cause of offence to the gentiles who do not profess christianity, Whither the Blacks from Africa, or the Native Inhabitants of this Continent: And here I was led into a close, laborious Enquiry, whether I as an individual kept clear from all things which tended to Stir up, or were connnected with wars, Either in this Land or Africa, and my heart was deeply concerned that in future I might in all things keep steadily to the pure Truth, & live and walk in the plainness and Simplicity of a Sincere follower of Christ. And in this lonely Journey, I did this day greatly bewail the spreading of a wrong Spirit, believing that the prosperous Conveniant Scituation of the English, requires a Constant Attention to Divine love & wisdom, to guide and Support us in a way answerable to the will of that Good, Gracious, & Almighty Being who hath an Equal regard to all mankind. And here Luxury and Covetousness, with the numerous Opressions and other evils attending them, appeared very Afflicting to me, and I felt in that which is Immutable that the Seeds of great

Calamity and desolation are Sown & growing fast on this Continent. Nor have I words sufficient to set forth that longing I then felt, that we who are placed along the Coast, & have tasted the Love and Goodness of God, might arise in his Strength, and like faithful Messengers Labour to check the growth of those Seeds that they may not ripen to the Ruin of our posterity.

3. John Woolman, "A Plea for the Poor"

"A Plea for the Poor," first published in 1793, expresses the full scope of Woolman's social philosophy: that if men would regard their daily bread as a gift from God, and be content with necessities, then wars caused by the strife for luxuries would end, and the exploitation of man by man would give way to universal love.

Chapter IX.

When our eyes are so single as to discern the selfish spirit clearly, we behold it the greatest of all Tyrants. Many thousand Innocent people under some of the Roman Emperors being confirmed in the truth of Christ's religion, from the powerful effects of His Holy Spirit upon them, and Scrupling to conform to Heathenish Rites, were therefore, by various kinds of Cruel & Lingering Torments put to Death, as is largely set forth by Eusebius.

"A Plea for the Poor," *The Journal and Essays of John Woolman,* ed. Amelia Mott Gummere (New York: Macmillan, 1922), Chapters IX, X, XI, pp. 416–421. This essay of sixteen chapters is presumed by Mrs. Gummere to have been written in 1763. Bracketed material in the text was supplied by Mrs. Gummere. Reprinted with the permission of Richard M. Gummere for the Estate of F. B. Gummere.

Now if we single out Domitian, Nero, or any other of these persecuting Emperors, the man though terrible in his time, Will appear a Tyrant of small consequence, compared with the Selfish Spirit. For though his bounds were large, yet a great part of the world was out of his reach. And though he grievously afflicted the Bodies of those Innocent people, yet the minds of many were Divinely Supported in their greatest Agonies; & being Faithfull unto Death, they were delivered from his Tyranny. His reign, though cruel for a time, was soon over and he considered in his greatest pomp, appears to have been a Slave to the Selfish Spirit. Thus Tyranny as applied to a man, rises up and is soon near an end. But if we consider the numerous Oppressions in many States, & the Calamities occasioned by Nation contending with Nation, in various parts and ages of the world, and remember that Selfishness hath been the Original Cause of them all; If we consider that those who are finally possessed with this Selfish Spirit, not only Afflict others, but are afflicted themselves, and have no real quietness in this life, nor in futurity, but according to the Saying of Christ, have their portion in that uneasie condition, "where the worm dieth not, and the fire is not quenched:" [Under all these Circumstances, how Terrible does this Selfishness appear?] If we consider the havock that is made in this age, & how numbers of people are hurried on, Striving to Collect Treasures to please that mind which wanders from perfect resignedness, and in that wisdom which is foolishness with God, are perverting the true use of things, Labouring as in the Fire, Contending with one another, even unto Blood, and Exerting their power to support ways of living, foreign to the life of one wholly Crucified to the world:

If we consider what great numbers of people are Employed in different Kingdoms preparing the materials of war, and the Labour & Toyl of armies set apart for protecting their respective Territories from the Incursions of others, and the Ex-

tensive miseries which attend their Engagements: While many
of those who Till the land, and are Employed in other useful
things: in Supporting themselves, Supporting those Employed
in Military Affairs, and some who own the soil, have great
hardships to encounter through too much Labour. While others
in several kingdoms are busied in fetching men to help Labour
from distant parts of the World, to spend the remainder of
their lives in the uncomfortable Condition of Slaves, and that
Self is at the bottom of these proceedings. Amidst all this Confusion and these Scenes of Sorrow and distress, can we remember the Prince of Peace, Remember that we are his Disciples,
& Remember that Example of Humility and plainness which
he set for us, without feeling an earnest desire to be disen-
tangled from everything connected with selfish customs, in
Food, in Raiment, in Houses, and all things else? That being
of Christ's family, and walking as he walked, we may Stand
in that uprightness wherein man was first made, and have no
fellowship with those Inventions which men in their fallen
wisdom have sought out.

In the selfish spirit standeth Idolatry. Did our blessed Redeemer enable his family to endure great reproaches, and suffer cruel torments even unto death for their testimony against
the idolatry of those times, and can we behold the prevalence
of Idolatry, though under a different appearance without being
jealous over ourselves lest we unwarily join in it?

Those faithful Martyrs refused to cast incense into the fire,
though by doing it, they might have escaped a cruel death.
Casting sweet-scented matter into the fire to make a comfortable smell, this considered separate from all circumstances,
would appear to be of small consequence: but as they would
thereby have signified their approbation of Idolatry, it was
necessarily refused by the faithful. Nor can we, in any degree
depart from pure universal Righteousness, and publicly continue in that which is not agreeable to the Truth, without

strengthening the hands of the unrighteous, and doing that which in the nature of the thing is like offering incense to an Idol.

Origen, a primitive Christian, it is reported of him, that in a time of unwatchfulness, being under great difficulty, he took incense into his hand, and a certain heathen to forward the work took hold of his hand and Cast the incense into the fire on the Altar, and that through thus far complying, he was released from his outward trouble, but afterward greatly bewailed his condition as one fallen from a good estate to that which was worse.

Thus it appears that a small degree of deliberate compliance with that which is wrong is very dangerous, and the case of Origen carries in it an Admonition worthy of our Notice.

Chapter X.

"Are not two Sparrows sold for a Farthing, and one of them shall not fall to the Ground without your Father."

The way of Carrying on Wars, common in the world, is so far distinguishable from the purity of Christ's Religion, that many scruple to joyn in them. Those who are so redeemed from the Love of the World, as to possess nothing in a Selfish Spirit, their "Life is hid with Christ in God," and these he preserves in resignedness, even in times of Commotion.

As they possess nothing but what pertains to His family, anxious thoughts about wealth or dominion hath little or nothing in them to work upon, and they learn contentment in being disposed of according to His Will, who being Omnipotent, and always mindful of his Children, causeth all things to work for their good. But where that spirit works which loves Riches; works, & in its working gathers wealth, and cleaves to customs which have their Root in self pleasing. This Spirit thus separating from Universal Love, seeks help from that power which stands in the Separation, and whatever name it hath, it still desireth to defend the Treasures thus gotten. This is like a Chain, where the end of one link encloses the end of another. The rising up of a desire to obtain wealth is the beginning. This desire being cherished moves to action, and riches thus gotten pleace self and while self hath a life in them it desires to have them defended.

Wealth is attended with Power, by which Bargains and proceedings contrary to Universal Righteousness are Supported, and here Oppression, carried on with worldly policy & order, cloathes itself with the name of Justice, and becomes like a seed of Discord in the soyl: and as this spirit which wanders from the pure Habitation prevails, so the seed of War Swells & Sprouts and grows & becomes Strong, till much fruit are ripened. Thus cometh the Harvest spoken of by the prophet, which "is a Heap, in the Day of Grief & of desperate Sorrow."

Oh! that we who declare against wars, and Acknowledge our trust to be in God only, may walk in the Light, and therein examine our Foundation & motives in holding great Estates: May we look upon our Treasures, and the furniture of our Houses, and the Garments in which we array ourselves, and try whether the seeds of war have any nourishment in these our possessions, or not. Holding Treasures in the Self pleasing Spirit is a Strong plant, the fruit whereof ripens fast.

A day of outward Distress is coming, and Divine Love calls to prepare for it. Hearken then, O ye Children who have known the Light, and come forth! Leave every thing which our Lord Jesus Christ does not own. Think not his pattern too plain or too coarse for you. Think not a Small portion in this life too little: but let us live in His Spirit, & walk as he walked, and he will preserve us in the greatest Troubles.

Chapter XI.

"The Heaven, even the Heavens are the Lord's; but the Earth hath he given to the children of men." Psal. 115:16.

As Servants of God, what Land or Estates we hold, we hold under him as his gifts; and in applying the profits, it is our duty to act consistently with the Design of Our Benefactor. Imperfect men may give on motives of Misguided Affection, but Perfect Wisdom & Goodness gives agreeable to his own Nature; nor is this gift absolute, but conditional, for us to occupy as dutiful Children, and not otherwise; for he alone is the true proprietor. "The World," saith He, "is mine, and the fulness thereof." Psal. xxiv. 1.

The Inspired Law giver directed that such of the Israelites as sold their Inheritance, should sell it for a term only; and that they or their Children should again enjoy it in the year of Jubilee, settled on every Fiftieth year. "The land shall not be sold for ever; for the Land is mine, saith the Lord, for ye are Strangers, and Sojourners with me." Levit. xxv. 23. The design of which was to prevent the Rich from Oppressing the poor, by too much engrossing the Land. And Our Blessed Redeemer said, "Till heaven and earth pass, one jot or one Tittle shall in no wise pass from the Law till all be fulfilled."

Where Divine love takes place in the Hearts of any people, and they steadily act on a principle of Universal Righteousness, there the true intent of the Law is fulfilled, though their outward modes of proceeding may be distinguishable from one another: But where men are possessed by that Spirit hinted at by the Prophet, and looking over their wealth, say in their hearts, "Have we not taken to us Horns by our own Strength?" Here they deviate from the Divine Law, and do not account their possessions so strictly God's, nor the weak & poor entitled to so much of the increase thereof, but that they may indulge their desires in conforming to worldly pomp. And thus where House is joined to House, and Field laid to Field, till there is no place, and the poor are thereby straitened; though this be done by Bargain & Purchase, yet so far as it Stands distinguished from Universal Love, so far that WO, prefixed by the Prophet will accompany their proceedings.

As He who first formed the Earth out of nothing was then

the true Proprietor of it, so He still remains; and though he
hath given it to the Children of men, so that multitudes of people have had sustenance from it, while they continued here,
yet he hath never Aliencd it, but his Right to give is as good as
the first, nor can any apply the increase of their possessions
contrary to Universal Love: nor dispose of Lands in a way
which they know tends to Exalt some, by Oppressing others,
without being justly chargeable with Usurpation.

4. Anthony Benezet,
Letter to the President of
the Continental Congress

Anthony Benezet (1713–1784) shared the peace and antislavery
concerns of his fellow Quakers, Penn and Woolman. A teacher, he
founded schools for girls and for Negroes. Benezet's writing against
slavery, detailing from travelers' accounts the horrors of the slave
trade, made a deep impression on Franklin, Patrick Henry, and other
prominent Americans. Benezet refused to pay taxes in support of the
French and Indian War, and when the War for Independence began
he opposed that, too.

Chesnut Street, 2d mo.
Feb. 7, 1779.

With affectionate respect I hereby salute thee, and take the
freedom to send thee the inclosed pamphlet, containing some
thoughts on war, slavery, &c. of which I earnestly request thy

---

Anthony Benezet to John Jay, President of the Congress, February 7,
1779, in George S. Brookes, *Friend Anthony Benezet* (Philadelphia: University of Pennsylvania Press, 1937), pp. 330–331.

serious perusal. Indeed the subject is of the greatest weight to all, even as human beings; but much more so to those who indeed believe the great truths of the Christian religion, God becoming man, and dying for mankind, even for his enemies, "leaving us, says the apostle, *an example that we should follow his footsteps."* This, and other arguments therein deduced, from the doctrines and nature of the Gospel, will I trust tend to soften, if not remove, any offence which Friends' refusal to take part in matters of a military nature may have raised in thy mind, and induce thee to distinguish between such who are active in opposition, and those who have been restrained from an apprehension of duty, and a persuasion that our common beneficent Father who has the hearts of all men in his power, and has in former times so eminently displayed his goodness in favour of these countries, if properly sought unto, would in his love and mercy have averted the evil effects of any attempt which might have been made to impede our real welfare. By the deplorable effects which attend on these dreadful contests, it is evident that it cannot be agreeable to God, who the apostle denominates under the appellation of Love, as thereby every noxious passion of the human mind, instead of being calmed by the benign influences of grace, the end and aim of Christianity, are inflamed into greater wrath, and evil of every kind; as has been verified in that destruction of morals, that waste of substance, but more particularly in the hasty death of so vast a number of our fellow men, hurried into eternity, many it is to be feared in that distracted state of mind which generally attends on war.

These are considerations which cannot but strike every thoughtful mind with awe, and which, from the kindness and considerateness of thy disposition, will I trust incite thee to advocate the cause of a number of innocent people of different religious persuasions, who from the above mentioned view of things, have not dared to give life or support to military operations, yet at the same time are indeed friends to, and really concerned for the true welfare of America, but willing to sacrifice their all, rather than do that whereby they apprehend they may offend that great and good Being, from whom alone they look for any permanent happiness for themselves or their afflicted country.

With affectionate desires, that the blessings of the peace maker, the peculiar favourite of Heaven, may be thine, I remain thy friend

ANTHONY BENEZET

PART II

Abolitionists

5. William Lloyd Garrison,
"Declaration of Sentiments, 1838"

Quiescent for a generation after the American Revolution, nonviolence revived during the widely unpopular War of 1812. After the
war the abolitionist movement, under the influence of William Lloyd
Garrison, adopted nonviolence as part of its creed.

Garrison (1805–1879) espoused the abolition of capital punishment, abstention from politics, and opposition to all war, as well as
emancipation of the slaves. Prompted by these beliefs, Garrison and
a few abolitionist friends split the American Peace Society in 1838 to
found the New England Non Resistance Society. The Society's statement of principles, which he drafted, illustrates the fact that Garrison
might eschew physical violence but was never hesitant to "assail
iniquity" with words.

Assembled in Convention, from various sections of the American Union, for the promotion of peace on earth and good will
among men, we, the undersigned, regard it as due to ourselves,
to the cause which we love, to the country in which we live,

"Declaration of Sentiments adopted by the [American] Peace Convention, held in Boston, September 18, 19 and 20, 1838,"*Selections from
the Writings and Speeches of William Lloyd Garrison* (Boston: R. F.
Wallcutt, 1852), pp. 72–77.

and to the world, to publish a Declaration, expressive of the principles we cherish, the purposes we aim to accomplish, and the measures we shall adopt to carry forward the work of peaceful and universal reformation.

We cannot acknowledge allegiance to any human government; neither can we oppose any such government, by a resort of physical force. We recognize but one King and Lawgiver, one Judge and Ruler of mankind. We are bound by the laws of a kingdom which is not of this world; the subjects of which are forbidden to fight; in which Mercy and Truth are met together, and Righteousness and Peace have kissed each other; which has no state lines, no national partitions, no geographical boundaries; in which there is no distinction of rank, or division of caste, or inequality of sex; the officers of which are Peace, its exactors Righteousness, its walls Salvation, and its gates Praise; and which is destined to break in pieces and consume all other kingdoms.

Our country is the world, our countrymen are all mankind. We love the land of our nativity, only as we love all other lands. The interests, rights, and liberties of American citizens are no more dear to us, than are those of the whole human race. Hence, we can allow no appeal to patriotism, to revenge any national insult or injury. The Prince of Peace, under whose stainless banner we rally, came not to destroy, but to save, even the worst of enemies. He has left us an example, that we should follow his steps. 'God commendeth his love towards us, in that while we were yet sinners, Christ died for us.'

We conceive, that if a nation has no right to defend itself against foreign enemies, or to punish its invaders, no individual possesses that right in his own case. The unit cannot be of greater importance than the aggregate. If one man may take life, to obtain or defend his rights, the same license must necessarily be granted to communities, states, and nations. If he may use a dagger or a pistol, they may employ cannon, bomb-shells, land and naval forces. The means of self-preservation must be in proportion to the magnitude of interests at stake, and the number of lives exposed to destruction. But if a rapacious and blood-thirsty soldiery, thronging these shores from abroad, with intent to commit rapine and destroy life, may not be resisted by the people or magistracy, then ought no resistance to be offered to domestic troublers of the public peace, or of private security. No obligation can rest upon Americans to regard foreigners as more sacred in their persons than themselves, or to give them a monopoly of wrong-doing with impunity.

The dogma, that all the governments of the world are approvingly ordained of God, and that the powers that be in the United States, in Russia, in Turkey, are in accordance with His will, is not less absurd than impious. It makes the impartial Author of human freedom and equality, unequal and tyrannical. It cannot be affirmed, that the powers that be, in any nation, are actuated by the spirit, or guided by the example of Christ, in the treatment of enemies: therefore, they cannot be agreeable to the will of God: and, therefore, their overthrow, by a spiritual regeneration of their subjects, is inevitable.

We register our testimony, not only against all wars, whether offensive or defensive, but all preparations for war; against every naval ship, every arsenal, every fortification; against the militia system and a standing army; against all military chieftains and soldiers; against all monuments commemorative of victory over a foreign foe, all trophies won in battle, all celebrations in honor of military or naval exploits; against all appropriations for the defence of a nation by force and arms on the part of any legislative body; against every edict of government, requiring of its subjects military service. Hence, we deem it unlawful to bear arms, or to hold a military office.

As every human government is upheld by physical strength, and its laws are enforced virtually at the point of the bayonet, we cannot hold any office which imposes upon its incumbent the obligation to do right, on pain of imprisonment or death.

We therefore voluntarily exclude ourselves from every legislative and judicial body, and repudiate all human politics, worldly honors, and stations of authority. If *we* cannot occupy a seat in the legislature, or on the bench, neither can we elect *others* to act as our substitutes in any such capacity.

It follows, that we cannot sue any man at law, to compel him by force to restore any thing which he may have wrongfully taken from us or others; but, if he has seized our coat, we shall surrender up our cloak, rather than subject him to punishment.

We believe that the penal code of the old covenant, An eye for an eye, and a tooth for a tooth, has been abrogated by Jesus Christ; and that, under the new covenant, the forgiveness, instead of the punishment of enemies, has been enjoined upon all his disciples, in all cases whatsoever. To extort money from enemies, or set them upon a pillory, or cast them into prison, or hang them upon a gallows, is obviously not to forgive, but to take retribution. 'Vengeance is mine—I will repay, saith the Lord.'

The history of mankind is crowded with evidences, proving that physical coercion is not adapted to moral regeneration; that the sinful disposition of man can be subdued only by love; that evil can be exterminated from the earth only by goodness; that it is not safe to rely upon an arm of flesh, upon man, whose breath is in his nostrils, to preserve us from harm; that there is great security in being gentle, harmless, long-suffering, and abundant in mercy; that it is only the meek who shall inherit the earth, for the violent, who resort to the sword, shall perish with the sword. Hence, as a measure of sound policy, of safety to property, life, and liberty, of public quietude and private enjoyment, as well as on the ground of allegiance to Him who is King of kings, and Lord of lords, we cordially adopt the non-resistance principle; being confident that it provides for all possible consequences, will ensure all things needful to us, is armed with omnipotent power, and must ultimately triumph over every assailing force.

We advocate no jacobinical doctrines. The spirit of jacobinism is the spirit of retaliation, violence and murder. It neither
fears God, nor regards man. We would be filled with the spirit
of Christ. If we abide by our principles, it is impossible for us
to be disorderly, or plot treason, or participate in any evil
work: we shall submit to every ordinance of man, for the
Lord's sake; obey all the requirements of government, except
such as we deem contrary to the commands of the gospel; and
in no wise resist the operation of law, except by meekly submitting to the penalty of disobedience.

But, while we shall adhere to the doctrines of non-resistance
and passive submission to enemies, we purpose, in a moral and
spiritual sense, to speak and act boldly in the cause of God; to
assail iniquity in high places and in low places; to apply our
principles to all existing civil, political, legal, and ecclesiastical
institutions; and to hasten the time, when the kingdoms of this
world shall become the kingdoms of our Lord and of his
Christ, and he shall reign for ever.

It appears to us a self-evident truth, that, whatever the
gospel is designed to destroy at any period of the world, being
contrary to it, ought now to be abandoned. If, then, the time is
predicted, when swords shall be beaten into plough-shares, and
spears into pruning-hooks, and men shall not learn the art of
war any more, it follows that all who manufacture, sell, or
wield those deadly weapons, do thus array themselves against
the peaceful dominion of the Son of God on earth.

Having thus briefly, but frankly, stated our principles and
purposes, we proceed to specify the measures we propose to
adopt, in carrying our object into effect.

We expect to prevail through the foolishness of preaching—
striving to commend ourselves unto every man's conscience, in
the sight of God. From the press, we shall promulgate our
sentiments as widely as practicable. We shall endeavor to secure the co-operation of all persons, of whatever name or sect.
The triumphant progress of the cause of Temperance and of

Abolition in our land, through the instrumentality of benevolent and voluntary associations, encourages us to combine our own means and efforts for the promotion of a still greater cause. Hence we shall employ lecturers, circulate tracts and publications, form societies, and petition our state and national governments in relation to the subject of Universal Peace. It will be our leading object to devise ways and means for effecting a radical change in the views, feelings and practices of society respecting the sinfulness of war, and the treatment of enemies.

In entering upon the great work before us, we are not unmindful that, in its prosecution, we may be called to test our sincerity, even as in a fiery ordeal. It may subject us to insult, outrage, suffering, yea, even death itself. We anticipate no small amount of misconception, misrepresentation, calumny. Tumults may arise against us. The ungodly and violent, the proud and pharisaical, the ambitious and tyrannical, principalities and powers, and spiritual wickedness in high places, may combine to crush us. So they treated the Messiah, whose example we are humbly striving to. imitate. If we suffer with him, we know that we shall reign with him. We shall not be afraid of their terror, neither be troubled. Our confidence is in the Lord Almighty, not in man. Having withdrawn from human protection, what can sustain us but that faith which overcomes the world? We shall not think it strange concerning the fiery trial which is to try us, as though some strange thing had happened unto us; but rejoice, inasmuch as we are partakers of Christ's sufferings. Wherefore, we commit the keeping of our souls to God, in well-doing, as unto a faithful Creator. 'For every one that forsakes houses, or brethren, or sisters, or father, or mother, or wife, or children, or lands, for Christ's sake, shall receive an hundred fold, and shall inherit everlasting life.'

Firmly relying upon the certain and universal triumph of the sentiments contained in this Declaration, however formidable may be the opposition arrayed against them, in solemn

testimony of our faith in their divine origin, we hereby affix
our signatures to it; commending it to the reason and conscience of mankind, giving ourselves no anxiety as to what may
befall us, and resolving, in the strength of the Lord God,
calmly and meekly to abide the issue.

6. Adin Ballou,

Christian Non-Resistance

Adin Ballou (1803–1890) was another of those early nineteenth-
century reformers who made the eradication of sin—whether in the
form of war, slavery, or intemperance—the business of their lives.
Ballou founded one of the first American utopian communities at
Hopedale, Massachusetts. It lasted from 1841 to 1856. In 1839, at
a meeting of the New England Non-Resistance Society, he delivered
a lecture on "Non-Resistance in Relation to Human Governments";
later he expanded these thoughts into a book, *Christian Non-Resistance*, here excerpted. Ballou's work contains many of the ideas made
famous by Thoreau's more celebrated essay. It ends with some interesting speculations about society without government, in which
the influence of the New England town meeting and the utopian
community movement are equally apparent.

Different Kinds of Non-Resistance.

What is Christian Non-Resistance? It is that original peculiar
kind of non-resistance, which was enjoined and exemplified by
Jesus Christ, according to the Scriptures of the New Testament. Are there other kinds of non-resistance? Yes. 1. Philo-

Adin Ballou, *Christian Non-Resistance, in All Its Important Bearings,
Illustrated and Defended* (Philadelphia: J. Miller M'Kim, 1846), pp.
9–13, 26–28, 104–105, 107–109, 144–145, 147–148, 165–168, 213–222,
224–226, 229–233.

sophical non-resistance of various hue, which sets at nought
divine revelation, disregards the authority of Jesus Christ as a
divine teacher, excludes all strictly religious considerations,
and deduces its conclusions from the light of nature, the supposed fitness of things and the expediency of consequences.
2. Sentimental non-resistance, also of various hue; which is
held to be the spontaneous dictate of man's higher sentiments
in the advanced stages of their development, *transcending* all
special divine revelations, positive instructions, ratiocination
and considerations of expediency. 3. Necessitous non-resistance, commonly expressed in the phrase, *"passive obedience
and non-resistance,"* imperiously preached by *despots* to their
subjects, as their indispensable duty and highest virtue; also
recommended by worldly prudence to the victims of oppression when unable to offer *successful* resistance to their injurers.
With this last mentioned kind Christian non-resistance has
nothing in common. With philosophical and sentimental non-
resistance it holds *much* in common; being, in fact, the *divine
original* of which they are human *adulterations,* and embrac-
ing all the *good* of *both* without the *evils* of *either.* This treatise
is an illustration and defence of Christian non-resistance,
properly so designated.

The Term Non-Resistance.

The term non-resistance itself next demands attention. It requires very considerable qualifications. I use it as applicable
only to the conduct of human beings towards human beings—
not towards the inferior animals, inanimate things, or satanic
influences. If an opponent, willing to make me appear ridiculous, should say—"You are a non-resistant, and therefore must
be *passive* to all assailing beings, things and influences, to
satan, man, beast, bird, serpent, insect, rocks, timbers, fires,
floods, heat, cold and storm,"—I should answer, *not so;* my
non-resistance relates solely to conduct between human beings.

This is an important limitation of the term. But I go further, and disclaim using the term to express *absolute passivity*, even towards *human* beings. I claim the right to offer the utmost *moral* resistance, not sinful, of which God has made me capable, to every manifestation of evil among mankind. Nay, I hold it my *duty* to offer such moral resistance. In this sense my very non-resistance becomes the highest kind of *resistance* to evil. This is another important qualification of the term. But I do not stop here. There is an uninjurious, benevolent *physical* force. There are cases in which it would not only be allowable, but in the highest degree commendable, to *restrain* human beings by this kind of force. Thus, maniacs, the insane, the delirious sick, ill natured children, the intellectually or *morally* non-compos mentis, the intoxicated and the violently passionate, are frequently disposed to perpetrate outrages and inflict injuries, either on themselves or others, which ought to be kindly and uninjuriously prevented by the muscular energy of their friends. And in cases where deadly violence is inflicted with deliberation and malice aforethought, one may nobly throw his body as a temporary barrier between the destroyer and his helpless victim, choosing to die in that position, rather than be a passive spectator. Thus another most important qualification is given to the term non-resistance. It is not non-resistance to animals and inanimate things, nor to satan, but only to human beings. Nor is it *moral* non-resistance to human beings, but chiefly physical. Nor is it physical non-resistance to all human beings, under all circumstances, but only so far as to abstain totally from the infliction of personal injury, as a means of resistance. It is simply non-resistance of injury with injury— evil with evil.

Will the opposer exclaim—"This is no non-resistance at all; the term is mischosen!" I answer. So said the old opposers of the Temperance Reformation, respecting the term *"total abstinence."* They began by insisting that the term *must* be taken unqualifiedly, and pronounced total abstinence an *absurdity*.

It was replied—"we limit its application to the use of ardent spirits and intoxicating liquours." "Then you exclude these substances from the arts and from external applications, do you?" rejoined the opposers. "No," replied the advocates of the cause, "we mean *total abstinence* from the *internal* use— the *drinking* of those liquors." "But are they not sometimes necessary for medical purposes?" said the opposers, "and *then* may they not be taken internally?" "Certainly, with proper precautions," was the reply; "we mean by *total abstinence,* precisely *this* and no more, the entire disuse of all ardent spirits and intoxicating liquors, *as a beverage.*" "That," exclaimed the objectors, (despairing of a reductio ad absurdam,) "is *no total* abstinence *at all;* the term is mischosen!" Nevertheless, it was a most significant term. It had in it an almost talismanic power. It expressed better than any other just what was meant, and wrought a prodigious change in public opinion and practice. The term *non-resistance* is equally significant and talismanic. It signifies total abstinence from all resistance of injury with injury. It is thus far *non-resistance*—no farther.

The almost universal opinion and practice of mankind has been on the side of resistance of injury *with* injury. It has been held justifiable and *necessary,* for individuals and nations to inflict any amount of *injury* which would effectually resist a supposed greater injury. The consequence has been universal suspicion, defiance, armament, violence, torture and bloodshed. The earth has been rendered a vast slaughter-field—a theatre of reciprocal cruelty and vengeance—strewn with human skulls, reeking with human blood, resounding with human groans, and steeped with human tears. Men have become drunk with mutual revenge; and they who could inflict the greatest amount of injury, in pretended defence of life, honor, rights, property, institutions and laws, have been idolized as the heroes and rightful sovereigns of the world. Non-resistance explodes this horrible delusion; announces the impossibility of overcoming evil with evil; and, making its appeal directly to all the *injured* of the human race, enjoins on them, in the name of God, never more to *resist injury with injury;* assuring them that by adhering to the law of love under all provocations, and scrupulously suffering wrong, rather than inflicting it, they shall gloriously "overcome evil with good," and exterminate all their enemies by turning them into faithful friends. . . .

What a Christian Non-Resistant Cannot Consistently Do.

It will appear from the foregoing exposition, that a true Christian non-resistant *cannot,* with deliberate intent, knowledge or conscious voluntariness, compromit his principles by either [any] of the following acts.

1. He cannot kill, maim or otherwise *absolutely injure* any human being, in personal self-defence, or for the sake of his family, or any thing he holds dear.

2. He cannot participate in any lawless conspiracy, mob, riotous assembly, or disorderly combination of individuals, to cause or countenance the commission of any such absolute personal injury.

3. He cannot be a member of any voluntary association, however orderly, respectable or allowable by law and general consent, *which declaratively* holds as *fundamental truth,* or claims as an essential right, or distinctly inculcates as sound doctrine, or approves as commendable in practice, *war, capital* punishment, or any other absolute personal injury.

4. He cannot be an officer or private, chaplain or retainer, in the army, navy or militia of any nation, state, or chieftain.

5. He cannot be an officer, elector, agent, legal prosecutor, passive constituent, or approver of any government, as a sworn or otherwise pledged supporter thereof, whose civil constitution and fundamental laws, require, authorize or tolerate war, slavery, capital punishment, or the infliction of any absolute personal injury.

6. He cannot be a member of any chartered corporation, or

body politic, whose articles of compact oblige or authorize its official functionaries to resort for compulsory aid, in the conducting of its affairs, to a government of constitutional violence.

7. Finally, he cannot do any act, either in person or by proxy; nor abet or encourage any act in others; nor demand, petition for, request, advise or approve the doing of any act, by an individual, association or government, *which* act would inflict, *threaten* to inflict, or *necessarily* cause to *be* inflicted *any absolute personal injury*, as herein before defined.

Such are the necessary bearings, limitations and applications of the doctrine of Christian non-resistance. Let the reader be careful not to misunderstand the positions laid down. The platform of principle and action has been carefully founded, and its essential peculiarities plainly delineated. Let it not be said that the doctrine goes against all religion, government, social organization, constitutions, laws, order, rules and regulations. It goes against none of these things, *per se*. It goes for them, in the highest and best sense. It goes only against *such* religion, government, social organization, constitutions, laws, order, rules, regulations and restraints, as are unequivocally contrary to the law of Christ; as sanction taking "life for life, eye for eye, tooth for tooth"; as are based on the assumption, that it is *right* to resist *injury with injury, evil with evil*. . . .

Non-Resistance Not Contrary to Nature.

The opposers of Non-Resistance with one voice confidently assert that it is contrary to the known laws of Nature, and therefore must be false, however plausibly defended from the Scriptures. It is the design of the present chapter to refute this confident assertion, and to demonstrate that Christian non-resistance is in perfect accordance with the laws of Nature considered in all their developments. I shall endeavor to do this with arguments sustained by numerous facts and illustrations drawn from real life.

Nature and the Laws of Nature Defined.

What is "Nature?" and what are "the laws of Nature?" These terms are in very common use with a certain class of persons. But they are more flippantly uttered than definitely understood. . . .

Self-Preservation the First Law of Nature.

It is reiterated that "self-preservation is the first law of nature." I grant it, and then what follows? "Self-defence against whatever threatens destruction or injury," says the opponent. I grant it, and what next follows? "Generally mutual personal conflict, injury, and, in extremities, *death.* Hence there are justifiable homicides, wars, injuries and penal inflictions. Nature impels them. Her law of self-preservation necessitates them. They are *right* in the very nature of things; and therefore non-resistance must be as *wrong*, as it is impracticable. It is contrary to nature, and cannot be brought into practice." Let us examine these bold assertions. I have granted that "self-preservation is the first law of nature." Also that this law prompts to self-defence against whatever threatens destruction or injury. I also admit the fact that generally men, in common with the lower animals, fight, injure, and frequently slay each other in self-defence, or for something supposed to be necessary to self-preservation. In granting this last, I only grant that men are generally very foolish and wicked.

What Is the True Method of Self-Preservation [?].

For it remains to be seen whether this *general* method of self-preservation be the *true* method. Whether it be not a very bad method. Whether it be not a method which absolutely defeats its own designed object. Let us inquire. If it be the true method, it must on the whole work well. It must preserve human life and secure mankind against injury, more certainly and effectually than any other possible method. Has it done this? I do not admit it. How happens it that, according to the lowest probable estimate, some fourteen thousand millions of human beings have been slain by human means, in war and otherwise? Here are enough to people eighteen planets like the earth with its present population. What inconceiveable miseries must have been endured by these worlds of people and their friends, in the process of those murderous conflicts which extinguished their earthly existence! Could all their dying groans be heard and their expiring throes be witnessed at once, by the existing generation of men; could their blood flow together into one vast lake, mingled with the tears of their bereaved relatives; could their corpses be seen piled up in one huge pyramid; or their skeletons be contemplated in a broad golgotha, would it be deemed conclusive evidence that mankind had practised the true method of self-preservation!! Would it encourage us still to confide in and pursue the same method? Would it suggest no inquiries, whether there were not "a more excellent way?" Should we not be impelled to conclude that this method was the offspring of a purblind instinct—the cherished salvo of ignorance—the fatal charm of deluded credulity —the *supposed preserver*, but the *real destroyer* of the human family? If this long-trusted method of self-preservation be indeed the best which nature affords to her children, their lot is most deplorable. To preserve what life has been preserved at such a cost, renders life itself a thing of doubtful value. If only a few thousands, or even a few millions, had perished by the two edged sword; if innocence and justice and right had uniformly triumphed; if aggression, injustice, violence, injury and insult, after a few dreadful experiences, had been overawed; if gradually the world had come into wholesome order—

a state of truthfulness, justice and peace; if the sword of self-defence had frightened the sword of aggression into its scabbard, there to consume in its rust; then might we admit that the common method of self-preservation was the true one. But now we have ample demonstration that *they who take the sword, perish with the sword.* Is it supposable that if no injured person or party, since the days of Abel, had lifted up a deadly weapon, or threatened an injury against an offending party, there would have been a thousandth part of the murders and miseries which have actually taken place on our earth? Take the worst possible view; resolve all the assailed and injured into the most passive non-resistants imaginable, and let the offenders have unlimited scope to commit all the robberies, cruelties and murders they pleased; would as many lives have been sacrificed, or as much real misery have been experienced by the human race, as have actually resulted from the general method of self-preservation, by personal conflict, and resistance of injury with injury? He must be a bold man who affirms it. The truth is, man has stood in his own light. He has frustrated his own wishes. He has been deceived, deluded, betrayed, and all but destroyed, by his own self conceited, evil imagination. He would not be taught of God. He would have his own way. He would be a fool, a spendthrift, a murderer and a suicide. Yet his Father still calls after him. He offers to make him wise, good and happy. He offers to teach him the true method of self-preservation. It is found in the non-resistance of Jesus Christ. But he is wretchedly wedded to his old idols, and will scarcely hear the voice of his only true friend. When he will hear, he shall live. . . .

The Safety of Non-Resistance.

I have been endeavoring to demonstrate in the preceding chapter that non-resistance, instead of being contrary to nature, is in perfect accordance with all her fundamental laws. I intend in the present chapter to complete that demonstration by an ample illustration of the superior general safety of non-resistance. This will be done by anecdotes and historical facts, showing its actual workings in many cases of imminent danger. I do not undertake to prove that the practice of non-resistance will *always* preserve the life and personal security of its adherents, but only that it *generally* will. Jesus, the apostles, and thousands of Christian martyrs were slain notwithstanding their non-resistance. Doubtless others will be wronged, outraged, and murdered in time to come, notwithstanding the same safeguard. Exceptions do not disprove a general rule. As the advocates of *deadly resistance* do not contend that it *always* ensures the preservation of life and personal security, so neither do I contend that Christian non-resistance will do it. They contend that discretionary resistance is safer than non-resistance; that its general tendency, despite of incidental failures, is to preserve life and render personal safety secure. I contend for the exact reverse. Here is an important issue. The deadly resistants affirm the superior safety of their principle of action; the non-resistants of *theirs.* The parties are in direct contradiction. Which of them is right? The resistants have lost, according to Dr. Dick, 14,000,000,000, and according to Mr. Burke, 35,000,000,000 of human lives, since their experiment commenced. Can non-resistants make a greater loss than this? Can their principle of action result in a greater expenditure of life and happiness? No. Under the most unfavorable circumstances they will not lose in the proportion of one to a thousand, and a few centuries of perseverance in their principle would totally extinguish the fires of human violence throughout the earth. Let me proceed to show that the practice of non-resistance is pre-eminently safe.

Robert Barclay and Leonard Fell.

Robert Barclay, the celebrated apologist of the Quakers, and Leonard Fell, a member of the same Society, were severally attacked by highwaymen in England, at different times. Both faithfully adhered to their non-resistance principles, and both signally triumphed. The pistol was levelled at Barclay, and a determined demand made for his purse. Calm and self-possessed, he looked the robber in the face, with a firm but meek benignity, assured him he was *his* and every man's friend, that he was willing and ready to relieve his wants, that he was free from the fear of death through a divine hope in immortality, and therefore was not to be intimidated by a deadly weapon; and then appealed to him, whether he could have heart to shed the blood of one who had no other feeling or purpose but to do him good. The robber was confounded; his eye melted; his brawny arm trembled; his pistol fell to his side; and he fled from the presence of the non-resistant hero whom he could no longer confront.

Fell was assaulted in a much more violent manner. The robber rushed upon him, dragged him from his horse, rifled his pockets, and threatened to blow out his brains on the spot, if he made the least resistance. This was the work of a moment. But Fell experienced no panic. His principles raised him above the fear of man and of death. Though forbidden to speak, he calmly but resolutely reproved the robber for his wickedness, warned him of the consequences of such a course of life, counselled him to reform, and assured him that while he forgave this wanton outrage on himself, he hoped for *his own* sake he would henceforth betake himself to an upright calling. His expostulation was so fearless, faithful and affectionate, that the robber was struck with compunction, delivered back his money and horse, and bade him go in peace. Then, with tears filling his eyes, he exclaimed,—"May God have mercy on a sinful wretch," and hastened out of sight. . . .

. . . Perhaps the severest test to which the peace principles were ever put, was in Ireland, during the memorable rebellion of 1798. During that terrible conflict, the Irish Quakers were continually between two fires. The protestant party viewed them with suspicion and dislike because they refused to fight or to pay military taxes; and the fierce multitude of insurgents deemed it sufficient cause of death, that they would neither profess belief in the Catholic religion nor help them fight for Irish freedom. Victory alternated between the two contending parties, and, as usual in civil war, the victors made almost indiscriminate havoc of those who did not march under their banners. It was a perilous time for all men; but the Quakers alone were liable to a raking fire from both sides. Foreseeing calamity, they had, nearly two years before the war broke out, publicly destroyed all their guns, and other weapons used for game. But this pledge of pacific intentions was not sufficient to satisfy the government, which required warlike assistance at their hands. Threats and insults were heaped upon them from all quarters; but they steadfastly adhered to their resolution of doing good to both parties, and harm to neither. Their houses were filled with widows and orphans, with the sick, the wounded and the dying, belonging both to the loyalists and the rebels. Sometimes, when the Catholic insurgents were victorious, they would be greatly enraged to find Quaker houses filled with Protestant families. They would point their pistols and threaten death, if their enemies were not immediately turned into the street to be massacred. But the pistol dropped, when the Christian mildly replied, "Friend, do what thou wilt, I will not harm thee, or any other human being." Not even amid the savage fierceness of civil war, could men fire at one who spoke such words as these. They saw that this was not cowardice, but bravery very much higher than their own.

On one occasion, an insurgent threatened to burn down a Quaker house unless the owner expelled the Protestant women and children who had taken refuge there. "I cannot help it," replied the Friend; "so long as I have a house, I will keep it open to succor the helpless and distressed, whether they belong to thy ranks, or to those of thy enemies. If my house is burned, I must be turned out with them, and share their affliction." The fighter turned away and did the Christian no harm.

The Protestant party seized the Quaker school-master of Ballitore, saying they could see no reason why he should stay at home in quiet, while they were obliged to defend his property. "Friends, I have asked no man to fight for me," replied the school-master. But they dragged him along, swearing that he should at least stop a bullet. His house and school-house were filled with women and children, who had taken refuge there; for it was an instructive fact, throughout this bloody contest, that *the houses of the men of peace were the only places of safety.* Some of the women followed the soldiers, begging them not to take away their friend and protector, a man who expended more for the sick and starving, than others did for arms and ammunition. The school-master said, "Do not be distressed, my friends. I forgive these neighbors; for what they do, they do in ignorance of my principles and feelings. They may take my life, but they cannot force me to do injury to one of my fellow creatures." As the Catholics had done, so did the Protestants; they went away, and left the man of peace safe in his divine armor.

The flames of bigotry were, of course, fanned by civil war. On one occasion, the insurgents seized a wealthy old Quaker, in very feeble health, and threatened to shoot him, if he did not go with them to a Catholic priest to be christened. They had not led him far, before he sank down from extreme weakness. "What do you say to our proposition?" asked one of the soldiers, handling his gun significantly. The old man quietly replied, "If thou art permitted to take my life I hope our Heavenly Father will forgive thee." The insurgents talked apart for a few moments, and then went away, restrained by a power they did not understand.

Deeds of kindness added strength to the influence of gentle words. The officers and soldiers of both parties had had some dying brother tended by the Quakers, or some starving mother who had been fed, or some desolate little ones who had been cherished. Whichever party marched into a village victorious, the cry was, "Spare the Quakers! They have done good to all, and harm to none." While flames were raging, and blood flowing in every direction, the houses of the peace makers stood uninjured.

It is a circumstance worthy to be recorded, that, during the fierce and terrible struggle, even in counties where Quakers were most numerous, but one of their society fell a sacrifice. That one was a young man, who, being afraid to trust peace principles, put on a military uniform, and went to the garrison for protection. The garrison was taken by the insurgents, and he was killed. "His dress and arms spoke the language of hostility," says the historian, "and therefore invited it. . . ."

Is Non-Resistance For or Against Human Government?

I propose to occupy the present chapter in treating on the relation of non-resistance to human government. Is non-resistance, as defined and expounded in this work, *for* or *against* human government *per se?* This depends on what sense is given to the adjective *human* when joined to the noun *government*. If *human* government be understood to imply or presuppose an *inherent, original,* ABSOLUTE power in *man* to make laws and exercise discretionary control *over* man, non-resistance is *against* it. It denies any such inherent, original, *absolute* power in *man,* and refers it to *God* only. In this sense all rightful government is essentially *divine;* man being ever a *subject*—not a *governor.* And whenever he assumes to *require* any thing repugnant to the divine law, he is a rebel against God, and a usurper over his co-equal fellow man. Man cannot rightfully legislate or govern *insubordinately* to his Creator. He can only govern *under* and *with* the divine sanction. If this position needs any defence, non-resistants are prepared to maintain it against the world. None, however, but atheists and *would-be Deicides,* the genuine *no-governmentists,* can be reckless enough to convert it.

But if *human* government be understood to imply only *di-*

vine government clothed in *human forms,* and administered by *human organizations,* with merely incidental human imperfections, non-resistance is *for* it *per se.* It has no *necessary* opposition to it whatever. It recognizes man as by nature a social being. It sees the ties and dependencies of husband and wife, parent and child, friend and neighbor, smaller and larger community; and is essentially friendly to all social organizations, founded on love to God and man. Human government in this sense would be an organization of society *Constitutionally* deferential to the highest known law of God. It would disclaim and denounce all assumption of power to set up and enforce any law, regulation, or usage in violation of the natural equality and brotherhood of mankind. It would inscribe on its main pillars, *No resistance of injury with injury—no rendering of evil for evil—evil can be overcome only with good!* It would pledge its entire religious, intellectual, moral, physical, industrial and pecuniary resources to the maintenance of the right education, good conduct, comfortable subsistence and general welfare of all its population. It would declare and treat all its officers as *servants* of their brethren, entitled to no other remuneration than an equal subsistence and dividend of general profits with the mass of unofficials. It would know no such thing as *government craft,* and have no separate interests of its functionaries to be fattened at the expense of their constituents. It would disclaim all *authority* of its *own,* and rest all its legislation, its judicial decrees, and its executive proceedings on their intrinsic rectitude and fitness to promote the public good. It would put off all external display, pomp, parade and childish insignia, and be a plain simple, business *concern,* provided with all things decent and convenient for its necessary use, and nothing more. It would incur no expense for distinction's sake—for show and dazzle. Man would make no wicked and foolish attempt to *appear a god* to his fellow-worms. The most exalted servant of the people would need to dwell in no better house, eat no better food, drink no costlier liquids, wear no richer livery, ride in no better carriage, under a wise and righteous government than would be proper for every common citizen. He would be ashamed to wish anything better. *"He that will be chief among you shall be as he that doth serve."* This is the pattern for the head of a Christian republic. Such a government would verify the prophetic prediction: *"I will also make thy officers peace, and thine exactors righteousness. Violence shall no more be heard in thy land, wasting nor destruction within thy borders."* Such a government there will *yet be* throughout the earth. It is coming in the dim distant future. Christian non-resistance is its forerunner, and will hail its arrival amid the welcome shouts of an enlightened world. Men will then look back on our present semi-barbarous governments, much as a philosopher now does on the picture of an Indian Sachem, smeared with paint, ornamented with feathers and wampum, and resting on his war club or tomahawk. Understanding then by *human* government *only* divine government *humanized* in its forms, applications and details, non-resistance is decidedly *for* it *per se.*

Human Government De Facto.

But is it *for* human government *as it is de facto?* This is now the practical question. No. Why not? Because it cannot be both *for* and *against itself.* *Non-resistance* cannot be for *war, capital punishment, slavery* and all sorts of *penal injury.* Nor can it be FOR any government which is fundamentally FOR *these things.* These things are not reconcileable with non-resistance. Its adherents cannot therefore be voluntary participators *in* existing governments. Not because they are opposed to government *per se;* but because they are utterly opposed to these fundamental *evils,* with which all that is good in existing governments is inseparably interwoven. They demand a removal of these anti-Christian articles from our national and state constitutions, before they can voluntarily participate in the government. Are they right in assuming this stand?

Objection.

"*No,*" says the objector, "you are not clearly right, to my apprehension, in charging our national and state constitution with being *necessarily* for *war, capital punishment, slavery* and *penal injury.* But if you are right in *this,* you are *positively wrong* in refusing to participate in the government till these things are expunged. If you will neither hold office, vote, nor bring actions at law under the government, how do you expect these evils are to be eradicated! You ought to take part in the government, if for nothing else, to effect the necessary amendments in our constitutions. Who is to remove these evils, if *you,* who see and feel them, refuse to lift a finger to dislodge them? Stay in the government and reform it. You frustrate your own aims by non-participation."

Answer.

War, capital punishment, slavery and many penal injuries have prevailed in the United States. They still prevail. Are they *contrary* to the fundamental law? Do they not flourish under its positive sanctions? I shall not go far out of my way to establish facts naked to universal observation. Without meddling with fine spun arguments, designed to show that the federal constitution is an anti-slavery instrument, or anticipating any ingenious plea which might be offered to demonstrate its consonance with Christianity in respect to capital punishment, I shall content myself with presenting an extract from the Constitution of Massachusetts, (a state in the vanguard of human improvement), and two or three from that of the United States. These will show whether non-resistance can endorse even republican constitutions—not to mention the written and unwritten ones of the old world.

Extract from the Constitution of Massachusetts.

"The Governor of this Commonwealth, for the time being, shall be the commander in chief of the army and navy, and of all the military forces of the State, by sea and land; and shall have full power, by himself, or by any commander, or other officer and officers, from time to time, to *train, instruct, exercise* and *govern* the militia and navy; and for the special defence and safety of the Commonwealth, *to assemble in martial array, and put in warlike posture*, the inhabitants thereof; and to lead and conduct them, and with them to encounter, repel, resist, expel, and pursue, *by force of arms*, as well by sea as by land, within or without the limits of this Commonwealth, and also to KILL, SLAY, AND DESTROY, if necessary, and conquer, by all fitting ways, enterprizes and means, *whatsoever*, all and every such person or persons as shall, at any time hereafter, in a hostile manner, attempt or enterprise the destruction, invasion, detriment or annoyance of this Commonwealth; and to use and exercise, over the army and navy, and over the militia in actual service, the law martial, in time of war and invasion, and also in time of rebellion declared by the Legislature to exist, as occasion shall necessarily require; and to take and surprise, by all ways and means *whatsoever*, all and every such person or persons, with their ships, arms, ammunition, and other goods, as shall, in a hostile manner, invade, or attempt the invading, conquering, or annoying this Commonwealth; and that the Governor be entrusted with all these and other powers, incident to the offices of captain general and commander in chief and admiral, to be exercised agreeably to the rules and regulations of the Constitution, and the laws of the land, and not otherwise."

Extracts from the U. S. Constitution.

"The Congress shall have power—to define and punish piracies and felonies committed on the high seas, and offences against the laws of nations.

To declare war; grant letters of marque and reprisal; and make rules concerning captures on land and water.

To raise and support armies.

To provide and maintain a navy.

To provide for calling forth the militia to execute the laws of the union, suppress insurrections and invasions.

To provide for organizing, arming and disciplining the militia," &c.

"The President shall be commander in chief of the army and navy of the United States, and of the militia of the several States, when called into actual service."

His oath shall be:—"I do solemnly swear (or affirm) that I will faithfully execute the office of President of the United States; and will, to the best of my ability, preserve, protect, and defend the Constitution of the United States."

"This Constitution, and the laws of the United States which shall be made in pursuance thereof, and all treaties made, or which shall be made, under the authority of the United States, shall be the SUPREME LAW of the land."

These extracts ought to make it clear to every man's apprehension that our State and National Constitutions authorize, provide for, and sanction war, preparations for war, and all the abominations incident to or consequent upon the murderous military system. The objector has no ground to stand on here.

Why Not Participate in Order to Reform?

But to come to the second part of the objection. If the non-resistants are right, as to the fundamental, *military and penal* character of the government, the objector declares they are *positively wrong* in refusing to participate in the government till these things are expunged. He wishes to know how, or by whom, we expect these evils to be eradicated, if we will neither hold office, vote nor bring actions at law. He bids us stay in the government to reform it; and tells us we frustrate our own aims by non-participation.

This will pass current with the mass of people for sound common sense; but I shall show it to be more specious than substantial. If our scruples related solely to minor details, and incidental defects in the existing governments, the objector's reasoning would be conclusive. For we do not exact absolute perfection, either theoretical or practical, in constitutions of government, as a condition of our participation in them. We can readily conceive of a radically Christian government with minor errors and defects in its details, and certainly with incidental abuses of administration arising out of human imperfection. In such governments we could conscientiously participate, and should feel bound to do so for the purpose of purifying them *entirely,* if possible, from errors and abuses.

But the governments now under notice are *radically, fundamentally* ANTI-CHRISTIAN. "The whole head is sick, and the whole heart faint." Military and injurious penal power is their very life-blood—the stamina of their existence. They are as repugnant to non-resistance, as pride is to humility, wrath to meekness, vengeance to forgiveness, death to life, destruction to salvation.

These Constitutions have the double character of *declarations and covenants.* They declare what is to be considered truth and duty, and are a solemn mutual covenant of the people with each other, as to what *may* or *shall* be done in their name. They are written out with great clearness and precision, so that no one may misunderstand them. When a man assents to them, or swears to support them, or acknowledges himself a party to the compact established by them, they become to all intents and purposes *declarations* of what *he* regards as truth and duty, and a pledge on his part that he will faithfully co-operate in carrying them into full effect. If they do not declare his sentiments, he makes himself a *liar* by endorsing, subscribing, or assenting to them. If he does not honestly mean to co-operate in giving them practical efficacy, he *perjures* himself by solemnly engaging to support the compact.

Cannot Lie and Commit Perjury.

Am I advised to *lie* and commit *perjury*, in order to reform an anti-Christian government? If I accept any office of distinction, I must swear or affirm to support the Constitution: not in *parts*, but *entire*. In fact, I cannot vote, without either actually taking such oath or affirmation, or at least *virtually* acknowledging myself to be under the highest obligations of allegiance. Government in this country is vested in the voters. They are leagued together by their common *declaration* of sentiments and mutual covenant—the Constitution—to conduct the government in a certain way, and to maintain its authority by military force. It seems to have been universally taken for granted that military force would be indispensable.

It is therefore a gross fraud and imposition for any man to appear at the ballot-box as a voter, who is at heart false to the Constitution, who does not mean in good faith to abide by and support it, and just as it is, till it can be constitutionally amended. This is what a non-resistant cannot do, without treason to the divine government; without trampling under foot the precepts of Jesus Christ.

Would the objector have me join an association of persons who covenant that their governor shall be "commander in chief of their army and navy, and of all their military forces by sea and land?" Whose army, navy and military forces? *Mine?* Am I, a non-resistant, in company with a combination who have armies, navies and military forces? And do I agree that our chief servant shall command these? That he may lead them forth to "KILL, SLAY and DESTROY" our enemies! Am I to vote for such an officer, and agree to have him put under oath to do *such* things! A most exemplary non-resistant indeed! Should I not speedily convince the common mind that I was amazingly opposed to war and all its kindred deeds!

Delegated Power to Declare War.

Will the objector insist that I shall proclaim to all the world my assent and agreement as a co-governing citizen of the United States, that "Congress shall have power to DECLARE WAR?" *My* representatives have power to do this wicked thing, in *my* name at their discretion! Power to turn the whole nation into impious robbers, murderers and desolators of the earth! Power to declare all this *lawful, just* and *right!* Power to authorize the perpetration of all the crimes and cruelties of war! *Never.* I will not agree or consent to any such thing. It is an abomination. I will hold office on no such conditions, I will not be a voter on such conditions. I will join no church or state, who hold such a creed or prescribe such a covenant for the subscription of their members. . . .

Legal and Political Action.

Many people seem to take for granted that *legal* and *political* action afford to *good men* indispensable instrumentalities for the promotion of moral reform, or at least for the maintenance of wholesome order in society. Hence we hear much said of the duty of enforcing certain penal laws, of voting for just rulers, and of rendering government "a terror to evil doers." Now I make no objection to any kind of legal or political action, which is truly *Christian* action. Nor do I deny that some local and temporary good has been done by prosecutions at law, voting in our popular elections, and exercising the functions of magistracy, under the prevailing system of human government. But I contend that there is very *little* legal and political action under this system, which is *strictly* CHRISTIAN action. And I deny that professedly good men do half as much to *promote* as they do to *subvert* moral reform and wholesome order in society, by legal and political action. The common notions respecting these matters are extremely superficial, delusive and mischievous. Look at facts:

1. Is it not a *fact*, that men strenuous for legal coercion, who devote themselves to the prosecution of law-breakers as an important duty, *generally* become incapable of benevolent, patient, suasory moral action? Do they not become *mere compulsionists?* Do they not become disagreeable to humble minds, and objects of *defiance* to the lawless? Is not this *generally* the case? I am sure it is. Reliance on injurious penal force costs more than it comes to, as an instrumentality for the promotion of moral reform. It works only a *little less* mischievously in *morals* than in *religion*.

2. Is it not a *fact*, that equally good men are divided among all the rival political parties, and that, under pretence of doing their duty to God and humanity, they vote point blank *for* and *against* the same men and measures, mutually thwarting, as far as possible, each others' preferences? Every man knows this. Does God make it their duty to practice this sheer contradiction and hostility of effort at the ballot-box! Does enlightened humanity prompt it! No; there must be a *cheat* somewhere in the game. The Holy Ghost does not blaspheme the Holy Ghost; nor Satan cast out Satan. Either the men are not *good*, or their notions of duty are *false*.

3. Is it not a *fact* that the most scrupulously moral and circumspect men in all the rival political parties are uniformly found, with very rare exceptions, either among the rank and file of their party, or in the *inferior* offices? Are our wisest and best men of each party put forward as *leaders?* Are not the managers—the real wire-pullers—generally selfish, unscrupulous men? Whatever may be the exceptions, is not this the *general rule?* We have all seen that it is. How then is it to be accounted for, on the supposition that political action is so

adapted to moral reform and wholesome order in society? The *facts* contradict the *theory*. The *good men* in political parties are not the *leaders*, but the *led*. They do not *use* political action to a noble end, but are themselves the *dupes* and *tools* of immoral managers—put *up* or put *down*, *foremost* or *rearmost*, in the *centre* or on the *flank*, just as they will *show* and *count* to the best advantage. All they are wanted for is to *show* and *count* against the same class in the other party. Their *use* is to give *respectability*, *weight of character* and *moral capital* to their party. They are the "stool pigeons," the "decoy ducks," the *take-ins* of their managers. The way they are used and the game of iniquity played off, are the proofs of this. Yet this is what many simple souls call *having influence*.

4. Is it not a *fact* that of the very *few* high-toned moral men, who happen to get into the head quarters of political distinction, not one in ten escapes *contamination*, or utter *disgust?* And now what do all these *facts* prove? That under the present system of government, legal and political action is generally anti-Christian. That *political good men* are influential chiefly as *tools* for mischief. And that *non-political* good men are the most likely to render *legalists* and *politicians* DECENT in the affairs of government. . . .

Injurious Force Not Essential to Government.

I shall now be told by the opposer, that I am a Utopian, a dreamer, a chimerist, to imagine any such thing as a government without a war-power in the last resort—without the power of deadly compulsion to suppress individual crime and mobocratic violence. That such a government would be a body without a soul—a house without a foundation—a powerless non-resistant abstraction; a something which can never have existence on earth, at least so long as human imperfection remains. I know that this is the common opinion respecting government. But it is false, the spawn of ignorance—a sheer delusion. A little reflection will show how utterly groundless it is. It derives all its plausibility from the exhibitions of past and remaining barbarism. Because men have been barbarous, and their laws and penalties barbarous, it is taken for granted that they *cannot* be otherwise; just as the African, in the centre of the torrid zone, assumed that there could be no such thing as ice because he had never seen any; and just as all your ignorant people assume that nothing can exist unlike what has come under their own observation.

Suppose one should confidently assert that there could be no such thing as a man, actually living and transacting business among mankind, without a military chapeau on his head, a sword dangling by his side, or a musket over his shoulder, or at least pistols or bowie knife about his person. That no man could live in the world without either *actually* fighting, or *threatening* to fight, or at least *being armed* for a fight. Who would not see the absurdity of the assertion? The man and the man's means of preserving his life, do not necessarily belong together. The Christian non-resistant is as much of a man as your sword and dagger character, and much less a *brute*. And the former stands a much better chance of long life, civil treatment and substantial happiness in the world, than the latter. Suppose some one should assert that there could be no such thing as a family, or good family government, without guns and dogs to defend them against marauders, and plenty of *switch-sticks* to wear up over the children's backs. Would it show any thing more than the ignorance and low moral development of the asserter? Suppose another should affirm that there can be no such thing as a church of Christ, without the *Inquisition* and *auto da fe?* Men of intelligence, reflection and Christianized moral feeling, know the contrary.

Under What Circumstances the Country Might Have a Non-Resistant Government.

Let us have two-thirds of the people of the United States, (including that portion who *are*, or would be *thought* Christians,

philanthropists, people of intelligence and orderly citizens)
once firmly committed to non-resistance, as explained and illustrated in this work, with even a large share of imperfection
still lingering about them, and the government might trium-
phantly dispense with its army, navy, militia, capital punishment, and all manner of *injurious* inflictions. Under the light
necessary to effect so general a change of public sentiment, a
considerable portion of the people would have reconstructed
neighborhood society by voluntary association, in such a manner as nearly to do away intemperance, idleness, debauchery,
miseducation, poverty and brutality, and to insure the requisite
inducements, means and opportunities for great self-improve-
ment and social usefulness. The consequence would be, that
very few poor creatures would remain without a strong moral
guardianship of wise and true friends to look after their welfare. Wholesome cure would be applied with vast success to
the ignorant and vicious, and at the same time powerful pre-
ventives beyond estimation applied to the new-born generation. Under such circumstances, suppose a truly Christian government to administer the general affairs of the several states,
and of the nation. How little would they have to do, how well
might they perform that little, and how trifling would be the
burthens of it either to officers or people? It would hardly require *thirty millions* of dollars to carry such a government
through a single year. They would not expend eighty per cent.
of all their receipts on ships of war, forts, arsenals, troops, &c.
&c. If they expended half this sum on the reformation of the
few remaining vicious, the right education of youth, and the
encouragement of virtue among the whole people, their work
would be cut short in righteousness. If here and there a disorderly individual broke over the bounds of decency, the whole
force of renovated public sentiment would surround and press
in upon him like the waters of the ocean, and slight *uninjurious*
force would prevent personal outrage in the most extreme
cases. And every day the causes of such extreme cases would

be undergoing the process of annihilation. Meantime England, and the other great nations, between whom and ourselves there is such a frequent and increasing familiarity of intercourse, would vie with ours, not which should have the strongest army and navy, and be able to do the most mischief, but which should lead off in the glorious work of reforming, improving and blessing the human race. Patriotism would then no longer strut in regimentals, recount its ruffian exploits, and provoke quarrels with fellow men for the crime of having been born over sea, or on the other side of a mountain or river. It would glory in superior justice, forbearance, meekness, forgiveness—*charity*. O glorious era, I see thee coming to smile on my country and the world. Thou art advancing in silent majesty on the remote verge of the blue horizon. Clouds of dust intervene between thee and the uncouth present. They conceal thee from the gaze of the boisterous and bustling multitude. The prophets even can but dimly discern thy beautiful outline. But thou are drawing nearer. Angels are thy heralds. The morning stars are singing together in thy train, and the sons of God shout for joy. In due time the heaven shall kiss the earth in thy presence, and the earth shall be restored to the bliss of heaven!

7. Henry David Thoreau, "Civil Disobedience"

Henry Thoreau (1817–1862) wrote his essay on civil disobedience after he served a night in jail, in 1846, for refusing to pay the Massachusetts poll tax. He believed that the war with Mexico, then going on, was intended to spread slavery; and that those who wished

---

Henry D. Thoreau, "Civil Disobedience," *A Yankee in Canada, with Anti-Slavery and Reform Papers* (Boston: Ticknor and Fields, 1866), pp. 123–151.

to do more than wish godspeed to the right as it went by them (as he put it) would have to put their bodies in the way.

Thoreau's essay owed much to the Christian anarchism of Garrison and Ballou. But while Garrison and Ballou disavowed "jacobinism," Thoreau deliberately proclaimed the need for revolution, albeit a revolution of one. And in contrast to the religious perfectionism of his predecessors, Thoreau put forward his doctrine as a creed for citizens: ". . . to speak practically and as a citizen, unlike those who call themselves no-government men, I ask for, not at once no government, but *at once* a better government." In effect Thoreau synthesized two previously divergent traditions: the Christian concept of civil disobedience, and John Locke's justification of the revolution. The essay on civil disobedience was first published in 1849 under the title "Resistance to Civil Government."

I heartily accept the motto,—"That government is best which governs least"; and I should like to see it acted up to more rapidly and systematically. Carried out, it finally amounts to this, which also I believe,—"That government is best which governs not at all"; and when men are prepared for it, that will be the kind of government which they will have. Government is at best but an expedient; but most governments are usually, and all governments are sometimes, inexpedient. The objections which have been brought against a standing army, and they are many and weighty, and deserve to prevail, may also at last be brought against a standing government. The standing army is only an arm of the standing government. The government itself, which is only the mode which the people have chosen to execute their will, is equally liable to be abused and perverted before the people can act through it. Witness the present Mexican war, the work of comparatively a few individuals using the standing government as their tool; for, in the outset, the people would not have consented to this measure.

This American government,—what is it but a tradition, though a recent one, endeavoring to transmit itself unimpaired to posterity, but each instant losing some of its integrity? It has not the vitality and force of a single living man; for a single man can bend it to his will. It is a sort of wooden gun to the people themselves. But it is not the less necessary for this; for the people must have some complicated machinery or other, and hear its din, to satisfy that idea of government which they have. Governments show thus how successfully men can be imposed on, even impose on themselves, for their own advantage. It is excellent, we must all allow. Yet this government never of itself furthered any enterprise, but by the alacrity with which it got out of its way. *It* does not keep the country free. *It* does not settle the West. *It* does not educate. The character inherent in the American people has done all that has been accomplished; and it would have done somewhat more, if the government had not sometimes got in its way. For government is an expedient by which men would fain succeed in letting one another alone; and, as has been said, when it is most expedient, the governed are most let alone by it. Trade and commerce, if they were not made of India-rubber, would never manage to bounce over the obstacles which legislators are continually putting in their way; and, if one were to judge these men wholly by the effects of their actions and not partly by their intentions, they would deserve to be classed and punished with those mischievous persons who put obstructions on the railroads.

But, to speak practically and as a citizen, unlike those who call themselves no-government men, I ask for, not at once no government, but *at once* a better government. Let every man make known what kind of government would command his respect, and that will be one step toward obtaining it.

After all, the practical reason why, when the power is once in the hands of the people, a majority are permitted, and for a long period continue, to rule, is not because they are most likely to be in the right, nor because this seems fairest to the minority, but because they are physically the strongest. But a government in which the majority rule in all cases cannot be based on justice, even as far as men understand it. Can there not be a government in which majorities do not virtually decide right and wrong, but conscience?—in which majorities decide only those questions to which the rule of expediency is applicable? Must the citizen ever for a moment, or in the least degree, resign his conscience to the legislator? Why has every man a conscience, then? I think that we should be men first, and subjects afterward. It is not desirable to cultivate a respect for the law, so much as for the right. The only obligation which I have a right to assume, is to do at any time what I think right. It is truly enough said, that a corporation has no conscience; but a corporation of conscientious men is a corporation *with* a conscience. Law never made men a whit more just; and, by means of their respect for it, even the well-disposed are daily made the agents of injustice. A common and natural result of an undue respect for law is, that you may see a file of soldiers, colonel, captain, corporal, privates, powder-monkeys, and all, marching in admirable order over hill and dale to the wars, against their wills, ay, against their common sense and consciences, which makes it very steep marching indeed, and produces a palpitation of the heart. They have no doubt that it is a damnable business in which they are concerned; they are all peaceably inclined. Now, what are they? Men at all? or small movable forts and magazines, at the service of some unscrupulous man in power? Visit the Navy-Yard, and behold a marine, such a man as an American government can make, or such as it can make a man with its black arts,—a mere shadow and reminiscence of humanity, a man laid out alive and standing, and already, as one may say, buried under arms with funeral accompaniments, though it may be,—

> "Not a drum was heard, not a funeral note,
>   As his corse to the rampart we hurried;
> Not a soldier discharged his farewell shot
>   O'er the grave where our hero we buried."

The mass of men serve the state thus, not as men mainly, but as machines, with their bodies. They are the standing army, and the militia, jailers, constables, posse comitatus, &c. In most cases there is no free exercise whatever of the judgment or of the moral sense; but they put themselves on a level with wood and earth and stones; and wooden men can perhaps be manufactured that will serve the purpose as well. Such command no more respect than men of straw or a lump of dirt. They have the same sort of worth only as horses and dogs. Yet such as these even are commonly esteemed good citizens. Others,—as most legislators, politicians, lawyers, ministers, and office-holders,—serve the state chiefly with their heads; and, as they rarely make any moral distinctions, they are as likely to serve the Devil, without *intending* it, as God. A very few, as heroes, patriots, martyrs, reformers in the great sense, and *men*, serve the state with their consciences also, and so necessarily resist it for the most part; and they are commonly treated as enemies by it. A wise man will only be useful as a man, and will not submit to be "clay," and "stop a hole to keep the wind away," but leave that office to his dust at least:—

> "I am too high-born to be propertied,
> To be a secondary at control,
> Or useful serving-man and instrument
> To any sovereign state throughout the world."

He who gives himself entirely to his fellow-men appears to them useless and selfish; but he who gives himself partially to them is pronounced a benefactor and philanthropist.

How does it become a man to behave toward this American government to-day? I answer, that he cannot without disgrace be associated with it. I cannot for an instant recognize that political organization as *my* government which is the *slave's* government also.

All men recognize the right of revolution; that is, the right to refuse allegiance to, and to resist, the government, when its tyranny or its inefficiency are great and unendurable. But almost all say that such is not the case now. But such was the case, they think, in the Revolution of '75. If one were to tell me that this was a bad government because it taxed certain foreign commodities brought to its ports, it is most probable that I should not make an ado about it, for I can do without them. All machines have their friction; and possibly this does enough good to counterbalance the evil. At any rate, it is a great evil to make a stir about it. But when the friction comes to have its machine, and oppression and robbery are organized, I say, let us not have such a machine any longer. In other words, when a sixth of the population of a nation which has undertaken to be the refuge of liberty are slaves, and a whole country is unjustly overrun and conquered by a foreign army, and subjected to military law, I think that it is not too soon for honest men to rebel and revolutionize. What makes this duty the more urgent is the fact, that the country so overrun is not our own, but ours is the invading army.

Paley, a common authority with many on moral questions, in his chapter on the "Duty of Submission to Civil Government," resolves all civil obligation into expediency; and he proceeds to say, "that so long as the interest of the whole society requires it, that is, so long as the established government cannot be resisted or changed without public inconveniency, it is the will of God that the established government be obeyed, and no longer. . . . This principle being admitted, the justice of every particular case of resistance is reduced to a computation of the quantity of the danger and grievance on the one side, and of the probability and expense of redressing it on the other." Of this, he says, every man shall judge for himself. But Paley appears never to have contemplated those cases to which the rule of expediency does not apply, in which a people, as well as an individual, must do justice, cost what it may. If I have unjustly wrested a plank from a drowning man, I must restore it to him though I drown myself. This, according to

Paley, would be inconvenient. But he that would save his life, in such a case, shall lose it. This people must cease to hold slaves, and to make war on Mexico, though it cost them their existence as a people.

In their practice, nations agree with Paley; but does any one think that Massachusetts does exactly what is right at the present crisis?

"A drab of state, a cloth-o'-silver slut,
    To have her train borne up, and her soul trail in the dirt."

Practically speaking, the opponents to a reform in Massachusetts are not a hundred thousand politicians at the South, but a hundred thousand merchants and farmers here, who are more interested in commerce and agriculture than they are in humanity, and are not prepared to do justice to the slave and to Mexico, *cost what it may.* I quarrel not with far-off foes, but with those who, near at home, co-operate with, and do the bidding of, those far away, and without whom the latter would be harmless. We are accustomed to say, that the mass of men are unprepared; but improvement is slow, because the few are not materially wiser or better than the many. It is not so important that many should be as good as you, as that there be some absolute goodness somewhere; for that will leaven the whole lump. There are thousands who are *in opinion* opposed to slavery and to the war, who yet in effect do nothing to put an end to them; who, esteeming themselves children of Washington and Franklin, sit down with their hands in their pockets, and say that they know not what to do, and do nothing; who even postpone the question of freedom to the question of free-trade, and quietly read the prices-current along with the latest advices from Mexico, after dinner, and, it may be, fall asleep over them both. What is the price-current of an honest man and patriot to-day? They hesitate, and they regret, and sometimes they petition; but they do nothing in earnest and with effect. They will wait, well disposed, for others to remedy the evil, that they may no longer have it to regret. At most, they

give only a cheap vote, and a feeble countenance and Godspeed, to the right, as it goes by them. There are nine hundred
and ninety-nine patrons of virtue to one virtuous man. But it
is easier to deal with the real possessor of a thing than with the
temporary guardian of it.

All voting is a sort of gaming, like checkers or backgammon,
with a slight moral tinge to it, a playing with right and wrong,
with moral questions; and betting naturally accompanies it.
The character of the voters is not staked. I cast my vote, perchance, as I think right; but I am not vitally concerned that
that right should prevail. I am willing to leave it to the
majority. Its obligation, therefore, never exceeds that of expediency. Even voting *for the right* is *doing* nothing for it. It is
only expressing to men feebly your desire that it should prevail. A wise man will not leave the right to the mercy of
chance, nor wish it to prevail through the power of the majority. There is but little virtue in the action of masses of men.
When the majority shall at length vote for the abolition of
slavery, it will be because they are indifferent to slavery, or
because there is but little slavery left to be abolished by their
vote. *They* will then be the only slaves. Only *his* vote can
hasten the abolition of slavery who asserts his own freedom by
his vote.

I hear of a convention to be held at Baltimore, or elsewhere,
for the selection of a candidate for the Presidency, made up
chiefly of editors, and men who are politicians by profession;
but I think, what is it to any independent, intelligent, and
respectable man what decision they may come to? Shall we not
have the advantage of his wisdom and honesty, nevertheless?
Can we not count upon some independent votes? Are there not
many individuals in the country who do not attend conventions? But no: I find that the respectable man, so called, has
immediately drifted from his position, and despairs of his country, when his country has more reason to despair of him. He
forthwith adopts one of the candidates thus selected as the

only *available* one, thus proving that he is himself *available* for any purposes of the demagogue. His vote is of no more worth than that of any unprincipled foreigner or hireling native, who may have been bought. O for a man who is a *man*, and, as my neighbor says, has a bone in his back which you cannot pass your hand through! Our statistics are at fault: the population has been returned too large. How many *men* are there to a square thousand miles in this country? Hardly one. Does not America offer any inducement for men to settle here? The American has dwindled into an Odd Fellow,—one who may be known by the development of his organ of gregariousness, and a manifest lack of intellect and cheerful self-reliance; whose first and chief concern, on coming into the world, is to see that the Almshouses are in good repair; and, before yet he has lawfully donned the virile garb, to collect a fund for the support of the widows and orphans that may be; who, in short, ventures to live only by the aid of the Mutual Insurance company, which has promised to bury him decently.

It is not a man's duty, as a matter of course, to devote himself to the eradication of any, even the most enormous wrong; he may still properly have other concerns to engage him; but it is his duty, at least, to wash his hands of it, and, if he gives it no thought longer, not to give it practically his support. If I devote myself to other pursuits and contemplations, I must first see, at least, that I do not pursue them sitting upon another man's shoulders. I must get off him first, that he may pursue his contemplations too. See what gross inconsistency is tolerated. I have heard some of my townsmen say, "I should like to have them order me out to help put down an insurrection of the slaves, or to march to Mexico;—see if I would go"; and yet these very men have each, directly by their allegiance, and so indirectly, at least, by their money, furnished a substitute. The soldier is applauded who refuses to serve in an unjust war by those who do not refuse to sustain the unjust government which makes the war; is applauded by those whose own act and authority he disregards and sets at naught; as if the State were penitent to that degree that it hired one to scourge it while it sinned, but not to that degree that it left off sinning for a moment. Thus, under the name of Order and Civil Government, we are all made at last to pay homage to and support our own meanness. After the first blush of sin comes its indifference; and from immoral it becomes, as it were, *unmoral*, and not quite unnecessary to that life which we have made.

The broadest and most prevalent error requires the most disinterested virtue to sustain it. The slight reproach to which the virtue of patriotism is commonly liable, the noble are most likely to incur. Those who, while they disapprove of the character and measures of a government, yield to it their allegiance and support, are undoubtedly its most conscientious supporters, and so frequently the most serious obstacles to reform. Some are petitioning the State to dissolve the Union, to disregard the requisitions of the President. Why do they not dissolve it themselves,—the union between themselves and the State,—and refuse to pay their quota into its treasury? Do not they stand in the same relation to the State, that the State does to the Union? And have not the same reasons prevented the State from resisting the Union, which have prevented them from resisting the State?

How can a man be satisfied to entertain an opinion merely, and enjoy *it?* Is there any enjoyment in it, if his opinion is that he is aggrieved? If you are cheated out of a single dollar by your neighbor, you do not rest satisfied with knowing that you are cheated, or with saying that you are cheated, or even with petitioning him to pay you your due; but you take effectual steps at once to obtain the full amount, and see that you are never cheated again. Action from principle, the perception and the performance of right, changes things and relations; it is essentially revolutionary, and does not consist wholly with anything which was. It not only divides states and churches, it di-

vides families; ay, it divides the *individual*, separating the diabolical in him from the divine.

Unjust laws exist: shall we be content to obey them, or shall
we endeavor to amend them, and obey them until we have
succeeded, or shall we transgress them at once? Men generally,
under such a government as this, think that they ought to wait
until they have persuaded the majority to alter them. They
think that, if they should resist, the remedy would be worse
than the evil. But it is the fault of the government itself that
the remedy *is* worse than the evil. *It* makes it worse. Why is it
not more apt to anticipate and provide for reform? Why does
it not cherish its wise minority? Why does it cry and resist before it is hurt? Why does it not encourage its citizens to be on
the alert to point out its faults, and *do* better than it would
have them? Why does it always crucify Christ, and excom-
municate Copernicus and Luther, and pronounce Washington
and Franklin rebels?

One would think, that a deliberate and practical denial of its
authority was the only offence never contemplated by government; else, why has it not assigned its definite, its suitable and
proportionate penalty? If a man who has no property refuses
but once to earn nine shillings for the State, he is put in prison
for a period unlimited by any law that I know, and determined
only by the discretion of those who placed him there; but if he
should steal ninety times nine shillings from the State, he is
soon permitted to go at large again.

If the injustice is part of the necessary friction of the machine of government, let it go, let it go: perchance it will wear
smooth,—certainly the machine will wear out. If the injustice
has a spring, or a pulley, or a rope, or a crank, exclusively for
itself, then perhaps you may consider whether the remedy
will not be worse than the evil; but if it is of such a nature that
it requires you to be the agent of injustice to another, then, I
say, break the law. Let your life be a counter friction to stop

the machine. What I have to do is to see, at any rate, that I do not lend myself to the wrong which I condemn.

As for adopting the ways which the State has provided for remedying the evil, I know not of such ways. They take too much time, and a man's life will be gone. I have other affairs to attend to. I came into this world, not chiefly to make this a good place to live in, but to live in it, be it good or bad. A man has not everything to do, but something; and because he cannot do *everything*, it is not necessary that he should do *something* wrong. It is not my business to be petitioning the Governor or the Legislature any more than it is theirs to petition me; and, if they should not hear my petition, what should I do then? But in this case the State has provided no way: its very Constitution is the evil. This may seem to be harsh and stubborn and unconciliatory; but it is to treat with the utmost kindness and consideration the only spirit that can appreciate or deserves it. So is all change for the better, like birth and death, which convulse the body.

I do not hesitate to say, that those who call themselves Abolitionists should at once effectually withdraw their support, both in person and property, from the government of Massachusetts, and not wait till they constitute a majority of one, before they suffer the right to prevail through them. I think that it is enough if they have God on their side, without waiting for that other one. Moreover, any man more right than his neighbors constitutes a majority of one already.

I meet this American government, or its representative, the State government, directly, and face to face, once a year—no more—in the person of its tax-gatherer; this is the only mode in which a man situated as I am necessarily meets it; and it then says distinctly, Recognize me; and the simplest, the most effectual, and, in the present posture of affairs, the indispensablest mode of treating with it on this head, of expressing your little satisfaction with and love for it, is to deny it then. My civil neighbor, the tax-gatherer, is the very man I have to deal

with,—for it is, after all, with men and not with parchment
that I quarrel,—and he has voluntarily chosen to be an agent
of the government. How shall he ever know well what he is
and does as an officer of the government, or as a man, until he
is obliged to consider whether he shall treat me, his neighbor,
for whom he has respect, as a neighbor and well-disposed man,
or as a maniac and disturber of the peace, and see if he can
get over this obstruction to his neighborliness without a ruder
and more impetuous thought or speech corresponding with his
action. I know this well, that if one thousand, if one hundred,
if ten men whom I could name,—if ten *honest* men only,—
ay, if *one* HONEST man, in this State of Massachusetts, *ceasing
to hold slaves,* were actually to withdraw from this copartner-
ship, and be locked up in the county jail therefor, it would be
the abolition of slavery in America. For it matters not how
small the beginning may seem to be: what is once well done
is done forever. But we love better to talk about it: that we
say is our mission. Reform keeps many scores of newspapers in
its service, but not one man. If my esteemed neighbor, the
State's ambassador, who will devote his days to the settlement
of the question of human rights in the Council Chamber, instead of being threatened with the prisons of Carolina, were
to sit down the prisoner of Massachusetts, that State which is
so anxious to foist the sin of slavery upon her sister,—though
at present she can discover only an act of inhospitality to be
the ground of a quarrel with her,—the Legislature would not
wholly waive the subject the following winter.

Under a government which imprisons any unjustly, the true
place for a just man is also a prison. The proper place to-day,
the only place which Massachusetts has provided for her freer
and less desponding spirits, is in her prisons, to be put out and
locked out of the State by her own act, as they have already
put themselves out by their principles. It is there that the fugitive slave, and the Mexican prisoner on parole, and the Indian
come to plead the wrongs of his race, should find them; on that

separate, but more free and honorable ground, where the State places those who are not *with* her, but *against* her,—the only house in a slave State in which a free man can abide with honor. If any think that their influence would be lost there, and their voices no longer afflict the ear of the State, that they would not be as an enemy within its walls, they do not know by how much truth is stronger than error, nor how much more eloquently and effectively he can combat injustice who has experienced a little in his own person. Cast your whole vote, not a strip of paper merely, but your whole influence. A minority is powerless while it conforms to the majority; it is not even a minority then; but it is irresistible when it clogs by its whole weight. If the alternative is to keep all just men in prison, or give up war and slavery, the State will not hesitate which to choose. If a thousand men were not to pay their tax-bills this year, that would not be a violent and bloody measure, as it would be to pay them, and enable the State to commit violence and shed innocent blood. This is, in fact, the definition of a peaceable revolution, if any such is possible. If the tax-gatherer, or any other public officer, asks me, as one has done, "But what shall I do?" my answer is, "If you really wish to do anything, resign your office." When the subject has refused allegiance, and the officer has resigned his office, then the revolution is accomplished. But even suppose blood should flow. Is there not a sort of blood shed when the conscience is wounded? Through this wound a man's real manhood and immortality flow out, and he bleeds to an everlasting death. I see this blood flowing now.

I have contemplated the imprisonment of the offender, rather than the seizure of his goods,—though both will serve the same purpose,—because they who assert the purest right, and consequently are most dangerous to a corrupt State, commonly have not spent much time in accumulating property. To such the State renders comparatively small service, and a slight tax is wont to appear exorbitant, particularly if they are obliged to earn it by special labor with their hands. If there were one who lived wholly without the use of money, the State itself would hesitate to demand it of him. But the rich man,—not to make any invidious comparison,—is always sold to the institution which makes him rich. Absolutely speaking, the more money, the less virtue; for money comes between a man and his objects, and obtains them for him; and it was certainly no great virtue to obtain it. It puts to rest many questions which he would otherwise be taxed to answer; while the only new question which it puts is the hard but superfluous one, how to spend it. Thus his moral ground is taken from under his feet. The opportunities of living are diminished in proportion as what are called the "means" are increased. The best thing a man can do for his culture when he is rich is to endeavor to carry out those schemes which he entertained when he was poor. Christ answered the Herodians according to their condition. "Show me the tribute-money," said he;—and one took a penny out of his pocket;—if you use money which has the image of Caesar on it, and which he has made current and valuable, that is, *if you are men of the State,* and gladly enjoy the advantages of Caesar's government, then pay him back some of his own when he demands it; "Render therefore to Caesar that which is Caesar's, and to God those things which are God's," —leaving them no wiser than before as to which was which; for they did not wish to know.

When I converse with the freest of my neighbors, I perceive that, whatever they may say about the magnitude and seriousness of the question, and their regard for the public tranquillity, the long and the short of the matter is, that they cannot spare the protection of the existing government, and they dread the consequences to their property and families of disobedience to it. For my own part, I should not like to think that I ever rely on the protection of the State. But, if I deny the authority of the State when it presents its tax-bill, it will soon take and waste all my property, and so harass me and my children without end. This is hard. This makes it impossible for a man to live honestly, and at the same time comfortably, in outward respects. It will not be worth the while to accumulate property; that would be sure to go again. You must hire or squat somewhere, and raise but a small crop, and eat that soon. You must live within yourself, and depend upon yourself always tucked up and ready for a start, and not have many affairs. A man may grow rich in Turkey even, if he will be in all respects a good subject of the Turkish government. Confucius said: "If a state is governed by the principles of reason, poverty and misery are subjects of shame; if a state is not governed by the principles of reason, riches and honors are the subjects of shame." No: until I want the protection of Massachusetts to be extended to me in some distant Southern port, where my liberty is endangered, or until I am bent solely on building up an estate at home by peaceful enterprise, I can afford to refuse allegiance to Massachusetts, and her right to my property and life. It costs me less in every sense to incur the penalty of disobedience to the State, than it would to obey. I should feel as if I were worth less in that case.

Some years ago, the State met me in behalf of the Church, and commanded me to pay a certain sum toward the support of a clergyman whose preaching my father attended, but never I myself. "Pay," it said, "or be locked up in the jail." I declined to pay. But, unfortunately, another man saw fit to pay it. I did not see why the schoolmaster should be taxed to support the priest, and not the priest the schoolmaster; for I was not the State's schoolmaster, but I supported myself by voluntary subscription. I did not see why the lyceum should not present its tax-bill, and have the State to back its demand, as well as the Church. However, at the request of the selectmen, I condescended to make some such statement as this in writing:—"Know all men by these presents, that I, Henry Thoreau, do not wish to be regarded as a member of any incorporated society which I have not joined." This I gave to the town clerk; and he has it. The State, having thus learned that I did not wish to be regarded as a member of that church, has never made a like demand on me since; though it said that it must adhere to its original presumption that time. If I had known how to name them, I should then have signed off in detail from all the societies which I never signed on to; but I did not know where to find a complete list.

I have paid no poll-tax for six years. I was put into a jail once on this account, for one night; and, as I stood considering the walls of solid stone, two or three feet thick, the door of wood and iron, a foot thick, and the iron grating which strained the light, I could not help being struck with the foolishness of that institution which treated me as if I were mere flesh and blood and bones, to be locked up. I wondered that it should have concluded at length that this was the best use it could put me to, and had never thought to avail itself of my services in some way. I saw that, if there was a wall of stone between me and my townsmen, there was a still more difficult one to climb or break through, before they could get to be as free as I was. I did not for a moment feel confined, and the walls seemed a great waste of stone and mortar. I felt as if I alone of all my townsmen had paid my tax. They plainly did not know how to treat me, but behaved like persons who are underbred. In every threat and in every compliment there was a blunder; for they thought that my chief desire was to stand the other side of that stone wall. I could not but smile to see how industriously they locked the door on my meditations, which followed them out again without let or hindrance, and *they* were really all that was dangerous. As they could not reach me, they had resolved to punish my body; just as boys, if they cannot come at some person against whom they have a spite, will abuse his dog. I saw that the State was half-witted, that it was timid as a lone woman with her silver spoons, and that it did not know its friends from its foes, and I lost all my remaining respect for it, and pitied it.

Thus the State never intentionally confronts a man's sense, intellectual or moral, but only his body, his senses. It is not armed with superior wit or honesty, but with superior physical strength. I was not born to be forced. I will breathe after my own fashion. Let us see who is the strongest. What force has a multitude? They can only force me who obey a higher law than I. They force me to become like themselves. I do not hear of *men* being *forced* to live this way or that by masses of men. What sort of life were that to live? When I meet a government which says to me, "Your money or your life," why should I be in haste to give it my money? It may be in a great strait, and not know what to do: I cannot help that. It must help itself; do as I do. It is not worth the while to snivel about it. I am not responsible for the successful working of the machinery of society. I am not the son of the engineer. I perceive that, when an acorn and a chestnut fall side by side, the one does not remain inert to make way for the other, but both obey their own laws, and spring and grow and flourish as best they can, till one, perchance, overshadows and destroys the other. If a plant cannot live according to its nature, it dies; and so a man.

The night in prison was novel and interesting enough. The prisoners in their shirt-sleeves were enjoying a chat and the evening air in the doorway, when I entered. But the jailer said, "Come, boys, it is time to lock up"; and so they dispersed, and I heard the sound of their steps returning into the hollow apartments. My room-mate was introduced to me by the jailer, as "a first-rate fellow and a clever man." When the door was locked, he showed me where to hang my hat, and how he managed matters there. The rooms were whitewashed once a month; and this one, at least, was the whitest, most simply furnished, and probably the neatest apartment in the town. He naturally wanted to know where I came from, and what brought me there; and, when I had told him, I asked him in my turn how he came there, presuming him to be an honest man,

of course; and, as the world goes, I believe he was. "Why,"
said he, "they accuse me of burning a barn; but I never did it."
As near as I could discover, he had probably gone to bed in a
barn when drunk, and smoked his pipe there; and so a barn
was burnt. He had the reputation of being a clever man, had
been there some three months waiting for his trial to come on,
and would have to wait as much longer; but he was quite
domesticated and contented, since he got his board for nothing,
and thought that he was well treated.

He occupied one window, and I the other; and I saw, that,
if one stayed there long, his principal business would be to
look out the window. I had soon read all the tracts that were
left there, and examined where former prisoners had broken
out, and where a grate had been sawed off, and heard the history of the various occupants of that room; for I found that
even here there was a history and a gossip which never cir-
culated beyond the walls of the jail. Probably this is the only
house in the town where verses are composed, which are afterward printed in a circular form, but not published. I was
shown quite a long list of verses which were composed by
some young men who had been detected in an attempt to
escape, who avenged themselves by singing them.

I pumped my fellow-prisoner as dry as I could, for fear I
should never see him again; but at length he showed me which
was my bed, and left me to blow out the lamp.

It was like travelling into a far country, such as I had never
expected to behold, to lie there for one night. It seemed to me
that I never had heard the town-clock strike before, nor the
evening sounds of the village; for we slept with the windows
open, which were inside the grating. It was to see my native
village in the light of the Middle Ages, and our Concord was
turned into a Rhine stream, and visions of knights and castles
passed before me. They were the voices of old burghers that I
heard in the streets. I was an involuntary spectator and auditor

of whatever was done and said in the kitchen of the adjacent village-inn,—a wholly new and rare experience to me. It was a closer view of my native town. I was fairly inside of it. I never had seen its institutions before. This is one of its peculiar institutions; for it is a shire town. I began to comprehend what its inhabitants were about.

In the morning, our breakfasts were put through the hole in the door, in small oblong-square tin pans, made to fit, and holding a pint of chocolate, with brown bread, and an iron spoon. When they called for the vessels again, I was green enough to return what bread I had left; but my comrade seized it, and said that I should lay that up for lunch or dinner. Soon after he was let out to work at haying in a neighboring field, whither he went every day, and would not be back till noon; so he bade me good-day, saying that he doubted if he should see me again.

When I came out of prison,—for some one interfered, and paid that tax,—I did not perceive that great changes had taken place on the common, such as he observed who went in a youth, and emerged a tottering and gray-headed man; and yet a change had to my eyes come over the scene,—the town, and State, and country,—greater than any that mere time could effect. I saw yet more distinctly the State in which I lived. I saw to what extent the people among whom I lived could be trusted as good neighbors and friends; that their friendship was for summer weather only; that they did not greatly propose to do right; that they were a distinct race from me by their prejudices and superstitions, as the Chinamen and Malays are; that, in their sacrifices to humanity, they ran no risks, not even to their property; that, after all, they were not so noble but they treated the thief as he had treated them, and hoped, by a certain outward observance and a few prayers, and by walking in a particular straight though useless path from time to time, to save their souls. This may be to judge my neighbors harshly; for I believe that many of them are not aware that they have such an institution as the jail in their village.

It was formerly the custom in our village, when a poor debtor came out of jail, for his acquaintances to salute him, looking through their fingers, which were crossed to represent the grating of a jail window, "How do ye do?" My neighbors did not thus salute me, but first looked at me, and then at one another, as if I had returned from a long journey. I was put into jail as I was going to the shoemaker's to get a shoe which was mended. When I was let out the next morning, I proceeded to finish my errand, and having put on my mended shoe, joined a huckleberry party, who were impatient to put themselves under my conduct; and in half an hour,—for the horse was soon tackled,—was in the midst of a huckleberry field, on one of our highest hills, two miles off, and then the State was nowhere to be seen.

This is the whole history of "My Prisons."

I have never declined paying the highway tax, because I am as desirous of being a good neighbor as I am of being a bad subject; and, as for supporting schools, I am doing my part to educate my fellow-countrymen now. It is for no particular item in the tax-bill that I refuse to pay it. I simply wish to refuse allegiance to the State, to withdraw and stand aloof from it effectually. I do not care to trace the course of my dollar, if I could, till it buys a man or a musket to shoot one with,—the dollar is innocent,—but I am concerned to trace the effects of my allegiance. In fact, I quietly declare war with the State, after my fashion, though I will still make what use and get what advantage of her I can, as is usual in such cases.

If others pay the tax which is demanded of me, from a sympathy with the State, they do but what they have already done in their own case, or rather they abet injustice to a greater extent than the State requires. If they pay the tax from a mistaken interest in the individual taxed, to save his property, or prevent his going to jail, it is because they have not considered wisely how far they let their private feelings interfere with the public good.

This, then, is my position at present. But one cannot be too much on his guard in such a case, lest his action be biased by obstinacy, or an undue regard for the opinions of men. Let him see that he does only what belongs to himself and to the hour.

I think sometimes, Why, this people mean well; they are only ignorant; they would do better if they knew how: why give your neighbors this pain to treat you as they are not inclined to? But I think again, this is no reason why I should do as they do, or permit others to suffer much greater pain of a different kind. Again, I sometimes say to myself, When many millions of men, without heat, without ill will, without personal feeling of any kind, demand of you a few shillings only, without the possibility, such is their constitution, of retracting or altering their present demand, and without the possibility, on your side, of appeal to any other millions, why expose yourself to this overwhelming brute force? You do not resist cold and hunger, the winds and the waves, thus obstinately; you quietly submit to a thousand similar necessities. You do not put your head into the fire. But just in proportion as I regard this as not wholly a brute force, but partly a human force, and consider that I have relations to those millions as to so many millions of men, and not of mere brute or inanimate things, I see that appeal is possible, first and instantaneously, from them to the Maker of them, and secondly, from them to themselves. But, if I put my head deliberately into the fire, there is no appeal to fire or to the Maker of fire, and I have only myself to blame. If I could convince myself that I have any right to be satisfied with men as they are, and to treat them accordingly, and not according, in some respects, to my requisitions and expectations of what they and I ought to be, then, like a good Mussulman and fatalist, I should endeavor to be satisfied with things as they are, and say it is the will of God. And, above all, there is this difference between resisting this and a purely brute or natural force, that I can resist this with some effect; but I cannot expect, like Orpheus, to change the nature of the rocks and trees and beasts.

I do not wish to quarrel with any man or nation. I do not wish to split hairs, to make fine distinctions, or set myself up as better than my neighbors. I seek rather, I may say, even an excuse for conforming to the laws of the land. I am but too ready to conform to them. Indeed, I have reason to suspect myself on this head; and each year, as the tax-gatherer comes round, I find myself disposed to review the acts and position of the general and State governments, and the spirit of the people, to discover a pretext for conformity.

> "We must affect our country as our parents;
> And if at any time we alienate
> Our love or industry from doing it honor,
> We must respect effects and teach the soul
> Matter of conscience and religion,
> And not desire of rule or benefit."

I believe that the State will soon be able to take all my work of this sort out of my hands, and then I shall be no better a patriot than my fellow-countrymen. Seen from a lower point of view, the Constitution, with all its faults, is very good; the law and the courts are very respectable; even this State and this American government are, in many respects, very admirable and rare things, to be thankful for, such as a great many have described them; but seen from a point of view a little higher, they are what I have described them; seen from a higher still, and the highest, who shall say what they are, or that they are worth looking at or thinking of at all?

However, the government does not concern me much, and I shall bestow the fewest possible thoughts on it. It is not many moments that I live under a government, even in this world. If a man is thought-free, fancy-free, imagination-free, that which *is not* never for a long time appearing *to be* to him, unwise rulers or reformers cannot fatally interrupt him.

I know that most men think differently from myself; but those whose lives are by profession devoted to the study of these or kindred subjects, content me as little as any. Statesmen and legislators, standing so completely within the institution, never distinctly and nakedly behold it. They speak of moving society, but have no resting-place without it. They may be men of a certain experience and discrimination, and have no doubt invented ingenious and even useful systems, for which we sincerely thank them; but all their wit and usefulness lie within certain not very wide limits. They are wont to forget that the world is not governed by policy and expediency. Webster never goes behind government, and so cannot speak with authority about it. His words are wisdom to those legislators who contemplate no essential reform in the existing government; but for thinkers, and those who legislate for all time, he never once glances at the subject. I know of those whose serene and wise speculations on this theme would soon reveal the limits of his mind's range and hospitality. Yet, compared with the cheap professions of most reformers, and the still cheaper wisdom and eloquence of politicians in general, his are almost the only sensible and valuable words, and we thank Heaven for him. Comparatively, he is always strong, original, and, above all, practical. Still his quality is not wisdom, but prudence. The lawyer's truth is not Truth, but consistency, or a consistent expediency. Truth is always in harmony with herself, and is not concerned chiefly to reveal the justice that may consist with wrong-doing. He well deserves to be called, as he has been called, the Defender of the Constitution. There are really no blows to be given by him but defensive ones. He is not a leader, but a follower. His leaders are the men of '87. "I have never made an effort," he says, "and never propose to make an effort; I have never countenanced an effort, and never mean to countenance an effort, to disturb the arrangement as originally made, by which the various States came into the Union." Still thinking of the sanction which the Constitution gives to slavery, he says, "Because it was a part of the original compact,—let it stand." Notwithstanding his special acuteness and ability, he is unable to take a fact out of its merely political relations, and behold it as it lies absolutely to be disposed of by the intellect,—what, for instance, it behooves a man to do here in America today with regard to slavery, but ventures, or is driven, to make some such desperate answer as the following, while professing to speak absolutely, and as a private man,—from which what new and singular code of social duties might be inferred? "The manner," says he, "in which the governments of those States where slavery exists are to regulate it, is for their own consideration, under their responsibility to their constituents, to the general laws of propriety, humanity, and justice, and to God. Associations formed elsewhere, springing from a feeling of humanity, or any other cause, have nothing whatever to do with it. They have never received any encouragement from me, and they never will."

They who know of no purer sources of truth, who have traced up its stream no higher, stand, and wisely stand, by the Bible and the Constitution, and drink at it there with reverence and humility; but they who behold where it comes trickling into this lake or that pool, gird up their loins once more, and continue their pilgrimage towards its fountain-head.

No man with a genius for legislation has appeared in America. They are rare in the history of the world. There are orators, politicians, and eloquent men, by the thousand; but the speaker has not yet opened his mouth to speak, who is capable of settling the much-vexed questions of the day. We love eloquence for its own sake, and not for any truth which it may utter, or any heroism it may inspire. Our legislators have not yet learned the comparative value of free-trade and of freedom, of union, and of rectitude, to a nation. They have no genius or talent for comparatively humble questions of taxation and finance, commerce and manufacturers and agriculture. If we were left solely to the wordy wit of legislators in Congress for our guidance, uncorrected by the seasonable experience and the effectual complaints of the people, America would not long retain her rank among the nations. For eighteen hundred years, though perchance I have no right to say it, the New Testament has been written, yet where is the legislator who has wisdom and practical talent enough to avail himself of the light which it sheds on the science of legislation?

The authority of government, even such as I am willing to submit to,—for I will cheerfully obey those who know and can do better than I, and in many things even those who neither know nor can do so well,—is still an impure one: to be strictly just, it must have the sanction and consent of the governed. It can have no pure right over my person and property but what I concede to it. The progress from an absolute to a limited monarchy, from a limited monarchy to a democracy, is a progress toward a true respect for the individual. Even the Chinese philosopher was wise enough to regard the individual as the basis of the empire. Is a democracy, such as we know it, the last improvement possible in government? Is it not possible to take a step further towards recognizing and organizing the rights of man? There will never be a really free and enlightened State, until the State comes to recognize the individual as a higher and independent power, from which all its own power and authority are derived, and treats him accordingly. I please myself with imagining a State at last which can afford to be just to all men, and to treat the individual with respect as a neighbor; which even would not think it inconsistent with its own repose, if a few were to live aloof from it, not meddling with it, nor embraced by it, who fulfilled all the duties of neighbors and fellow-men. A State which bore this kind of fruit, and suffered it to drop off as fast as it ripened, would prepare the way for a still more perfect and glorious State, which also I have imagined, but not yet anywhere seen.

8. Wendell Phillips,
"Philosophy of the Abolition Movement"

Next to Garrison, Wendell Phillips (1811–1884) was the most prominent New England abolitionist. He was also perhaps the most effective orator in the great age of American oratory.

Phillips was drawn into the abolitionist movement in 1835 when he witnessed a mob leading Garrison through the streets of Boston with a noose around his neck. For thirty years thereafter his public role was that of loyal lieutenant to his friend. From the beginning, however, there were significant differences in the thinking of the two men.

Phillips attempted to steer a middle course between Garrison's Christian anarchism and the political abolitionism of men like Charles Sumner and Thaddeus Stevens. In the "Philosophy of the Abolition Movement," Phillips was particularly concerned to defend Garrison's practice of personally villifying individual slaveholders. "We must plead guilty, if there be guilt in not knowing how to separate the sin from the sinner." Within a few years this conception led Phillips to complete support for the Union Army in the Civil War.

MR. CHAIRMAN: I have to present, from the business committee, the following resolution:—

"*Resolved,* That the object of this society is now, as it has always been, to convince our countrymen, by arguments addressed to their hearts and consciences, that slaveholding is a heinous crime, and that the duty, safety, and interest of all concerned demand its immediate abolition, without expatriation."

Wendell Phillips, "Philosophy of the Abolition Movement," Speech before the Massachusetts Antislavery Society, Boston, January 27, 1853, *Speeches, Lectures, and Letters* (Boston: James Redpath, Publisher, 1863), pp. 98–100, 106–110, 134–136, 139–140, 151–153.

I wish, Mr. Chairman, to notice some objections that have been made to our course ever since Mr. Garrison began his career, and which have been lately urged again, with considerable force and emphasis, in the columns of the London Leader, the able organ of a very respectable and influential class in England. . . .

. . . The charges to which I refer are these: that, in dealing with slaveholders and their apologists, we indulge in fierce denunciations, instead of appealing to their reason and common sense by plain statements and fair argument;—that we might have won the sympathies and support of the nation, if we would have submitted to argue this question with a manly patience; but, instead of this, we have outraged the feelings of the community by attacks, unjust and unnecessarily severe, on its most valued institutions, and gratified our spleen by indiscriminate abuse of leading men, who were often honest in their intentions, however mistaken in their views;—that we have utterly neglected the ample means that lay around us to convert the nation, submitted to no discipline, formed no plan, been guided by no foresight, but hurried on in childish, reckless, blind, and hot-headed zeal,—bigots in the narrowness of our views, and fanatics in our blind fury of invective and malignant judgment of other men's motives.

. . . I need not waste time by repeating the superfluous confession that we are men, and therefore do not claim to be perfect. Neither would I be understood as denying that we use denunciation, and ridicule, and every other weapon that the human mind knows. We must plead guilty, if there be guilt in not knowing how to separate the sin from the sinner. With all the fondness for abstractions attributed to us, we are not yet capable of that. We are fighting a momentous battle at desperate odds,—one against a thousand. Every weapon that ability or ignorance, wit, wealth, prejudice, or fashion can command, is pointed against us. The guns are shotted to their lips. The arrows are poisoned. Fighting against such an array, we cannot afford to confine ourselves to any one weapon. The cause is not ours, so that we might, rightfully, postpone or put in peril the victory by moderating our demands, stifling our convictions, or filing down our rebukes, to gratify any sickly taste of our own, or to spare the delicate nerves of our neighbor. Our clients are three millions of Christian slaves, standing dumb suppliants at the threshold of the Christian world. They have no voice but ours to utter their complaints, or to demand justice. The press, the pulpit, the wealth, the literature, the prejudices, the political arrangements, the present self-interest of the country, are all against us. God has given us no weapon but the truth, faithfully uttered, and addressed, with the old prophets' directness, to the conscience of the individual sinner. The elements which control public opinion and mould the masses are against us. We can but pick off here and there a man from the triumphant majority. We have facts for those who think, arguments for those who reason; but he who cannot be reasoned out of his prejudices must be laughed out of them; he who cannot be argued out of his selfishness must be shamed out of it by the mirror of his hateful self held up relentlessly before his eyes. We live in a land where every man makes broad his phylactery, inscribing thereon, "All men are created equal,"—"God hath made of one blood all nations of men." It seems to us that in such a land there must be, on this question of slavery, sluggards to be awakened, as well as doubters to be convinced. Many more, we verily believe, of the first than of the last. There are far more dead hearts to be quickened, than confused intellects to be cleared up,—more dumb dogs to be made to speak, than doubting consciences to be enlightened. [Loud cheers.] We have use, then, sometimes, for something beside argument.

What is the denunciation with which we are charged? It is endeavoring, in our faltering human speech, to declare the enormity of the sin of making merchandise of men,—of separating husband and wife,—taking the infant from its mother, and selling the daughter to prostitution,—of a professedly Christian nation denying, by statute, the Bible to every sixth man and woman of its population, and making it illegal for "two or three" to meet together, except a white man be present! What is this harsh criticism of motives with which we are charged? It is simply holding the intelligent and deliberate actor responsible for the character and consequences of his acts. Is there anything inherently wrong in such denunciation or such criticism? This we may claim—we have never judged a man but out of his own mouth. We have seldom, if ever, held him to account, except for acts of which he and his own friends were proud. All that we ask the world and thoughtful men to note are the principles and deeds on which the American pulpit and American public men plume themselves. We always allow our opponents to paint their own pictures. Our humble duty is to stand by and assure the spectators that what they would take for a knave or a hypocrite is really, in American estimation, a Doctor of Divinity or Secretary of State.[1]

---

[1] A paragraph from the New England Farmer, of this city, has gone the rounds of the press, and is generally believed. It says:—

"We learn, on reliable authority, that Mr. Webster confessed to a warm political friend, a short time before his death, that the great mistake of his life was the famous Seventh of March Speech, in which, it will be remembered, he defended the Fugitive Slave Law, and fully committed himself to the Compromise Measures. Before taking his stand on that occasion, he is said to have corresponded with Professor Stuart, and other eminent divines, to ascertain how far the religious sentiment of the North would sustain him in the position he was about to assume."

Some say this "warm political friend" was a clergyman! Consider a moment the language of this statement, the form it takes on every lip and in every press. "The great *mistake* of his life"! Seventy years old, brought up in New England churches, with all the culture of the world at his command, his soul melted by the repeated loss of those dearest to him, a great statesman, with a heart, according to his admirers, yet tender and fresh,—one who bent in such agony over the death-bed of his first daughter,—he looks back on this speech, which his friends say changed the feelings of ten millions of people, and made it possible to enact and execute the Fugitive Slave Law. He sees that it flooded the hearth-stones of thousands of colored men with wretchedness and despair,—crazed the

The South is one great brothel, where half a million of
women are flogged to prostitution, or, worse still, are degraded
to believe it honorable. The public squares of half our great
cities echo to the wail of families torn asunder at the auction-
block; no one of our fair rivers that has not closed over the
negro seeking in death a refuge from a life too wretched to
bear; thousands of fugitives skulk along our highways, afraid
to tell their names, and trembling at the sight of a human
being; free men are kidnapped in our streets, to be plunged
into that hell of slavery; and now and then one, as if by miracle, after long years, returns to make men aghast with his
tale. The press says, "It is all right"; and the pulpit cries,
"Amen." They print the Bible in every tongue in which man
utters his prayers; and get the money to do so by agreeing
never to give the book, in the language our mothers taught us,
to any negro, free or bond, south of Mason and Dixon's line.

---

mother, and broke the heart of the wife,—putting the virtue of woman
and the liberty of man in the power of the vilest,—and all, as he at least
now saw, for nothing. Yet one who, according to his worshippers, was
"the grandest growth of our soil and our institutions," looked back on
such an act, and said—what? With one foot in the grave, said what of
it? "I did wrong"? "I committed a foul outrage on my brother man"?
"I sported too carelessly with the welfare of the poor"? Was there no
moral chord in that heart, "the grandest growth of our soil and our institutions"? No! He said, "I made a mistake!" Not, "I was false in my stew-
ardship of these great talents and this high position!" No! But on the
chess-board of the political game, I made a bad move! I threw away my
chances! A gambler, I did not understand my cards! And to whom does
he offer this acknowledgment? To a clergyman! the representative of the
moral sense of the community! What a picture! We laugh at the lack of
heart in Talleyrand, when he says, "It is worse than a crime, a blunder."
Yet all our New-Englander can call this momentous crime of his life is—
a *mistake!*

Whether this statement be entirely true or not, we all know it is
exactly the tone in which all about us talk of that speech. If the statement
be true, what an entire want of right feeling and moral sensibility it
shows in Mr. Webster! If it be unfounded, still the welcome it has
received, and the ready belief it has gained, show the popular appreciation of him, and of such a crime. Such is the public with which
Abolitionists have to deal.

The press says, "It is all right"; and the pulpit cries, "Amen." The slave lifts up his imploring eyes, and sees in every face but ours the face of an enemy. Prove to me now that harsh rebuke, indignant denunciation, scathing sarcasm, and pitiless ridicule are wholly and always unjustifiable; else we dare not, in so desperate a case, throw away any weapon which ever broke up the crust of an ignorant prejudice, roused a slumbering conscience, shamed a proud sinner, or changed, in any way, the conduct of a human being. Our aim is to alter public opinion. Did we live in a market, our talk should be of dollars and cents, and we would seek to prove only that slavery was an unprofitable investment. Were the nation one great, pure church, we would sit down and reason of "righteousness, temperance, and judgment to come." Had slavery fortified itself in a college, we would load our cannons with cold facts, and wing our arrows with arguments. But we happen to live in the world,—the world made up of thought and impulse, of self-conceit and self-interest, of weak men and wicked. To conquer, we must reach all. Our object is not to make every man a Christian or a philosopher, but to induce every one to aid in the abolition of slavery. We expect to accomplish our object long before the nation is made over into saints or elevated into philosophers. To change public opinion, we use the very tools by which it was formed. That is, all such as an honest man may touch.

All this I am not only ready to allow, but I should be ashamed to think of the slave, or to look into the face of my fellow-man, if it were otherwise. It is the only thing which justifies us to our own consciences, and makes us able to say we have done, or at least tried to do, our duty. . . .

. . . Sir, when a nation sets itself to do evil, and all its leading forces, wealth, party, and piety, join in the career, it is impossible but that those who offer a constant opposition should be hated and maligned, no matter how wise, cautious, and well planned their course may be. We are peculiar suf-

ferers in this way. The community has come to hate its reprov-
ing Nathan so bitterly, that even those whom the relenting
part of it is beginning to regard as standard-bearers of the anti-
slavery host think it unwise to avow any connection or sympathy with him. I refer to some of the leaders of the political
movement against slavery. They feel it to be their mission to
marshal and use as effectively as possible the present convictions of the people. They cannot afford to encumber themselves
with the odium which twenty years of angry agitation have
engendered in great sects sore from unsparing rebuke, parties
galled by constant defeat, and leading men provoked by unexpected exposure. They are willing to confess, privately, that
our movement produced theirs, and that its continued existence is the very breath of their life. But, at the same time, they
would fain walk on the road without being soiled by too close
contact with the rough pioneers who threw it up. They are
wise and honorable, and their silence is very expressive.

When I speak of their eminent position and acknowledged
ability, another thought strikes me. Who converted these men
and their distinguished associates? It is said we have shown
neither sagacity in plans, nor candor in discussion, nor ability.
Who, then, or what, converted Burlingame and Wilson, Sumner and Adams, Palfrey and Mann, Chase and Hale, and Phillips and Giddings? Who taught the Christian Register, the
Daily Advertiser, and that class of prints, that there were such
things as a slave and a slaveholder in the land, and so gave
them some more intelligent basis than their mere instincts to
hate William Lloyd Garrison? [Shouts and laughter.] What
magic wand was it whose touch made the toadying servility of
the land start up the real demon that it was, and at the same
time gathered into the slave's service the professional ability,
ripe culture, and personal integrity which grace the Free Soil
ranks? We never argue! These men, then, were converted by
simple denunciation! They were all converted by the "hot,"
"reckless," "ranting," "bigoted," "fanatic" Garrison, who never

troubled himself about facts, nor stopped to argue with an opponent, but straightway knocked him down! [Roars of laughter and cheers.] My old and valued friend, Mr. Sumner, often boasts that he was a reader of the Liberator before I was. Do not criticise too much the agency by which such men were converted. That blade has a double edge. Our reckless course, our empty rant, our fanaticism, has made Abolitionists of some of the best and ablest men in the land. We are inclined to go on, and see if even with such poor tools we cannot make some more. [Enthusiastic applause.] . . .

Caution is not always good policy in a cause like ours. It is said that, when Napoleon saw the day going against him, he used to throw away all the rules of war, and trust himself to the hot impetuosity of his soldiers. The masses are governed more by impulse than conviction; and even were it not so, the convictions of most men are on our side, and this will surely appear, if we can only pierce the crust of their prejudice or indifference. I observe that our Free Soil friends never stir their audience so deeply as when some individual leaps beyond the platform, and strikes upon the very heart of the people. Men listen to discussions of laws and tactics with ominous patience. It is when Mr. Sumner, in Faneuil Hall, avows his determination to disobey the Fugitive Slave Law, and cries out, "I was a man before I was a Commissioner,"—when Mr. Giddings says of the fall of slavery, quoting Adams, "Let it come; if it must come in *blood,* yet I say let it come!"—that their associates on the platform are sure they are wrecking the party,—while many a heart beneath beat its first pulse of antislavery life.

These are brave words. When I compare them with the general tone of Free Soil men in Congress, I distrust the atmosphere of Washington and of politics. These men move about, Sauls and Goliaths among us, taller by many a cubit. There they lose port and stature. Mr. Sumner's speech in the Senate unsays no part of his Faneuil Hall pledge. But, though discussing the same topics, no one would gather from any word or argument that the speaker ever took such ground as he did in Faneuil Hall. It is all through, the *law*, the *manner* of the surrender, not the surrender itself, of the slave, that he objects to. As my friend Mr. Pillsbury so forcibly says, so far as anything in the speech shows, he puts the slave behind the jury trial, behind the *habeas corpus* act, and behind the new interpretation of the Constitution, and says to the slave claimant: "You must get through all these, before you reach him; but if you *can* get through all these, you may have him!" It was no tone like this which made the old Hall rock! Not if he got through twelve jury trials, and forty *habeas corpus* acts, and constitutions built high as yonder monument, would he permit so much as the shadow of a little finger of the slave claimant to touch the slave! [Loud applause.] At least, so he was understood. In an elaborate discussion, by the leader of the political antislavery party, of the whole topic of fugitive slaves, you do not find one protest against the surrender itself, one frank expression on the constitutional clause, or any indication of the speaker's final purpose, should any one be properly claimed under that provision. It was under no such uncertain trumpet that the antislavery host was originally marshalled. The tone is that of the German soldiers whom Napoleon routed. They did not care, they said, for the defeat, but only that they were not beaten according to rule. . . .

. . . Every thoughtful and unprejudiced mind must see that such an evil as slavery will yield only to the most radical treatment. If you consider the work we have to do, you will not think us needlessly aggressive, or that we dig down unnecessarily deep in laying the foundations of our enterprise. A money power of two thousand millions of dollars, as the prices of slaves now range, held by a small body of able and desperate men; that body raised into a political aristocracy by special constitutional provisions; cotton, the product of slave labor, forming the basis of our whole foreign commerce, and the commercial class thus subsidized; the press bought up, the pulpit reduced to vassalage, the heart of the common people chilled by a bitter prejudice against the black race; our leading men bribed, by ambition, either to silence or open hostility;—in such a land, on what shall an Abolitionist rely? On a few cold prayers, mere lip-service, and never from the heart? On a church resolution, hidden often in its records, and meant only as a decent cover for servility in daily practice? On political parties, with their superficial influence at best, and seeking ordinarily only to use existing prejudices to the best advantage? Slavery has deeper root here than any aristocratic institution has in Europe; and politics is but the common pulse-beat, of which revolution is the fever-spasm. Yet we have seen European aristocracy survive storms which seemed to reach down to the primal strata of European life. Shall we, then, trust to mere politics, where even revolution has failed? How shall the stream rise above its fountain? Where shall our church organizations or parties get strength to attack their great parent and moulder, the Slave Power? Shall the thing formed say to him that formed it, Why hast thou made me thus? The old jest of one who tried to lift himself in his own basket, is but a tame picture of the man who imagines that, by working solely through existing sects and parties, he can destroy slavery. Mechanics say nothing but an earthquake, strong enough to move all Egypt, can bring down the Pyramids.

Experience has confirmed these views. The Abolitionists who have acted on them have a "short method" with all unbelievers. They have but to point to their own success, in contrast with every other man's failure. To waken the nation to its real state, and chain it to the consideration of this one duty, is half the work. So much we have done. Slavery has been made the question of this generation. To startle the South to madness, so that every step she takes, in her blindness, is one step more toward ruin, is much. This we have done. Witness Texas and the

Fugitive Slave Law. To have elaborated for the nation the only plan of redemption, pointed out the only exodus from this "sea of troubles," is much. This we claim to have done in our motto of IMMEDIATE, UNCONDITIONAL EMANCIPATION ON THE SOIL. The closer any statesmanlike mind looks into the question, the more favor our plan finds with it. The Christian asks fairly of the infidel, "If this religion be not from God, how do you explain its triumph, and the history of the first three centuries?" Our question is similar. If our agitation has not been wisely planned and conducted, explain for us the history of the last twenty years! Experience is a safe light to walk by, and he is not a rash man who expects success in future from the same means which have secured it in times past.

9. Elihu Burritt,

"Passive Resistance"

Elihu Burritt (1810–1879) snatched time from his work as a blacksmith to learn Latin, Greek, French, Spanish, Italian, German, Hebrew, Chaldaic, Samaritan, Ethiopic, and a number of other languages. During one three-month period he studied near (but not at) Yale University; later he took a foundry job in Worcester, Massachusetts, so as to be able to borrow grammars and lexicons from the American Antiquarian Society.

As Burritt's learning became publicly recognized, he devoted himself increasingly to writing and lecturing on behalf of temperance, abolitionism, and world peace. Never forgetting his own origins, Burritt also called on workingmen for a worldwide general strike

Elihu Burritt, *Thoughts and Things at Home and Abroad* (Boston: Phillips, Sampson, and Co., 1854), pp. 269–286.

against war. "We hope," he declared in 1867, "the day will come when the working-men of Christendom will form one vast Trades Union, and make a universal and simultaneous *strike* against the whole war system." The concern for mass use of nonviolence, as opposed to the individual action of a Woolman or Thoreau, is evident throughout Burritt's essays on "Passive Resistance."

The Power of Passive Resistance.

The full power revealed and prescribed in that simple and sublime precept of the Gospel, *"overcome evil with good,"* has never been tested by any people, population, or community, in subduing the evils and enemies that beset and oppressed them, either from within or without. To put it into full operation, requires a capacity of good-will, of forgiveness of injuries, of abnegation of natural instincts, which the population of no town, or province, or state, has ever acquired. But, at long intervals, and a little more frequently of late, a case has occurred here and there, in which a considerable community has acquired the ability of sustaining for awhile the lowest, feeblest, manifestation of this power, or a condition of *passive resistance* to oppression, armed with a force which could instantly crush any violent opposition they might attempt to array against it. Within the last two or three years, several of these cases have transpired in different parts of the world. In one of these, a little English colony at the Cape of Good Hope, *passively,* but successfully, *resisted* the great Government of the British empire, backed with all its navies and armies, in its attempt to make the home of their small population a receptacle of criminals, crime, and convicts from England. Then, almost simultaneously with this successful experiment with the force of passive resistance, there comes the report of another, from the distant islands of the Pacific Ocean, tried under circumstances of more imminent peril and oppression, and crowned with more illustrious triumph. The weak little Government of the Sand-

wich Islands, in order to diminish the use and effect of intoxicating liquors among their people, imposed a heavy tax upon
French brandy and wine. This irritated the French, and they
sent thither a great ship of war to compel the government to
remove the tax; and the captain gave them but a few hours to
comply with the demand. But they absolutely refused to obey.
Then they must take the consequences, and these would be
terrible. The lady of the French consul—good, kind, compassionate woman—went with her husband from house to house,
and entreated the foreign residents to take refuge on board the
French ship, for the island was to be blown up, or sunk, to
punish the wicked government for taxing French brandy, and
making drunkenness a dearer luxury to the people! But not a
single person accepted of the refuge. The government held fast
to its resolution without wavering for a moment. The French
commander landed with his marines in battle array. Men with
lighted matches stood at the great cannons of the ship. The
hour of vengeance had come. Poor little people! what will become of you now? What will you do to defend yourselves
against this resistless force? Do? do nothing but *endure*. "The
King," says the report, "gave peremptory orders to his people
to *oppose no resistance* to the Frenchmen. The gallant commander, therefore, landed his marines and took possession of
the fort, custom-house, and some other Government buildings,
no resistance being offered. All was still and peaceful in the
streets, business going on as usual. Here they remained for
some days; when, finding that the government would not ac-
cede at all to their demands, though they offered to leave the
whole question to an umpire, the chivalrous Frenchmen went
to work to dismantle the fort, and destroyed everything within
its walls. After having finished this Vandal-like work, they
marched off with flying colors." How full of illustration is this
case of passive resistance! The simple, quiet force of *endurance*
which the government opposed to the French, wet their pow-
der and turned their bayonets to straw. Against this unexpected

force the marines were powerless. They had no arms to contend with such an enemy. All their weapons, and discipline,
and bravery, were fitted only to overcome brute force; and of
this they found none, except its shadow in the fort and its
equipments; and with great valor they fell upon this shadow,
and mutilated it terribly, and then marched back with flying
colors! So far was this invasion of bayonet-power from induc-
ing a settlement to the advantage of the French, that the
government even refused their offer to submit the question to
arbitration, or to put the law at any hazard of modification, in
face of all the brute force that France could marshal against it.

These are examples of the irresistible power of *passive resistance,* when opposed by a people to foreign enemies and oppression. But almost simultaneously with these, we have examples of this kind of resistance when arrayed against domestic
oppression, or the despotic acts of dynasties that have at their
command vast military organizations, ready to do their will.
The most striking of these is the case of Hesse Cassel. Here,
the force of resistance has been tested for a longer period, and
by a larger population than ever have illustrated its virtue before. The result has not yet transpired, nor can we conclude
what it will be. We can hardly believe that it will be crowned
with complete success; for we cannot believe that the Hessians
will be able to *endure* unto the end which they seek. We fear
they will lose their impregnable strength, by being seduced
into a manifestation of brute force. But the teaching of their
experiment, even up to this stage, will be invaluable to the people and the cause of popular freedom everywhere on the
Continent of Europe. It has established the fact that despotism,
backed by the mightiest armies, cannot serf or subdue a people or a population, or rob them of their rights, or barricade
their way to rational freedom, if they can only acquire the
capacity of a *passive resistance,* which the most aggravated
oppression can never weary out. Up to this hour, the Hessians
have manifested this capacity, and practised this virtue; and

the bristling bayonets which virtually surrounded them have become as stubble. While they possess their souls in patience, and refrain from the slightest act of violence, the whole soldiery of the continent will be powerless against them. How full of glorious illustration and consequence is this spectacle! The eyes of despotism, like those of beasts of prey, are glaring upon them from every side, watching to spring upon them at a single bound, the first moment that they venture from their stronghold of *passive resistance!* What a sublime sight in the moral world! It is said that the poor peasants, and the poorest day-laborers in Cassel have signed a pledge to abstain from intoxicating drinks, and that they are watching over each other with the keenest vigilance, lest, in an evil hour, some sudden act of oppression should make them mad, and they should fall from the grace of patience, and peril their country's all by a deed of violence! Contrast that discipline with the spirit and deeds of a brute-force revolution! How the people rise, rise, rise to the highest stature of moral being, under such a process of self-education! "Better is he that ruleth his spirit than he that taketh a city." Yes; the Elector may take the city of Cassel, with 60,000 Austrian and Bavarian troops; but they will be to him as mere shadows, so long as the Hessians shall be able to rule their spirits after this fashion. The cause of popular freedom, progress, and prosperity has an immense interest at stake in the issue of this grand experiment with a force which the God of the poor and the oppressed has given to them in his great Gospel of love:—"I SAY UNTO YOU, RESIST NOT EVIL, BUT OVERCOME EVIL WITH GOOD."

The Dignity of Passive Resistance.

We have recently dwelt at some length upon the irresistible power of *passive resistance,* when opposed to oppression, either from home or from abroad, by any population or people, great or small. We contemplated its capacity as a force, which any community or country might employ successfully in repelling and disarming despotism, whatever amount of bayonet power it might have at its command. This was illustrated by the example of the little community at the Cape of Good Hope, in thwarting the attempt of the British Government to make their country a penal settlement; of the Sandwich islanders, in repelling the aggressions of the French; and of the people of Hesse Cassel, in resisting the despotism of a dynasty, threatening to trample their rights under the feet of foreign soldiery. But, it will be said, in these cases, the people *"made a virtue of necessity."* Passive resistance was all they could oppose to these acts of oppression. Very good. But, as it was effective to this end, would it have been less a *virtue*, if it had not been a *necessity?* If the king of the Sandwich Islands had at his command a standing army of 100,000 men, and a Gibraltar full of cannon, could he have more completely expelled, chastised, and humbled the French than he did, by putting them into the condition of pirates before the world, and by forcing them to fight the air, and then retreat to their ships from very shame at the result of their martial prowess? We can see many lips curl at this proposition. What! stand by with 100,000 armed men, and see a regiment of foreign soldiers land, to compel the Government to abrogate its laws, without opposing that physical force resistance organized at great expense for such an emergency! Would not "endurance cease to be a virtue" at such a point? Could passive resistance, friend Broadbrim, be compatible with a nation's dignity in such a case? Neighbor Firelock, thou thinkest these to be hard questions, and hard to be answered by human nature. And so they are; but religion, and even reason, can do it easily. But from what Scriptures comes that precept, "There is a point at which endurance ceases to be a virtue?" There is no divinity in the Scriptures from which that maxim is taken; they are human, in a very low manifestation of reason and experience. Christianity says, "endure unto the end; not to the end of your patience, but to the end of wrong, evil and oppression—to the goal, to the crown of your triumph and rejoicing. Now, neighbor Firelock, before we proceed to consider these hard questions, let us examine the maxim which thou hast quoted, as if it were from the New Testament,—"There is a point at which *endurance* ceases to be a *virtue*." Then what does it become, when it ceases to be a *virtue?*—a *crime!* Says the maxim, the endurance of wrong and oppression is really a virtue up to a certain point. From the starting, to this terminating point of patience, the greater the oppression, the more virtuous is its endurance. To this extent the virtue of patience is measured by the pressure of wrong which it sustains; but when it reaches this point, and confronts a severer trial, it becomes criminal in it not to give way and relinquish the struggle, although it possesses the capacity of enduring, unto the end, all the wrongs and outrages which oppression can oppose to its resistance. For the maxim speaks only of a contingency in which endurance ceases to be a *virtue,* not a *possibility.* Now, what would become of society and its moralities, if all the other virtues should follow the course prescribed to this? If men were to be taught, by maxims couched in a Bible *tournure,* that "There is a point at which truth, temperance, or honesty ceases to be a *virtue!*—that there are trials and temptations to which it is virtuous to yield!— tests too severe for purity, probity, or any other grace, before which it is graceful to fall!" Surely, the evidence of such a false maxim must be rejected from the consideration of the question. Let us, then, look at the case of the Sandwich Islands, in the light of national independence, dignity and honor.

The Government had enacted a law, for the good of the people, which diminished the use and sale of French brandy and wines. The French attempted to compel the Government by violence, to repeal that law. It was a direct and aggravated attack upon the sovereignty of the Sandwich Island State. That attack was repelled and thwarted by the *passive* resistance of the Government and people. But that was the only resistance which they had in their power to oppose to their assailants, it is urged. Grant it; but was it not as effective as would have been the broadsides of fifty ships of the line, if such a fleet had been at the command of the king? But, says another, passive resistance invites attack and insult, and repetition of outrage. Prove this, if you can, by any evidence drawn from history, or any argument from philosophy; prove it by the result of this very experiment. See if the French venture again to compel this little Government, by force, to repeal or modify one of its laws to their commercial advantage. But, if the Sandwich islanders had possessed an army of 100,000 men, would passive resistance, in such a case, have been compatible with their national dignity, even if it had been more efficient and success-ful than the strongest array of brute force? In this question comes the tug of the principle, in the minds of thousands, who can follow it to a certain length. The greatest dignity that a nation can acquire, is to be always in the right. Right is not only its highest dignity, but its moral power. This dignity and power combine to create in a nation's heart an indomitable will to maintain them. Now, passive resistance puts in force all the energies of this will, and raises the smallest nation to the foremost rank among the great powers of the earth. It de-fends its territory, its rights, its honors and dignity, by the sheer force of its will. It conquers and triumphs by its will. Did ever Alexander, Caesar, Bonaparte, or Nicholas, more than this? On the other hand, brute-force resistance weakens the will of a nation—dethrones it from its first place and power —subordinates it to precarious contingencies—throws it head-long among the veriest hap-hazards of the battle-field—in a word, compromises its dignity, by pitting it against the blind-est chances of success. The Sandwich islanders repelled the attack upon their rights, by the mere force of their will. Compatible with their dignity! Why, that will was the embodi-ment and energy of their dignity; and they not only main-tained, but elevated it, by the passive resistance which they opposed to their assailants. The French retreated before that dignity—the quiet dignity of right. They, too, had a will, when they left their ship-of-war, and drew up their forces on the shore, for the attack; but they had no dignity to sustain it, nor force to carry it into execution. But they hoped to acquire both, before they had marched twenty yards. How? from whom? From the Sandwich islanders themselves. They expected and intended to tempt the Government from its impregnable position of passive resistance; to descend from its dignity, or share it with them by ordering them to be fired upon. The discharge of a single musket, on the part of the islanders, would have transferred the transaction to the ground of a regular contest, in which right and wrong would be in equilibrium; in which the former relinquishes all its moral advantage over the latter, and hazards its all upon the even chances of a die, the result of which cannot be affected by any moral discriminations between the contending parties.

To conquer by the moral manifestation of the will, is to conquer like a God. To conquer by the manifestation of brute force, is to conquer like a beast. The dignity of passive resistance lies between these parallels.

The Patriotism of Passive Resistance.

We have considered the power and dignity of passive resistance, when opposed to assaults from without, or oppression from within. We have tried to show that necessity does not make it a virtue in any case; but that its inherent virtue always makes it a necessity. We now proceed to demonstrate its patriotism. We deem it due to the principles and advocates of peace, to rebut the charge that is often brought against them, that they are "the complacent allies of despotism—that they would stand by and see, without concern or remonstrance, communities, peoples, and nations manacled hand and foot, by tyrants; their rights, liberties, hopes, and aspirations, trodden

out of existence by the iron heel of oppression." The imputa-
tion of cowardice, unmanly imbecility, a crouching, abject
spirit, is involved in this charge. "What! would you have us
lie down in the dust, and be trampled upon by these despotic
powers and governments! Would you have us permit them to
enslave us, and hold out our arms and feet to the fettering
without a struggle or a murmur?" And then, having filled their
bosoms to bursting with patriotic indignation at the course and
disposition described interrogatively by these triumphant questions, they exclaim, "No! we would spill the last drop of our
blood;—we would see our cities burned with fire;—we would
perish with arms in our hands on the battle-field, or pine in
exile in Siberia or Botany Bay, before we would tamely submit
to be slaves! Liberty or death!" These are the most striking
and usual terms of comparison in the vocabulary of martial
patriotism. Frequently the sentiments they express take a
figurative form more fearful still. We recollect one employed
by the editor of an American journal, pending the Oregon controversy, to this effect: "Sooner than relinquish our just rights
to the disputed territory, we would shed every drop of blood in
the heart of the nation!" Mr. Borrow, agent of the Bible Society, records "a broken prayer for my native land, which, after
my usual thanksgiving, I breathed forth to the Almighty, ere
retiring to rest that Sunday night at Gibraltar;" a prayer *for*
his native country which contains this passage—"May'st thou
sink, if thou dost sink, amidst blood and flame, with a mighty
noise, causing more than one nation to participate in thy down-
fall!" And these are regarded as the outbursts of a patriotic
feeling—of a love of country so intense that they would see it
engulfed in fire and blood, and even the last vein of the
nation's heart pierced, and its existence extinguished, rather
than endure insult, injury, or oppression! They measure their
attachment and devotion to their country and its institutions
by the awful calamities which they would bring upon it, in
defending its honor and rights. What a fearful antithesis of

alternatives! How many peoples and nations have "sunk, amidst blood and flame, and with a mighty noise," in the abyss which yawns between these alternative conditions! How many patriots of this order have seen their country a smoking sea of ruin, without finding a bulrush ark in which to float "the immediate jewel of its soul"—the charter of its existence as a nation!

We wish no one to accept or share the responsibility of our convictions, or of the views we wish to express in reference to this aspect of the subject. If peace has its victories no less than war, it has its heroism and its patriotism. The men of peace can find no attribute, in the great Gospel principles of their faith, that can side with despotism, or wink with indifference at oppression. They are not cowards. They counsel no tame, unmanly submission to wrong; but to oppose to wrong a courage of the human will that shall never faint or waver at any extremity of endurance;—aye, to "resist unto blood," if it be unavoidable,—to give their own necks to the axe or to the halter, on the block or the scaffold, but never to shed themselves a single drop, or perpetrate a single act of malevolent injury on any human being, under the severest pressure of despotic rule. Peace has its heroism, serene and dauntless, that neither trembles nor pales before the guillotine, the halter, or the knout. Peace has its patriotism; deep, earnest, unselfish, self-sacrificing, and sensitive,—a love of country that would bleed to the last vein, but never wound, for its rights, honor, and prosperity. Peace has its battle-fields; bloodless, but brave to a degree of heroic endurance of wrong and outrage to which martial courage could never attain. The patriotism of peace, like the first grace of Christianity, "is first pure, then peaceable;" pure from those intense emotions of selfishness which are generally the heart and soul of the patriotism of the warrior. The history of nations, from its first to its last chapter, is full of the examples of those who have gloried in dying for their country. These last years have produced multitudes of the like. This patriotic sentiment is popularized among the millions, and set to the music of the songs of labor; and the hardy, humble men of the sewers often cheer the hours of their toil by singing, *sotto voce*, the joy and the glory *"Mourir pour sa patrie."* The leaders of the depressed peoples of Europe, who have struggled, again and again, to recover their freedom and independence by the sword, are loud in the profession of their readiness to die for their country, and thousands of their countrymen echo the same sentiment. But under what circumstances would you die for your nation's freedom? Would you mount the scaffold, and die for your country, as Jesus Christ died on the cross for the world, amid the scoffs and scorn, and cutting taunts of your own countrymen? How would your patriotism stand the test of such an ordeal? How would the military heroes of the world, who have acquired fame for dying on the battle-field for their country's good, have trembled and recoiled like cowards from such a scaffold! Tried by such a test, how often would the patriotism of the warrior be seen to be nothing more or better than an intense love of self, the eager ambition for a name that shall outlive the memory of the good!

The Protecting Power of Peace Principles.

The principles of peace, as a protection and defence, are equal to any enemy or emergency. They are a safe resort in "extreme cases." They carried William Penn through as an extreme case as any Christian nation can fear to get into. Armed with these divine principles—trusting to no Egyptian reeds of steel, no mailed arm of flesh—he came among the red savages, whose bare breasts had been scarred in their long and bloody wars with the puritans of New England, and the *Long Knives* of Maryland and Virginia. The memory of burnt wigwams, and the cry of their children as they were thrust into the flames on the bayonets of professing Christians were fresh in their hearts. —Among their painted chieftains, strode many a *Logan*, sombre, stern, with long-brooding revenge rankling in his bosom. Penn came among them from the land of their deadliest foes; he spoke their language, and his face was pale like theirs. But he came with peace in his eyes and peace on his lips. He took hold of their rough red hands, and called them brethren; and their strong hearts grew soft at his words. And there they sat down and held sweet counsel together. There they burnished the silver chain of friendship bright; for the music of the good man's voice was peace. And their old men called him father, and their children, and their children's children called him father. No oaths were used in that covenant of peace, and none were broken.

The Economy of Passive Resistance.

Here, for example, is a people that have been subjected to a foreign and despotic rule, which has become intolerable to them. They are penetrated with a sense of the wrong and outrage which are inflicted upon them. They arrive at the con clusion to wage a desperate struggle to shake off the yoke of their servitude, and to regain or acquire their freedom as a nation. Unanimity of will and purpose, a strong and common sentiment of the justice of their cause, the concentrated and enduring energy of the whole population, are indispensably requisite to give such a struggle a possibility of success. Now, then, what are their position and their prospects? What are their forces, and what are those of the despotic power with which they have to contend? They have the right and the will to defend it. The powerful Government that oppresses them has the wrong, and the military force on its side to maintain it. What, then, are the chances of the battlefield? In the trial by battle, right has not the slightest advantage over wrong. So the prime force of the oppressed people is virtually put *hors du combat* in the struggle; and their will falls to the ground powerless, with the weapons they lifted to sustain it. At the disastrous issue of brute force with their colossal oppressor, they fall, not half-way, but to a lower depth of depression than before. When they entered on the struggle, they felt the hazard of the fearful odds; they knew the issue would be doubtful; successful or discomfited, they expected to suffer great calamities; to sacrifice thousands of human lives; to consume the resources of the nation, and bring wailing, desolation, and ruin, to numberless homes. But so strong was the will of the people, that they tried "the hazard of the die" of battle, in face of these terrible and visible certainties. Now, then, let us suppose the same people, with the same deep sense of right, and the same unanimous will to maintain it, at the cost of any amount of suffering, shake off the yoke of the oppressor, and oppose to his power the mere moral or passive resistance of that will. Simultaneously, as at the declaration of war, every man, woman and child secedes from obedience to the despotic Government, and prepares for the consequences. No tri-colored banner is raised; no bodies of men are marched through the streets to the sound of martial music. The only battle-word of the nation is written on the doorposts of every house:—*"No political change is worth a single crime, or a single drop of human blood!"* The only soldiers employed are like the peasant-sentinels of Cassel, who watched over their fellows, lest oppression should make them mad, and, in a sudden trial of their patience, they might fall to an act or word of violence. Now what force can the despotic Government employ to subdue the will of that people, arrayed against it in this impregnable state of opposition? It has no moral force, that is clear; and every act of violence puts it more and more in the wrong; that is, increases its moral weakness, and the moral power and dignity of the other side. Its soldiery is powerless, because every breast in the nation is defenceless, and every man possesses his soul in quiet patience, and withholds his hand from the slightest act of violence. Its generals and officers can find no other field of glory or prowess than the scaffold, where they may superintend the hanging of a few leaders of the revolution, for exciting in the people a spirit of patience under oppression;

for saying on the platform, or in the journals of the country—
"Endure unto the end; but do violence to no man." How is
this people to be subjugated? It cannot be hung, put in prison,
or transported, entire, or by sections. A dozen or two, in every
considerable town, might be hung, hundreds imprisoned, and
hundreds exiled. Thousands might be spoiled of their goods.
But all this loss of life and treasure, and calamity of other
species, would not equal the bloody casualties of a single battle. Not a farthing's expense is imposed upon them by their
own Government or leaders to sustain this struggle. No agricultural laborer is called away from the plough, no mechanic
from the loom or the anvil. Every soldier's post in the conflict
is in his own field, workshop, or counting-room; and every
man of the people, and every woman and child that can endure, is a soldier. In these long campaigns of patience, there
is no individual subjected to the despotism of military rule, or
to the inequalities of the camp. The heroes of this warfare are
those who have best ruled their spirits under the sharpest
trials. The veterans to be remembered and rewarded, when
the crown of their freedom is attained, are such as have given
to the people the most illustrious examples of endurance of
wrong, of a patience which oppression could not tire, of a
capacity to rule their own spirits under the pressure of the
most stinging provocations. Could the dignity, power and
courage of the human will be combined and presented in a
sublimer manifestation, than in such a spectacle? Here patriotism puts off self, and walks serene in the pure white robe of
its majesty. Here the steady bravery of the human heart looks
gigantic despotism in the face with an eye that makes it cower
in the midst of its Cossacks. National independence! 'tis more
than gained and guaranteed; that people has conquered it by
its will. Democracy! it is already established, with attributes of
popular sovereignty which ally it to Omnipotence. Democracy!
that term falls below the dignity of this people's prerogative
and power, even while the faggot blazes, and the block drips
with the blood of their patriots and heroes, in every town and

village of their land. The experience of ages has given a meaning to that word too gross and physical to describe the sovereignty and freedom of this self-governing people. With them it signifies not the brute force of the mass, not the capricious sway of its impulses, but "THE POWER OF GOD WITH MEN." With them it is true, for the first time in the history of humanity, "*vox populi est vox Dei;*" because the battle-word of their conflict and conquest is the sublime voice of His Gospel, "*Resist not evil, but overcome evil with good.*" Is there any man who aspires in his heart to see "*Liberty, Equality, Fraternity,*" illustrated in the life and being of a republic? Here you have those conditions realized to the full. The armies of the aliens, the banded despotisms of the world, may encamp around such a nation; but they can no more withhold from it the freedom it has won by its capacity to enjoy it, than they can withhold the communion and friendship of the Holy Spirit from the individual soul that has worked out its own salvation with fear and trembling.

We do not believe that despotism, in any of its manifestations, has foes more decided and unwavering, or popular freedom and progress friends more earnest or efficient, than are the advocates of peace, on both sides of the Atlantic. For one, we trust that the last experiment to win liberty by the sword, to attain to the capacity and dignity of self-government, by unchaining and stimulating to frenzy the worst passions of the people, has been tried and found wanting. The fearful and sanguinary struggles of the last few years, we hope, will serve to this evidence, without a repetition of these terrible lessons. If there be any oppressed and aggrieved people, that are nourishing in their heart the determination to struggle again for the national being and freedom they have lost, there is only one way given under heaven among men by which they may reach the consummation of their longings; and that is, *Passive Resistance.*

PART III

Anarchists

10. Michael Schwab and August Spies,
Speeches in Court, 1886

On May 3, 1886, Chicago police fired into a crowd of strikers at the
McCormick Harvester works. A protest meeting was held the next
day in front of the Haymarket. Somebody threw a bomb which killed
seven policemen. Michael Schwab, August Spies, and six other anarchist leaders were arrested, tried, and convicted, despite a total
lack of evidence as to the murderer's identity. Spies was hanged;
Schwab's sentence was commuted to life imprisonment, and in 1893
he was pardoned by Illinois Governor John Peter Altgeld.

The Haymarket Anarchists were hardly advocates of nonviolence.
Yet, while urging that workers arm themselves in response to the
habitual violence of businessmen, they also envisioned a society in
which the coercion of governments and armies would wither away.

The obvious miscarriage of injustice in this incident shocked re-
form-minded Americans much as Elijah Lovejoy's murder in the
1830's electrified abolitionists. Among authors represented in this
volume, Emma Goldman and William Haywood both considered
Haymarket the decisive event in shaping their radical convictions.

*The Chicago Martyrs. The Famous Speeches Of The Eight Anarchists
In Judge Gary's Court, October 7, 8, 9, 1886* . . . (San Francisco: Free
Society, Publishers, 1899), pp. 14, 19–20.

[*Schwab*]

"Anarchy" is Greek, and means, verbatim, without rulership; not being ruled. According to our vocabulary, anarchy is a state of society in which the only government is reason; a state of society in which all human beings do right for the simple reason that it is right, and hate wrong because it is wrong. In such a society, no laws, no compulsion will be necessary. The attorney of the State was wrong when he said: "Anarchy is dead." Anarchy, up to the present day, has existed only as a doctrine, and Mr. Grinnell has not the power to kill any doctrine whatever. You may call anarchy, as defined by us, an idle dream, but that dream was dreamed by Gotthold Ephraim Lessing, one of the three great German poets and the most celebrated German critic of the last century. If anarchy were the thing the State's attorney makes it out to be, how could it be that such eminent scholars as Prince Kropotkine and the greatest living geographer, Elisee Reclus, were avowed anarchists, even editors of anarchistic newspapers? Anarchy is a dream, but only in the present. It will be realized. Reason will grow in spite of all obstacles. Who is the man that has the cheek to tell us that human development has already reached its culminating point? I know that our ideal will not be accomplished this or next year, but I know that it will be accomplished as near as possible, some day, in the future. It is entirely wrong to use the word anarchy as synonymous with violence. Violence is one thing and anarchy another. In the present state of society violence is used on all sides, and, therefore, we advocated the use of violence against violence, but against violence only, as a necessary means of defence.

[*Spies*]

Society will reclaim its own, even though you erect a gibbet on every street corner. And anarchism, this terrible "ism," deduces that under a co-operative organization of society, under economic equality and individual independence, the "state" —the political state—will pass into barbaric antiquity. And we will be where all are free, where there are no longer masters and servants, where intellect stands for brute force; there will no longer be any use for the policemen and militia to preserve the so called "peace and order"—the order that the Russian general speaks of when he telegraphed to the Czar after he had massacred half of Warsaw, "Peace reigns in Warsaw." Anarchism does not mean bloodshed; does not mean, robbery, arson, etc. These monstrosities are, on the contrary, the characteristic features of capitalism. Anarchism means peace and tranquillity to all. Anarchism means the reorganization of society upon scientific principles and the abolition of causes which produce vice and crime.

11. Benjamin Tucker,

"Relation of the State to the Individual"

Benjamin Tucker (1854–1939) was the most important American exponent of individualist or philosophical anarchism. The son of radical Unitarian parents, Tucker attended a Friends Academy in New Bedford, Massachusetts and the Massachusetts Institute of Technology. He espoused prohibition, women's suffrage, and the eight-hour day before a decisive meeting with Josiah Warren in 1872. Thereafter he edited the *Radical Review* (1877–1878) and *Liberty* (1881–1908), and translated Proudhon's *What is Property?*, Ba-

Benjamin R. Tucker, "Relation of the State to the Individual," address delivered October 14, 1890, Salem, Mass., in *Instead of a Book By A Man Too Busy to Write One; a fragmentary exposition of Philosophical Anarchism* (New York: Benj. R. Tucker, 1893), pp. 21–27.

kunin's *God and the State,* and *What is to be Done?* by the Russian Populist Nicholas Tchernishevsky.

Like Burritt, Tucker advocated "non-resistance" and "passive resistance," instancing the Irish Land League as an example of successful mass nonviolence. He condemned the violence of the Haymarket Anarchists and Garfield's assassin Guiteau, and also of the state which condemned them to death. Tucker viewed the state not merely (like Thoreau) as unnecessary, but as a dangerous "invasive" agency.

. . . Anarchism, in dealing with this subject, has found it necessary, first of all, to define its terms. . . . Take the term "State," for instance, with which we are especially concerned to-day. It is a word that is on every lip. But how many of those who use it have any idea of what they mean by it? And, of the few who have, how various are their conceptions! We designate by the term "State" institutions that embody absolutism in its extreme form and institutions that temper it with more or less liberality. We apply the word alike to institutions that do nothing but aggress and to institutions that, besides aggressing, to some extent protect and defend. But which is the State's essential function, aggression or defence, few seem to know or care. Some champions of the State evidently consider aggression its principle, although they disguise it alike from themselves and from the people under the term "administration," which they wish to extend in every possible direction. Others, on the contrary, consider defence its principle, and wish to limit it accordingly to the performance of police duties. Still others seem to think that it exists for both aggression and defence, combined in varying proportions according to the momentary interests, or maybe only whims, of those happening to control it. Brought face to face with these diverse views, the Anarchists, whose mission in the world is the abolition of aggression and all the evils that result therefrom, perceived that, to be understood, they must attach some definite and avowed significance to the terms which they are obliged to employ, and especially to the words "State" and "government." Seeking, then, the elements common to all the institutions to which the name "State" has been applied, they have found them two in number: first, aggression; second, the assumption of sole authority over a given area and all within it, exercised generally for the double purpose of more complete oppression of its subjects and extension of its boundaries. That this second element is common to all States, I think, will not be denied,—at least, I am not aware that any State has ever tolerated a rival State within its borders; and it seems plain that any State which should do so would thereby cease to be a State and to be considered as such by any. The exercise of authority over the same area by two States is a contradiction. That the first element, aggression, has been and is common to all States will probably be less generally admitted. Nevertheless, I shall not attempt to re-enforce here the conclusion of Spencer, which is gaining wider acceptance daily,—that the State had its origin in aggression, and has continued as an aggressive institution from its birth. Defence was an afterthought, prompted by necessity; and its introduction as a State function, though effected doubtless with a view to the strengthening of the State, was really and in principle the initiation of the State's destruction. Its growth in importance is but an evidence of the tendency of progress toward the abolition of the State. Taking this view of the matter, the Anarchists contend that defence is not an essential of the State, but that aggression is. Now what is aggression? Aggression is simply another name for government. Aggression, invasion, government, are interconvertible terms. The essence of government is control, or the attempt to control. He who attempts to control another is a governor, an aggressor, an invader; and the nature of such invasion is not changed, whether it is made by one man upon another man, after the manner of the ordinary criminal, or by one man upon all other men, after the manner of an absolute monarch, or by all other men upon one man, after the manner of a modern democracy. On the other hand, he who resists another's attempt to control is not an aggressor, an invader, a governor, but simply a defender, a protector; and the nature of such resistance is not changed whether it be offered by one man to another man, as when one repels a criminal's onslaught, or by one man to all other men, as when one declines to obey an oppressive law, or by all other men to one man, as when a subject people rises against a despot, or as when the members of a community voluntarily unite to restrain a criminal. This distinction between invasion and resistance, between government and defence, is vital. Without it there can be no valid philosophy of politics. Upon this distinction and the other considerations just outlined, the Anarchists frame the desired definitions. This, then, is the Anarchistic definition of government: the subjection of the non-invasive individual to an external will. And this is the Anarchistic definition of the State: the embodiment of the principle of invasion in an individual, or a band of individuals, assuming to act as representatives or masters of the entire people within a given area. As to the meaning of the remaining term in the subject under discussion, the word "individual," I think there is little difficulty. Putting aside the subtleties in which certain metaphysicians have indulged, one may use this word without danger of being misunderstood. Whether the definitions thus arrived at prove generally acceptable or not is a matter of minor consequence. I submit that they are reached scientifically, and serve the purpose of a clear conveyance of thought. The Anarchists, having by their adoption taken due care to be explicit, are entitled to have their ideas judged in the light of these definitions.

Now comes the question proper: What relations should exist between the State and the individual? The general method of determining these is to apply some theory of ethics involving a basis of moral obligation. In this method the Anarchists have no confidence. The idea of moral obligation, of inherent rights and duties, they totally discard. They look upon all obligations, not as moral, but as social, and even then not really as obligations except as these have been consciously and voluntarily assumed. If a man makes an agreement with men, the latter may combine to hold him to his agreement; but, in the absence of such agreement, no man, so far as the Anarchists are aware, has made any agreement with God or with any other power of any order whatsoever. The Anarchists are not only utilitarians, but egoists in the farthest and fullest sense. So far as inherent right is concerned, might is its only measure. Any man, be his name Bill Sykes or Alexander Romanoff, and any set of men, whether the Chinese highbinders or the Congress of the United States, have the right, if they have the power, to kill or coerce other men and to make the entire world subservient to their ends. Society's right to enslave the individual and the individual's right to enslave society are unequal only because their powers are unequal. This position being subversive of all systems of religion and morality, of course I cannot expect to win immediate assent thereto from the audience which I am addressing to-day; nor does the time at my disposal allow me to sustain it by an elaborate, or even a summary, examination of the foundations of ethics. Those who desire a greater familiarity with this particular phase of the subject should read a profound German work, "*Der Einzige und sein Eigenthum*," written years ago by a comparatively unknown author, Dr. Caspar Schmidt, whose *nom de plume* was Max Stirner. Read only by a few scholars, the book is buried in obscurity, but is destined to a resurrection that perhaps will mark an epoch.

If this, then, were a question of right, it would be, according to the Anarchists, purely a question of strength. But, fortunately, it is not a question of right: it is a question of expediency, of knowledge, of science,—the science of living together, the science of society. The history of humanity has been largely one long and gradual discovery of the fact that the individual is the gainer by society exactly in proportion as society is free, and of the law that the condition of a permanent and harmonious society is the greatest amount of individual liberty compatible with equality of liberty. The average man of each new generation has said to himself more clearly and consciously than his predecessor: "My neighbor is not my enemy, but my friend, and I am his, if we would but mutually recognize the fact. We help each other to a better, fuller, happier living; and this service might be greatly increased if we would cease to restrict, hamper, and oppress each other. Why can we not agree to let each live his own life, neither of us transgressing the limit that separates our individualities?" It is by this reasoning that mankind is approaching the real social contract, which is not, as Rousseau thought, the origin of society, but rather the outcome of a long social experience, the fruit of its follies and disasters. It is obvious that this contract, this social law, developed to its perfection, excludes all aggression, all violation of equality of liberty, all invasion of every kind. Considering this contract in connection with the Anarchistic definition of the State as the embodiment of the principle of invasion, we see that the State is antagonistic to society; and, society being essential to individual life and development, the conclusion leaps to the eyes that the relation of the State to the individual and of the individual to the State must be one of hostility, enduring till the State shall perish.

"But," it will be asked of the Anarchists at this point in the argument, "what shall be done with those individuals who undoubtedly will persist in violating the social law by invading their neighbors?" The Anarchists answer that the abolition of the State will leave in existence a defensive association, resting no longer on a compulsory but on a voluntary basis, which will restrain invaders by any means that may prove necessary. "But that is what we have now," is the rejoinder. "You really want, then, only a change of name?" Not so fast, please. Can it be soberly pretended for a moment that the State, even as it exists here in America, is purely a defensive institution? Surely not, save by those who see of the State only its most palpable manifestation,—the policeman on the street-corner. And one would not have to watch him very closely to see the error of this claim. Why, the very first act of the State, the compulsory assessment and collection of taxes, is itself an aggression, a violation of equal liberty, and, as such, vitiates every subsequent act, even those acts which would be purely defensive if paid for out of a treasury filled by voluntary contributions. How is it possible to sanction, under the law of equal liberty, the confiscation of a man's earnings to pay for protection which he has not sought and does not desire? And, if this is an outrage, what name shall we give to such confiscation when the victim is given, instead of bread, a stone, instead of protection, oppression? To force a man to pay for the violation of his own liberty is indeed an addition of insult to injury. But that is exactly what the State is doing. Read the "Congressional Record"; follow the proceedings of the State legislatures; examine our statute-books; test each act separately by the law of equal liberty,—you will find that a good nine-tenths of existing legislation serves, not to enforce that fundamental social law, but either to prescribe the individual's personal habits, or, worse still, to create and sustain commercial, industrial, financial, and proprietary monopolies which deprive labor of a large part of the reward that it would receive in a perfectly free market. "To be governed," says Proudhon, "is to be watched, inspected, spied, directed, law-ridden, regulated, penned up, indoctrinated, preached at, checked, appraised, sized, censured, commanded, by beings who have neither title nor knowledge nor virtue. To be governed is to have every operation, every transaction, every movement noted, registered, counted, rated, stamped, measured, numbered, assessed, licensed, refused, authorized, indorsed, admonished, prevented, reformed, redressed, corrected. To be governed is, under pretext of public utility and in the name of the general interest, to be laid under contribution, drilled, fleeced, exploited, monopolized, extorted from, exhausted, hoaxed, robbed; then, upon the slightest resistance, at the first word of complaint, to be repressed, fined, vilified, annoyed, hunted down, pulled about, beaten, disarmed, bound, imprisoned, shot, mitrailleused, judged, condemned, banished, sacrificed, sold, betrayed, and, to crown all, ridiculed, derided, outraged, dishonored." And I am sure I do not need to point out to you the existing laws that correspond to and justify nearly every count in Proudhon's long indictment. How thoughtless, then, to assert that the existing political order is of a purely defensive character instead of the aggressive State which the Anarchists aim to abolish!

This leads to another consideration that bears powerfully upon the problem of the invasive individual, who is such a bugbear to the opponents of Anarchism. Is it not such treatment as has just been described that is largely responsible for his existence? I have heard or read somewhere of an inscription written for a certain charitable institution:

"This hospital a pious person built,
But first he made the poor wherewith to fill't."

And so, it seems to me, it is with our prisons. They are filled with criminals which our virtuous State has made what they are by its iniquitous laws, its grinding monopolies, and the horrible social conditions that result from them. We enact many laws that manufacture criminals, and then a few that punish them. Is it too much to expect that the new social conditions which must follow the abolition of all interference with the production and distribution of wealth will in the end so change the habits and propensities of men that our jails and prisons, our policemen and our soldiers,—in a word, our whole machinery and outfit of defence,—will be superfluous? That, at least, is the Anarchists' belief. . . .

12. Emma Goldman, "Anarchism: What It Really Stands For"

Emma Goldman (1869–1940) was born in Russia, and moved to St. Petersburg at the age of thirteen, one year after the assassination of Czar Alexander II. In 1886 she emigrated to the United States where she obtained work in a clothing factory at a wage of $2.50 a week. In 1892 she assisted Alexander Berkman in his attempt to assassinate Henry Clay Frick of United States Steel during the Homestead strike in Pittsburgh. Arrested for sedition in June 1917, she was deported to revolutionary Russia two years later. Emma Goldman's disillusionment with the Russian Revolution is recorded in *My Disillusionment in Russia* (1923) and other books.

Toward the end of her life this fiery but compassionate rebel reconsidered her attitude toward violence, writing to Berkman in 1928 that she wished that she could adopt the nonviolence of Gandhi and Tolstoy: "I feel violence in whatever form never has and probably never will bring constructive results." The following essay, published in 1910, condemns violence indirectly in its critique of the penal system. But anarchism's most important contribution to the nonviolent tradition was its doctrine of "direct action," which Miss Goldman here expounds.

The history of human growth and development is at the same time the history of the terrible struggle of every new idea heralding the approach of a brighter dawn. In its tenacious hold on tradition, the Old has never hesitated to make use of the foulest and cruelest means to stay the advent of the New, in whatever form or period the latter may have asserted itself. Nor need we retrace our steps into the distant past to realize the enormity of opposition, difficulties, and hardships placed in

---

Emma Goldman, "Anarchism: What It Really Stands For," *Anarchism And Other Essays* (New York: Mother Earth Publishing Association, 1910), pp. 53–73.

the path of every progressive idea. The rack, the thumbscrew, and the knout are still with us; so are the convict's garb and the social wrath, all conspiring against the spirit that is serenely marching on.

Anarchism could not hope to escape the fate of all other ideas of innovation. Indeed, as the most revolutionary and uncompromising innovator, Anarchism must needs meet with the combined ignorance and venom of the world it aims to reconstruct.

To deal even remotely with all that is being said and done against Anarchism would necessitate the writing of a whole volume. I shall therefore meet only two of the principal objections. In so doing, I shall attempt to elucidate what Anarchism really stands for.

The strange phenomenon of the opposition to Anarchism is that it brings to light the relation between so-called intelligence and ignorance. And yet this is not so very strange when we consider the relativity of all things. The ignorant mass has in its favor that it makes no pretense of knowledge or tolerance. Acting, as it always does, by mere impulse, its reasons are like those of a child. "Why?" "Because." Yet the opposition of the uneducated to Anarchism deserves the same consideration as that of the intelligent man.

What, then, are the objections? First, Anarchism is impractical, though a beautiful ideal. Second, Anarchism stands for violence and destruction, hence it must be repudiated as vile and dangerous. Both the intelligent man and the ignorant mass judge not from a thorough knowledge of the subject, but either from hearsay or false interpretation.

A practical scheme, says Oscar Wilde, is either one already in existence, or a scheme that could be carried out under the existing conditions; but it is exactly the existing conditions that one objects to, and any scheme that could accept these conditions is wrong and foolish. The true criterion of the practical, therefore, is not whether the latter can keep intact the wrong or foolish; rather is it whether the scheme has vitality enough to leave the stagnant waters of the old, and build, as well as sustain, new life. In the light of this conception, Anarchism is indeed practical. More than any other idea, it is helping to do away with the wrong and foolish; more than any other idea, it is building and sustaining new life.

The emotions of the ignorant man are continuously kept at a pitch by the most blood-curdling stories about Anarchism. Not a thing too outrageous to be employed against this philosophy and its exponents. Therefore Anarchism represents to the unthinking what the proverbial bad man does to the child,—a black monster bent on swallowing everything; in short, destruction and violence.

Destruction and violence! How is the ordinary man to know that the most violent element in society is ignorance; that its power of destruction is the very thing Anarchism is combating? Nor is he aware that Anarchism, whose roots, as it were, are part of nature's forces, destroys, not healthful tissue, but parasitic growths that feed on the life's essence of society. It is merely clearing the soil from weeds and sagebrush, that it may eventually bear healthy fruit.

Someone has said that it requires less mental effort to condemn than to think. The widespread mental indolence, so prevalent in society, proves this to be only too true. Rather than to go to the bottom of any given idea, to examine into its origin and meaning, most people will either condemn it altogether, or rely on some superficial or prejudicial definition of non-essentials.

Anarchism urges man to think, to investigate, to analyze every proposition; but that the brain capacity of the average reader be not taxed too much, I also shall begin with a definition, and then elaborate on the latter.

ANARCHISM:—The philosophy of a new social order based on liberty unrestricted by manmade law; the theory that all forms of government rest on violence, and are therefore wrong and harmful, as well as unnecessary.

The new social order rests, of course, on the materialistic basis of life; but while all Anarchists agree that the main evil today is an economic one, they maintain that the solution of that evil can be brought about only through the consideration of *every phase* of life,—individual, as well as the collective; the internal, as well as the external phases.

A thorough perusal of the history of human development will disclose two elements in bitter conflict with each other; elements that are only now beginning to be understood, not as foreign to each other, but as closely related and truly harmonious, if only placed in proper environment: the individual and social instincts. The individual and society have waged a relentless and bloody battle for ages, each striving for supremacy, because each was blind to the value and importance of the other. The individual and social instincts,—the one a most potent factor for individual endeavor, for growth, aspiration, self-realization; the other an equally potent factor for mutual helpfulness and social well-being.

The explanation of the storm raging within the individual, and between him and his surroundings, is not far to seek. The primitive man, unable to understand his being, much less the unity of all life, felt himself absolutely dependent on blind, hidden forces ever ready to mock and taunt him. Out of that attitude grew the religious concepts of man as a mere speck of dust dependent on superior powers on high, who can only be appeased by complete surrender. All the early sagas rest on that idea, which continues to be the *leit-motif* of the biblical tales dealing with the relation of man to God, to the State, to society. Again and again the same motif, *man is nothing, the powers are everything.* Thus Jehovah would only endure man on condition of complete surrender. Man can have all the glories of the earth, but he must not become conscious of himself. The State, society, and moral laws all sing the same refrain: Man can have all the glories of the earth, but he must not become conscious of himself.

Anarchism is the only philosophy which brings to man the consciousness of himself; which maintains that God, the State, and society are non-existent, that their promises are null and void, since they can be fulfilled only through man's subordination. Anarchism is therefore the teacher of the unity of life; not merely in nature, but in man. There is no conflict between the individual and the social instincts, any more than there is between the heart and the lungs: the one the receptacle of a precious life essence, the other the repository of the element that keeps the essence pure and strong. The individual is the heart of society, conserving the essence of social life; society is the lungs which are distributing the element to keep the life essence—that is, the individual—pure and strong.

"The one thing of value in the world," says Emerson, "is the active soul; this every man contains within him. The soul active sees absolute truth and utters truth and creates." In other words, the individual instinct is the thing of value in the world. It is the true soul that sees and creates the truth alive, out of which is to come a still greater truth, the re-born social soul.

Anarchism is the great liberator of man from the phantoms that have held him captive; it is the arbiter and pacifier of the two forces for individual and social harmony. To accomplish that unity, Anarchism has declared war on the pernicious influences which have so far prevented the harmonious blending of individual and social instincts, the individual and society.

Religion, the dominion of the human mind; Property, the dominion of human needs; and Government, the dominion of human conduct, represent the stronghold of man's enslavement and all the horrors it entails. Religion! How it dominates man's mind, how it humiliates and degrades his soul. God is everything, man is nothing, says religion. But out of that nothing God has created a kingdom so despotic, so tyrannical, so cruel, so terribly exacting that naught but gloom and tears and blood have ruled the world since gods began. Anarchism rouses man to rebellion against this black monster. Break your mental fetters, says Anarchism to man, for not until you think and judge for yourself will you get rid of the dominion of darkness, the greatest obstacle to all progress.

Property, the dominion of man's needs, the denial of the right to satisfy his needs. Time was when property claimed a divine right, when it came to man with the same refrain, even as religion, "Sacrifice! Abnegate! Submit!" The spirit of Anarchism has lifted man from his prostrate position. He now stands erect, with his face toward the light. He has learned to see the insatiable, devouring, devastating nature of property, and he is preparing to strike the monster dead.

"Property is robbery," said the great French Anarchist, Proudhon. Yes, but without risk and danger to the robber. Monopolizing the accumulated efforts of man, property has robbed him of his birthright, and has turned him loose a pauper and an outcast. Property has not even the time-worn excuse that man does not create enough to satisfy all needs. The A B C student of economics knows that the productivity of labor within the last few decades far exceeds normal demand a hundredfold. But what are normal demands to an abnormal institution? The only demand that property recognizes is its own gluttonous appetite for greater wealth, because wealth means power: the power to subdue, to crush, to exploit, the power to enslave, to outrage, to degrade. America is particularly boastful of her great power, her enormous national wealth. Poor America, of what avail is all her wealth, if the individuals comprising the nation are wretchedly poor? If they live in squalor, in filth, in crime, with hope and joy gone, a homeless, soilless army of human prey.

It is generally conceded that unless the returns of any business venture exceed the cost, bankruptcy is inevitable. But those engaged in the business of producing wealth have not yet learned even this simple lesson. Every year the cost of production in human life is growing larger (50,000 killed, 100,000 wounded in America last year); the returns to the masses, who help to create wealth, are ever getting smaller. Yet America continues to be blind to the inevitable bankruptcy of our business of production. Nor is this the only crime of the latter. Still more fatal is the crime of turning the producer into a mere particle of a machine, with less will and decision than his master of steel and iron. Man is being robbed not merely of the products of his labor, but of the power of free initiative, of originality, and the interest in, or desire for, the things he is making.

Real wealth consists in things of utility and beauty, in things that help to create strong, beautiful bodies and surroundings inspiring to live in. But if man is doomed to wind cotton around a spool, or dig coal, or build roads for thirty years of his life, there can be no talk of wealth. What he gives to the world is only gray and hideous things, reflecting a dull and hideous existence,—too weak to live, too cowardly to die. Strange to say, there are people who extol this deadening method of centralized production as the proudest achievement of our age. They fail utterly to realize that if we are to continue in machine subserviency, our slavery is more complete than was our bondage to the King. They do not want to know that centralization is not only the death knell of liberty, but also of health and beauty, of art and science, all these being impossible in a clocklike, mechanical atmosphere.

Anarchism cannot but repudiate such a method of production: its goal is the freest possible expression of all the latent powers of the individual. Oscar Wilde defines a perfect personality as "one who develops under perfect conditions, who is not wounded, maimed, or in danger." A perfect personality, then, is only possible in a state of society where man is free to choose the mode of work, the conditions of work, and the freedom to work. One to whom the making of a table, the building of a house, or the tilling of the soil, is what the painting is to the artist and the discovery to the scientist,—the result of inspiration, of intense longing, and deep interest in work as a creative force. That being the ideal of Anarchism, its economic arrangements must consist of voluntary productive and distributive associations, gradually developing into free communism, as the best means of producing with the least waste of human energy. Anarchism, however, also recognizes the right of the individual, or numbers of individuals, to arrange at all times for other forms of work, in harmony with their tastes and desires.

Such free display of human energy being possible only under complete individual and social freedom, Anarchism directs its forces against the third and greatest foe of all social equality; namely, the State, organized authority, or statutory law,—the dominion of human conduct.

Just as religion has fettered the human mind, and as property, or the monopoly of things, has subdued and stifled man's needs, so has the State enslaved his spirit, dictating every phase of conduct. "All government in essence," says Emerson, "is tyranny." It matters not whether it is government by divine right or majority rule. In every instance its aim is the absolute subordination of the individual.

Referring to the American government, the greatest American Anarchist, David Thoreau, said: "Government, what is it but a tradition, though a recent one, endeavoring to transmit itself unimpaired to posterity, but each instance losing its integrity; it has not the vitality and force of a single living man. Law never made man a whit more just; and by means of their respect for it, even the well disposed are daily made agents of injustice."

Indeed, the keynote of government is injustice. With the arrogance and self-sufficiency of the King who could do no wrong, governments ordain, judge, condemn, and punish the most insignificant offenses, while maintaining themselves by the greatest of all offenses, the annihilation of individual liberty. Thus Ouida is right when she maintains that "the State only aims at instilling those qualities in its public by which its demands are obeyed, and its exchequer is filled. Its highest attainment is the reduction of mankind to clockwork. In its atmosphere all those finer and more delicate liberties, which require treatment and spacious expansion, inevitably dry up and perish. The State requires a taxpaying machine in which there is no hitch, an exchequer in which there is never a deficit, and a public, monotonous, obedient, colorless, spiritless, moving humbly like a flock of sheep along a straight high road between two walls."

Yet even a flock of sheep would resist the chicanery of the State, if it were not for the corruptive, tyrannical, and oppressive methods it employs to serve its purposes. Therefore Bakunin repudiates the State as synonymous with the surrender of the liberty of the individual or small minorities,—the destruction of social relationship, the curtailment, or complete denial even, of life itself, for its own aggrandizement. The State is the altar of political freedom and, like the religious altar, it is maintained for the purpose of human sacrifice.

In fact, there is hardly a modern thinker who does not agree that government, organized authority, or the State, is necessary *only* to maintain or protect property and monopoly. It has proven efficient in that function only.

Even George Bernard Shaw, who hopes for the miraculous from the State under Fabianism, nevertheless admits that "it is at present a huge machine for robbing and slave-driving of the poor by brute force." This being the case, it is hard to see why the clever prefacer wishes to uphold the State after poverty shall have ceased to exist.

Unfortunately there are still a number of people who continue in the fatal belief that government rests on natural laws, that it maintains social order and harmony, that it diminishes crime, and that it prevents the lazy man from fleecing his fellows. I shall therefore examine these contentions.

A natural law is that factor in man which asserts itself freely and spontaneously without any external force, in harmony with the requirements of nature. For instance, the demand for nutrition, for sex gratification, for light, air, and exercise, is a natural law. But its expression needs not the machinery of government, needs not the club, the gun, the handcuff, or the prison. To obey such laws, if we may call it obedience, requires only spontaneity and free opportunity. That governments do not maintain themselves through such harmonious factors is proven by the terrible array of violence, force, and coercion all governments use in order to live. Thus Blackstone is right when he says, "Human laws are invalid, because they are contrary to the laws of nature."

Unless it be the order of Warsaw after the slaughter of thousands of people, it is difficult to ascribe to governments any capacity for order or social harmony. Order derived through submission and maintained by terror is not much of a safe guaranty; yet that is the only "order" that governments have ever maintained. True social harmony grows naturally out of solidarity of interests. In a society where those who always work never have anything, while those who never work enjoy everything, solidarity of interests is non-existent; hence social harmony is but a myth. The only way organized authority meets this grave situation is by extending still greater privileges to those who have already monopolized the earth, and by still further enslaving the disinherited masses. Thus the entire arsenal of government—laws, police, soldiers, the courts, legislatures, prisons,—is strenuously engaged in "harmonizing" the most antagonistic elements in society.

The most absurd apology for authority and law is that they serve to diminish crime. Aside from the fact that the State is itself the greatest criminal, breaking every written and natural law, stealing in the form of taxes, killing in the form of war and capital punishment, it has come to an absolute standstill in coping with crime. It has failed utterly to destroy or even minimize the horrible scourge of its own creation.

Crime is naught but misdirected energy. So long as every institution of today, economic, political, social, and moral, conspires to misdirect human energy into wrong channels; so long as most people are out of place doing the things they hate to do, living a life they loathe to live, crime will be inevitable, and all the laws on the statutes can only increase, but never do away with, crime. What does society, as it exists today, know of the process of despair, the poverty, the horrors, the fearful struggle the human soul must pass on its way to crime and degradation. Who that knows this terrible process can fail to see the truth in these words of Peter Kropotkin:

"Those who will hold the balance between the benefits thus attributed to law and punishment and the degrading effect of the latter on humanity; those who will estimate the torrent of depravity poured abroad in human society by the informer, favored by the Judge even, and paid for in clinking cash by governments, under the pretext of aiding to unmask crime; those who will go within prison walls and there see what human beings become when deprived of liberty, when subjected to the care of brutal keepers, to coarse, cruel words, to a thousand stinging, piercing humiliations, will agree with us that the entire apparatus of prison and punishment is an abomination which ought to be brought to an end."

The deterrent influence of law on the lazy man is too absurd to merit consideration. If society were only relieved of the waste and expense of keeping a lazy class, and the equally great expense of the paraphernalia of protection this lazy class requires, the social tables would contain an abundance for all, including even the occasional lazy individual. Besides, it is well to consider that laziness results either from special privileges, or physical and mental abnormalities. Our present insane system of production fosters both, and the most astounding phenomenon is that people should want to work at all now. Anarchism aims to strip labor of its deadening, dulling aspect, of its gloom and compulsion. It aims to make work an instrument of joy, of strength, of color, of real harmony, so that the poorest sort of a man should find in work both recreation and hope.

To achieve such an arrangement of life, government, with its unjust, arbitrary, repressive measures, must be done away with. At best it has but imposed one single mode of life upon all, without regard to individual and social variations and needs. In destroying government and statutory laws, Anarchism proposes to rescue the self-respect and independence of the individual from all restraint and invasion by authority. Only in freedom can man grow to his full stature. Only in freedom will he learn to think and move, and give the very best in him. Only in freedom will he realize the true force of the social bonds which knit men together, and which are the true foundation of a normal social life.

But what about human nature? Can it be changed? And if not, will it endure under Anarchism?

Poor human nature, what horrible crimes have been committed in thy name! Every fool, from king to policeman, from the flatheaded parson to the visionless dabbler in science, presumes to speak authoritatively of human nature. The greater the mental charlatan, the more definite his insistence on the wickedness and weaknesses of human nature. Yet, how can any one speak of it today, with every soul in a prison, with every heart fettered, wounded, and maimed?

John Burroughs has stated that experimental study of animals in captivity is absolutely useless. Their character, their habits, their appetites undergo a complete transformation when torn from their soil in field and forest. With human nature caged in a narrow space, whipped daily into submission, how can we speak of its potentialities?

Freedom, expansion, opportunity, and, above all, peace and repose, alone can teach us the real dominant factors of human nature and all its wonderful possibilities.

Anarchism, then, really stands for the liberation of the human mind from the dominion of religion; the liberation of the human body from the dominion of property; liberation from the shackles and restraint of government. Anarchism stands for a social order based on the free grouping of individuals for the purpose of producing real social wealth; an order that will guarantee to every human being free access to the earth and full enjoyment of the necessities of life, according to individual desires, tastes, and inclinations.

This is not a wild fancy or an aberration of the mind. It is the conclusion arrived at by hosts of intellectual men and women the world over; a conclusion resulting from the close and studious observation of the tendencies of modern society: individual liberty and economic equality, the twin forces for the birth of what is fine and true in man.

As to methods. Anarchism is not, as some may suppose, a theory of the future to be realized through divine inspiration. It is a living force in the affairs of our life, constantly creating new conditions. The methods of Anarchism therefore do not comprise an iron-clad program to be carried out under all circumstances. Methods must grow out of the economic needs of each place and clime, and of the intellectual and temperamental requirements of the individual. The serene, calm character of a Tolstoy will wish different methods for social reconstruction than the intense, overflowing personality of a Michael Bakunin or a Peter Kropotkin. Equally so it must be apparent that the economic and political needs of Russia will dictate more drastic measures than would England or America. Anarchism does not stand for military drill and uniformity; it does, however, stand for the spirit of revolt, in whatever form, against everything that hinders human growth. All Anarchists agree in that, as they also agree in their opposition to the political machinery as a means of bringing about the great social change.

"All voting," says Thoreau, "is a sort of gaming, like checkers, or backgammon, a playing with right and wrong; its obligation never exceeds that of expediency. Even voting for the right thing is doing nothing for it. A wise man will not leave the right to the mercy of chance, nor wish it to prevail through the power of the majority." A close examination of the machinery of politics and its achievements will bear out the logic of Thoreau.

What does the history of parliamentarism show? Nothing but failure and defeat, not even a single reform to ameliorate the economic and social stress of the people. Laws have been passed and enactments made for the improvement and protection of labor. Thus it was proven only last year that Illinois, with the most rigid laws for mine protection, had the greatest mine disasters. In States where child labor laws prevail, child exploitation is at its highest, and though with us the workers enjoy full political opportunities, capitalism has reached the most brazen zenith.

Even were the workers able to have their own representatives, for which our good Socialist politicians are clamoring, what chances are there for their honesty and good faith? One has but to bear in mind the process of politics to realize that its path of good intentions is full of pitfalls: wire-pulling, intriguing, flattering, lying, cheating; in fact, chicanery of every description, whereby the political aspirant can achieve success. Added to that is a complete demoralization of character and conviction, until nothing is left that would make one hope for anything from such a human derelict. Time and time again the people were foolish enough to trust, believe, and support with their last farthing aspiring politicians, only to find themselves betrayed and cheated.

It may be claimed that men of integrity would not become corrupt in the political grinding mill. Perhaps not; but such men would be absolutely helpless to exert the slightest influence in behalf of labor, as indeed has been shown in numerous instances. The State is the economic master of its servants. Good men, if such there be, would either remain true to their political faith and lose their economic support, or they would cling to their economic master and be utterly unable to do the slightest good. The political arena leaves one no alternative, one must either be a dunce or a rogue.

The political superstition is still holding sway over the hearts and minds of the masses, but the true lovers of liberty will have no more to do with it. Instead, they believe with Stirner that man has as much liberty as he is willing to take. Anarchism therefore stands for direct action, the open defiance of, and resistance to, all laws and restrictions, economic, social, and moral. But defiance and resistance are illegal. Therein lies the salvation of man. Everything illegal necessitates integrity, self-reliance, and courage. In short, it calls for free, independent spirits, for "men who are men, and who have a bone in their backs which you cannot pass your hand through."

Universal suffrage itself owes its existence to direct action. If not for the spirit of rebellion, of the defiance on the part of the American revolutionary fathers, their posterity would still wear the King's coat. If not for the direct action of a John Brown and his comrades, America would still trade in the flesh of the black man. True, the trade in white flesh is still going on; but that, too, will have to be abolished by direct action. Trade unionism, the economic arena of the modern gladiator, owes its existence to direct action. It is but recently that law and government have attempted to crush the trade union movement, and condemned the exponents of man's right to organize to prison as conspirators. Had they sought to assert their cause through begging, pleading, and compromise, trade unionism would today be a negligible quantity. In France, in Spain, in Italy, in Russia, nay even in England (witness the growing rebellion of English labor unions) direct, revolutionary, economic action has become so strong a force in the battle for industrial liberty as to make the world realize the tremendous importance of labor's power. The General Strike, the supreme expression of the economic consciousness of the workers, was ridiculed in America but a short time ago. Today every great strike, in order to win, must realize the importance of the solidaric general protest.

Direct action, having proved effective along economic lines, is equally potent in the environment of the individual. There a hundred forces encroach upon his being, and only persistent resistance to them will finally set him free. Direct action against the authority in the shop, direct action against the authority of the law, direct action against the invasive, meddlesome authority of our moral code, is the logical, consistent method of Anarchism.

Will it not lead to a revolution? Indeed, it will. No real social change has ever come about without a revolution. People are either not familiar with their history, or they have not yet learned that revolution is but thought carried into action.

Anarchism, the great leaven of thought, is today permeating every phase of human endeavor. Science, art, literature, the drama, the effort for economic betterment, in fact every individual and social opposition to the existing disorder of things, is illumined by the spiritual light of Anarchism. It is the philosophy of the sovereignty of the individual. It is the theory of social harmony. It is the great, surging, living truth that is reconstructing the world, and that will usher in the Dawn.

PART IV

Progressives

---

13. William James,
"The Moral Equivalent of War"

Next to Thoreau's essay on civil disobedience, "The Moral Equivalent of War" by William James (1842–1910) is probably the most influential statement in the history of American nonviolence. The American Friends Service Committee, the Civilian Conservation Corps, and the Peace Corps all derive from the central thought of James' argument.

According to James, the pacifist will never succeed merely by preaching against war. His task must be to find another mode whereby the energies of men can be elicited, involving risk, voluntary poverty, and service to the state. James suggested that young people be conscripted for a period of years in a war against nature rather than against man. Such labor would redirect warlike impulses toward more constructive ends: "Great indeed is Fear; but it is not . . . the only stimulus known for awakening the higher ranges of men's spiritual energy."

First written as a pamphlet for the American Association for International Conciliation, "The Moral Equivalent of War" was also published in 1910 by McClure's Magazine and The Popular Science Monthly.

William James, The Moral Equivalent of War (New York: American Association for International Conciliation, 1910), Leaflet No. 27.

The war against war is going to be no holiday excursion or camping party. The military feelings are too deeply grounded to abdicate their place among our ideals until better substitutes are offered than the glory and shame that come to nations as well as to individuals from the ups and downs of politics and the vicissitudes of trade. There is something highly paradoxical in the modern man's relation to war. Ask all our millions, north and south, whether they would vote now (were such a thing possible) to have our war for the Union expunged from history, and the record of a peaceful transition to the present time substituted for that of its marches and battles, and probably hardly a handful of eccentrics would say yes. Those ancestors, those efforts, those memories and legends, are the most ideal part of what we now own together, a sacred spiritual possession worth more than all the blood poured out. Yet ask those same people whether they would be willing in cold blood to start another civil war now to gain another similar possession, and not one man or woman would vote for the proposition. In modern eyes, precious though wars may be, they must not be waged solely for the sake of the ideal harvest. Only when forced upon one, only when an enemy's injustice leaves us no alternative, is a war now thought permissible.

It was not thus in ancient times. The earlier men were hunting men, and to hunt a neighboring tribe, kill the males, loot the village and possess the females, was the most profitable, as well as the most exciting, way of living. Thus were the more martial tribes selected, and in chiefs and peoples a pure pugnacity and love of glory came to mingle with the more fundamental appetite for plunder.

Modern war is so expensive that we feel trade to be a better avenue to plunder; but modern man inherits all the innate pugnacity and all the love of glory of his ancestors. Showing war's irrationality and horror is of no effect upon him. The horrors make the fascination. War is the *strong* life; it is life *in extremis;* war-taxes are the only ones men never hesitate to pay, as the budgets of all nations show us.

History is a bath of blood. The Iliad is one long recital of how Diomedes and Ajax, Sarpedon and Hector *killed*. No detail of the wounds they made is spared us, and the Greek mind fed upon the story. Greek history is a panorama of jingoism and imperialism—war for war's sake, all the citizens being warriors. It is horrible reading, because of the irrationality of it all—save for the purpose of making "history"—and the history is that of the utter ruin of a civilization in intellectual respects perhaps the highest the earth has ever seen.

Those wars were purely piratical. Pride, gold, women, slaves, excitement, were their only motives. In the Peloponnesian war, for example, the Athenians ask the inhabitants of Melos (the island where the "Venus of Milo" was found), hitherto neutral, to own their lordship. The envoys meet, and hold a debate which Thucydides gives in full, and which, for sweet reasonableness of form, would have satisfied Matthew Arnold. "The powerful exact what they can," said the Athenians, "and the weak grant what they must." When the Meleans say that sooner than be slaves they will appeal to the gods, the Athenians reply: "Of the gods we believe and of men we know that, by a law of their nature, wherever they can rule they will. This law was not made by us, and we are not the first to have acted upon it; we did but inherit it, and we know that you and all mankind, if you were as strong as we are, would do as we do. So much for the gods; we have told you why we expect to stand as high in their good opinion as you." Well, the Meleans still refused, and their town was taken. "The Athenians," Thucydides quietly says, "thereupon put to death all who were of military age and made slaves of the women and children. They then colonized the island, sending thither five hundred settlers of their own."

Alexander's career was piracy pure and simple, nothing but an orgy of power and plunder, made romantic by the character of the hero. There was no rational principle in it, and the moment he died his generals and governors attacked one another. The cruelty of those times is incredible. When Rome

finally conquered Greece, Paulus Aemilius was told by the
Roman Senate to reward his soldiers for their toil by "giving"
them the old kingdom of Epirus. They sacked seventy cities
and carried off a hundred and fifty thousand inhabitants as
slaves. How many they killed I know not; but in Etolia they
killed all the senators, five hundred and fifty in number.
Brutus was "the noblest Roman of them all," but to reanimate
his soldiers on the eve of Philippi he similarly promises to give
them the cities of Sparta and Thessalonica to ravage, if they
win the fight.

Such was the gory nurse that trained societies to cohesiveness. We inherit the warlike type; and for most of the capaci-
ties of heroism that the human race is full of we have to thank
this cruel history. Dead men tell no tales, and if there were
any tribes of other type than this they have left no survivors.
Our ancestors have bred pugnacity into our bone and marrow,
and thousands of years of peace won't breed it out of us. The
popular imagination fairly fattens on the thought of wars. Let
public opinion once reach a certain fighting pitch, and no ruler
can understand it. In the Boer war both governments began
with bluff, but couldn't stay there, the military tension was too
much for them. In 1898 our people had read the word WAR
in letters three inches high for three months in every newspaper. The pliant politician McKinley was swept away by their
eagerness, and our squalid war with Spain became a necessity.

At the present day, civilized opinion is a curious mental mixture. The military instincts and ideals are as strong as ever, but
are confronted by reflective criticisms which sorely curb their
ancient freedom. Innumerable writers are showing up the
bestial side of military service. Pure loot and mastery seem no
longer morally avowable motives, and pretexts must be found
for attributing them solely to the enemy. England and we, our
army and navy authorities repeat without ceasing, arm solely
for "peace," Germany and Japan it is who are bent on loot and
glory. "Peace" in military mouths to-day is a synonym for "war

expected." The word has become a pure provocative, and no government wishing peace sincerely should allow it ever to be printed in a newspaper. Every up-to-date Dictionary should say that "peace" and "war" mean the same thing, now *in posse*, now *in actu*. It may even reasonably be said that the intensely sharp competitive *preparation* for war by the nations *is the real war*, permanent, unceasing; and that the battles are only a sort of public verification of the mastery gained during the "peace"-interval.

It is plain that on this subject civilized man has developed a sort of double personality. If we take European nations, no legitimate interest of any one of them would seem to justify the tremendous destructions which a war to compass it would necessarily entail. It would seem as though common sense and reason ought to find a way to reach agreement in every conflict of honest interests. I myself think it our bounden duty to believe in such international rationality as possible. But, as things stand, I see how desperately hard it is to bring the peace-party and the war-party together, and I believe that the difficulty is due to certain deficiencies in the program of pacificism which set the militarist imagination strongly, and to a certain extent justifiably, against it. In the whole discussion both sides are on imaginative and sentimental ground. It is but one utopia against another, and everything one says must be abstract and hypothetical. Subject to this criticism and caution, I will try to characterize in abstract strokes the opposite imaginative forces, and point out what to my own very fallible mind seems the best utopian hypothesis, the most promising line of conciliation.

In my remarks, pacificist tho' I am, I will refuse to speak of the bestial side of the war-régime (already done justice to by many writers) and consider only the higher aspects of militaristic sentiment. Patriotism no one thinks discreditable; nor does any one deny that war is the romance of history. But inordinate ambitions are the soul of every patriotism, and the possibility of violent death the soul of all romance. The militarily patriotic and romantic-minded everywhere, and especially the professional military class, refuse to admit for a moment that war may be a transitory phenomenon in social evolution. The notion of a sheep's paradise like that revolts, they say, our higher imagination. Where then would be the steeps of life? If war had ever stopped, we should have to reinvent it, on this view, to redeem life from flat degeneration.

Reflective apologists for war at the present day all take it religiously. It is a sort of sacrament. Its profits are to the vanquished as well as to the victor; and quite apart from any question of profit, it is an absolute good, we are told, for it is human nature at its highest dynamic. Its "horrors" are a cheap price to pay for rescue from the only alternative supposed, of a world of clerks and teachers, of co-education and zoophily, of "consumer's leagues" and "associated charities," of industrialism unlimited, and feminism unabashed. No scorn, no hardness, no valor any more! Fie upon such a cattleyard of a planet!

So far as the central essence of this feeling goes, no healthy minded person, it seems to me, can help to some degree partaking of it. Militarism is the great preserver of our ideals of hardihood, and human life with no use for hardihood would be contemptible. Without risks or prizes for the darer, history would be insipid indeed; and there is a type of military character which every one feels that the race should never cease to breed, for every one is sensitive to its superiority. The duty is incumbent on mankind, of keeping military characters in stock —of keeping them, if not for use, then as ends in themselves and as pure pieces of perfection,—so that Roosevelt's weaklings and mollycoddles may not end by making everything else disappear from the face of nature.

This natural sort of feeling forms, I think, the innermost soul of army-writings. Without any exception known to me, militarist authors take a highly mystical view of their subject, and regard war as a biological or sociological necessity, uncontrolled by ordinary psychological checks and motives. When the time of development is ripe the war must come, reason or no reason, for the justifications pleaded are invariably fictitious. War is, in short, a permanent human *obligation*. General Homer Lea, in his recent book "the Valor of Ignorance," plants himself squarely on this ground. Readiness for war is for him the essence of nationality, and ability in it the supreme measure of the health of nations.

Nations, General Lea says, are never stationary—they must necessarily expand or shrink, according to their vitality or decrepitude. Japan now is culminating; and by the fatal law in question it is impossible that her statesmen should not long since have entered, with extraordinary foresight, upon a vast policy of conquest—the game in which the first moves were her wars with China and Russia and her treaty with England, and of which the final objective is the capture of the Philippines, the Hawaiian Islands, Alaska, and the whole of our Coast west of the Sierra Passes. This will give Japan what her ineluctable vocation as a state absolutely forces her to claim, the possession of the entire Pacific Ocean; and to oppose these deep designs we Americans have, according to our author, nothing but our conceit, our ignorance, our commercialism, our corruption, and our feminism. General Lea makes a minute technical comparison of the military strength which we at present could oppose to the strength of Japan, and concludes that the islands, Alaska, Oregon, and Southern California, would fall almost without resistance, that San Francisco must surrender in a fortnight to a Japanese investment, that in three or four months the war would be over, and our republic, unable to regain what it had heedlessly neglected to protect sufficiently, would then "disintegrate," until perhaps some Caesar should arise to weld us again into a nation.

A dismal forecast indeed! Yet not unplausible, if the mentality of Japan's statesmen be of the Caesarian type of which history shows so many examples, and which is all that General

Lea seems able to imagine. But there is no reason to think that women can no longer be the mothers of Napoleonic or Alexandrian characters; and if these come in Japan and find their opportunity, just such surprises as "the Valor of Ignorance" paints may lurk in ambush for us. Ignorant as we still are of the innermost recesses of Japanese mentality, we may be foolhardy to disregard such possibilities.

Other militarists are more complex and more moral in their considerations. The "Philosophie des Krieges," by S. R. Steinmetz is a good example. War, according to this author, is an ordeal instituted by God, who weighs the nations in its balance. It is the essential form of the State, and the only function in which peoples can employ all their powers at once and convergently. No victory is possible save as the resultant of a totality of virtues, no defeat for which some vice or weakness is not responsible. Fidelity, cohesiveness, tenacity, heroism, conscience, education, inventiveness, economy, wealth, physical health and vigor—there isn't a moral or intellectual point of superiority that doesn't tell, when God holds his assizes and hurls the peoples upon one another. *Die Weltgeschichte ist das Weltgericht;* and Dr. Steinmetz does not believe that in the long run chance and luck play any part in apportioning the issues.

The virtues that prevail, it must be noted, are virtues anyhow, superiorities that count in peaceful as well as in military competition; but the strain on them, being infinitely intenser in the latter case, makes war infinitely more searching as a trial. No ordeal is comparable to its winnowings. Its dread hammer is the welder of men into cohesive states, and nowhere but in such states can human nature adequately develop its capacity. The only alternative is "degeneration."

Dr. Steinmetz is a conscientious thinker, and his book, short as it is, takes much into account. Its upshot can, it seems to me, be summed up in Simon Patten's word, that mankind was nursed in pain and fear, and that the transition to a "pleasure-economy" may be fatal to a being wielding no powers of defense against its disintegrative influences. If we speak of the *fear of emancipation from the fear-regime*, we put the whole situation into a single phrase; fear regarding ourselves now taking the place of the ancient fear of the enemy.

Turn the fear over as I will in my mind, it all seems to lead back to two unwillingnesses of the imagination, one aesthetic, and the other moral: unwillingness, first to envisage a future in which army-life, with its many elements of charm, shall be forever impossible, and in which the destinies of peoples shall nevermore be decided quickly, thrillingly, and tragically, by force, but only gradually and insipidly by "evolution"; and, secondly, unwillingness to see the supreme theatre of human strenuousness closed, and the splendid military aptitudes of men doomed to keep always in a state of latency and never show themselves in action. These insistent unwillingnesses, no less than other esthetic and ethical insistencies have, it seems to me, to be listened to and respected. One cannot meet them effectively by mere counter-insistency on war's expensiveness and horror. The horror makes the thrill, and when the question is of getting the extremest and supremest out of human nature, talk of expense sounds ignominious. The weakness of so much merely negative criticism is evident—pacificism makes no converts from the military party. The military party denies neither the bestiality nor the horror, nor the expense; it only says that these things tell but half the story. It only says that war is *worth* them; that, taking human nature as a whole, its wars are its best protection against its weaker and more cowardly self, and that mankind cannot *afford* to adopt a peace-economy.

Pacificists ought to enter more deeply into the esthetical and ethical point of view of their opponents. Do that first in any controversy, says J. J. Chapman, *then move the point*, and your opponent will follow. So long as anti-militarists propose no substitute for war's disciplinary function, no *moral equivalent* of war, analogous, as one might say, to the mechanical equivalent of heat, so long they fail to realize the full inwardness of the situation. And as a rule they do fail. The duties, penalties, and sanctions pictured in the utopias they paint are all too weak and tame to touch the military-minded. Tolstoy's pacificism is the only exception to this rule, for it is profoundly pessimistic as regards all this world's values, and makes the fear of the Lord furnish the moral spur provided elsewhere by the fear of the enemy. But our socialistic peace-advocates all believe absolutely in this world's values; and instead of the fear of the Lord and the fear of the enemy, the only fear they reckon with is the fear of poverty if one be lazy. This weakness pervades all the socialistic literature with which I am acquainted. Even in Lowes Dickinson's exquisite dialogue, high wages and short hours are the only forces invoked for overcoming man's distaste for repulsive kinds of labor. Meanwhile men at large still live as they always have lived, under a pain-and-fear economy—for those of us who live in an ease-economy are but an island in the stormy ocean—and the whole atmosphere of present-day utopian literature tastes mawkish and dishwatery to people who still keep a sense for life's more bitter flavors. It suggests, in truth, ubiquitous inferiority.

Inferiority is always with us, and merciless scorn of it is the keynote of the military temper. "Dogs, would you live forever?" shouted Frederick the Great. "Yes," say our utopians, "let us live forever, and raise our level gradually." The best thing about our "inferiors" to-day is that they are as tough as nails, and physically and morally almost as insensitive. Utopianism would see them soft and squeamish, while militarism would keep their callousness, but transfigure it into a meritorious characteristic, needed by "the service," and redeemed by that from the suspicion of inferiority. All the qualities of a man acquire dignity when he knows that the service of the collectivity that owns him needs them. If proud of the collectivity, his own pride rises in proportion. No collectivity is like an army for nourishing such pride; but it has to be con-

fessed that the only sentiment which the image of pacific cos-
mopolitan industrialism is capable of arousing in countless
worthy breasts is shame at the idea of belonging to *such* a
collectivity. It is obvious that the United States of America as
they exist to-day impress a mind like General Lea's as so much
human blubber. Where is the sharpness and precipitousness,
the contempt for life, whether one's own, or another's? Where
is the savage "yes" and "no," the unconditional duty? Where
is the conscription? Where is the blood-tax? Where is anything
that one feels honored by belonging to?

Having said thus much in preparation, I will now confess
my own utopia. I devoutly believe in the reign of peace and
in the gradual advent of some sort of a socialistic equilibrium.
The fatalistic view of the war-function is to me nonsense, for I
know that war-making is due to definite motives and subject
to prudential checks and reasonable criticisms, just like any
other form of enterprise. And when whole nations are the
armies, and the science of destruction vies in intellectual re-
finement with the sciences of production, I see that war becomes absurd and impossible from its own monstrosity. Ex
travagant ambitions will have to be replaced by reasonable
claims, and nations must make common cause against them. I
see no reason why all this should not apply to yellow as well
as to white countries, and I look forward to a future when acts
of war shall be formally outlawed as between civilized peoples.

All these beliefs of mine put me squarely into the anti-
militarist party. But I do not believe that peace either ought to
be or will be permanent on this globe, unless the states pacifi-
cally organized preserve some of the old elements of army-
discipline. A permanently successful peace-economy cannot be
a simple pleasure-economy. In the more or less socialistic future towards which mankind seems drifting we must still subject ourselves collectively to those severities which answer to
our real position upon this only partly hospitable globe. We
must make new energies and hardihoods continue the manli-

ness to which the military mind so faithfully clings. Martial virtues must be the enduring cement; intrepidity, contempt of softness, surrender of private interest, obedience to command, must still remain the rock upon which states are built—unless, indeed, we wish for dangerous reactions against commonwealths fit only for contempt, and liable to invite attack whenever a centre of crystallization for military-minded enterprise gets formed anywhere in their neighborhood.

The war-party is assuredly right in affirming and reaffirming that the martial virtues, although originally gained by the race through war, are absolute and permanent human goods. Patriotic pride and ambition in their military form are, after all, only specifications of a more general competitive passion. They are its first form, but that is no reason for supposing them to be its last form. Men now are proud of belonging to a conquering nation, and without a murmur they lay down their persons and their wealth, if by so doing they may fend off subjection. But who can be sure that *other aspects of one's country* may not, with time and education and suggestion enough, come to be regarded with similarly effective feelings of pride and shame? Why should men not some day feel that it is worth a blood-tax to belong to a collectivity superior in *any* ideal respect? Why should they not blush with indignant shame if the community that owns them is vile in any way whatsoever? Individuals, daily more numerous, now feel this civic passion. It is only a question of blowing on the spark till the whole population gets incandescent, and on the ruins of the old morals of military honour, a stable system of morals of civic honour builds itself up. What the whole community comes to believe in grasps the individual as in a vise. The war-function has graspt us so far; but constructive interests may some day seem no less imperative, and impose on the individual a hardly lighter burden.

Let me illustrate my idea more concretely. There is nothing to make one indignant in the mere fact that life is hard, that

men should toil and suffer pain. The planetary conditions once
for all are such, and we can stand it. But that so many men, by
mere accidents of birth and opportunity, should have a life of
nothing else but toil and pain and hardness and inferiority imposed upon them, should have *no* vacation, while others
natively no more deserving never get any taste of this campaigning life at all,—*this* is capable of arousing indignation in
reflective minds. It may end by seeming shameful to all of us
that some of us have nothing but campaigning, and others
nothing but unmanly ease. If now—and this is my idea—there
were, instead of military conscription a conscription of the
whole youthful population to form for a certain number of
years a part of the army enlisted against *Nature,* the injustice
would tend to be evened out, and numerous other goods to
the commonwealth would follow. The military ideals of hardihood and discipline would be wrought into the growing fibre of
the people; no one would remain blind as the luxurious classes
now are blind, to man's real relations to the globe he lives on,
and to the permanently sour and hard foundations of his higher
life. To coal and iron mines, to freight trains, to fishing fleets
in December, to dish-washing, clothes-washing, and window-
washing, to road-building and tunnel-making, to foundries and
stoke-holes, and to the frames of skyscrapers, would our gilded
youths be drafted off, according to their choice, to get the
childishness knocked out of them, and to come back into society with healthier sympathies and soberer ideas. They would
have paid their blood-tax, done their own part in the immemo-
rial human warfare against nature, they would tread the earth
more proudly, the women would value them more highly, they
would be better fathers and teachers of the following generation.

Such a conscription, with the state of public opinion that
would have required it, and the many moral fruits it would
bear, would preserve in the midst of a pacific civilization the
manly virtues which the military party is so afraid of seeing

disappear in peace. We should get toughness without callousness, authority with as little criminal cruelty as possible, and
painful work done cheerily because the duty is temporary, and
threatens not, as now, to degrade the whole remainder of one's
life. I spoke of the "moral equivalent" of war. So far, war has
been the only force that can discipline a whole community,
and until an equivalent discipline is organized, I believe that
war must have its way. But I have no serious doubt that the
ordinary prides and shames of social man, once developed to a
certain intensity, are capable of organizing such a moral
equivalent as I have sketched, or some other just as effective
for preserving manliness of type. It is but a question of time,
of skillful propagandism, and of opinion-making men seizing
historic opportunities.

The martial type of character can be bred without war.
Strenuous honour and disinterestedness abound elsewhere.
Priests and medical men are in a fashion educated to it, and
we should all feel some degree of it imperative if we were
conscious of our work as an obligatory service to the state. We
should be *owned,* as soldiers are by the army, and our pride
would rise accordingly. We could be poor, then, without
humiliation, as army officers now are. The only thing needed
henceforward is to inflame the civic temper as past history has
inflamed the military temper. H. G. Wells, as usual, sees the
centre of the situation. "In many ways," he says, "military organization is the most peaceful of activities. When the contemporary man steps from the street, of clamorous insincere
advertisement, push, adulteration, underselling and intermit-
tent employment, into the barrack-yard, he steps on to a higher
social plane, into an atmosphere of service and co-operation
and of infinitely more honourable emulations. Here at least
men are not flung out of employment to degenerate because
there is no immediate work for them to do. They are fed and
drilled and trained for better services. Here at least a man is
supposed to win promotion by self-forgetfulness and not by

self-seeking. And beside the feeble and irregular endowment of research by commercialism, its little short-sighted snatches at profit by innovation and scientific economy, see how remarkable is the steady and rapid development of method and appliances in naval and military affairs! Nothing is more striking than to compare the progress of civil conveniences which has been left almost entirely to the trader, to the progress in military apparatus during the last few decades. The house-appliances of to-day for example, are little better than they were fifty years ago. A house of today is still almost as ill-ventilated, badly heated by wasteful fires, clumsily arranged and furnished as the house of 1858. Houses a couple of hundred years old are still satisfactory places of residence, so little have our standards risen. But the rifle or battleship of fifty years ago was beyond all comparison inferior to those we possess; in power, in speed, in convenience alike. No one has a use now for such superannuated things."

Wells adds that he thinks that the conceptions of order and discipline, the tradition of service and devotion, of physical fitness, unstinted exertion, and universal responsibility, which universal military duty is now teaching European nations, will remain a permanent acquisition, when the last ammunition has been used in the fireworks that celebrate the final peace. I believe as he does. It would be simply preposterous if the only force that could work ideals of honour and standards of efficiency into English or American natures should be the fear of being killed by the Germans or the Japanese. Great indeed is Fear; but it is not, as our military enthusiasts believe and try to make us believe, the only stimulus known for awakening the higher ranges of men's spiritual energy. The amount of alteration in public opinion which my utopia postulates is vastly less than the difference between the mentality of those black warriors who pursued Stanley's party on the Congo with their cannibal war-cry of "Meat! Meat!" and that of the "general-staff" of any civilized nation. History has seen the latter interval bridged over: the former one can be bridged over much more easily.

14. Clarence Darrow,
Marx vs. Tolstoi

Clarence Darrow (1857–1938) came to Chicago in the late 1880's and took part in the campaign for amnesty to the surviving Haymarket Anarchists. He was named corporation counsel for the city of Chicago, then general attorney for the Chicago and Northwestern Railroad. But when his employer became involved in the great railway strike of 1894, Darrow resigned to represent Eugene Debs and the striking workers.

Thus began his celebrated career as "attorney for the damned." Among the criminals he defended were Nathan Leopold and Richard Loeb, wealthy Chicago youths, and "Big Bill" Haywood, poor and persecuted leader of Western miners. Darrow's interest in nonviolence grew from his observation of crime and punishment in American courts and jails. In the excerpts that follow, from a debate between Darrow and the Socialist Arthur Lewis concerning the relative merits of the Marxist and Tolstoyan social philosophies, he presents nonviolence as "the opposite to the theory of punishment, or the theory of vengeance," and goes on to argue that while the state "was born in force and violence" yet "the only force that can win is determination, non-resistance, peaceable force." These views earned Darrow a reputation as America's foremost exponent of nonviolence in the years just prior to World War I. He expounded them more at length in books such as *Resist Not Evil* (1903) and *An Eye for an Eye* (1905).

Marx vs Tolstoi. A Debate Between Clarence S. Darrow and Arthur M. Lewis, People's Pocket Series No. 157 (Girard, Kansas: Appeal to Reason [*ca.* 1910]), pp. 5–16, 38–40.

As this is Sunday morning, and a semi-religious question, I take for my text the 38th and 39th verses in the 5th chapter of Matthew. I cannot quote it literally. It is quite a time since I have read it. But I know the import of it.

"Ye have heard it hath been said," I am quoting from Matthew, "An eye for an eye, and a tooth for a tooth. But I say unto you: Resist not evil. But whosoever shall smite you on the right cheek, turn to him the other also."

I do not quote this because Matthew wrote it. I really do not know whether he did or not; and I care a great deal less. I could not find out whether Matthew wrote it, unless I should read Professor Foster's works on religion, and that would take too long. But I quote it because throughout all the Western world this has been the accepted statement of the doctrine of non-resistance. It is, perhaps, as good a statement of that theory as one can find in a few short sentences. Matthew had no patent on it, of course. There are very few thoughts in this world that are patented, and those are not worth it. It was undoubtedly very old before Matthew lived—if he lived. And it has been repeated a great many times since he died—if he died.

The theory of non-resistance is taken, generally, as the opposite to the theory of punishment, or the theory of vengeance, which, up to the time of the Christian religion, was the theory of the world—and since that time has been doubly the theory of the world. Its announcement, as generally admitted by those who have written and spoken upon the subject, has reference, first, to the treatment of those whom society calls criminals; next, perhaps, to governments in their relations to each other and to their subjects; and then to women and children, insane, prisoners, and the like. It relates to the way those who have the power have generally exercised that power in relation to the rest of the world.

Now, I might say in the beginning that I am not quite sure of this theory, or of any other theory. I used to be a good deal more positive than I am today. And especially, I am not at all sure that there is any theory in philosophy, or morals (or laws), that works out in sociology. The science of society, if there is such a science, is not an exact science. You cannot demonstrate any theory of society the way you can demonstrate the multiplication table, unless it is Socialism—and you cannot demonstrate that in the same way unless you are speaking to an audience of Socialists. You might demonstrate Single Tax to a Single Taxer, but you could not do it to anybody else. Exact science has little to do—something to do, but little to do, with the ways in which man organizes himself on the planet. He does not move in straight lines, or in regular curves, or even in crooked lines, that can be depended upon. When he learns what the crooked line is he goes straight. And no theory of life, no theory of society can be worked out as to communal life, in the same way that you can work out the science of mathematics, or of astronomy, or geology, or any science dealing with anything that keeps still.

But the question is, whether the theory of punishment, as opposed to the theory of non-resistance, is most in harmony with life, and tends to the progress of the world; whether human life in its slow evolution is going toward the theory of non-resistance, or is going toward the theory of violence, and force, and punishment.

If one looks back to the origin of the State we do not find that it had the immaculate birth that most people believe. It was born in force and violence. The strong took a club and made a state for himself. It was a simple state, kept there by the force of the strong man's club and his will. From that it has gone on until it takes a good many strong clubs, together with a good many armies, navies, policemen, lawyers, judges, etc., to keep the state in order. But through it all has run the theory of force, and through it all the power has come not from the people who ask it, but from the people who took it because they were the stronger. In the beginning the chief preserved order and the law, by saying what should be the law and enforcing order himself with his club.

In modern society the controlling forces arrange things as they want them, and provide that certain things are criminal. Sometimes those things have a semblance of natural crime, and sometimes not. The largest number of crimes are crimes against property. Sometimes you may trace them more or less directly to the violation of some law that is in the natural world. But the fact is that the class which rules society come together and say what men must do, and what they must not do. And the man who violates it commits crime.

There are in society, and always have been, a large number of people, due mainly to conditions of society, who are what we call defectives; who are anti-social in their nature; whose life and conduct tend toward the disintegration of society, instead of the life of society. Very largely the treatment of crime is a question of treatment of these anti-social individuals. It is a question of treatment of those who persevere, in one way or another, in violating the rules of the game which society has made.

Way back under the Mosaic Law—and Moses did not have a patent on it either, but under the law of the world, the doctrine of an "Eye for an eye, a tooth for a tooth," prevailed. If a man killed another his life should be taken. If he stole something he should be punished. If he burglarized, then it meant something else, generally death. If he did something, the world would do something to him. And they would do that something that the world at that time thought was the right thing to do to him. In this way, even down to a hundred years ago, there were in England about two hundred crimes punishable by death. Almost everything that could be conceived was punished by death. And the lawyers, and judges, and preachers of that day had no thought that society could hang together if men were not hanged regularly for stealing sheep and anything that happened. The old doctrine of an eye for an eye, and a tooth for a tooth, was the common doctrine of the world, and that doctrine prevails today.

All penal codes are really built upon that doctrine. When you trace penal codes back to the beginning, they mean one thing, and only one, i. e., vengeance. . . . In the early stages, if some one slew another, the members of his tribe had the right to go and take the life of any member of the other tribe in return. It did not matter whether he had been guilty or not. It was the law of vengeance, the law of punishment—and punishment and vengeance have always meant the same thing in the world, no matter where it has been.

Punishments of crimes have always been arbitrary. One man would say that for stealing a horse the somebody stealing it should go to jail for thirty days. Another would say that he should go to the penitentiary for a year; another would say five years; and somebody else would say he should be hanged by the neck until dead. Punishments have never depended upon the act done, but upon the man who saw the act done and the mind possessed by the ruling power. Or half a dozen judges given authority to administer punishment for a certain act no two judges would administer the same kind of punishment. One would say thirty days, another thirty years; just according to the mind he has. Some judge might give you less after breakfast than he would before. And another judge might give you more if he had attended a banquet through the small hours in the morning preceding, and did not feel well when he administered the sentence. All those things enter into it, and when you come to sum it all up, the real theory of it is a question of vengeance: The individual has done something. How much shall we do to him in return? How much will we make him suffer, because he has made some one else suffer?

Now, the non-resistant says, there is no such thing as crime, i. e., some of them say that. And they say that all punishment is bad, not heavy punishment alone—but all punishment; that man has no right to punish his fellow man, that only evil results from it; that the theory of vengeance and the theory of punishment is wrong; that it cures nobody, it does not tend to benefit society, it does not tend to change the defective, it does not tend to build up society. It is wrong and untrue in its whole theory; and the theory of non-resistance is the true theory as to crime. Whatever you may think of the theory, the world has been steadily going that way. It has been abolishing the death penalty, until today in most civilized countries there are only one or two crimes punishable by death; and it is very rarely that death is meted out for those.

Punishment has been growing less severe, and the methods of inflicting punishment are less severe. Of course, in the old day when men were less squeamish and more honest they had their hangings in broad daylight. Today we do not do it, not because we are better, but because we are squeamish. We have hangings in the jail, so that the effects of the punishment will be entirely lost to the community.

Our terms of imprisonment are not so long. Our methods of treating the imprisoned are more humane. We sentence a man to prison. Of course, in the old time he used to be put into a vile place, where he would be half clad and half fed, and where he would be covered with rags full of vermin, and where he would suffer all sorts of physical pain. Today we send him to jail, and we have the jail steam heated and electric lighted. We have a doctor to take care of him if so, perchance, the penalty is death he won't die before his time comes; and if he is to be hanged he gets better food than he ever did before. So far as men are entrusted with the power of carrying out these provisions they do it as humanely as they can do it.

In the old times the insane were treated like criminals. They were locked up in cells; they were loaded with chains; they WERE criminals, because the rest of the world did not understand them. We have gotten over that. We have learned to treat them as human beings, and to treat them as those suffering from ailment, whereas once in the history of the world they were visited with the old law of vengeance, the law of force. The world some time will learn to treat all of its defectives, and all those who violate the code, the same as they treat the insane and the ill today. And we are learning it, more and more, every day. .

The theory of non-resistance does not, necessarily, say that a man cannot be restrained, although very likely that would not be necessary under any decent law of society. It is possible there are some who are so born, and have been so treated by society, that they would need to be restrained just as those afflicted with small-pox may be restrained in a hospital. But to restrain them and treat them until cured is one thing; to say that men because of some inherent wickedness deserve punishment is another thing. It would be absurd to restrain men suffering from small-pox and turn them out from a hospital in six weeks, whether cured or not. If hospitals were run in the same way as jails, we would send them up for thirty days; and if they got well in a week we would keep them there.

The whole theory of punishment, so far as there is any theory in it—and there is not much in it, except the idea of vengeance—but the whole theory, so far as there is one, comes from the religious conception; that some people are made inherently bad, that their minds are evil, or their souls for that matter, or whatever is the intangible thing about them that makes them evil. And they deserve punishment, because they have a "wicked, abandoned and malignant heart." We always have to put that "wicked, abandoned and malignant heart" in the indictment; otherwise it is no good. If he has that in his heart he can be punished. When twelve jurors and a judge get together, how can they tell whether his heart is bad or not? You could tell better if you dissect him. It goes upon the theory that man is apart from all the other beings that inhabit the universe; that he is a free moral agent; that he is a sort of a wild train running at large through the universe; that he is not governed by rules and conditions like the rest of the universe about us. But that the Lord created him, put a mind in him, a good heart in some of them; a wicked, abandoned and malignant heart in others; and sent them out to run wild independent of all the universe about them. And whenever the good people catch up with these wicked, abandoned and malignant people then we punish the wicked because, intrinsically, they are bad, because they chose the evil instead of the good. They could do better if they wanted to be better but they did not choose. Society sends them to jail, just as brutal parents whip their children because they are bad instead of good. As a matter of fact, science and evolution teach us that man is an animal, a little higher than the other orders of animals; that he is governed by the same natural laws that govern the rest of the universe; that he is governed by the same laws that govern animal life, aye, and plant life; that free moral agency is a myth, a delusion, and a snare. It teaches us that he is surrounded by environment the product of all the past, the product of all the present; that he is here just like any other subject of natural law; and that it is not goodness, it is not badness, that makes him what he is. It is the condition of life in which he lives. And if he lives unwisely, if he is a defective, if he is anti-social, it is not that he chose it; but it is due to a thousand conditions over which he has not the slightest control. And the wise society seeks to change his environment, to place him in harmony with life. They know that they can only change the man by changing the conditions under which he lives; that good and evil, so far as he is concerned, do not exist; that right and wrong are religious myths; that it is a question of the adaptability of the individual to society life, and a gradual change of the environment under which he lives.

With the state is the same thing. The theory of force and violence applied to the state has drenched the world in blood. It has built great navies, and great armies. One nation builds a great navy and a great army, and destroys the resources of its people to build armies and navies. And another nation must build a greater navy and a greater army, because of the first. It makes of the nations of the earth armed camps, and the stronger the one arms itself, the stronger must the rest. England builds her wonderful navy out of the toil of the poor, out of what should buy food for the men who produce it. And when she builds it, then Germany must build one as large, and so must France and so must Russia build one, too. And of course patriotic America must build one. We need a navy for fear that a band of Senegambians might send a fleet to devastate Chicago some night. The theory of force and violence as applied to political states has built up the navies and armies of the world, and has caused most of the bloodshed of the human race. Is there any doubt but what nations would be stronger if they burned their battleships instead of building new ones? Can you increase the power of one nation by building ships when you simply make others build larger? You never change the relative proportion, which alone makes the strength. If instead of adding to the navies the world over, we gradually got rid of them, the relative strength would be what it was before.

In industrial life it is the same thing. The reign of force, and the reign of violence, means competition, means industrial strife; is responsible for the greed and selfishness and avarice for the fortunes of the great and the poverty of the poor. It is only in these later days, when the world is looking to something better, when they are learning that force and violence is wrong, that it is wrong that merchants compete and cut each other's throats and workmen compete against each other to show how much less they can work for; and that it is better to organize society on a co-operative basis where each man is to help his fellowman instead of fighting his fellowman.

The dreams of the world may be far off, and we must fit every dream to every reality. For the world is imperfect. But if, as society progresses, there shall one day be a civilization better than the world has known, it will be a society where force and violence and bloodshed and cruelty have disappeared. It will be a world of brotherhood. A world not of destruction, of competition, of violence, of hatred, of enmity; but a world of co-operation, of mutual help, of love, of brotherliness; and that alone makes for the progress of the world.

. . . Those who think that non-resistance is a milk-and-water theory have got another guess. It is not. I was talking the other day with a man who had been a colonel in the war. I said: "I do not know how you could get up courage to go up in the face of cannons and bayonets and take your life in your hands." He says: "I did it because I was too big a coward to run away." And that is why most all men go to war. They are too big cowards to stay at home. That is why men fight. They are too big cowards not to fight. Do you think it is a brave man who fights; or is it the brave man who does not fight? I will show you ten thousand men who are willing to go up in the face of hostile cannon, where you cannot find one man who will take one stick of criticism in a daily newspaper. There is not anything on earth so cheap as physical courage. Why even a bulldog can fight, but it has not got much brain. Fighting has nothing to do with the labor question, or with the question of capital and labor. How is it applied to the question as it exists today?

In order to change social conditions you say you must get rid of the ruling class, by force or some other way—one way or the other. Now, the weak are the poorest ones in the world to fight. They have no guns; the other fellow has them all. They have no organization. They have no chance in a fight. But they can fight. Workingmen of today can fight. If all of them would refuse to work or the great majority would refuse to work and enter into passive resistance—non-resistance—quit feeding the race; that is all you need to do. You cannot, of course. Wait until you can. You can get a small minority to arm themselves with brickbats and guns. What happens? You are sending a small force, poorly armed and equipped, against all the power of the state, and you cannot succeed, and you never have succeeded.

The only force that can win is determination, non-resistance, peaceable force. There is such a thing as peaceable force that is more forcible than forcible force.

Let me give you a few illustrations. What makes life? The cold, hard, stern winter; or the sunshine and the warm rain of the summer and the spring? The one means death, and the other means life. Repression and death go together. Love and sunshine and life are born together. Do you want to change the conduct of men, whether grown individuals or children; take a child and whip a child, can you change his conduct? You may change his conduct, but can you change his heart? Conduct is only the outward manifestation of the inward individual. To change the individual you must change the heart, and then the conduct must be free. Can you cure hatred with hatred? Everybody knows it in their own life. You may force men against their will to do certain things, but their hearts are a seething mass waiting for a time when they may accomplish other things by violence. Do you think you can do something for a man by sending him to the penitentiary? Gentleness is the law that makes life. Cruelty and hatred and coldness is the law that makes death. The question of non-resistance or resistance means a choice between those two laws.

15. Suffragettes,
Letters from Prison, 1917

The struggle for women's rights began as a phase of the abolitionist movement. Garrison insisted that women be permitted to participate in antislavery meetings, and women leaders such as Susan B. Anthony and Lucretia Mott urged freedom for both the slave and the

Doris Stevens, *Jailed For Freedom* (New York: Boni and Liverwright, 1920), pp. 175, 177–178, 184–191.

unfranchised female. After the Civil War most male abolitionists concluded that the vote for women should be deferred so that the vote for the Negro could be won. Victory in the women's suffrage struggle came fifty years later, during World War I. Led now by a new and more militant group of spokesmen, such as Alice Paul, the suffragettes did not hesitate to press their domestic concern in a world at war. They picketed persistently in Washington, D. C. When arrested, they continued their protest in jail. The following passages, from a book by a participant in the movement, de scribe prison protest, first by petition, then by a refusal to work and eat. The suffering of the suffragettes moved the nation, prompted the resignation of the Collector of Customs for the Port of New York, contributed to the passage of the Nineteenth Amendment, and established significant precedents for later nonviolent demonstrators.

Political Prisoners

Finding that a Suffrage Committee in the House and a report in the Senate had not silenced our banners, the Administration cast about for another plan by which to stop the picketing. This time they turned desperately to longer terms of imprisonment. They were indeed hard pressed when they could choose such a cruel and stupid course.

Our answer to this policy was more women on the picket line, on the outside, and a protest on the inside of prison.

We decided, in the face of extended imprisonment, to demand to be treated as political prisoners. We felt that, as a matter of principle, this was the dignified and self-respecting thing to do, since we had offended politically, not criminally. We believed further that a determined, organized effort to make clear to a wider public the political nature of the offense would intensify the Administration's embarrassment and so accelerate their final surrender.

It fell to Lucy Burns, vice chairman of the organization, to be the leader of the new protest. . . . She had no sooner begun to organize her comrades for protest than the officials sensed a "plot," and removed her at once to solitary confinement. But they were too late. Taking the leader only hastened the rebellion. A forlorn piece of paper was discovered, on which was written their initial demand. It was then passed from prisoner to prisoner through holes in the wall surrounding leaden pipes, until a finished document had been perfected and signed by all the prisoners.

This historic document—historic because it represents the first organized group action ever made in America to establish the status of political prisoners—said:

To the Commissioners of the District of Columbia:

As political prisoners, we, the undersigned, refuse to work while in prison. We have taken this stand as a matter of principle after careful consideration, and from it we shall not recede.

This action is a necessary protest against an unjust sentence. In reminding President Wilson of his pre-election promises toward woman suffrage we were exercising the right of peaceful petition, guaranteed by the Constitution of the United States, which declares peaceful picketing is legal in the District of Columbia. That we are unjustly sentenced has been well recognized—when President Wilson pardoned the first group of suffragists who had been given sixty days in the workhouse, and again when Judge Mullowny suspended sentence for the last group of picketers. We wish to point out the inconsistency and injustice of our sentences—some of us have been given sixty days, a later group thirty days, and another group given a suspended sentence for exactly the same action.

Conscious, therefore, of having acted in accordance with the highest standards of citizenship, we ask the Commissioners of the District to grant us the rights due political prisoners.

We ask that we no longer be segregated and confined under locks and bars in small groups, but permitted to see each other, and that Miss Lucy Burns, who is in full sympathy with this letter, be released from solitary confinement in another building and given back to us.

We ask exemption from prison work, that our legal right to consult counsel be recognized, to have food sent to us from outside, to supply ourselves with writing material for as much correspondence as we may need, to receive books, letters, newspapers, our relatives and friends.

Our united demand for political treatment has been delayed, because on entering the workhouse we found conditions so very bad that before we could ask that the suffragists be treated as political prisoners, it was necessary to make a stand for the ordinary rights of human beings for all the inmates. Although this has not been accomplished we now wish to bring the important question of the status of political prisoners to the attention of the commissioners, who, we are informed, have full authority to make what regulations they please for the District prison and workhouse.

The Commissioners are requested to send us a written reply so that we may be sure this protest has reached them.

Signed by,

MARY WINSOR, LUCY BRANHAM, ERNESTINE HARA, HILDA BLUMBERG, MAUD MALONE, PAULINE F. ADAMS, ELEANOR A. CALNAN, EDITH AINGE, ANNIE ARNEIL, DOROTHY J. BARTLETT, MARGARET FOTHERINGHAM.

The Commissioners' only answer to this was a hasty transfer of the signers and the leader, Miss Burns, to the District Jail, where they were put in solitary confinement. The women were not only refused the privileges asked but were denied some of the usual privileges allowed to ordinary criminals. . . .

The Hunger Strike—A Weapon

When the Administration refused to grant the demand of the prisoners and of that portion of the public which supported them, for the rights of political prisoners, it was decided to resort to the ultimate protest-weapon inside prison. A hunger strike was undertaken, not only to reinforce the verbal demand for the rights of political prisoners, but also as a final protest against unjust imprisonment and increasingly long sentences. This brought the Administration face to face with a more acute embarrassment. They had to choose between more stubborn resistance and capitulation. They continued for a while longer on the former path.

Little is known in this country about the weapon of the hunger strike. And so at first it aroused tremendous indignation. "Let them starve to death," said the thoughtless one, who did not perceive that that was the very thing a political administration could least afford to do. "Mad fanatics," said a kindlier critic. The general opinion was that the hunger strike was "foolish."

Few people realize that this resort to the refusal of food is almost as old as civilization. It has always represented a passionate desire to achieve an end. There is not time to go into the religious use of it, which would also be pertinent, but I will cite a few instances which have tragic and amusing likenesses to the suffrage hunger strike.

According to the Brehon Law,[1] which was the code of ancient Ireland by which justice was administered under ancient Irish monarchs (from the earliest record to the 17th century), it became the duty of an injured person, when all else failed, to inflict punishment directly, for wrong done. "The plaintiff 'fasted on' the defendant." He went to the house of the defendant and sat upon his doorstep, remaining there without food to

---

[1] Joyce, *A Social History of Ancient Ireland*, Vol. I, Chapter VIII.

force the payment of a debt, for example. The debtor was compelled by the weight of custom and public opinion not to let the plaintiff die at his door, and yielded. Or if he did not yield, he was practically outlawed by the community, to the point of being driven away. A man who refused to abide by the custom not only incurred personal danger but lost all character.

If resistance to this form of protest was resorted to it had to take the form of a counter-fast. If the victim of such a protest thought himself being unjustly coerced, he might fast in opposition, "to mitigate or avert the evil."

"Fasting on a man" was also a mode of compelling action of another sort. St. Patrick fasted against King Trian to compel him to have compassion on his [Trian's] slaves.[2] He also fasted against a heretical city to compel it to become orthodox.[3] He fasted against the pagan King Loeguire to "constrain him to his will."[4]

This form of hunger strike was further used under the Brehon Law as compulsion to obtain a request. For example, the Leinstermen on one occasion fasted on St. Columkille till they obtained from him the promise that an extern King should never prevail against them.

It is interesting to note that this form of direct action was adopted because there was no legislative machinery to enforce justice. These laws were merely a collection of customs attaining the force of law by long usage, by hereditary habit, and by public opinion. Our resort to this weapon grew out of the same situation. The legislative machinery, while empowered to give us redress, failed to function, and so we adopted the fast.

The institution of fasting on a debtor still exists in the East. It is called by the Hindoos "sitting dharna."

---

2 *Tripartite Life of St. Patrick,* CLXXVII, p. 218.
3 *Ibid.,* CLXXVII, p. 418.
4 *Ibid.,* CLXXVII, p. 556.

The hunger strike was continuously used in Russia by prisoners to obtain more humane practices toward them. Kropotkin[5] cites an instance in which women prisoners hunger struck to get their babies back. If a child was born to a woman during her imprisonment the babe was immediately taken from her and not returned. Mothers struck and got their babies returned to them.

He cites another successful example in Kharkoff prison in 1878 when six prisoners resolved to hunger strike to death if necessary to win two things—to be allowed exercise and to have the sick prisoners taken out of chains.

There are innumerable instances of hunger strikes, even to death, in Russian prison history. But more often the demands of the strikers were won. Breshkovsky[6] tells of a strike by 17 women against outrage, which elicited the desired promises from the warden.

As early as 1877 members of the Land and Liberty Society[7] imprisoned for peaceful and educational propaganda, in the Schlusselburg Fortress for political prisoners, hunger struck against inhuman prison conditions and frightful brutalities and won their points.

During the suffrage campaign in England this weapon was used for the double purpose of forcing the release of imprisoned militant suffragettes, and of compelling the British government to act.

Among the demonstrations was a revival of the ancient Irish custom by Sylvia Pankhurst, who in addition to her hunger strikes within prison, "fasted on" the doorstep of Premier Asquith to compel him to see a deputation of women on the granting of suffrage to English women. She won.

Irish prisoners have revived the hunger strike to compel either release or trial of untried prisoners and have won. As

---

[5] See *In Russian and French Prisons*, P. Kropotkin.
[6] *For Russia's Freedom*, by Ernest Poole,—An Interview with Breshkovsky.
[7] See *The Russian Bastille*, Simon O. Pollock.

I write, almost a hundred Irish prisoners detained by England for alleged nationalist activities, but not brought to trial, hunger struck to freedom. As a direct result of this specific hunger strike England has promised a renovation of her practices in dealing with Irish rebels.

And so it was that when we came to the adoption of this accelerating tactic, we had behind us more precedents for winning our point than for losing. We were strong in the knowledge that we could "fast on" President Wilson and his powerful Administration, and compel him to act or "fast back."

Among the prisoners who with Alice Paul led the hunger strike was a very picturesque figure, Rose Winslow (Ruza Wenclawska) of New York, whose parents had brought her in infancy from Poland to become a citizen of "free" America. At eleven she was put at a loom in a Pennsylvania mill, where she wove hosiery for fourteen hours a day until tuberculosis claimed her at nineteen. A poet by nature she developed her mind to the full in spite of these disadvantages, and when she was forced to abandon her loom she became an organizer for the Consumers' League, and later a vivid and eloquent power in the suffrage movement.

Her group preceded Miss Paul's by about a week in prison.

These vivid sketches of Rose Winslow's impressions while in the prison hospital were written on tiny scraps of paper and smuggled out to us, and to her husband during her imprisonment. I reprint them in their original form with cuts but no editing.

"If this thing is necessary we will naturally go through with it. Force is so stupid a weapon. I feel so happy doing my bit for decency—for *our* war, which is after all, real and fundamental."

"The women are all so magnificent, so beautiful. Alice Paul is as thin as ever, pale and large-eyed. We have been in solitary for five weeks. There is nothing to tell but that the days go by somehow. I have felt quite feeble the last few days—faint, so that I could hardly get my hair brushed, my arms ached so. But to-day I am well again. Alice Paul and I talk back and forth though we are at opposite ends of the building and a hall door also shuts us apart. But occasionally—thrills—we escape from behind our iron-barred doors and visit. Great laughter and rejoicing!"

[To her husband]
"My fainting probably means nothing except that I am not strong after these weeks. I know you won't be alarmed.

"I told about a syphilitic colored woman with one leg. The other one was cut off, having rotted so that it was alive with maggots when she came in. The remaining one is now getting as bad. They are so short of nurses that a little colored girl of twelve, who is here waiting to have her tonsils removed, waits on her. This child and two others share a ward with a syphilitic child of three or four years, whose mother refused to have it at home. It makes you absolutely ill to see it. I am going to break all three windows as a protest against their confining Alice Paul with these!

"Dr. Gannon is chief of a hospital. Yet Alice Paul and I found we had been taking baths in one of the tubs here, in which this syphilitic child, an incurable, who has his eyes bandaged all the time, is also bathed. He has been here a year. Into the room where he lives came yesterday two children to be operated on for tonsillitis. They also bathed in the same tub. The syphilitic woman has been in that room seven months. Cheerful mixing, isn't it? The place is alive with roaches, crawling all over the walls, everywhere. I found one in my bed the other day. . . ."

"There is great excitement about my two syphilitics. Each nurse is being asked whether she told me. So, as in all institutions where an unsanitary fact is made public, no effort is made to make the wrong itself right. All hands fall to, to find the culprit, who made it known, and he is punished."

"Alice Paul is in the psychopathic ward. She dreaded forcible feeding frightfully, and I hate to think how she must be feeling. I had a nervous time of it, gasping a long time afterward, and my stomach rejecting during the process. I spent a bad, restless night, but otherwise I am all right. The poor soul who fed me got liberally besprinkled during the process. I heard myself making the most hideous sounds. . . . One feels so forsaken when one lies prone and people shove a pipe down one's stomach."

"This morning but for an astounding tiredness, I am all right. I am waiting to see what happens when the President realizes that brutal bullying isn't quite a statesmanlike method for settling a demand for justice at home. At least, if men are supine enough to endure, women—to their eternal glory—are not.

"They took down the boarding from Alice Paul's window yesterday, I heard. It is so delicious about Alice and me. Over in the jail a rumor began that I was considered insane and would be examined. Then came Doctor White, and said he had come to see 'the thyroid case.' When they left we argued about the matter, neither of us knowing which was considered 'suspicious.' She insisted it was she, and, as it happened, she was right. Imagine any one thinking Alice Paul needed to be 'under observation!' The thick-headed idiots!"

"Yesterday was a bad day for me in feeding. I was vomiting continually during the process. The tube has developed an irritation somewhere that is painful.

"Never was there a sentence[8] like ours for such an offense

---

[8] Sentence of seven months for "obstructing traffic."

as ours, even in England. No woman ever got it over there even for tearing down buildings. And during all that agitation *we* were busy saying that never would such things happen in the United States. The men told us they would not endure such frightfulness."

"Mary Beard and Helen Todd were allowed to stay only a minute, and I cried like a fool. I am getting over that habit, I think.

"I fainted again last night. I just fell flop over in the bathroom where I was washing my hands and was led to bed when I recovered, by a nurse. I lost consciousness just as I got there again. I felt horribly faint until 12 o'clock, then fell asleep for awhile."

"I was getting frantic because you seemed to think Alice was with me in the hospital. She was in the psychopathic ward. The same doctor feeds us both, and told me. Don't let them tell you we take this well. Miss Paul vomits much. I do, too, except when I'm not nervous, as I have been every time against my will. I try to be less feeble-minded. It's the nervous reaction, and I can't control it much. I don't imagine bathing one's food in tears very good for one.

"We think of the coming feeding all day. It is horrible. The doctor thinks I take it well. I hate the thought of Alice Paul and the others if I take it well."

"We still get no mail; we are 'insubordinate.' It's strange, isn't it; if you ask for food fit to eat, as we did, you are 'insubordinate'; and if you refuse food you are 'insubordinate.' Amusing. I am really all right. If this continues very long I perhaps won't be. I am interested to see how long our so-called 'splendid American men' will stand for this form of discipline.

"All news cheers one marvelously because it is hard to feel anything but a bit desolate and forgotten here in this place.

"All the officers here know we are making this hunger strike that women fighting for liberty may be considered political prisoners; we have told them. God knows we don't want other women ever to have to do this over again."

There have been sporadic and isolated cases of hunger strikes in this country but to my knowledge ours was the first to be organized and sustained over a long period of time. . . .

PART V

Conscientious Objectors,
World War I

16. Roger Baldwin and Others,
Statements of Conscientious Objection,
1917–1918

Of the approximately 4,000 conscientious objectors in World War I,
some 1,300 eventually entered noncombatant military service in the
Medical Corps, the Quartermaster Corps, and the Engineer Service.
About 1,200 were given furloughs to do farm work, 100 were
assigned to Quaker war relief work in France, 500 were court-
martialed and convicted. Of these 500, seventeen were sentenced to
death (but none actually executed) and 142 to life imprisonment.
In 1933 President Roosevelt pardoned all those still in prison.

The statements of conscientious objectors that follow illustrate
the variety of their motives. The political objector, Carl Haessler,
and the religious objector, Maurice Hess, were or became college
professors; Roger Baldwin was then director of the Civil Liberties
Bureau and later became the first president of the American Civil
Liberties Union.

From Norman Thomas, *The Conscientious Objector in America* (New
York: B. W. Heubsch, 1923), pp. 23–28. Reprinted with the permission
of Norman Thomas.

1 [*Carl Haessler*]

I, Carl Haessler, Recruit, Machine Gun Company, 46th Infantry, respectfully submit the following statement in extenuation in connection with my proposed plea of guilty to the charge of violation of the 64th Article of War, the offense having been committed June 22, 1918, in Camp Sheridan, Ala.

The offense was not committed from private, secret, personal, impulsive, religious, pacifist or pro-German grounds. An admixture of quasi-personal motives is admitted, but they were in no sense the guiding or controlling factors. I have evidence for each of these assertions, should it be required.

The willful disobedience of my Captain's and of my Lieutenant-Colonel's orders to report in military uniform arose from a conviction which I hesitate to express before my country's military officers but which I nevertheless am at present unable to shake off, namely, that America's participation in the World War was unnecessary, of doubtful benefit (if any) to the country and to humanity, and accomplished largely, though not exclusively, through the pressure of the Allied and American commercial imperialists.

Holding this conviction, I conceived my part as a citizen to be opposition to the war before it was declared, active efforts for a peace without victory after the declaration, and a determination so far as possible to do nothing in aid of the war while its character seemed to remain what I thought it was. I hoped in this way to help bring the war to an earlier close and to help make similar future wars less probable in this country.

I further believe that I shall be rendering the country a service by helping to set an example for other citizens to follow in the matter of fearlessly acting on unpopular convictions instead of forgetting them in time of stress. The crumbling of American radicalism under pressure in 1917 has only been equalled by that of the majority of German socialist leaders in August, 1914.

Looking at my case from the point of view of the administration and of this court, I readily admit the necessity of exemplary punishment. I regret that I have been forced to make myself a nuisance and I grant that this war could not be carried on if objections like mine were recognized by those conducting the war. My respect for the administration has been greatly increased by the courteous and forbearing treatment accorded me since having been drafted, but my view of international politics and diplomacy, acquired during my three years of graduate study in England, has not altered since June, 1917, when I formally declared that I could not accept service if drafted. Although officers have on three occasions offered me noncombatant service if I would put on the uniform, I have regretfully refused each time on the ground that "bomb-proof" service on my part would give the lie to my sincerity (which was freely granted by Judge Julian Mack when he and his colleagues examined me at Camp Gordon). If I am to render any war services, I shall not ask for special privileges.

I wish to conclude this long statement by reiterating that I am not a pacifist or pro-German, not a religious or private objector, but regard myself as a patriotic political objector, acting largely from public and social grounds.

I regret that, while my present view of this war continues, I cannot freely render any service in aid of the war. I shall not complain about the punishment that this court may see fit to mete out to me.

II [*Maurice Hess*]

I do not believe that I am seeking martyrdom. As a young man, life and its hopes and freedom and opportunities for service are sweet to me. I want to go out into the world and make use of what little talent I may have acquired by long and laborious study.

But I know that I dare not purchase these things at the price of eternal condemnation. I know the teaching of Christ, my Savior. He taught us to resist not evil, to love our enemies, to bless them that curse us, and do good to them that hate us. Not only did he teach this, but he also practiced it in Gethsemane, before Pilate, and on Calvary. We would indeed be hypocrites and base traitors to our profession if we would be unwilling to bear the taunts and jeers of a sinful world, and its imprisonment, and torture or death, rather than to participate in war and military service. We know that obedience to Christ will gain for us the glorious prize of eternal life. We cannot yield, we cannot compromise, we must suffer.

Two centuries ago our people were driven out of Germany by religious persecution, and they accepted the invitation of William Penn to come to his colony where they might enjoy the blessing of religious liberty which he promised them. This religious liberty was later confirmed by the Constitution of Pennsylvania, and the Constitution of the United States.

If the authorities now see fit to change those fundamental documents and take away our privilege of living in accordance with the teaching of the scriptures of God, then we have no course but to endure persecution as true soldiers of Christ.

If I have committed anything worthy of bonds or death, I do not refuse to suffer or to die.

I pray God for strength to remain faithful.

III [Roger N. Baldwin]

The compelling motive for refusing to comply with the draft act is my uncompromising opposition to the principle of conscription of life by the state for any purpose whatever, in time of war or peace. I not only refuse to obey the present conscription law, but I would in future refuse to obey any similar statute which attempts to direct my choice of service and ideals. I regard the principle of conscription of life as a flat contradiction of all our cherished ideals of individual freedom, democratic liberty, and Christian teaching.

I am the more opposed to the present act, because it is for the purpose of conducting war. I am opposed to this and all other wars. I do not believe in the use of physical force as a method of achieving any end, however good. . . .

I am not complaining for myself or others. I am merely advising the court that I understand full well the penalty of my heresy, and am prepared to pay it. The conflict with conscription is irreconcilable. Even the liberalism of the President and Secretary of War in dealing with objectors leads those of us who are "absolutists" to a punishment longer and severer than that of desperate criminals.

But I believe most of us are prepared even to die for our faith, just as our brothers in France are dying for theirs. To them we are comrades in spirit—we understand one another's motives, though our methods are wide apart. We both share deeply the common experience of living up to the truth as we see it, whatever the price.

Though at the moment I am of a tiny minority, I feel myself just one protest in a great revolt surging up from among the people—the struggle of the masses against the rule of the world by the few—profoundly intensified by the war. It is a struggle against the political state itself, against exploitation, militarism, imperialism, authority in all forms. . . .

Having arrived at the state of mind in which those views mean the dearest things in life to me, I cannot consistently, with self-respect, do other than I have, namely, to deliberately violate an act which seems to me to be a denial of everything which ideally and in practice I hold sacred.

17. Jane Addams,
"Personal Reactions During War"

Another important opponent of the First World War was Jane Addams (1860–1935). Best known as the founder of one of America's first settlement houses, Jane Addams also helped to organize the Women's International League for Peace and Freedom and in 1931 received the Nobel Prize. Her "Personal Reactions During War" is a moving statement of a liberal driven to radicalism by persevering in her convictions in time of crisis.

After the United States had entered the war there began to appear great divergence among the many types of pacifists, from the extreme left, composed of non-resistants, through the middle-of-the-road groups, to the extreme right, who could barely be distinguished from mild militarists. There were those people, also, who although they felt keenly both the horror and the futility of war, yet hoped for certain beneficent results from the opportunities afforded by the administration of war; they were much pleased when the government took over the management of the railroads, insisting that governmental ownership had thus been pushed forward by decades; they were also sure that the War Labor Policies Board, the Coal Commission and similar war institutions would make an enormous difference in the development of the country, in short, that militarism might be used as an instrument for advanced social ends. Such justifications had their lure and one found old

Jane Addams, "Personal Reactions During War," *Peace and Bread in Time of War*, Chapter VII (Boston: G. K. Hall, 1960), pp. 132–151. Permission has been given to quote copyrighted material from *Peace and Bread in Time of War*, copyright 1922 by the Macmillan Company, 1945 by the Women's International League for Peace and Freedom of which Jane Addams was the first international president.

pacifist friends on all the war boards and even in the war
department itself. Certainly we were all eager to accept whatever progressive social changes came from the quick reorganization demanded by war, and doubtless prohibition was one
of these, as the granting of woman suffrage in the majority of
the belligerent nations, was another. But some of us had suspected that social advance depends as much upon the process
through which it is secured as upon the result itself, if railroads
are nationalized solely in order to secure rapid transit of ammunition and men to points of departure for Europe, when
that governmental need no longer exists what more natural
than that the railroads should no longer be managed by the
government?

My temperament and habit had always kept me rather in the
middle of the road; in politics as well as in social reform I had
been for "the best possible." But now I was pushed far toward
the left on the subject of the war and I became gradually convinced that in order to make the position of the pacifist clear
it was perhaps necessary that at least a small number of us
should be forced into an unequivocal position. If I sometimes
regretted having gone to the Woman's Congress at The Hague
in 1915, or having written a book on Newer Ideals of Peace in
1911 which had made my position so conspicuously clear, certainly far oftener I was devoutly grateful that I had used such
unmistakable means of expression before the time came when
any spoken or written word in the interests of Peace was
forbidden.

It was on my return from The Hague Congress in July, 1915,
that I had my first experience of the determination on the part
of the press to make pacifist activity or propaganda so absurd
that it would be absolutely without influence and its authors
so discredited that nothing they might say or do would be regarded as worthy of attention. I had been accustomed to
newspaper men for many years and had come to regard them
as a good natured fraternity, sometimes ignorant of the subject

on which they asked an interview, but usually quite ready to report faithfully albeit somewhat sensationally. Hull-House had several times been the subject of sustained and inspired newspaper attacks, one, the indirect result of an exposure of the inefficient sanitary service in the Chicago Health Department had lasted for many months; I had of course known what it was to serve unpopular causes and throughout a period of campaigning for the Progressive Party I had naturally encountered the "opposition press" in various parts of the country, but this concerted and deliberate attempt at misrepresentation on the part of newspapers of all shades of opinion was quite new in my experience. After the United States entered the war, the press throughout the country systematically undertook to misrepresent and malign pacifists as a recognized part of propaganda and as a patriotic duty. We came to regard this misrepresentation as part of the war technique and in fact an inevitable consequence of war itself, but we were slow in the very beginning to recognize the situation, and I found my first experience which came long before the United States entered the war rather overwhelming.

Upon our return from the Woman's International Congress at The Hague in 1915, our local organization in New York City with others, notably a group of enthusiastic college men, had arranged a large public meeting in Carnegie Hall. Dr. Anna Howard Shaw presided and the United States delegates made a public report of our impressions in "war stricken Europe" and of the moral resources in the various countries we visited that might possibly be brought to bear against a continuation of the war. We had been much impressed with the fact that it was an old man's war, that the various forms of doubt and opposition to war had no method of public expression and that many of the soldiers themselves were far from enthusiastic in regard to actual fighting as a method of settling international difficulties. War was to many of them much more anachronistic than to the elderly statesmen who were primarily responsible for the soldiers' presence in the trenches.

It was the latter statement which was my undoing, for in illustration of it I said that in practically every country we had visited, we had heard a certain type of young soldier say that it had been difficult for him to make the bayonet charge (enter into actual hand to hand fighting) unless he had been stimulated; that the English soldiers had been given rum before such a charge, the Germans ether and that the French were said to use absinthe. To those who heard the address it was quite clear that it was not because the young men flinched at the risk of death but because they had to be inflamed to do the brutal work of the bayonet, such as disembowelling, and were obliged to overcome all the inhibitions of civilization.

Dr. Hamilton and I had notes for each of these statements with the dates and names of the men who had made them, and it did not occur to me that the information was new or startling. I was, however, reported to have said that no soldier could go into a bayonet charge until he was made half drunk, and this in turn was immediately commented upon, notably in a scathing letter written to the New York Times by Richard Harding Davis, as a most choice specimen of a woman's sentimental nonsense. Mr. Davis himself had recently returned from Europe and at once became the defender of the heroic soldiers who were being traduced and belittled. He lent the weight of his name and his very able pen to the cause, but it really needed neither, for the misstatement was repeated, usually with scathing comment, from one end of the country to the other.

I was conscious, of course, that the story had struck athwart the popular and long-cherished conception of the nobility and heroism of the soldier as such, and it seemed to me at the time that there was no possibility of making any explanation, at least until the sensation should have somewhat subsided. I might have repeated my more sober statements with the explanation that whomsoever the pacifist held responsible for war, it was certainly not the young soldiers themselves who were, in a sense, its most touching victims, "the heroic youth of the world whom a common ideal tragically pitted against each other." Youth's response to the appeal made to their self-sacrifice, to their patriotism, to their sense of duty, to their high-hearted hopes for the future, could only stir one's admiration, and we should have been dull indeed had we failed to be moved by this most moving spectacle in the world. That they had so responded to the higher appeals only confirms Ruskin's statement that "we admire the soldier not because he goes forth to slay but to be slain." The fact that many of them were obliged to make a great effort to bear themselves gallantly in the final tests of "war's brutalities" had nothing whatever to do with their courage and sense of devotion. All this, of course, we had realized during our months in Europe.

After the meeting in Carnegie Hall and after an interview with President Wilson in Washington, I returned to Chicago to a public meeting arranged in the Auditorium; I was met at the train by a committee of aldermen appointed as a result of a resolution in the City Council. There was an indefinite feeling that the meeting at The Hague might turn out to be of significance, and that in such an event its chairman should have been honored by her fellow citizens. But the bayonet story had preceded me and every one was filled with great uneasiness. To be sure, a few war correspondents had come to my rescue—writing of the overpowering smell of ether preceding certain German attacks; the fact that English soldiers knew when a bayonet charge was about to be ordered because rations of rum were distributed along the trenches. Some people began to suspect that the story, exaggerated and grotesque as it had become, indicated not cowardice but merely an added sensitiveness which the modern soldier was obliged to overcome. Among the many letters on the subject which filled my mail for weeks, the bitter and abusive were from civilians or from the old men to whom war experiences had become a reminiscence, the larger number and the most understanding ones came from soldiers in active service.

Only once did I try a public explanation. After an address

in Chautauqua, New York, in which I had not mentioned
bayonets, I tried to remake my original statement to a young
man of the associated press only to find it once more so
garbled that I gave up in despair, quite unmoved by the young
man's letter of apology which followed hard upon the published report of his interview.

I will confess that the mass psychology of the situation interested me even then and continued to do so until I fell ill
with a serious attack of pleuro-pneumonia, which was the beginning of three years of semi-invalidism. During weeks of
feverish discomfort I experienced a bald sense of social op-
probrium and wide-spread misunderstanding which brought
me very near to self pity, perhaps the lowest pit into which
human nature can sink. Indeed the pacifist in war time, with
his precious cause in the keeping of those who control the
sources of publicity and consider it a patriotic duty to make all
types of peace propaganda obnoxious, constantly faces two
dangers. Strangely enough he finds it possible to travel from
the mire of self pity straight to the barren hills of self-righteousness and to hate himself equally in both places.

From the very beginning of the great war, as the members
of our group gradually became defined from the rest of the
community, each one felt increasingly the sense of isolation
which rapidly developed after the United States entered the
war into that destroying effect of "aloneness," if I may so
describe the opposite of mass consciousness. We never ceased
to miss the unquestioning comradeship experienced by our fellow citizens during the war, nor to feel curiously outside the
enchantment given to any human emotion when it is shared
by millions of others. The force of the majority was so overwhelming that it seemed not only impossible to hold one's own
against it, but at moments absolutely unnatural, and one
secretly yearned to participate in "the folly of all mankind."
Our modern democratic teaching has brought us to regard popular impulses as possessing in their general tendency a valu-

able capacity for evolutionary development. In the hours of doubt and self-distrust the question again and again arises, has the individual or a very small group, the right to stand out against millions of his fellow countrymen? Is there not a great value in mass judgment and in instinctive mass enthusiasm, and even if one were right a thousand times over in conviction, was he not absolutely wrong in abstaining from this communion with his fellows? The misunderstanding on the part of old friends and associates and the charge of lack of patriotism was far easier to bear than those dark periods of faint-heartedness. We gradually ceased to state our position as we became convinced that it served no practical purpose and, worse than that, often found that the immediate result was provocative.

We could not, however, lose the conviction that as all other forms of growth begin with a variation from the mass, so the moral changes in human affairs may also begin with a differing group or individual, sometimes with the one who at best is designated as a crank and a freak and in sterner moments is imprisoned as an atheist or a traitor. Just when the differing individual becomes the centro-egotist, the insane man, who must be thrown out by society for its own protection, it is impossible to state. The pacifist was constantly brought sharply up against a genuine human trait with its biological basis, a trait founded upon the instinct to dislike, to distrust and finally to destroy the individual who differs from the mass in time of danger. Regarding this trait as the basis of self-preservation it becomes perfectly natural for the mass to call such an individual a traitor and to insist that if he is not for the nation he is against it. To this an estimated nine million people can bear witness who have been burned as witches and heretics, not by mobs, for of the people who have been "lynched" no record has been kept, but by order of ecclesiastical and civil courts.

There were moments when the pacifist yielded to the suggestion that keeping himself out of war, refusing to take part in its enthusiasms, was but pure quietism, an acute failure to adjust himself to the moral world. Certainly nothing was clearer than that the individual will was helpless and irrelevant. We were constantly told by our friends that to stand aside from the war mood of the country was to surrender all possibility of future influence, that we were committing intellectual suicide, and would never again be trusted as responsible people or judicious advisers. Who were we to differ with able statesmen, with men of sensitive conscience who also absolutely abhorred war, but were convinced that this war for the preservation of democracy would make all future wars impossible, that the priceless values of civilization which were at stake could at this moment be saved only by war? But these very dogmatic statements spurred one to alarm. Was not war in the interest of democracy for the salvation of civilization a contradiction of terms, whoever said it or however often it was repeated?

Then, too, we were always afraid of fanaticism, of preferring a consistency of theory to the conscientious recognition of the social situation, of a failure to meet life in the temper of a practical person. Every student of our time had become more or less a disciple of pragmatism and its great teachers in the United States had come out for the war and defended their positions with skill and philosophic acumen. There were moments when one longed desperately for reconciliation with one's friends and fellow citizens; in the words of Amiel, "Not to remain at variance with existence but to reach that understanding of life which enables us at least to obtain forgiveness." Solitude has always had its demons, harder to withstand than the snares of the world, and the unnatural desert into which the pacifist was summarily cast out seemed to be peopled with them. We sorely missed the contagion of mental activity, for we are all much more dependent upon our social environment and daily newspaper than perhaps any of us realize. We also doubtless encountered, although subconsciously, the temptations described by John Stuart Mill: "In respect to the persons and affairs of their own day, men insensibly adopt the modes of feeling and judgment in which they can hope for sympathy from the company they keep."

The consciousness of spiritual alienation was lost only in moments of comradeship with the like minded, which may explain the tendency of the pacifist in war time to seek his intellectual kin, his spiritual friends, wherever they might be found in his own country or abroad.

It was inevitable that in many respects the peace cause should suffer in public opinion from the efforts of groups of people who, early in the war, were convinced that the country as a whole was for peace and who tried again and again to discover a method for arousing and formulating the sentiment against war. I was ill and out of Chicago when the People's Council held a national convention there, which was protected by the city police but threatened with dispersion by the state troops, who, however, arrived from the capital several hours after the meeting had adjourned. The incident was most sensational and no one was more surprised than many of the members of the People's Council who thus early in the war had supposed that they were conducting a perfectly legitimate convention. The incident gave tremendous "copy" in a city needing rationalizing rather than sensationalizing at that moment. There is no doubt that the shock and terror of the "anarchist riots" occurring in Chicago years ago have left their traces upon the nervous system of the city somewhat as a nervous shock experienced in youth will long afterwards determine the action of a mature man under widely different circumstances.

On the whole, the New York groups were much more active and throughout the war were allowed much more freedom both of assembly and press, although later a severe reaction followed expressed through the Lusk Committee and other agencies. Certainly neither city approximated the freedom of

London and nothing surprised me more in 1915 and again in 1919 than the freedom of speech permitted there.

We also read with a curious eagerness the steadily increasing number of books published from time to time during the war, which brought a renewal of one's faith or at least a touch of comfort. These books broke through that twisting and suppressing of awkward truths, which was encouraged and at times even ordered by the censorship. Such manipulation of news and motives was doubtless necessary in the interest of war propaganda if the people were to be kept in a fighting mood. Perhaps the most vivid books came from France, early from Romain Rolland, later from Barbusse, although it was interesting to see how many people took the latter's burning indictment of war merely as a further incitement against the enemy. On the scientific side were the frequent writings of David Starr Jordan and the remarkable book of Nicolai on "The Biology of War." The latter enabled one, at least in one's own mind, to refute the pseudo-scientific statement that war was valuable in securing the survival of the fittest. Nicolai insisted that primitive man must necessarily have been a peaceful and social animal and that he developed his intelligence through the use of the tool, not through the use of the weapon; it was the primeval community which made the evolution of man possible, and coöperation among men is older and more primitive than mass combat which is an outgrowth of the much later property instinct. No other species save ants, who also possess property, fights in masses against other masses of its own kind. War is in fact not a natural process and not a struggle for existence in the evolutionary sense. He illustrated the evolutionary survival of the fittest by two tigers inhabiting the same jungle or feeding ground, the one who has the greater skill and strength as a hunter survives and the other starves, but the strong one does not go out to kill the weak one, as the war propagandist implied; or by two varieties of mice living in the same field or barn; in the biological struggle, the variety which grows a thicker coat survives the winter while the other variety freezes to extinction, but if one variety of mice should go forth to kill the other, it would be absolutely abnormal and quite outside the evolutionary survival which is based on the adjustment of the organism to its environment. George Nasmyth's book on Darwinism and the Social Order was another clear statement of the mental confusion responsible for the insistence that even a biological progress is secured through war. Mr. Brailsford wrote constantly on the economic results of the war and we got much comfort from John Hobson's "Toward International Government," which gave an authoritative account of the enormous amount of human activity actually carried on through international organizations of all sorts, many of them under governmental control. Lowes Dickenson's books, especially the spirited challenge in "The Choice Before Us," left his readers with the distinct impression that "war is not inevitable but proceeds from definite and removable causes." From every such book the pacifist was forced to the conclusion that none save those interested in the realization of an idea are in a position to bring it about and that if one found himself the unhappy possessor of an unpopular conviction, there was nothing for it but to think as clearly as he was able and be in a position to serve his country as soon as it was possible for him to do so.

But with or without the help of good books a hideous sensitiveness remained, for the pacifist, like the rest of the world, has developed a high degree of suggestibility, sharing that consciousness of the feelings, the opinions and the customs of his own social group which is said to be an inheritance from an almost pre-human past. An instinct which once enabled the man-pack to survive when it was a question of keeping together or of perishing off the face of the earth, is perhaps not underdeveloped in any of us. There is a distinct physical as well as moral strain when this instinct is steadily suppressed or at least ignored.

The large number of deaths among the older pacifists in all the warring nations can probably be traced in some measure to the peculiar strain which such maladjustment implies. More than the normal amount of nervous energy must be consumed in holding one's own in a hostile world. These older men, Kier Hardie and Lord Courtney in England, Jenkin Lloyd Jones, Rauchenbusch, Washington Gladden in the United States, Lammasch and Fried in Austria, had been honored by their fellow citizens because of marked ability to interpret and understand them. Suddenly to find every public utterance wilfully misconstrued, every attempt at normal relationship repudiated, must react in a baffled suppression which is health-destroying even if we do not accept the mechanistic explanation of the human system. Certainly by the end of the war we were able to understand, although our group certainly did not endorse the statement of Cobden, one of the most convinced of all internationalists: "I made up my mind during the Crimean War that if ever I lived in the time of another great war of a similar kind between England and another power, I would not as a public man open my mouth on the subject, so convinced am I that appeals to reason, conscience or interest have no force whatever on parties engaged in war, and that exhaustion on one or both sides can alone bring a contest of physical force to an end."

On the other hand there were many times when we stubbornly asked ourselves, what after all, has maintained the human race on this old globe despite all the calamities of nature and all the tragic failings of mankind, if not faith in new possibilities, and courage to advocate them. Doubtless many times these new possibilities were declared by a man who, quite unconscious of courage, bore the "sense of being an exile, a condemned criminal, a fugitive from mankind." Did every one so feel who, in order to travel on his own proper path had been obliged to leave the traditional highway? The pacifist, during the period of the war could answer none of these questions but he was sick at heart from causes which to him were hidden and impossible to analyze. He was at times devoured by a veritable dissatisfaction with life. Was he thus bearing his share of blood-guiltiness, the morbid sense of contradiction and inexplicable suicide which modern war implies? We certainly had none of the internal contentment of the doctrinnaire, the ineffable solace of the self-righteous which was imputed to us. No one knew better than we how feeble and futile we were against the impregnable weight of public opinion, the appalling imperviousness, the coagulation of motives, the universal confusion of a world at war. There was scant solace to be found in this type of statement: "The worth of every conviction consists precisely in the steadfastness with which it is held," perhaps because we suffered from the fact that we were no longer living in a period of dogma and were therefore in no position to announce our sense of security! We were well aware that the modern liberal having come to conceive truth of a kind which must vindicate itself in practice, finds it hard to hold even a sincere and mature opinion which from the very nature of things can have no justification in works. The pacifist in war time is literally starved of any gratification of that natural desire to have his own decisions justified by his fellows.

That, perhaps, was the crux of the situation. We slowly became aware that our affirmation was regarded as pure dogma. We were thrust into the position of the doctrinnaire, and although, had we been permitted, we might have cited both historic and scientific tests of our so-called doctrine of Peace, for the moment any sanction even by way of illustration was impossible.

It therefore came about that ability to hold out against mass suggestion, to honestly differ from the convictions and enthusiasms of one's best friends did in moments of crisis come to depend upon the categorical belief that a man's primary allegiance is to his vision of the truth and that he is under obligation to affirm it.

18. Ammon Hennacy,
"Atlanta Prison—1917"

Ammon Hennacy opposed World War I as a socialist but was converted to Christian pacifism while in prison. Later he became a leader of the Catholic Worker movement, founded in 1933 by Peter Maurin and Dorothy Day, a movement that played an important part in anti-war protests after World War II by encouraging nonpayment of taxes, civil disobedience against war preparations, and voluntary poverty.

I was arrested when I spoke against the coming war at Broad and High in Columbus, Ohio before about 10,000 people on the evening of April 5, 1917. The next day war was declared and I was released for trial May 30. Meanwhile I distributed leaflets over Ohio for the Socialist Party, advising young men to refuse to register for the draft. When I was picked up again I asked to see a lawyer but was told I could not see one. Detective Wilson said that unless I registered for the draft by June 5th, which was registration day, I was to be shot on orders from Washington. I was shown a copy of the local paper with headlines "Extreme Penalty for Traitors." I only saw it through

From *Two Agitators: Peter Maurin—Ammon Hennacy,* ed. Ammon Hennacy (New York: *The Catholic Worker,* 1959), pp. 6–19. Reprinted with the permission of *The Catholic Worker.*

the bars and was not allowed to read it. The detective said that the young Socialists arrested with me for refusing to register had all given in and registered. (Later I found out that he had also told them that I had registered.) I felt that if they gave in someone had to stick, and I was that one. Spike Moore, an I.W.W., the radical union of that day: the Industrial Workers of the World, founded by Debs, Haywood and others, from Pittsburgh who was in Columbus, sneaked me a note and a clipping from the paper in which a reporter asked my mother if she was not frightened because I was to be shot soon. Her reply was that the only thing she was afraid of was that they might scare me to give in. This gave me added courage. June 5th passed and no move was made to shoot me. Detective Wilson said that the Government had postponed my execution thinking I would give the names of those who had helped me distribute the leaflets. I pled guilty for my refusal to register. My partner and I each got 2 years in Atlanta. After this term was served I was to do 9 months in Delaware, Ohio County Jail nearby for refusal to register. The two guards who accompanied us to Atlanta chained us to our Pullman berths and gave us sandwiches prepared by their women folks, kidding us that they were marking up good meals on their expense accounts.

Friday, July 3, 1917 was the date of my arrival in Atlanta. My number was 7438. I was sent to the top floor of the old cell house, to a certain cell. This was occupied by someone else it seemed, for pictures of chorus girls were on the wall, and magazines and cigarette stubs on the floor. This cell was 8 feet long, 8 feet high, and 4½ feet wide and was made of steel. In half an hour a large, burly, but good natured man of about 40 came in.

"Hello kid, my name's Brockman, Peter Brockman from Buffalo, doin' a six bit for writing my name on little pieces of paper. Got one to go yet. How do you like our little home? What's your name?"

The next morning after breakfast, Blackie, the runner in the block, brought me a note, saying that he knew the prisoner who had written the note, and had done time with him in Alleghaney prison years ago. I read:

"Blackie, who gave you this note is o.k. See me in the yard this afternoon if it does not rain; otherwise come to the Catholic Mass tomorrow and I will talk to you there. Your cell mate has paid $5 worth of tobacco to the screw in your cell block to get the first young prisoner coming in to be his cell mate. You are the 'lucky' one. Watch him, for he is one of the worst perverts in the prison. There is no use making a fuss for you may 'accidentally' fall down four tiers. Get $5 worth of tobacco from the store and give it to Blackie and he will give it to the guard and pull strings to have you transferred out of the cell. This will take weeks; meantime get along the best you can.

Yours for the revolution, A. B."

A note from Alexander Berkman, the great Anarchist! I read it over and over again and then destroyed it, per the first rule in prison: don't keep any unnecessary contraband. For the first time in my life when I had read a book I had sat down at once and written to the author. This was in Warren, Ohio, in 1916, when I had read Berkman's *Memoirs*. I did not get an answer, but now I was to meet him personally. Hundreds of workers had been killed by the Pinkertons, a notorious detective agency, at Homestead, Pa. Frick was manager of Carnegie Steel at Homestead. Berkman, then a young anarchist, had stabbed and shot Frick, and had done 14 years and ten months actual time in Alleghaney prison, 3½ years of this in solitary in a dark hole. He had been in prison before I was born and here he was again with a fighting spirit that jails could not kill. I had read his paper *The Blast*. I had but a faint idea of the word pervert, and I wondered how and why I could talk to Berkman in a Catholic chapel.

The sun shone brightly that afternoon on the packed ground of the prison yard. In the shadow along one prison wall Blackie had pointed out Berkman to me. I hastened to greet him. His kindly smile made me feel that I had a friend. He told me of a means of getting out letters, *sub rosa*, and explained how to talk in your throat without moving your lips. He said that on rainy Saturdays, when we could not meet, we could see each other at the Catholic chapel, as the chaplain was an ex-prizefighter who was sympathetic to workers and did not mind those who came to visit each other. He gave me four things to remember. "(1) Don't tell a lie. (2) Don't tell on another prisoner; it's the job of the screws to find out what is going on, not yours. (3) Draw your line as to what you will do and will not do and don't budge, for if you begin to weaken they will beat you. (4) Don't curse the guards. They will try to get you to strike them and they will have the excuse to beat you up; and if one can't, two can; and if two can't; ten can. They are no good or they wouldn't take such a job. Just smile. Obey them in unimportant details but never budge an inch on principle. Don't be seen talking to me very often, for the guards are watching and will make trouble. Write to me by way of Blackie and I will do the same."

John, in my cell, was boss of the paint gang and was from Columbus, Ohio. He had me transferred to his gang, and when he left in about six months I was made boss of the gang. I had a pass to go anywhere I wanted inside the prison. The editor of the prison paper, *Good Words*, asked me to give him something to print. I told him that was what I got in for, printing things in papers, and that my ideas were too radical for him. He insisted so I gave this quote which, believe it or not, appeared in a box underneath the editorial caption of the Department of Justice on April 1, 1918: "*A prison is the only house in a slave state where a free man can abide with honor.*" *Thoreau.* This had the o.k. of the warden and was not sneaked in. The ignorant official thought it praised prisons. *The Conservator,* edited by the radical Horace Traubel, literary executor of Walt Whitman, was allowed in because they thought it was conservative. The *Irish World* which was much against the war came to the Catholic chaplain and he got copies to us radicals through John Dunn, a conscientious objector and Catholic, from Providence, R.I., who was boss of the plumbing gang. The conscientious objectors were scattered in different gangs and cell houses over the prison. The warden told me that the orders from Washington were to put us all in one place, but he knew better and scattered us out, for if we were in one place we would plot. This reminded me of the farmer who caught the ground-mole and said, "Hanging's too good; burning's too good; I'll bury you alive." So we conscientious objectors were scattered around where we could do propaganda instead of being segregated where we would argue among ourselves. John Dunn and I were good friends. His number was 7979 and he got 20 years. After his release he studied for the priesthood and is now a priest in Portsmouth, Ohio, and a reader of the *Catholic Worker*. Paul was a young, Russian born Socialist who had quit a good job to come to prison. Morris was a quiet, very short Russian Jewish anarchist, whom I met often at the vegetarian diet table. Louis was just the opposite; an erratic boisterous Nietzschean who felt that everything that you had was his and what he had was his own. Morris was deported at the same time as Emma Goldman and Alexander Berkman, after the war. Louis after many years came to an appreciation of God, but finally committed suicide. Tony was a Russian who did not speak English, but whose quiet manner marked him as some kind of a religious sectarian. Walter was a college man who came from an old anarchist family, and who had despised his father's ideas until the crisis of war brought him to prison. His partner was John, a seaman who belonged to the I.W.W. maritime branch. He had been banished from Australia as a radical, and had refused to register for the draft. Theodore and Adolph were young Socialists from Rhode Island who were enthusiastic and helpful in any prison rebellion. Gilbert was an Italian I.W.W. who spoke little English. He worked in the stone gang. I never met him personally; we just smiled from a distance. Al and Fred were two older comrades who had unwittingly been sent to prison. They were not left wingers, but were in official position in the Socialist Party, where the extreme conservatism of their communities made them martyrs. They were not active in any plans that we younger rebels formed. Francisco was the only local comrade from Atlanta in prison against the war; he was a Puerto Rican and had the advantage of his family coming to see him often. The young Hollander from Vermont was not a radical in the accepted sense of the term; he simply refused to fight against relatives who were in the German army. Fritz was a young Russian Socialist who was also quiet, but who went along with us in any of our plans.

The Russelites came along later when I was in solitary and I never saw any of them. Their leader Judge Rutherford was with them and they came to be called Jehovah's Witnesses. Nicholas, the Mexican, was dying of tuberculosis. I only saw him from a distance for he lived by himself in a tent the year around. He was a Mexican revolutionist. Two Negro objectors from some Holiness sect in the Carolinas would not mix with us. I sent candy to them but they did not respond. We were not religious and I suppose we shocked them. My especial friend was William McCoy of the McCoy-Hatfield feudists in Kentucky. He claimed to have killed six Hatfields. He could not write and I wrote his letters home for him. He had started out with Phillips, a friend, to shoot up the government when he heard that a war was on. The warden told me he was afraid of him.

Before the transfer had come through for my work on the paint gang I had worked with hundreds of others on the construction gang, wheeling "Georgia buggies," a slang for wheelbarrows, full of concrete mixture and pouring it into the foundation walls for a mill to make duck for mail sacks. There were about 80 of us in a line. The platforms had been built in such a way that we had to make a mighty run to get to the top. Complaining did no good. So John, the "wob" from Australia and I took turns slowing up the line; stopping to tie a shoe lace, to look intently at the wheel as if something was wrong with it, etc. About the time one of us would have the whole line waiting he would behave and the other one would take up the sabotage action. One afternoon of this and the boss took the hint and made the runways like they should have been in the first place. . . .

. . . A white man and a Negro had been killed by guards and I was incensed about it. My cell mates laughed and said I should worry about the living, for the dead were dead and no one could do anything about it. That if I wanted anything to do I should raise a fuss about the poor fish served on Fridays by the new mess guard, who was accused of making his rake-off by charging for good food and giving us junk. Accordingly I got cardboard from John Dunn and painted signs which I put up in all of the toilets around the place telling the prisoners to work on Fridays, but to stay in their cells and refuse to go to dinner or to eat the rotten fish. The guards and stoolpigeons tore the signs down, but I made others and put them up. The first Friday 20 of us stayed in our cells. The guards came around and asked us if we were sick. We said we were sick of that damn fish. The next Friday 200 stayed in their cells; and the next Friday 600. That was too many people thinking alike, so on the next Thursday the warden came to the second mess and said that those who did not come to dinner the next day would be put in the hole. Some kid squeaked out in a shrill voice: "You can't do it warden; there's only 40 solitary cells and there's a thousand of us." The next day 900 out of the 1,100 who ate at this shift stayed in their cells.

The next Monday I was called to the office and was told that I had been seen plotting to blow up the prison with dynamite, and was promptly sent to the dark hole. This was on June 21,

1918. I was left in my underwear, and lying in the small, three cornered, dark hole. I got a slice of cornbread and a cup of water each day. I kept a count of the days as I heard the men marching to work, and at the end of ten days I was put in the light hole. White bread, which I got then, tasted like cake. This cell was on the ground floor, back of the deputy's office. It was about 18 feet long, 15 feet high, and 6 feet wide. A small dirty window near the top to the east faced a tall building, which kept sunlight from coming in, except on very bright days. A bunk was attached to the wall to the right; a plain chair and a small table, with a spoon, plate, and cup on it. There was a toilet; and a wash basin attached to the wall. A small 20 watt light was screwed in the high ceiling and was turned off and on from the outside. There was a door of bars and an extra wooden door with a funnel shaped peephole through which guards could watch me at any time. I walked around examining my new home. The cell was exactly 8½ steps from corner to corner. The walls were dirty, and initials and home made calendars with days crossed off had been left by former inmates.

After the dark hole this cell was a relief. A Negro lifer brought in meals, three times a day, and ladled grits, beans, raisins, etc. out of a large bucket onto my plate, while Johnson, the fat guard, stood at the door. The Negro found out that I did not eat meat and he always grabbed my portion. Perhaps this helped him in his favorable attitude toward me, for he gave me notes and candy from Berkman and Dunn, and took my notes in return. The first morning I said "hello" to the guard, but he did not answer me; after a few days of silence on his part I ceased to bother him with a greeting.

When I had first come to prison I had met the Protestant chaplain. My red-headed cousin Georgia, who was his daughter-in-law, had told him about me. He wanted to know what church I belonged to, and when I told him I was an atheist he would have nothing to do with me, even when I was in solitary.

Catholics were taken care of by the priest and the Protestant had all the rest, so I sent a note to him for a Bible to read in solitary, for I was not allowed anything else, or to send or receive mail. After a few weeks a Bible with good print and maps and references in the back was sent to me. After a few days this was taken away and one with very small print and no maps was given to me in its place. I asked Johnson, the guard, why I was given a Bible with small print, as this was more difficult to read with the small light 15 feet above me, and he simply grunted. The colored trusty later spoke, down in his throat without moving his lips, in the manner we all learned, and told me that anything was done which would make it more difficult for those in solitary. I do not think that the chaplain had anything to do with this; probably the deputy or the guard took this means of teasing one of their caged animals. You hear the groans of fellow prisoners and when you do not know how many months you may remain in solitary you have a weight over you that precludes any joyfulness of spirit.

Here is the way my day went in solitary:

I hear the six o'clock gong ring for the early mess. I know at 7:20 I will get my mush. I am not sleepy, but I stretch out and relax. In a minute I wash and pull on my few articles of clothing. I pick up my chair and swing it thirty times-up-right-left-down, up-right-left-down. Then I walk 100 steps back and forth in my cell—arms-up-arms-out-arms-clenched-arms-down, as I walk back and forth. This I repeat several times. It is now 7 o'clock. I make my bed and then wash my face and hands again. Then I hear the clanging of the door and I know that breakfast is on the way. I hear the doors open and shut and the jangling of the keys and the rattling of utensils. I sit and watch the door like a cat watching a mouse. The shadows of the guard and the Negro trusty lengthen under my door; the key turns in the lock; the wooden door opens and Johnson, the fat guard, stands back after he has opened the iron barred door. The Negro steps in and ladles out my oatmeal, hands me a couple slices of bread, and pours out a large cup of coffee. To-day he has no note for me; tomorrow he may have one. He smiles to me as he turns his back to Johnson and I smile in return. I look up at Johnson but he scowls; no fraternizing it seems. The trusty leaves and the doors are locked. I am not very hungry, and I prolong the breakfast as much as possible to take up my time. At last the food is gone. I leisurely wash the dishes and dry them. Perhaps I spin my plate a dozen times, and see how long I can count before it falls to the floor off the table. I lean back in my chair and think of Selma, my girl in Milwaukee, and of my folks at home. Then I realize that I am within these four walls: a jail in a jail. I walk back and forth for 5 or 10 minutes and then throw myself on my bunk; take off my shoes and hunch up on my bunk. In a few minutes I am restless and turn on my side. I hear the men marching to work and stand near the outer wall hoping to hear a word or two but I only hear mumbled voices and the shouts of the guards. I hear the whistle of the train in the distance. I kneel by the door and strain my eyes seeking to discern some-one in the tailor shop on the second floor next door, but every-thing is a blur. I walk around the walls reading the poetry I have written on the wall and all the inscriptions others have engraved.

I try to figure out what the possible history of this or that initial may mean, but soon give it up as waste time. I hear the voice of the deputy in the hall greeting the guard in charge. It is now 9 a.m. and according to my schedule, time to read the Bible. I lie on my bunk for half an hour reading the chapter for that morning. Then I sit on the toilet and take my pencil which I found the first day hidden in a small crack in the plaster, back of the toilet. A pencil is precious, you either have one or you don't. The toilet is near the door and the only place in the cell where a full view of the occupant cannot be gained through the peephole. I do not want to be caught with my precious pencil. I place the toilet paper on which I have written my notes in the Bible and sit on my chair and study what I have written. Then I return to the toilet seat and write some conclusions. Then I lie on my bunk and with my eyes closed think over what I have read.

I try to sleep for half an hour but become restless and walk back and forth in my cell for a mile and a half and take my exercises. I spin my plate again. I look up to the dirty window many times but can see nothing. For fifteen minutes I look steadily, after I have noticed a bird flying near the window, hoping that it may return. But why should a bird stop by my dusty window? It is now 11:15 and the guards are outside watching the men enter for the first mess. I feel that this is the opportune time to write a few words, which I have not finished, on the wall. I sharpen my spoon on the floor and stealthily carve two letters when I hear a step in the hall and cease my carving. I walk aimlessly around my cell for fifteen minutes and then sit and wait for the door to open for my dinner. Beans, oleo, bread and coffee. I eat the beans carefully, for often I break my teeth from biting against the stones which are included in the beans. I again wash my dishes leisurely, rest on my bunk for half an hour, then become restless again and walk to and fro for a mile or two. I read for an hour as the afternoon passes slowly. Then make notes and think about the subject matter for a time. I hear the train at 2 p.m. I am tired of thinking and tired of exercising. I again walk aimlessly about my cell, examining the walls. Perhaps I take some toilet paper, wet it, and wash a section of the wall to see if there is a message written underneath the grime; perhaps I figure out a calendar six months ahead to discover on what day of the week Selma's birthday occurs.

I think again of those on the outside and of the radical movement. An hour passes by in this manner and I try to sleep for half an hour but turn from one side to the other. I hear Popoff rattle his chains and groan in the next cell. He is a Bulgarian, a counterfeiter. He invented some kind of a gun and offered the plans to the War Department but they never answered him. He does not speak English and did not explain his sickness to the doctor so it could be understood at once, and was put into solitary for faking. He had sent a poem to the prison paper and this was sent back. He sassed the guards and was beaten up. What with all this he thought if he knocked the deputy warden down someone would then come from Washington and then he could tell them about his invention. He struck harder than he thought and the deputy died. He got life imprisonment, but it was not supposed to be hanging by his wrists from the bars. He was not a pacifist or a radical, and when he called the guards names they strung him up.

I take strenuous exercises punching an imaginary punching bag; I try walking on my hands; I sing a song or recite some poetry for another hour. Finally a break in my day comes with the first mess marching by at 4:30. Supper comes and is soon over. I walk aimlessly around my cell. The guards change for the night shift. Now the other fellows in jail, outside of solitary, are getting their evening papers and mail; visiting with each other; playing games on the sly and having a good time. It is dark and the night guard, Dean, turns on the light. Again I read the Bible for an hour and take notes on what I have read. I rest on my bunk; sing some songs; perhaps curse a little if I feel like it; walk back and forth. Finally it is 8:30 p.m. and my light is turned out. I undress and go to bed. The lonesome whistle of the train howls in the distance. I lie on my back; then on one side; then on the other. Sometimes I cry; sometimes I curse; sometimes I pray to whatever kind of God listens to those in solitary. I think it must be night when the door opens and Dean flashes the light on to see if I am in my cell and shouts to the other guard, "o.k. all in at 10 p.m." I toss about, am nearly asleep when the bedbugs commence. I finally pass a night of fitful sleeping and dreaming. Again it is 6 a.m. and I cross off another day on my calendar.

I had read the Bible once when I belonged to the Baptist

church, and now that was all I had to read. I commenced with Genesis and read at least twenty chapters a day. I also walked what I figured was four and a half miles a day. Berkman sent me a copy of Edwin Markham's "The Man with the Hoe," and I learned it by heart and recited it aloud several times a day. For the first few weeks the time did not go so slowly, as I was busy planning a routine. I found that on one day, perhaps a Thursday or Friday, I would suddenly be called by the guard to go across the hall and get a bath. Meanwhile my cell would be searched for contraband. For three minutes at some other odd time in the week I would be taken across the hall to be shaved. It was summer time and I asked to have my hair shaved off to make my head cooler. I could not see myself and whatever the trusty or Johnson thought of my appearance did not make any difference to me. Once when I was going to get a shave I saw Popoff entering his cell with his head bandaged. This must have been the result of the blows which I had heard faintly the day before. He was mistreated for a year or more until he went insane. Selma and I visited him in 1921 at St. Elizabeth's Hospital in Washington, D.C. He did not recognize me until I said "Johnson, the guard." I sent notes to my sister Lola for the newspapers about the treatment of Popoff. I heard the chains fall which bound him to the bars and then the thump of his body to the floor. I was told that papers in Atlanta printed something about it but no official investigation was ever made. My mood was to curse the damned capitalist system, the guards and everyone connected with the government and prisons. Once in a while I would crouch by the door of my cell, on bright sunny mornings, and see the top of Berkman's bald head as he worked at his regular table by the west window of the tailor shop on the second floor of the building next to my solitary. I thought that if he did 3½ years in solitary, in Alleghaney prison, in a cell with slimy walls, I could do the balance of my time in this comparatively clean dry cell.

It was now nearly three months that I had been in solitary.

Fred Zerbst, the warden, came in and asked me to sign a paper. It was registration for the second war draft. I told him that I had not changed my mind about the war. He said I wouldn't get anything around here acting that way. I told him that I wasn't asking for anything around here: I was just doing time. He said that I would get another year back in the hole for this second refusal to register. I told him that was o.k. It was September 21, 1918. The warden came in again and said this was all the longer they kept prisoners in solitary and that he would let me out in the regular prison the next day; if I would not plot to blow up any more prisons.

"You know I didn't do that," I said.

"I know you didn't," he replied, "but what do you suppose I am warden for? If I had told the prisoners that you were put in solitary for leading in that food sit-down, all of them would be your friends. When you are accused of plotting to blow up the prison they are all afraid to know you. Why didn't you come and tell me about the food?"

"Why didn't you come in the kitchen and find out? No one but stoolies go to your office," I answered. He left hurriedly.

In about five minutes he returned, saying, "I forgot to ask you something, Hennacy. I'll leave you out tomorrow just the same."

"What's on your mind?" I asked.

"Have you been sneaking any letters out of this prison?" he asked in an angry tone.

"Sure," I replied, smiling.

"Who is doing it for you?" he demanded.

"A friend of mine," I answered.

"What is his name?" was the query.

"That is for you and your guards and stool pigeons to find out."

He stormed around my cell, somewhat taken back by the fact that I had not lied or given in.

"You'll stay in here all your good time and get another year, you stubborn fool," he said as he left.

I picked up the Bible and threw it in a corner, pacing back and forth, thinking and mumbling to myself: the liars, the double-crossers, tempting me with freedom and then telling me the only way to obtain it was by being a rat. This was bad enough, but to talk the Golden Rule and religion, as they did whenever outsiders came around. Love your enemies, turn the other cheek; fine stuff, after they frame you, and admit it. The world needs a Samson to pull down their whole structure of lies. Debs is arrested near my home town in Ohio for defending my comrades Ruthenberg, Wagenknecht and Baker who were doing time in Canton jail and he will come to Atlanta soon. He did time when he was a young man. He's not so bitter; but then, he's older, and won't allow the capitalist class to tramp on him either.

That night I was nervous and tore the buttons from my clothing in order to have something to do to sew them on again. I paced my eight and a half steps back and forth for hours and finally flung myself on the bunk. It must have been the middle of the night when I awoke. I had not had a note from anyone for a month. Were my friends forgetting me? I felt weak, lonesome and alone in the world. Here I had been singing defiance at the whole capitalist world but a few hours before, and had boasted to the warden how I would bravely do my time; now I wondered if anyone really cared. Perhaps by this time Selma might be married to someone else with a real future ahead of him instead of being lost in a jail. The last letter I had received from her was rather formal. Would she understand why I did not write; and could I be sure that some of the letters I had sent her had been received, with the officials opening the mail I had sent to my sister Lola? How could one end it all? The sharp spoon with which I had carved poems and my calendar on the wall could cut my wrist and I would bleed to death before a guard arrived. But then that would be such a messy death. Then the warden would be sorry for the lies he had told me and the tricks he had tried to play. The last thing I could remember before falling asleep was the long wailing whistle of the freight train as it echoed in the woods nearby.

The next day the deputy came to my cell and said that I was looking very pale, that number 7440, a man just two numbers from me who had come in the same day with me, had died of the flu, and that thirty others were buried that week. If I did not get out and breathe the fresh air it was likely that I would die sooner than the others, he said. Why should I not tell what I knew and get out? In reply I asked the deputy to talk about the weather, as I was not interested in achieving the reputation of a rat. He asked me if it was a prisoner or a guard who had sent out my letters. I walked up to him closely and in a confidential tone said, "It was a prisoner or a guard." I did not know the nature of the flu but thought that this might be a good way to die if I could only get it. Fate seemed to seal me up in a place where I couldn't get any germs. Late that afternoon I was called across the hall to take a bath. The guard accidently left my wooden door open when he was called to answer a telephone. I could not see anywhere except across the hall to the solid door of another cell, but I could hear Popoff in the next cell groaning and calling for water. He was still hanging from his hands for the eight hours a day as he had been for months. As the guard came down the hall he opened Popoff's door, dipping his tin cup in the toilet and threw the dirty water in Popoff's face. Then he came and slammed my door shut and locked it. How soon would I be strung to the bars? How long could a fellow stand such treatment? As soon as it was dark I sharpened my spoon again and tried it gently on my wrist. The skin seemed to be quite tough, but then I could press harder. If I cut my wrist at midnight I could be dead by morning. I thought I ought to write a note to Selma and my mother and I couldn't see to do it until morning. Well, I had waited that long, I could wait a day longer. That night my dreams were a mixture of Victor Hugo's stories of men hiding in the sewers of Paris; I.W.W. songs; blood flowing from the pigs that had been butchered on the farm when I was a boy; and the groans of Popoff.

The sun shone brightly in my cell the next morning for the first time in weeks. I crouched again by the door and saw Berkman's bald head. Tears came into my eyes and I felt ashamed of myself for my cowardly idea of suicide just because I had a few reverses. Here was Berkman who had passed through much more than I would ever have to endure if I stayed two more years in solitary. How was the world to know more about the continued torture of Popoff and others if I gave up? The last two verses of the I.W.W. prison song now had a real meaning to me as I sang them again. I was through with despair. I wanted to live to make the world better. Just because most prisoners, and for all that, most people on the outside, did not understand and know what solitary meant was all the more reason why I should be strong. I sang cheerfully:

> "By all the graves of Labor's dead,
> By Labor's deathless flag of red,
> We make a solemn vow to you,
> We'll keep the faith, we will be true.
> For freedom laughs at prison bars,
> Her voice reechoes from the stars;
> Proclaiming with the tempest's breath
> A Cause beyond the reach of death."

Two months later I heard the whistles blow and shouts resound throughout the prison. The war was over. The Armistice had been signed. It was not until then that I was informed in a note from Berkman that November 11 was also an anarchist anniversary: the date of the hanging of the Chicago anarchists of the Haymarket in 1887. I had ceased by this time my nervous running back and forth like a squirrel in my cell and was now taking steady walks in my cell each day, and also hours of physical exercise. I was going to build myself up and not get sick and die. I would show my persecutors that I would be a credit to my ideals. I had painted the ceiling of the Catholic chapel in flat work before I got in solitary, and had left no brush marks. The priest appreciated my good work. He knew I was an Irishman who was not a Catholic, but he never tried to convert me. Now, as I studied the Bible, I was not thinking of any church but just wanted to see what might be worthwhile in it. I had now read it through four times and had read the New Testament many times and the Sermon on the Mount scores of times. I had made up games with pages and chapters and names of characters in the Bible to pass away the time. I had memorized certain chapters and that I liked. As I read of Isaiah, Ezekiel, Micah and other of the prophets and of Jesus, I could see that they had opposed tyranny. I had also spent many days reviewing all of the historical knowledge that I could remember and trying to think through a philosophy of life. I had passed through the idea of killing myself. This was an escape, not any solution to life. The remainder of my two years in solitary must result in a clear-cut plan whereby I could go forth and be a force in the world. I could not take any halfway measures. If assassination, violence and revolution was the better way, then military tactics must be studied and a group of fearless rebels organized. I remembered again what Slim, the sort of Robin Hood Wobblie who was in on some larceny charge, had told me once to the effect that one could not be a good rebel unless he became angry and vengeful. Then I heard Popoff curse the guards and I heard them beat him. I remembered the Negro who had sworn at the guard in the tailor shop and was killed. I had read of riots in prison over food and I remembered the peaceful victory which we had in our strike against the spoiled fish. I also remembered what Berkman had said about being firm, but quiet. He had tried

violence but did not believe in it as a wholesale method. I read
of the wars and hatred in the Old Testament. I also read of
the courage of Daniel and the Hebrew children who would not
worship the golden image: of Peter who chose to obey God
rather than the properly constituted authorities who placed
him in jail; and of the victory of these men by courage and
peaceful methods. I read of Jesus, who was confronted with a
whole world empire of tryanny and chose not to overturn the
tyrant and make Himself King, but to change the hatred in
the hearts of men to love and understanding—to overcome
evil with goodwill.

I had called loudly for the sword and mentally listed those
whom I desired to kill when I was free. Was this really the
universal method which should be used? I would read the
Sermon on the Mount again. When a child I had been frightened by hell fire into proclaiming a change of life. Now I spent
months making a decision; there was no sudden change. I had
all the time in the world and no one could talk to me or influence me, I was deciding this idea for myself. Gradually I
came to gain a glimpse of what Jesus meant when He said,
"The Kingdom of God is within you." In my heart now after
six months I could love everybody in the world but the warden,
but if I did not love him then the Sermon on the Mount meant
nothing at all. I really saw this and felt it in my heart but I was
too stubborn to admit it in my mind. One day I was walking
back and forth in my cell when, in turning, my head hit the
wall. Then the thought came to me: "Here I am locked up in a
cell. The warden was never locked up in any cell and he never
had a chance to know what Jesus meant. Neither did I until
yesterday. So I must not blame him. I must love him." Now
the whole thing was clear. This Kingdom of God must be in
everyone: in the deputy, the warden, in the rat and the pervert—and now I came to know it—in myself. I read and reread, the Sermon on the Mount: the fifth, sixth and seventh
chapters of Matthew thus became a living thing to me. I tried

to take every sentence and apply it to my present problems. The warden had said that he did not understand political prisoners. He and the deputy, in plain words, did not know any better; they had put on the false face of sternness and tyranny because this was the only method which they knew. It was my job to teach them another method: that of goodwill overcoming their evil intentions, or rather habits. The opposite of the Sermon on the Mount was what the whole world had been practicing, in prison and out of prison; and hate piled on hate had brought hate and revenge. It was plain that this system did not work. I would never have a better opportunity than this to try out the Sermon on the Mount right now in my cell. Here was deceit, hatred, lust, murder, and every kind of evil in this prison. I reread slowly and pondered each verse: "ye have heard that it hath been said an eye for an eye, and a tooth for a tooth . . . whoever shall smite thee on thy right cheek turn to him the other also . . . take therefore no thought for the morrow . . . therefore all things whatsoever ye would that men should do to you, do ye even so to them."

I fancied what my radical friends in and out of prison would say when I spoke of the above teachings of Jesus. I knew that I would have to bear their displeasure, just as I had born the hysteria of the patriots and the silence of my friends when I was sent to prison. This did not mean that I was going to "squeal" and give in to the officials, but in my heart I would try to see the good in them and not hate them. Jesus did not give in to His persecutors. He used strong words against the evil doers of His time, but He had mercy for the sinner. I now was not alone fighting the world for I had Him as my helper. I saw that if I held this philosophy for myself I could not engage in violence for a revolution—a good war, as some might call it—but would have to renounce violence even in my thought. Would I be ready to go the whole way? At that time I had not heard of Tolstoy and his application of Christ's teachings to society. Berkman had just mentioned his name along with other anarchists and he might have told me more if I had had a lengthy conversation with him; but I never saw him again. I could see the warden's honesty in admitting that he had "framed" me. I could even see that the deputy had only been used to violence in his years of supervising the chain gang. I did not know much about the outside world and it was up to me now day by day to solve this problem of repressed hatred, and when I was finally released to see in what manner I could apply my new ideals to conditions as I found them. The most difficult animosity for me to overcome was a dislike of the hypocrites and church people who had so long withheld the real teachings of Jesus. I could see no connection between Jesus and the church.

I continued my study of the Bible. Popoff was still being manhandled. My teeth ached much of the time in solitary and I asked the deputy to allow the prison dentist to fix my teeth. The prison doctor gave one pint of dreadful tasting salts for whatever ailed a prisoner. Very few men would fake a sick call with this dose in view. However, the dentist could not give me a pint of physic for my toothache, and neither could he bring his dental chair to solitary. The deputy replied that I knew how I could get my teeth fixed; that was to tell what I knew; otherwise I could ache for all he cared. So loving my enemies was not altogether a theoretical matter.

It was now in February of 1919 and I had been in solitary for 7½ months. Mr. Duehay, Superintendent of Federal Prisons from Washington, and his secretary, and Warden Zerbst came to my cell. Duehay wanted to know why I was being held so long here. I told him I was telling the world of evil conditions in the prison and would not divulge the source of my outlet for contraband mail. He felt that I was an intelligent and educated man who was foolish to endanger my health in solitary by trying to better the conditions for a lot of bums in prison who would sell me for a dime. I told him I was learning to take it. I had read a poem in *The Appeal to Reason* years before and had remembered it and written it on the wall. He and the warden read it and laughed.

SURPLUS VALUE

The Merchant calls it Profit and winks the other eye;
The Banker calls it Interest and heaves a cheerful sigh;
The Landlord calls it Rent as he tucks it in his bag;
But the honest old Burglar he simply calls it Swag.

Duehay changed his tactics and began to swing his arms and berate me as a fool and a coward. The warden had called me names often but he disliked to hear an outsider do so.

"If he's a fool or a coward he must be a different kind, for no one ever stood more than three months in the hole without giving in. He must be a God's fool or a God's coward."

Years later I was to write an account of my prison life and call it "God's coward." Portions of it were printed in the November and December *Catholic Worker* in 1941. It must have seemed especial advice for those about to oppose World War II.

I did not lose my temper or fight back at the warden and Mr. Duehay; just smiled and held my ground. Suddenly Duehay turned to the warden saying, "Let's make out parole papers for this stubborn fellow. Half of the time I can't trust my own men. This Hennacy is honest and can't be bribed. I will give him a job in the secret service."

The warden nodded and smiled, I shook my head saying I wanted no job hunting down radicals and criminals for I was on their side and not that of the oppressor. The secretary of Duehay was taking all this down in shorthand. Finally they left. The next morning a runner came down from the office to measure me for an outgoing suit, saying: "The warden told us, 'that damn Hennacy wouldn't tell anything in 7½ months; he won't tell anything in 7½ years. Get him the hell out of here;

give him back his good time and let him go to his other jail.
He is too much of a nuisance.' "

The next month went very quickly. It was now March 19,
1919, and I was to be released the next day. That night the
deputy came in and said:

"Going out tomorrow, Hennacy?"

"That's what they say; sure a fine feeling," I replied.

"We give; we take. You tell who is getting out your contraband mail or you'll stay here another 5½ months and lose your
good time and then another year for refusing to register. You
don't think we will allow anyone to get by in bucking us, do
you?"

Tears came to my eyes as I chokingly replied, "I can do it.
Go away and don't bother me any more." After he left I wept,
but I was at the stage where I felt strong enough to take it.

The next morning after breakfast I wrote on the wall that I
was beginning to do the "good time" that I had lost, when the
door opened suddenly and old Johnson smiled for once, saying,
"Going out of this jail, Hennacy." I did not believe him; and
even while the barber was shaving me I thought it was some
trick to bedevil me. I was given my outgoing suit and an overcoat. It is customary for the warden to shake hands with those
who leave and to admonish them to live a good life out in the
world. A guard gave me my $10 outgoing money and a bun-
dle of letters that had come to me while I was in solitary, but
the warden never appeared.

When I walked out of prison a plain clothes man met me
saying that I was being arrested for refusing to register for
the draft in August 1918 and would be taken to the county
tower to await trial. We took a street car there, at the end of
South Pryor street and walked a few blocks before we got to
the tower. A second hand clothing merchant noticed my prison
clothes and asked if I wanted to sell my overcoat. I was not
handcuffed but I guess my white face from my months of solitary was sign enough to anyone as to my being an ex-convict.

I was ushered into a cell where Joe Webb, a mountain boy, also slept. He had been found guilty of murder, and was to be executed. Through influential friends I was able to get him a new trial, and he got life on the chain gang instead. I asked for radical books to read and among other books Tolstoy's *Kingdom of God Is Within You* was brought.

Debs had entered Moundsville, West Virginia prison to start his twenty years. He could not be allowed to receive letters from another convict so I wrote to his brother Theodore in Terre Haute expressing my admiration for one who in his old age was still a rebel. Sam Castleton, who was to be Debs lawyer in Atlanta, was also my lawyer. My case came up for trial after seven weeks. Castleton told me that if I was not too radical he might get me off with six months. I was asked if I had really refused to register for the first and second drafts and if I had not changed my mind and would I be ready to register for the third draft if and when it came along. I replied that I had entered prison an atheist and not a pacifist. I would fight in a revolution but not in a capitalist war. I had got locked up with the Bible in solitary and read it and became a Christian and a pacifist. If I had been locked up with the phone book, the cook book, or the Book of Mormon I might have come out an expert on these, but my study of the Bible had made me see that Christ was the greatest Revolutionist. And a few weeks ago I had read Tolstoy and had become an anarchist.

"What's an anarchist?" asked the judge. My lawyer shook his head and put his finger to his lips as a warning for me not to be too radical.

"An anarchist is one who doesn't have to have a cop to make him behave. It is the individual, the family, or the small co-operative group as a unit rather than the State." And, I continued for about ten minutes to quote Tolstoy to the effect that one had to obey God rather than man. The District Attorney, Hooper Alexander, an old fashioned looking southerner, came up to the judge and whispered, and the judge said, "case dismissed." I looked around to see whose case it was and it was mine. My lawyer seemed bewildered and so was I. I had approached the court this time with love for my enemy and had never thought I would get my freedom, for he allowed me to go 10 days on my own before I reported to the court in Columbus, Ohio, to do my 9 months in Delaware County jail for my first refusal to register.

PART VI

Trade Unionists

19. William Haywood,
Testimony Before The Industrial Relations
Commission, 1915

In this remarkable testimony before a government commission studying labor strife in 1915, William ("Big Bill") Haywood (1869–
1928) also sketched the story of his early life. Born in Salt Lake
City, he lost an eye at the age of nine as a child laborer in the mines.
Emerging as a leader of the Western Federation of Miners during a
series of violent strikes, he also helped to organize the Industrial
Workers of the World, or "Wobblies," in 1905. In 1906 Haywood
ran as Socialist candidate for governor of Colorado while imprisoned
on a false charge of assassinating the ex-governor of Idaho. Prominent both in the IWW and in the radical wing of the Socialist Party,
Haywood opposed America's entry into World War I and was arrested for "sedition" in September 1917. He jumped bail by going
to the Soviet Union in 1921. There, like Emma Goldman, he was
disillusioned with the first fruits of the revolutionary movement he
had sacrificed so much to create.

The IWW, and Haywood as its principal spokesman, are important to the history of nonviolence because of their thoroughgoing

*Testimony of William D. Haywood Before The Industrial Relations
Commission* (Chicago: I. W. W. Publishing Bureau, [*ca.* 1915]), pp. 3–5,
8–17, 23–24, 26–29, 35–37, 43–47, 54–56, 70–71.

syndicalism: the vision of a future society in which workingmen would control their own industrial destinies, created by the direct action of a general strike. In his testimony Haywood also stresses the need for direct action to ensure that laws are enforced, a conviction shared by civil rights workers half a century later. "Filling the jails" was a tactic introduced to America not by SNCC but by Wobblies like Haywood.

Chairman Walsh: Will you please state your full name?
   Mr. Haywood: William D. Haywood.
Chairman Walsh: Where do you reside, Mr. Haywood?
   Mr. Haywood: Denver is my home.
Chairman Walsh: Denver, Colo.?
   Mr. Haywood: Yes, sir.
Chairman Walsh: Where were you born?
   Mr. Haywood: Salt Lake City, Utah.
Chairman Walsh: And what is your Age?
   Mr. Haywood: Born in 1869—February.
Chairman Walsh: At what age did you begin work?
   Mr. Haywood: Nine years old.
Chairman Walsh: And in what industry, or what occupation?
   Mr. Haywood: In the mining industry.
Chairman Walsh: Whereabouts?
   Mr. Haywood: Utah—Ophir Canyon.
Chairman Walsh: Would you be kind enough, Mr. Haywood, just to sketch your history as a worker and a miner, up to the time you became a member of the association of the Western Federation of Miners?
   Mr. Haywood: Well, after the first short period, we moved from there back to Salt Lake City, where I worked at different kinds of work until I went to the State of Nevada, when I was 15 years old.
Chairman Walsh: Well, now, in a general way, what sort of work did you work at, between the ages of 9 and 15?
   Mr. Haywood: Why, I worked at driving delivery wagons,

as a messenger boy, in a hotel as elevator boy and bell boy. It was when I was in the latter part of it, the fifteenth year, that I went to Nevada, and went to work in the mines permanently.

Chairman Walsh: At the age of 15?

Mr. Haywood: Yes, sir.

Chairman Walsh: Will you kindly pitch your voice a little louder; the reporters seem to have difficulty in hearing you, and there are a number of spectators who would like to hear you. So you will speak a little louder.

Mr. Haywood: I went to work for the Ohio Mining Company in Willow Creek, Nevada, and worked there until I was 19; and then drifted around into the different mining camps of Utah, Colorado, Idaho, and back to Nevada again.

Chairman Walsh: Are you familiar with the formation of the Western Federation of Miners?

Mr. Haywood: Yes; being a miner, of course I kept acquainted with what the miners were doing and remember when that federation of miners was organized, and have since become acquainted with all of the circumstances that brought about the federation of miners.

Chairman Walsh: Will you please describe the conditions that led to the formation of the Western Federation of Miners?

Mr. Haywood: It was organized as the result of a strike that occurred in the Coeur d'Alene.

Chairman Walsh: What form of organization did they have prior to that time, if any?

Mr. Haywood: Local unions, and mostly branches or assemblies of the Knights of Labor.

The miners of the Coeur d'Alene had gone on strike against a reduction of wages, and the mine owners called in armed thugs, armed men from outside territory. There was a pitched battle between these guards and the miners, and in the course of the fight there was a mill blown up. This was charged to the miners, and the mine owners called on the governor for the militia. The militia was sent in there and martial law was declared, and nearly 1,000 men were arrested and placed in what they called the "bull pen." That was a hurriedly erected two-story structure built out of rough lumber, and these men were crowded in there with scarcely room to lie down—so many—with cracks in the floor above permitting the excrement from the men to drop on those below. The result of that incarceration, there were many of them who sickened and died from the diseases that they caught there. At one period of this strike an injunction was issued and 14 of the leaders were arrested and sent to Ada County; 2 of them, I think, were sent to Detroit to serve terms.

It was while these men were in Boise that they conceived the idea of federating all of the miners of the West into one general organization. After they were released, being in jail for six or seven months, they called a convention, that was held in Butte, in May, 1893, and it was there the Western Federation of Miners was started. . . .

. . . In 1902 and 1903 came the strike that is so well known as the Cripple Creek strike, and that strike was in the nature of a sympathetic strike. The men who were working in the mills in Colorado City, although entitled to the benefits of the 8-hour law which had been passed in Colorado at that time, were working 12 hours a day 11 hours on the day shift and 13 hours on the night shift.

This condition prevails in the smelting plants of Colorado at the present time, and in some of the milling plants. They went out on strike in September, I think, 1902.

Chairman Walsh: Was the attention of the authorities called to the condition—that is, that the law was being violated with reference to the hours of labor?

Mr. Haywood: Oh, yes, indeed.

Chairman Walsh: Was the law inoperative, or why didn't they prosecute the officials?

Mr. Haywood: The smelter officials, or mine owners, do you mean?

Chairman Walsh: Yes.

Mr. Haywood: Did you ever hear of a mine owner or of a manufacturer being prosecuted for violation of a law? Well, they were not, anyway. The courts don't work that way.

In the following March the miners of Cripple Creek who were producing the ore that was reduced at Colorado City, went on strike. . . .

. . . They were striking as they struck ten years before, for the enforcement of a state law. The laws at that time were inoperative at Cripple Creek. The militia ran the district. They threw the officers out of office. Sheriff Robinson, I remember, had a rope thrown at his feet and was told to resign or they would hang him; and others officers were treated in the same way, and some 400 men were deported from their homes. Seventy-six of them were placed aboard trains and escorted by soldiers over into the State of Kansas, where they were dumped out on the prairie and told that they must never come back. Habeas corpus was denied. I recall Judge Seed's court, where he had three men brought in that were being held by the militia. While his court was in session it was surrounded by soldiers who had their gatling guns and rifles trained on the door. He ordered those three prisoners released, and the soldiers went after them and they were taken back to jail. That strike was not won. . . .

. . . It was during the period of those strikes that the Western Federation of Miners realized the necessity of labor getting together in one big union. We were on strike in Cripple Creek, the miners; the mill men were on strike in Colorado Springs. There were scabs in the mines and scabs in the mills, and there were union railroaders that were the connecting link between those two propositions. There seemed to be no hope for such a thing as that among any of the existing labor organizations, and in 1905 the officials of the Western Federation of Miners took part in a conference we called—the convention of the Industrial Workers of the World. That convention was held in Chicago in June, 1905, and the Western Federation of Miners, among other labor organizations, became a part of that movement. . . . The Industrial Workers, when organized, became first involved in a strike of serious proportions at McKees Rocks, Pa. There was the first time that we went up against what were called the Cossacks, the black plague of that State. The Industrial Workers met them on a different basis to what other labor organizations had done, and told them, "For every man you kill of us, we will kill one of you," and with the death of one or two of the Cossacks their brutality became less.

I am trying to think of these incidents in sequence, as near as I can.

I think the next instance where the Industrial Workers had to contend with the law was perhaps the free speech fight in Spokane, where the members of the organization insisted on speaking on the streets in front of the employment agency offices. They were telling what the employment sharks—what they were doing; how they would employ men; that these men would go up to take jobs that they had picked for them; that they would be discharged and other gangs sent out. The authorities of the city took up the side of the employment sharks, and between 500 and 600 men and women, members of the organization, were thrown into prison. Several of them were killed. They were put in the hot box and then removed and put into a cold cell. Several died from pneumonia. They got no relief from the court, but, as the members of the organization persisted in carrying on the fight, finally the City of Spokane compromised by saying that they would let them all out of jail provided that the organization would not prosecute certain cases that had been made against the officers. I think that it was the following year that the free speech fight occurred in Fresno, California. There the authorities started to arrest men merely for speaking on the street corner, not causing a congestion of traffic. If I have it correctly, there was between 150 and 200 men thrown into prison there. They were crowded to more than the capacity of the prison. The hose of the fire department was turned on them. I am told that one night they were compelled to stand up to their knees in water, but they won that fight. . . .

. . . I think this will bring us down to the time of the Lawrence strike, in which the Industrial Workers took charge. There, of course, as everywhere, I might say, that I have seen courts in action; they took the side of the capitalists. There were between 800 and 900 people arrested—men and women, girls and boys—there were some convictions, but a small proportion for the large number that were arrested. In Massachusetts they have a system of State Police, something similar to that of Pennsylvania, though they are not mounted. When the strike was called the State police came, and the park police, the municipal police from other cities, and then they brought in the militia. Several of the strikers were killed, none of the employers were, but they arrested two of the leaders of the strike for the death of Anna ———; she was one of the girls that was on strike. They had those men in jail for nine months and would probably have convicted them if it had not been for the general strike on the part of the workers. After the strike had been settled and the demands had been gained, they added to their former demands that Ettor, Caruso, and Giovannitti be released from prison; they were finally acquitted. During the Lawrence strike there were strikes at Clinton and many other places in the textile industry.

At Clinton the police were again used by the mill owners, and they shot into a crowd of striking girls, wounding many of them seriously. In Little Falls the same treatment was accorded the strikers by the police, which is also true of the great strike at Paterson. Nearly everyone is acquainted with the details of that strike and its outcome.

Since the Paterson strike there has been trouble in Wheatland, California, where members of the Industrial Workers of the World organized 2,500 hop pickers, asking for better conditions in the hop fields of the Durst Brothers ranches. As the outcome of that demand two young married men, Ford and Suhr were arrested and charged with the killing of the district attorney. They were convicted, and have been sentenced to prison for life terms.

This, I think, briefly outlines the main strikes of the organization that I have been affiliated with and, I think, clearly portrays a condition that this commission should understand, and that is that there is a class struggle in society, with workers on one side of that struggle and the capitalists on the other; that the workers have nothing but their labor power and the capitalists have the control of and the influence of all branches of government—legislative, executive, and judicial; that they have on their side of the question all of the forces of law; they can hire detectives, they can have the police force for the asking or the militia, or the Regular Army.

There are workers who have come to the conclusion that there is only one way to win this battle. We don't agree at all with the statement that you heard reiterated here day after day—that there is an indentity of interests between capital and labor. We say to you frankly that there can be no identity of interests between labor, who produces all by their own labor power and their brains, and such men as John D. Rockefeller, Morgan, and their stockholders, who neither by brain or muscle or by any other effort contribute to the productivity of the industries that they own. We say that this struggle will go on in spite of anything that this commission can do or anything that you may recommend to Congress; that the struggle between the working class and the capitalist class is an inevitable battle; that it is a fight for what the capitalistic class has control of—the means of life, the tools and machinery of production. These, we contend should be in the hands of and controlled by the working class alone, independent of anything that capitalists and their shareholders and stockholders may say to the contrary.

Personally, I don't think that this can be done by political action. First, for the very good reason that the wage earner or producing class are in the minority; second, that they are not educated in the game of politics; that their life is altogether industrial. That while they are the only valuable unit of society, still their efforts must be confined to the jobs where they work. A dream that I have in the morning and at night and during the day is that there will be a new society sometime in which there will be no battle between capitalist and wage earner, but that every man will have free access to land and its resources. In that day there will be no political government, there will be no States, and Congress will not be composed of lawyers and preachers as it is now, but it will be composed of experts of the different branches of industry, who will come together for the purpose of discussing the welfare of all the people and discussing the means by which the machinery can be made the slave of the people instead of a part of the people being made the slave of machinery or the owners of machinery.

I believe that there will come a time when the workers will realize what the few of us are striving for—and that is industrial freedom.

Chairman Walsh: In how many of these places that you have spoken of—

Commissioner O'Connell: Just let me carry out this point if you please, Mr. Chairman. You say you don't believe it can be done by political action?

Mr. Haywood: No, sir.

Commissioner O'Connell: Have you in mind some other method by which it can?

Mr. Haywood: Yes sir; I think it can be done by direct action. I mean by organization of the forces of labor. Take, for instance, the organization that you know, the United Mine Workers of America. They have about one-half of the miners of this country organized. At least a sufficient number to control them all. I think the United Mine Workers can say to the mine owners, "You must put these mines in order, in proper shape, or we won't work in them." They can compel the introduction of safety appliances, of ventilation systems, and save in that way thousands of lives every year. I don't think anybody will deny that they have that power to bring about that improvement. If they have the power to bring that about by direct action, they have the power to reduce their hours; they have the power to increase or at least to better the laboring conditions around the mines and have better houses. It seems to me there is no reason in the world why the miner should not enjoy, even in a mining camp, some of the advantages that the worker has in the city. And I think that free organization of miners, organized in one big union, having no contract with the boss, have no right to enter into a contract with the employer or any other combination of labor, to my mind. There can be each division of industry, each subdivision, be brought into a whole, and that will bring about the condition that I have described to you.

Commissioner O'Connell: You mean by that, that these economic organizations would create, or control questions of hours and things of that kind you spoke of, but as to the ownership, the right of ownership, what is the method that you have in mind of your organization in connection with the method of taking over?

Mr. Haywood: Taking over through the organization. If you are strong enough to exact the things I speak of, you are strong enough to say, "Here, Mr. Stockholder, we won't work for you any longer. You have drawn dividends out of our hides long enough; we propose that you shall go to work now, and under the same opportunities that we have had."

Commissioner O'Connell: Well, you propose by your strength and numbers to declare ownership?

Mr. Haywood: Yes; exactly; through the organized efforts of the working class. . . .

Commissioner Weinstock: Well, then, summing up we find that I. W. W.'ism teaches the following:

(a) That the workers are to use any and all tactics that will get the results sought with the least possible expenditure of time and energy.

(b) The question of right or wrong is not to be considered.

(c) The avenging sword is to be unsheathed, with all hearts resolved on victory or death.

(d) The workman is to help himself when the proper time comes,

(e) No agreement with an employer is to be considered by the worker as sacred or inviolable.

(f) The worker is to produce inferior goods and kill time in getting tools repaired and in attending to repair work; all by a silent understanding.

(g) The worker is to look forward to the day when he will confiscate the factories and drive out the owners.

(h) The worker is to get ready to cause national industrial paralysis with a view of confiscating all industries, meanwhile taking forcible possession of all things that he may need.

(i) Strikers are to disobey and to treat with contempt all judicial injunction.

If that is the creed of the I. W. W., do you think the American people will ever stand for it? . . .

Mr. Haywood: Read me that over again.

Commissioner Weinstock (reading): "(a) That the workers are to use any and all tactics that will get the results sought with the least possible expenditure of time and energy."

Mr. Haywood: Yes; I believe in the worker using any kind of tactics that will get the results. I do not care what those tactics are when the working class had arrived at that stage of efficiency and organization, I do not care whether it means revolution. That is exactly the very—

Commissioner Weinstock (interrupting): "(b) The question of right or wrong is not to be considered."

Mr. Haywood: What is right and wrong? What I think is right in my mind or what you think is right in your mind?

Commissioner Weinstock: "(c) The avenging sword is to be unsheathed, with all hearts resolved on victory or death."

Mr. Haywood: What that means is a general strike.

Commissioner Weinstock: "(d) The workman is to help himself when the proper time comes."

Mr. Haywood: When the proper time comes, when he needs it let him go and get it.

Commissioner Weinstock: "(e) No agreement with an employer of labor is to be considered by the worker as sacred or inviolable."

Mr. Haywood: No agreement?

Commissioner Weinstock: Yes.

Mr. Haywood: He never wants to enter into an agreement. Let me explain something about an agreement. I heard you talk to Kobylak yesterday. What would a union man say if some member of that union entered into an agreement with the boss? He would say he was a bad man, wouldn't he? And that he ought to stand by the rest of the members of his union. Now, we say that union has only a little nucleus of industry; we say that a union has no right to enter into an agreement because the rest of the men employed in that industry ought to be considered. We say that no union has a right to enter into an agreement with the employers because they are members of the working class; and finally we say that the working class has no right to enter into an agreement because it is the inherent mission of the working class to overthrow capitalism and establish itself in its place.

You can let that about contract and agreement stand.

Commissioner Weinstock: "(f) The worker is to produce inferior goods and kill time"—we will cut that out, that which relates to the production of inferior goods and killing time; that is out of the subject.

Mr. Haywood: Yes.

Commissioner Weinstock: "(g) The worker is to look forward to the day when he will confiscate the factories and drive out the owners."

Mr. Haywood: I would drive them in instead of out.

Commissioner Weinstock: I think that was your own quotation.

Mr. Haywood: I would make an arrangement to take every owner on the inside and give him a job alongside of me.

Commissioner Weinstock: Have you changed your views any since you delivered this speech on March 16, 1911, in which, among other things, you said this:

"I hope to see the day when the man who goes out of the factory will be the one who will be called a scab, when the good union man will stay in the factory, whether the capitalists like it or not; when we lock the bosses out and run the factories to suit ourselves. That is our program. We will do it." Are your views the same today as when you said that?

Mr. Haywood: I hope we can do that tomorrow.

Commissioner Weinstock: The next is, "(h) The worker is to get ready to cause national industrial paralysis, with a view of confiscating all industries, meanwhile taking forcible possession of all things that he may need."

Mr. Haywood: I do not understand the necessity of causing industrial paralysis; that is, when the workers are sufficiently organized they have got control of the machinery; you never saw a capitalist with his hand on the throttle; you never saw him on the stormy end of a No. 2 shovel; you read of him on his way to Europe and going down with the Luisitania or the Titanic; they are not interested in work. It is the workers who have control now of all of the machinery if they would only make up their minds to hold that control and maintain it for themselves.

Commissioner Weinstock: I take it, then, that you take no issue as a member of the I. W. W. with that statement here?

Mr. Haywood: No; I will let that go.

Commissioner Weinstock: And the last is, "(i) Strikers are to disobey and treat with contempt all judicial injunction."

Mr. Haywood: Well, I have been plastered up with injunctions until I do not need a suit of clothes, and I have treated them with contempt.

Commissioner Weinstock: And you advocate that?

Mr. Haywood: I do not believe in that kind of law at all. I think that is a usurpation on the part of the courts of a function that was never vested in the courts by the Constitution.

Commissioner Weinstock: Therefore you would have no hesitancy in advising your fellow I. W. W.'ists to do as you have done.

Mr. Haywood: I do not like to advise too much, but I would do it myself. . . .

Commissioner Weinstock: Let me see if I understand the distinction correctly between socialism and I. W. W.'ism.

As I understand it, I. W. W.'ism is socialism, with this difference—

Mr. Haywood (interrupting): With its working clothes on.

Commissioner Weinstock: As an I. W. W., are you a believer in free speech?

Mr. Haywood: Yes, sir.

Commissioner Weinstock: Are you a believer in free press?

Mr. Haywood: Yes, sir.

Commissioner Weinstock: Now, if your idea prevails and you went to bed tonight under the capitalistic system and woke up tomorrow morning under your system, the machinery of production and distribution would belong to all the people?

Mr. Haywood: Under our system it would be under the management of the working class.

Commissioner Weinstock: There would be collective ownership?

Mr. Haywood: Yes, sir.

Commissioner Weinstock: Of course, you are not anarchistic, you believe in organization, you believe in government?

Mr. Haywood: Yes, sir.

Commissioner Weinstock: Well, the anarchists believe in individualism, and carries it to the limit, without government?

Mr. Haywood: Yes, sir.

Commissioner Weinstock: And if you believe in government, then you would have to have a ruler—

Mr. Haywood: Would you?

Commissioner Weinstock: You would have to have superiors; otherwise, how could you have government?

Mr. Haywood: It has been run at times without bosses.

Commissioner Weinstock: Without any officials of any kind?

Mr. Haywood: Without any officials; it was the glass workers of Italy.

Commissioner Weinstock: Taking society as we find it, as you know it and I know it, if you have organization you have to have officers?

Chairman Walsh: Let us have the glass workers' illustration; I never heard of it.

Mr. Haywood: The glass workers of Italy went on strike, and while on strike they determined to run competitive factories, and they built factories of their own, owned by the members of the glass blowers' union. They went to work in those factories; each man knew his work—what there was to do. If you have any surplus and different interests to divide up, then there is some occasion for a boss; but if—suppose, now, that these men who are working in glass factories cooperate, as in this instance, and had some occasion for a boss, they would elect him wouldn't they?

Commissioner Weinstock: Yes, sir; they would elect him, that is guaranteed, and would put certain responsibilities on him to carry out certain rules and regulations or laws that they might adopt.

Mr. Haywood: I cannot conceive of much rules and regulations that would need to be applied with a man of common sense. There would be sanitary regulations around the mine. They would not shoot during shift; they would keep the places well ventilated and clean and well timbered. What other regulations do you want?

Commissioner Weinstock: If this group in this room organized, it can not reasonably be expected to carry out its object unless it elected representatives and officers to carry out its wishes.

Mr. Haywood: But you take a motly group like this; no one can carry out its wishes, because they change every time they turn around.

But you take the workers that work in one industry; their interests can be well carried out.

Commissioner Weinstock: Now, would you confine this great army of workers, organized in one body, would you confine their functions and their efforts to industrial matters pure and simple, or would you at the same time have them also deal with the political conditions, with the government of our municipalities, of our Commonwealths, or our Republic?

Mr. Haywood: There would be neither county or State or National lines.

Commissioner Weinstock: There would be no political sub-division?

Mr. Haywood: Only what existed in the community.

Commissioner Weinstock: That is incomprehensible to me, Mr. Haywood; you will have to explain it a little more definitely.

Mr. Haywood: What is the government of the country? The government of many cities have been changed to the commission form.

Commissioner Weinstock: Yes, sir.

Mr. Haywood: The commissioner has the fire department, the public safety, and public improvement. Those are the different divisions. Why not have that same thing under industrial—

Commissioner Weinstock: Have it nationally?

Mr. Haywood: You have no community that is national in scope.

Commissioner Weinstock: How, then, would you have it?

Mr. Haywood: Have this group or this community wherever the industry was located. Do you suppose under normal conditions that there would be communities like New York or Chicago with great skyscrapers sticking up in the air?

Commissioner Weinstock: What would you say would be the size of the community?

Mr. Haywood: Some 50,000 or 60,000, where the people in that industry would dwell. There would be no lawyers or preachers or stockholders like built New York. . . .

Commissioner Weinstock: Let me make sure, Mr. Haywood, that I certainly understand the objective of I. W. W.'ism. I have assumed,—I will admit that I have assumed in my presentation to you—that I. W. W.'ism was socialism with a plus; that is, that I. W. W.'ism in—

Mr. Haywood (interrupting): I would very much prefer that you would eliminate the reference to socialism in referring to I. W. W.'ism, because from the examples we have, for instance, in Germany, socialism has, or at least the Social Democratic Party, has been very much discredited in the minds of workers of other countries. They have gone in for war, and those of us who believe we are Socialists are opposed to war. So if you don't mind we will discuss industrialism on its own basis.

Commissioner Weinstock: Well, in order that I at least may better understand the purpose, aims, and objects of industrialism, I must, in order to bring out the differences and compare it with the socialistic doctrine—you may not believe in the socialistic doctrine any more, and I do not; but my purpose is, so that we do not have a misunderstanding of the meaning of words. Now, let me briefly state to you what I understand socialism stands for, and what I understand I. W. W.'ism stands for. The Socialists, as I understand it, is striving for the co-operative commonwealth, striving to bring about a situation whereby all the machinery of production and distribution shall be owned by all the people, where there shall be but one employer, and that employer shall be all the people, and everything shall be conducted substantially as the Army and Navy are conducted under our form of government. I understand that I. W. W.'ism believes in exactly the same objectives but differs in the methods—

Mr. Haywood, (interrupting): In the first place, I. W. W.'ism has no such thing as an army or navy, and certainly not as the Army and Navy are conducted at the present time.

Commissioner Weinstock: Well, I did not say that the Socialists believe in a continuation of the Army and Navy—

Mr. Haywood, (interrupting): Some of them do.

Commissioner Weinstock: I said that they believed that everything would be managed as we now manage the Army and Navy. All the people manage the Army and Navy—

Mr. Haywood (interrupting): But you make a statement that is not true.

Commissioner Weinstock: The soldier and sailor has but one employer, and that employer is all the people. Now the only distinction that I have been able to discover between the aims and objects of those representing the I. W. W. doctrine, and those representing the so-called socialistic doctrines, is the methods of getting to the ends. The Socialists believe in getting it through education and political action, and you believe in doing it through direct action—

Mr. Haywood, (interrupting): And education.

Commissioner Weinstock, (continuing): And the general strike.

Mr. Haywood: Yes.

Commissioner Weinstock: Therefore, the ends are the same, but to be reached through different pathways?

Mr. Haywood: No; the ends are not the same. Now, Socialists, while they present an industrial democracy, they hope to follow the forms of existing governments, having industries controlled by the government, eventually, however, sloughing the State. They will tell you the State is of no further use; and when industries are controlled by the workers the State will no longer function.

Commissioner Weinstock: Well, then, am I to understand this, Mr. Haywood? I want that made very clear to me, because if the objective is as I understand you have tried to indicate, then I have been laboring under a misapprehension. Am I to understand that it is not the objective of the I. W. W. to have the State-owned industries?

Mr. Haywood: It certainly is not.

Commissioner Weinstock: I see. Then there is a radical difference between the I. W. W.'s and the Socialists, Mr. Haywood?

Mr. Haywood: Yes.

Commissioner Weinstock: The Socialist wants the State to own all the industries.

Mr. Haywood: Yes, sir.

Commissioner Weinstock: And the I. W. W., then, as you now explain it, proposes to have those industries not owned by the State but by the workers—

Mr. Haywood, (interrupting): By the workers.

Commissioner Weinstock, (continuing): Independent of the State.

Mr. Haywood: Independent of the State. There will be no such thing as the State or States. The industries will take the place of what are now existing States. Can you see any necessity for the States of Rhode Island and Connecticut, and two capitols in the smallest State in the Union?

Commissioner Weinstock: Except that of home rule.

Mr. Haywood: Well, you have home rule anyhow, when you place it in the people who are interested, and that is in the industries.

Commissioner Weinstock: Well, then, will you briefly outline to us, Mr. Haywood, how would you govern and direct the affairs under your proposed system of 100,000,000 of people, as we are in this country today?

Mr. Haywood: Well, how are the affairs of the hundred million people conducted at the present time? The workers have no interest, have no voice in anything except the shops. Many of the workers are children. They certainly have no interest and no voice in the franchise. They are employed in the shops, and of course my idea is that children who work should have a voice in the way they work—in the hours they work, in the wages that they should receive—that is, under the present conditions children should have that voice, children who labor. The same is true of women. The political state, the Government, says that women are not entitled to vote—that is, except in the 10 free States of the West; but they are industrial units; they are productive units; from millions of women. My idea is that they should have a voice in the control or disposition of their labor power, and the only place where they can express themselves is in their labor union halls, and there they express themselves to the fullest as citizens of industry, if you will, as to the purpose of their work and the conditions under which they will labor. Now, you recognize that in conjunction with women and children.

The black men of the South are on the same footing. They are all citizens of this country, but they have no voice in its government. Millions of black men are disfranchised, who if organized would have a voice in saying how they should work and how the conditions of labor should be regulated. But unorganized they are as helpless and in the same condition of slavery as they were before the war. This is not only true of women and children and black men, but it extends to the foreigner who comes to this country and is certainly a useful member of society. Most of them at once go into industries, but for five years they are not citizens. They plod along at their work and have no voice in the control or use of their labor power. And as you have learned through this commission there are corporations who direct the manner in which these foreigners shall vote. Certainly you have heard something of that in connection with the Rockefeller interests in the Southern part of Colorado. You know that the elections there were never carried on straight, and these foreigners were directed as to how their ballot should be placed.

They are not the only ones who are disfranchised, but there is also the workingman who is born in this country, who is shifted about from place to place by industrial depressions; their homes are broken up and they are compelled to go from one city to another, and each State requires a certain period of residence before a man has the right to vote. Some States say he must be a resident 1 year, others say 2 years; he must live for a certain length of time in the county; he must live for 30 days or such a matter in the precinct before he has any voice in the conduct of government. Now, if a man was not a subject of a State or Nation, but a citizen of industry, moving from place to place, belonging to his union, wherever he went he would step in the union hall, show his card, register, and he at once has a voice in the conduct of the affairs pertaining to his welfare. That is the form of society I want to see, where the men who do the work, and who are the only people who are worth while—understand me, Mr. Weinstock, I think that the workingman, even doing the meanest kind of work, is a more important member of society than any judge on the Supreme Bench and other useless members of society. I am speaking for the working class, and I am a partisan to the workers. . . .

Commissioner Harriman: Mr. Haywood. I understand from what you have said today, and from what you have said before, that you do not believe in war. Now, if you don't believe in war, why do you believe in violence in labor disputes? One is war between nations, and the other is war between—

Mr. Haywood, (interrupting): You say I believe in violence?

Commissioner Harriman: Yes, sir; one of your contemporaries, I think St. John, I asked him the direct question last spring, if the I. W. W. believed in violence, and he said yes.

Mr. Haywood: But you said I believe in violence?

Commissioner Harriman: I thought you did.

Mr. Haywood: Probably I do; but I don't want it to be taken for granted without giving me an opportunity to explain what violence means. I think you will agree that there is nothing more violent that you can do to the capitalist than to drain his pocketbook. In that sort of violence I believe, and we are trying to make it impossible for the growth of more capitalists, and to make useful citizens out of the existing capitalists. I give you an illustration of what I think violence is:

In Sioux City, Iowa, last month the authorities of that town came to the hall of the union and told a man, a member of the Industrial Workers of the World, that the chief wanted to see him. He said, knowing his rights as an American citizen, he said, "If the chief wants to see me, tell him where I am." He said, "No; you will have to go to the office." He said, "Have you a warrant?" "No." "Well, I will not go." The detective went downstairs and got a crowd of uniformed policemen and they came to the hall and took this man and all the other members that were in the hall and went to headquarters with them. The men were put in jail temporarily without a hearing. They were all thrown into jail, and the next morning refused a jury trial, refused a change of venue, and were sentenced to $100 fine or 30 days in jail. One of them remarked to the judge, "Why don't you make it a hundred?" And he said, "In your case, I will just double the sentence." Those men were put in jail, and word went out to the other locals throughout the country, and footloose members started for Sioux City. They came in groups of twos and threes, and tens and fifteens, and fifties and hundreds, until the Sioux City jails, both the city and the county were crowded to capacity. The authorities thinking to make use of the labor power of these men purchased from Sioux Falls, South Dakota, three carloads of granite, which they expected the members of the I. W. W. to break, making little ones out of big ones. This they refused to do. They went on hunger strike. Some 75 of those men were 86 hours without eating. The authorities found that they could not do anything with them, so they appointed a committee, or a commission, to go to see the men in jail, and asked them up on what terms things could be settled. The men said, "Unequivocal release from prison, the re-establishment of the right of free speech," and one of the boys said, "Now clothes for the ones the 'bulls' have destroyed," and upon those terms they were released. Those men were released from the prison in the face of the fact that they had been sentenced to jail by judges. That I regard as action more violent than the discharge of bombs in St. Patrick's Cathedral in New York, because they enforced the rights that this country gave to them; they compelled the authorities who are supposed to uphold those rights in seeing that they were granted. I believe in that kind of violence . . .

Chairman Walsh: That is all, Mr. Haywood, and you will be excused permanently. We thank you.

Mr. Haywood: I have here the Preamble of the Industrial Workers of the World that I wanted to make a part of the record, I would like to read it in.

Chairman Walsh: We will be very glad to have it put in the record.

Mr. Haywood, (reading): "Mr. Chairman, in view of the attempt on the part of Commissioner Weinstock yesterday to create an erroneous impression relative to the methods and aims of the I. W. W., and in view of the further fact that Commissioner Weinstock read into the record in the form of questions propounded to me portions of a biased report on the

I. W. W. prepared some years ago by himself in California, I
desire at this time to read for the enlightenment of the commission the very brief Preamble of the Industrial Workers of
the World.

"I. W. W. Preamble

"The working class and the employing class have nothing in
common.

"There can be no peace so long as hunger and want are
found among millions of the working people, and the few who
make up the employing class have all the good things of life.

"Between these two classes a struggle must go on until the
workers of the world organize as a class, take possession of the
earth, and the machinery of production, and abolish the wage
system.

"We find that the centering of the management of industries
into fewer and fewer hands makes the trade-unions unable to
cope with the ever-growing power of the employing class.

"The trade-unions foster a state of affairs which allows one
set of workers to be pitted against another set of workers in the
same industry, thereby helping to defeat one another in wage
wars.

"Moreover the trade-unions aid the employing class to mis-
lead the workers into the belief that the working class have
interests in common with their employers.

"These conditions can be changed and the interests of the
working class upheld only by an organization formed in such a
way that all its members in any one industry, or in all industries, if necessary, cease work whenever a strike or lockout is
on in any department thereof, thus making an injury to one
an injury to all.

"Instead of the conservative motto, 'A fair day's wage for a
fair day's work,' we must inscribe on our banner the revolutionary watchword, 'Abolition of the wage system.'

"It is the historic mission of the working class to do away with capitalism.

"The army of production must be organized, not only for the everyday struggle with the capitalists, but also to carry on production when capitalism shall have been overthrown.

"By organizing industrially we are forming the structure of a new society within the shell of the old."

20. Joel Seidman,
Sit-Down

The campaign of the Congress of Industrial Organizations (CIO) to organize workers in mass production industries had as a dramatic by-product, the "sit-down strike." In a sit-down, workingmen not only quit work but also refused to leave the factory. Sustained by food from friends and relations outside the plant, sit-downers attempted to live and sleep at their work place until the demand for union recognition was granted.

Sit-down strikes reached their peak between September 1936 and May 1937, when 485,000 workingmen were involved. Like the activists of the 1960's, the strikers of the 1930's were accused of trespassing on private property. Like the later "sit-inners," the strikers maintained that human rights come first. Document 20, a report published by the socialist-oriented League for Industrial Democracy, graphically describes the methods and spirit of the sit-down technique.

Joel Seidman, *Sit-Down* (New York: The League for Industrial Democracy, 1937), pp. 3, 5–19, 22–31. Reprinted with the permission of the League for Industrial Democracy, Inc.

When they tie the can to a union man,
Sit down! Sit down!
When they give him the sack, they'll take him back,
Sit down! Sit down!
Chorus
Sit down, just take a seat,
Sit down, and rest your feet,
Sit down, you've got 'em beat.
Sit down! Sit down!

A new strike technique has swept the country, arousing enthusiasm among workers, and bewilderment among employers. In industry after industry, in state after state, the workers remain at their posts but refuse to work. No longer is it possible to introduce strikebreakers, for the workers are in possession. Nor are the workers readily dispersed, for they can barricade themselves in a strong defensive position. If strikebreakers or police storm the factory gate, they are clearly responsible in the eyes of the public for whatever violence may occur. The employer cannot too easily afford to alienate public opinion, nor risk damage to his machinery. And so the workers remain in possession of the plant, in much more comfort and security than on the picket line. . . .

The rubber workers of Akron have engaged in more sit-down strikes than have any other group of workers in this country, and probably in the world. Their attitude is well expressed by Sherman H. Dalrymple, president of the United Rubber Workers of America:

Sit-downs do not occur in plants where true collective bargaining exists. Where management does not attempt to destroy unionism by financing company unions, by the formation of vigilante groups, and by placing other obstacles in the path of legitimate union growth, there is such a spirit of cooperation between the union and management that cessations of work do not occur.

Recent sit-downs in Akron have occurred because management either did not enter into fair negotiations on certain grievances or deliberately postponed decisions until resentment of the workers grew so keen that they resorted to sit-downs as a last resort.

The fact that these grievances were settled satisfactorily immediately after the sit-downs definitely indicates that they could have been settled just as easily before if management had negotiated fairly with the union committee in their efforts to secure peaceful settlement of the issues involved.

It is our contention that the only way these sit-downs can be avoided in the future is through the proper application of all the rules of true collective bargaining in a spirit of fair play.

Early Uses of the Sit-Down in America

It is impossible to determine accurately when and where the sit-down strike was first used. It seems such a logical tactic for workers to employ that there are probably many unrecorded instances, each one short in duration, going back almost as far as our modern industrial civilization. The wonder is that its use did not become widespread much earlier.

In at least two American industries it has long been common for workers to stop work without leaving their place of employment. In the anthracite coal fields the breaker boys, whose task it was to remove impurities from the coal, early formed the practice of stopping work without leaving their places when they were dissatisfied. Similarly miners have stopped loading coal when they were not adequately supplied with timber for safety protection.

In the women's garment industry, as far back as 1910, workers have ceased operations without leaving the shop. Partly this has been done when a contract forbade strikes, the workers arguing that a mere stoppage was not a violation. These stoppages, as they were called, attracted little attention because they were usually settled within a few hours, and lacked the drama and publicity value of a picket line. Seldom, if ever, did the workers remain at their places over night, though stoppages often continue for several days. In the Schenectady, N. Y., plant of the General Electric Company, similarly, a sit-down strike occurred as early as 1906. In 1933, 2,500 employees of the Hormel Packing Company in Austin, Minnesota, sat down for three days and won their strike against speed-up, for shorter hours and better wages. Many other instances doubtless occurred in other industries. During the depression the unemployed in New Jersey and elsewhere, took possession of legislative chambers, in an effort to dramatize their plight and force more adequate relief policies.

Seamen used the sit-down strike on the Pacific coast early in 1936. Seamen on the Panama Pacific liner *California* had signed on at the Atlantic coast rates. In an effort to obtain the higher Pacific coast rates, they struck for three days while the ship was at the San Pedro, California docks. The men remained on board, but refused to work. Had they struck while the ship was at sea, they would have been subject to a charge of mutiny. As it was, they narrowly escaped arrest on that charge. The line refused to reemploy the strikers when the ship reached New York, and a long strike against the International Mercantile Marine Company was the result.

Sit-Downs Abroad

In a number of miners' strikes in European countries during the depression, the sit-down technique has been coupled with a hunger strike in order to force concessions from the employer. Workers do not deliberately starve themselves unless low wages have forced them to the point of desperation. The coal miners of Terbovlyé, Jugoslavia, reached that point in the summer of 1934. Whole families had lived on the equivalent of a dollar a week, and yet another wage cut was announced. Strikes and demonstrations were not allowed, and most unions had been outlawed. Five thousand miners entered the mine on the morning of July 3 and remained there without working or eating. Signs were nailed over the entrance of the shaft: "We, workers in these mines, decline all food until the latest wage reduction is rescinded. We prefer quick to slow starvation. Our families will not be much worse off without us." In the afternoon the company rescinded the reduction order, and the workers emerged triumphant.

Three months later, 1,200 coal miners of Pecs, Hungary, brought the sit-down, or rather stay-in, strike sharply to the attention of the world. The miners had lived for years at the bare subsistence level. For some time they had been working only two days weekly, receiving about $2 as their weekly income. They decided that quick starvation was better than the slow torture to which they had been subjected, and in October, 1934, they went on a hunger strike within the mine. For more than 100 hours they remained in the mine, without food or water. Five unionists who were sent into the mine by Premier Gomboes to confer with the men were held below as hostages. It was reported that crazed men were chained to posts to prevent suicide. Lajos Molnar, a 72-year old miner, described the suffering of the men in this fashion:

> The pangs of hunger maddened us to such an extent that we ate leather belts, and gnawed at shoes. We couldn't even have the mercy of sleep because the corridors of the pits are so narrow that we were forced to stand up on each side of the corridor.

The heroism and determination of the miners won concessions from the company that owned the mine, and on the fifth day the men emerged. Some were brought out on stretchers, and 110 in all were rushed to the hospitals. The men won a bonus of $3 to each miner who worked through the winter and a Christmas bonus of the same amount. A wage cut was averted. In February, 1937, a second combination sit-down and hunger strike was conducted by the Pecs miners.

In late October, 1934, 60 miners in Katowice, Poland, conducted a hunger strike in a coal mine to prevent the dismissal of the entire force and the abandonment of the mine. As the year ended 370 employees, including a number of women, barricaded themselves in a tobacco factory in Saloniki, Greece, determined not to leave until their wages were increased. The police surrounded the plant, and refused to allow food to reach the strikers. The water supply was also shut off, as was electrical current. A general strike was declared in Saloniki in sympathy with the besieged strikers. In the following summer 3,000 copper miners, in an effort to force higher wages, took possession of the Rio Tinto mines near Huelva, Spain. After ten days they came to the surface, but the strike continued.

In the fall of 1935 it was 71 Welsh miners at the Nine-Mile Point Colliery in Monmouthshire who conducted a stay-down strike. The miners were not far above the subsistence level, and even their poor standards were threatened by the employment of cheap non-union labor. In protest the men struck. They stayed in the mine slightly more than a week, living on sandwiches and tea sent down by their families and friends. They held daily religious services, and sang and debated to pass the time away. Meanwhile the strike spread, until 20,000 miners had stopped work. At the Taff-Merthyr colliery strikebreakers, with police protection, went into the mine and conquered stay-down strikers after a fierce battle 800 feet below the surface. Forty men were wounded in that struggle. The Nine-Mile Point strikers came up when the Mineworkers' Federation of Great Britain decided to take a strike ballot in all the English, Scotch, and Welsh coal fields.

Elsewhere in Scotland and Wales stay-down strikes of coal miners occurred in 1936. In August, 1936, both Polish and French miners conducted stay-down strikes, the former also going on a hunger strike in an effort to collect back wages due them. The French miners sought the discharge of overseers charged with brutality. Several months earlier rubber workers at Cracow, Poland, had conducted a sit-down strike in the course of which six were killed and twenty wounded.

In far-off India the sit-down made its appearance in June, 1936. Five thousand textile workers at Pondicherry, angered by the non-payment of overtime wages and the failure to raise pay, took possession of the plant. After a week the strike ended with victory for the workers.

Rubber Workers Sit Down

It remained for the Akron rubber workers to popularize the sit-down in the United States. According to Louis Adamic it was first used by ball teams of union rubber workers, who sat down on the grass or on benches and refused to play until they were provided with an umpire who was a union man. Later a dozen of them remembered this technique when they were dissatisfied with working conditions. The paralysis spread through the plant, and within an hour the dispute was settled.

The sit-down played a part in the circumstances that led up to the big Goodyear Tire and Rubber Company strike of February-March, 1936. Fundamentally it was insecurity, speed-up, the threat of lower wages and longer hours, and the refusal of the company to engage in genuine collective bargaining that caused the strike. The immediate cause was the laying off of 70 men in the tire division, which convinced the workers that the company planned to change from the six-hour to the eight-hour day. In protest against the lay-off 137 men engaged in a sit-down strike, whereupon they were dismissed. Mass meetings were called, and the company under pressure agreed to rehire the 137 and reconsider the suspension of the 70. Nevertheless a strike acquired momentum and mass picketing closed down the entire plant, with 14,000 workers idle. The strike was started spontaneously and was then officially sanctioned by the union.

The rubber workers are new and enthusiastic unionists. The sit-down technique works, and so they use it as soon as an issue arises. Their officers are urging them not to stop production without first bringing their grievance to the attention of the union and the company through the regular channels. During 1936 there was scarcely a week that did not witness at least one sit-down in the rubber plants. In a single plant in less than a year no less than 58 were counted, ranging in length from an hour or less to two or three days. Following one sit-down 31 Goodyear strikers were charged with inciting to riot, but the charges were later dismissed. As the rubber workers become more experienced and more disciplined unionists, the sit-downs over petty issues will doubtless disappear.

"A Million Frenchmen Can't Be Wrong"

What European miners and American rubber workers had done on a small scale, the French workers did on a mass basis, in one of the most amazing strike waves of history. The strike wave, though largely spontaneous and unorganized, could not have been better timed. Had it begun earlier than May, 1936, the police would have been sent against it, and large quantities of blood would have been spilled. Had it come later it would have weakened the Popular Front government. It started at the most opportune moment, when Leon Blum and his associates were about to take power. With the workers bringing steady economic pressure on the employers, the Popular Front government was able to enact a remarkable series of labor laws.

The strike wave began in the metal industry in the Paris area. The workers, most of them unorganized, struck because hours were long, wages low, and the cost of living high. Since the pattern of occupying the plants was set by the first group, all others followed. In all directions and to all industries the movement spread. Once the workers had occupied the plants, they turned to the unions for aid and experienced leadership. The unions grew remarkably. The National Federation of Salaried Employees, for example, grew from 18,000 to 220,000. The

French Confederation of Labor rose to 5,000,000, doubling its membership. Automobile factories, department stores, munitions plants, shipyards, textile factories—all were occupied. At the peak about 1,000,000 workers were in possession of their plants. The cabinet in adjoining Belgium warned its workers not to follow the French example. The movement spread to Tunis, the French dependency in northern Africa. Even before the great wave of sit-downs began in France, it is interesting to note, the huge Michelin tire plant had been occupied by its workers. The Michelin workers were familiar with the Akron strikes, and were directly influenced by them.

Despite the magnitude of the strike wave, there was practically no violence. The strikers maintained perfect discipline, and took excellent care of the plants. Disregarding the employers' pleas that he evict the strikers with force, Premier Blum insisted that their just grievances be remedied. Since the employers balked at signing contracts with their workers, the Chamber of Deputies rushed through legislation restoring wage cuts, establishing the 40-hour week and the right of labor to bargain collectively, and granting vacations with pay and special tax exemptions. Through this legislation the sit-downers of France have left an impress upon labor relations that will long endure. Later Blum, under pressure from the right, promised that further occupation of factories would not be tolerated. The workers, however, dissatisfied with the terms offered them, continued to occupy some of the plants.

U. A. W. A.; 1937 Model

The next chapter, one of the most stirring in the history of the sit-down strike, was written in the United States. Automobile workers took the new weapon, adapted and developed it, and with its aid brought the powerful and anti-union General Motors Corporation to terms.

A short sit-down strike had occurred in the automobile industry as early as spring, 1934, in the White plant in Cleveland. This strike was settled within several hours. The first strike in which automobile workers stayed in the plant over night occurred in the Bendix plant in South Bend, Indiana. On November 17, 1936, workers in several Bendix departments, influenced by the successful sit-downs in the Akron rubber industry, stopped work but remained at their machines. The company ordered all workers to assemble outside the plant, to decide whether they wished to work. To forestall this attempted lockout, the Bendix workers determined to remain in the plant until the management came to terms. In a week victory was won.

The same day the Bendix strike ended, 900 workers in the Midland Steel plant in Detroit sat down. This strike had been planned as a stay-in, to utilize the technique used so effectively in South Bend. This strike marked the first use of the stay-in technique by automobile workers in Michigan. Again the strike ended in a smashing victory for the union. In mid-December the sit-down movement spread to the workers of the Kelsey-Hayes Wheel Company of Detroit. Two short sit-downs ended with the company's promise to negotiate; on its failure to live up to its promise the workers sat down again, this time with the determination not to resume work until they had won their demands. There was also a brief sit-down strike in the Windsor, Ontario, plant of the Kelsey Wheel Company, Ltd., a subsidiary of the Kelsey-Hayes Wheel Company. In the meantime other sit-downs were occurring in Detroit, in the plants of the Aluminum Company of America, Bohn Aluminum, and Gordon Bakery. Thus the stage was set for the big sit-down strike in Flint.

In November and December, 1936, the campaign of the United Automobile Workers of America to organize the General Motors Corporation workers was nearing a climax. The auto workers enjoyed the backing of the progressive unions of the Committee for Industrial Organization. In the warfare between non-union mass production industry and the C.I.O., the

General Motors strike was the first major battle. Realizing that much might depend upon the outcome, both sides unstintingly threw their resources into the struggle.

In December the union requested a conference with the heads of the General Motors Corporation, to engage in collective bargaining on behalf of all the corporation's employees. This request was denied, and the union was told to take up grievances with individual plant managers. At this point, in the Fisher Body plant of the corporation in Flint, Michigan, a sit-down that began inauspiciously enough was destined to have far-reaching consequences.

On December 29 the union presented a proposed contract to the plant manager, in Flint, requesting an answer within a week. The next morning a sit-down began in the No. 2 plant, when inspectors were transferred to other jobs because they would not leave the union. Late the same day the men in No. 1 were alarmed to see dies placed on box cars bound for Pontiac and Grand Rapids, where the union is weaker. To protect their jobs they kept the line from starting up again, and remained in possession of the plant. Slowly the tie-up spread through the vast General Motors system, as more and more plants were affected by strikes or the shortage of necessary parts. By early February almost all of the 200,000 General Motors employees were idle, and the weekly production of cars had declined to 1,500 from the mid-December peak of 53,000.

Behind the General Motors strike there was a long record of efforts by the United Automobile Workers of America to bargain collectively, with delays and evasions on the part of the corporation. Especially did the workers rebel against the speeding up of production and the spy system employed by the company. Repeated efforts of the union to win recognition and obtain a union contract came to naught, and in the meantime discrimination against union members continued. Complaints were made to the National Labor Relations Board that General Motors had violated the law by discharging employees for union activity, using industrial spies, and dominating a company union in its St. Louis plant. Scarcely had the hearing gotten under way when the corporation sought an injunction to restrain the board from proceeding further. The injunction was denied in the federal district court, but a subsequent appeal and stay prevented the board from proceeding. Six months later, when the strike began, the hands of the board were still bound.

From the first the corporation officials insisted that they would not negotiate so long as the strikers held the plants. The men suspected a ruse, knowing that if they left the plants they would lose their power to prevent production. They agreed to leave, however, if the company pledged itself not to try to operate the plant or to move machinery while negotiations were in progress. The company refused.

Injunctions and Tear Gas in Flint

On January 2 the struggle entered a new phase. Upon the company's petition, Judge Edward S. Black issued a sweeping injunction restraining the union from continuing to remain in the plant, from picketing, and from interfering in any manner with those who wished to enter the plant to work. To obey the injunction would be to concede the loss of the strike. The injunction exposed the hollowness of the company's complaint against possession of its plant, for a stay-out strike would have been crushed as surely as the sit-down, had the writ been obeyed. Later, in Cleveland, the corporation was to seek an injunction against strikers who had left the plant to form a picket line. Small wonder that when the sheriff read the injunction to the Flint strikers and asked them to leave voluntarily he was laughed out of the plant. Three days later it was discovered that the injunction judge owned stock in General Motors. The union charged that he owned 3,665 shares, worth $219,900 at the current market quotation, and the judge admitted ownership of 1,000 shares. The union thereupon petitioned the state legislature to impeach Judge Black, for his violation of the statute forbidding a judge from sitting in a case in which he has an interest. The company, sensing its weak position, did not apply for the writs of body attachment which would have required the sheriff to attempt to arrest the sit-down strikers for contempt of court.

Suddenly, on January 11, the company changed its tactics Heat in the plant was shut off, and city police mobilized in the area. Company police attempted to starve out the sit-downers, attacking carriers of food and removing the ladders by means of which food had been brought in. The sit-downers, in return, captured the gates from the company police. The city police, who had cleared nearby streets in advance, then attacked in an effort to recapture the gates. Tear gas bombs were hurled against the sit-downers and their sympathizers outside. Strikers used the fire hoses within the plant to direct streams of water on the police and on the gas bombs. During the battle the sit-downers, who had until then occupied only the second floor of the plant, took possession of the entire building. For four hours the strikers fought the police, who used clubs, tear gas, and riot guns. Fourteen workers were wounded by the police gunfire, one of them seriously, and dozens were tear-gassed. Within the sound truck union organizers took turns at the microphone, shouting encouragement to the strikers, and giving direction to the battle. When the battle ended the strikers remained in victorious possession of the plants.

The county prosecuting attorney, who owned 61 shares of General Motors stock, jailed the wounded as they were released from the hospital, and obtained 1,200 John Doe warrants under which any strike sympathizer could be arrested. Seven of the Flint strike leaders were arrested, charged with unlawful assembly and malicious destruction of property. The union demand for the arrest of the police, company guards, and others who had been responsible for the attack was disregarded. In the meantime National Guardsmen were mobilized and sent to Flint.

At this point, the public was relieved to learn that a truce had been arranged. General Motors agreed to enter into negotiations with the union in an effort to settle the strike, and the union in return agreed to evacuate all plants held by it, whether in Flint or elsewhere. One of the most important matters to be considered in the negotiations was whether the United Automobile Workers should be recognized as the sole bargaining agency for the workers. Thirty minutes before the sit-downers were to march out of the Flint plants, and after other plants had already been evacuated, the union discovered that W. S. Knudsen, executive vice-president of the corporation, had agreed to bargain collectively with the Flint Alliance, a semi-company union, semi-vigilante strikebreaking organization inspired by the company. Regarding this as a violation of the truce, the union refused to evacuate the plants, and General Motors thereupon cancelled the scheduled conference. Several days later the corporation announced that 110,000 workers had signed petitions asking to be returned to work, but this number was exaggerated and the union showed that large numbers of the signatures had been obtained by intimidation.

On February 1 came the turning point in the strike. General Motors had taken the offensive, and the union had suffered defeats in Anderson, Indiana, and Saginaw, Michigan. Hearings on another application for an injunction were in progress, this time before Judge Gadola. The Flint Alliance was becoming dangerous, and there was some fear that the back-to-work movement inspired by the company might spread. Something had to be done to bolster morale. The union had again to take the offensive.

The Chevrolet plant in Flint, the scene of discrimination against union members provided the opportunity. Of most strategic importance was plant No. 4, in which all Chevrolet motors are assembled. A hundred feet from this plant, however, was the personnel building, headquarters of company police and hired gunmen. The strategy decided upon was to make a sham attack upon plant No. 9, in the far corner of the tract. At 3:30 p.m. a sit-down started there, and the excitement brought the company police on the run. At 3:35 the union men in plant No. 6, starting to No. 9 to help, were instead directed by union leaders in the sound truck into No. 4, where a sit-down simultaneously began. The Company police arrived too late, and the union was in control of the key plant, without which no production was possible. The Women's Emergency Brigade, made up of wives, mothers and sisters of the strikers, played a heroic and important part in the battle, both at No. 9 and No. 4. They smashed windows of the plant to keep the men from being suffocated by tear gas, and with locked arms barred the police attack upon the main gate of No. 4.

On the following day Judge Gadola issued the injunction requested by the company. Though not a stockholder, as Judge Black had been, he proved himself just as willing a servant. His injunction, similar in many ways to that issued by Judge Black a month before, was much more drastic. It ordered the union officers and the sit-downers, under penalty of $15,000,000 to evacuate the plants by 3 p.m. the following day, and to refrain from picketing and from interfering with the operation of the plants or the entry of strikebreakers. The sheriff was ordered to evacuate the plants within 24 hours. Again the strikers refused to budge, and the judge ordered them all arrested. Sheriff Wolcott, explaining that he lacked a sufficient number of deputies, refused to carry out the order unless Governor Murphy provided the aid of the National Guard.

Meanwhile sit-downers within Fisher Body plant No. 2 and Chevrolet No. 4 were in a virtual state of siege. National Guardsmen surrounded the plants, and refused to allow friends and relatives to speak to the men at the factory gates. A hunger siege at first imposed by the Guardsmen was lifted in less than a day. Reporters who tried to speak to the strikers at the gates were escorted out of the military zone at the point of bayonets. At Fisher No. 1, on the contrary, the strikers were able to receive visitors and come and go as they pleased, under no restrictions except those imposed by their own shop council.

The stumbling block to peaceful settlement of the strike remained the issue of recognition. The union, which first asked recognition as sole bargaining agent for all General Motors employees, later surrendered that claim and asked merely to be sole bargaining agent in 20 plants closed by the strike. The union proposed that, if this was agreed upon, all plants immediately resume operations, and all other points at issue be settled in conference. This the company likewise refused. Company spokesmen favored a plebiscite to determine the wishes of the men, but refused to recognize the union as sole bargaining agent in those plants where it might win a majority.

Finally, on February 11, an agreement was reached and the strike ended. Much of the credit for its settlement without further bloodshed belonged to Governor Murphy, who proved a skillful and patient mediator. Under the agreement the United Automobile Workers was recognized as bargaining agent for its members, and the company agreed not to bargain on matters of general corporate policy with any other group from 20 struck plants without the governor's sanction. There was to be no discrimination against union men, and all court proceedings were to be dropped. Collective bargaining negotiations were to begin on February 16. The union, on its part, was to evacuate the occupied plants, refrain from recruiting on company property, and exhaust every possibility of negotiating before calling any other strike. At the same time the company announced an increase in the average wage rate of five cents an hour, swelling its normal annual wage bill by $25,000,000.

The strikers hailed the settlement as a signal victory for them. For the first time the giant General Motors Corporation had been fought to a stand-still by its workers, and forced to engage in collective bargaining with them. After 44 days the sit-downers marched out of the plant, heads and spirits high, singing "Solidarity Forever." Out they came, two by two, with a large American flag at the head of the procession, to the cheers of 2,000 sympathizers assembled at the plants.

Other Sit-Downs

Akron, Detroit, and Flint were not the only cities to witness the sit-down strike in the United States. Late in 1936 and early in 1937, as its popularity increased, it was employed by many other groups of workers. Automobile workers in many cities, notably Toledo, South Bend, and Kansas City, have used the sit-down technique. Glass workers in Illinois, W.P.A. workers in New York City and Chicago, bakers in Detroit, rubber workers in Illinois and Maryland, building service workers in New York City, and motion picture extras in California have used the same method. Other companies to experience sit-down tactics on the part of their workers include the Aluminum Company of America in its Detroit plant, the American Casting Company of Birmingham, the Briggs Manufacturing Company of Detroit, the United Wall Paper Company of Joliet, and the Wahl-Eversharp Pen Company of Chicago. Even a daily paper, the Detroit News, has experienced a sit-down strike, in this case, of its printing pressmen. A chain of retail tire shops in Chicago has also witnessed a sit-down. Submarine builders, aircraft workers, and motion picture operators are others to use the sit-down technique. Salesgirls employed by F. W. Woolworth sat down in Detroit. There are other instances too numerous to mention.

Even hospital workers have used the sit-down strike. Early in February, 1937, maintenance and service employees in a Brooklyn hospital engaged in a sit-down, demanding $15 a month for the cost of living outside. They continued to serve and feed the patients, but refused to serve doctors and nurses. Fifteen workers in the hospital laundry barricaded themselves within it to prevent its further use. After two days a compromise settlement was reached.

What are the causes of sit-down strikes? The same grievances that cause other strikes. Wages, hours, working conditions, discrimination, speed-up, lay-offs, espionage—all of these have played a part. Some unusual grievances have likewise caused sit-down protests. Akron rubber workers sat down when their union president, Sherman H. Dalrymple, was beaten in Gadsden, Alabama, by thugs employed by the Goodyear Tire and Rubber Company. The Bendix employees in South Bend were aroused by favoritism to company union members and anti-union propaganda by company union leaders. Goodrich workers in Akron have sat down to force the removal of non-union workers. Hollywood extras sat down because casting directors were hiring society girls at low wages. Employees of the Brownhill-Kramer Hosiery Company of Philadelphia sat down to prevent removal of the machinery and moving of the business to non-union territory. Every type of grievance has produced its quota of sit-downs. . . .

Keeping Comfortable

Sit-downers have had a host of new problems to solve, not the least of which have been living in factory buildings. Food, sleeping quarters, and sanitation are matters that must be properly attended to if morale is to be kept up and health maintained for long. The necessary work must be done, and facilities for recreation provided. In all of these respects our experience with sit-downs, brief though it has been, is illuminating.

With hundreds or perhaps several thousands of sit-downers in a plant, the problem of food becomes urgent. The union must assume responsibility for seeing that the workers receive three meals a day. This is a severe strain on the union treasury, but thus far adequate meals have been furnished. Indeed, in some strikes most of the sit-downers have gained weight. One of the most important committees in many sit-down strikes is the chiseling committee, which seeks donations from food merchants. It calls for resourcefulness when the committee is unable to obtain the food for the menu as planned, and the cook must prepare whatever is brought back. The Midland Steel Products Company sit-downers in Detroit were aided by a daily donation of 30 gallons of milk by the milk drivers' union. Often the meals furnished by the union are supplemented by food brought to individual strikers by their families or friends.

Usually the food is cooked in a nearby hall or restaurant, and brought in milk cans, kettles, or other large containers to the plant. In the case of the Wahl-Eversharp Pen Company of Chicago, police refused to allow friends of the strikers to bring food into the plant. The sit-downers then lowered a rope from an upper window to the roof of an adjoining bakery, and obtained food in this fashion. The menu of sit-downers is usually simple, but adequate. Barrels, kegs, and whatever else is suitable are used for chairs, and tables are likewise improvised. Newspapers sometimes serve as tablecloths. Liquor is strictly forbidden.

Usually the cooking is done by a committee of the strikers' wives. In large strikes, however, a professional cook may be obtained. The cook in the Flint strike, for example, was sent there to help by the Cooks' Union of Detroit. He had previously cooked for four other sit-down strikes. For the Flint strike the union installed new kitchen equipment worth more than $1,000.

"The food goes into the factories in twenty kettles of various sizes," the cook reported. "The amount of food the strikers use is immense. Five hundred pounds of meat, one thousand pounds of potatoes, three hundred loaves of bread, one hundred pounds of coffee, two hundred pounds of sugar, thirty gallons of fresh milk, four cases of evaporated milk!"

In Detroit a cooperative kitchen was established to feed 800 sit-down strikers in the Bohn Aluminum, Cadillac, and Fleetwood plants:

The kitchen runs on efficient lines, not speed-up, in two shifts. About 50 men and women comprise the working crew; the first shift working from 7:00 until 2:00 in the afternoon, the second from 11:00 in the morning until 6:00 in the afternoon. Everyone attends the meetings held at 2:00 o'clock daily at I.A.S. Hall where the various committees make their reports. There is the kitchen committee, which takes care of preparing the food, with a chef from the Cooks' Union, Local No. 234, to supervise the preparation of it. Then there is a finance committee, with two treasurers, working in shifts, one from the Cadillac plant and one from the Bohn Aluminum plant.

Other important committees were the drivers' committee, which delivered the food, and the chiseling committee, which covered the city for donations of food or money. About two-thirds of the supplies were obtained in this fashion.

One of the important problems is to obtain comfortable sleeping quarters. Sit-down strikers in an automobile body or final assembly plant are fortunate in this regard, for they may sleep on the floor of the cars, removing the seats if necessary or arranging the seats between the conveyor lines. In the Midland steel plant some of the men tied burlap to machines, and so rigged up cots. Elsewhere tables have been made to serve. Sometimes cots have been brought to the plants by friends, and usually all have obtained blankets after the first night. Standard Cotton Products Company sit-downers in Flint built houses of cardboard packing boxes, and made beds of cotton padding designed for automobile seats. Their houses were in two rows, one labeled "Union Street" and the other "Cotton Street."

Most visitors to sit-down strikes have been impressed by the neatness of the men and the tidy appearance of the plants. One of the important jobs is to see that the factories are kept clean. The machinery is kept in good order, for the sit-downers wish to return to work as soon as possible after the strike ends. Often a former barber is found among the strikers, and he is made to resume his old trade. In the Kelsey-Hayes plant a wheelbarrow on a platform served as a barber chair. In one sit-down strike where there were women employees, a beauty parlor was opened for them by a former worker in such an establishment. Washing is often a problem, however, for in most plants only ordinary washbowls are available. One sit-down, in the Detroit plant of the Aluminum Company of America, had to be transformed into a walk-out because a number of the men became ill and lack of sufficient sanitary facilities made further stay in the plant hazardous to health.

Obeying the Rules

A certain amount of work is required, for meals must be served, the place kept clean, a watch kept, and discipline maintained. For recreation the men play cards, listen to the radio, or provide their own entertainment program. There are dancers, singers, and musicians in every large group, and often an orchestra can be formed. Frequently the sit-downers write songs about their own strikes. A bowling alley was set up in one plant, and horse shoes pitched in others. Basket-ball courts have been improvised, hockey games played, and boxing and wrestling matches promoted. Where the company has provided a recreation room, with ping-pong tables and other games, these facilities are used to the utmost.

Those who are studiously inclined may prefer to read. The educational director of the United Automobile Workers has organized regular classes for the sit-downers, with parliamentary procedure, public speaking, and trade unionism among the popular subjects. Even where no formal classes are organized the sit-down has considerable educational value, for the workers must set up their own community government, and solve the many problems that arise. In some cases church services have been held regularly. Loud speaker systems are rigged up, so that announcements made at the gate or in the nearby union office may be heard by all. Pep speeches are made in the same manner, and entertainment is similarly broadcast. Often the sit-downers amuse themselves, at the very start of the strike, by hanging up the "No Help Wanted" sign.

Where both men and women are employed, the sit-downers must be extremely careful to avoid the charge of immorality. Usually the women have been sent home, partly for this reason and partly because the hardships were more difficult for them. Often the married women had to leave in any event, because of their family responsibilities. Where women have stayed in the plant, strict chaperonage rules have been established. In the Kelsey-Hayes strike the girls were not permitted to leave their dormitory after 11 p.m. The sit-downers asked that two of the regular plant matrons be placed in charge of the women's dormitory, and this request was complied with. The girls in this strike were not permitted to go through a dark tunnel that connected two buildings. Sit-down strikers of the Brownhill-Kramer Hosiery Company of Philadelphia included both men and women. The latter entered the factory each morning at 8 and stayed until 6 p.m., and only the men remained in the plant all night. Most sit-downers have not permitted women to enter the buildings at all. In several cases, however, the overwhelming majority of the sit-down strikers have been women. This was true, for example, in the cigar plant of Webster-Eisenlohr, Inc., of Detroit. "This is a woman's sit-down," said one of the strikers. "The men are just around— that's all."

Discipline and morale are of vital importance. Those who do not conform to the rules may be sentenced to extra clean-up duty for minor offenses, and ejected for serious violations. In the General Motors strike in Flint, court was held each morning, with bringing in liquor and circulating rumors the most frequent offenses. Elsewhere it may be overstaying leaves that is most frequently punished. In the Standard Cotton Products Company strike in Flint the judge himself was twice convicted of breaking the rules, and had to do extra dish washing as the penalty. Sometimes foremen and other company officials are allowed to converse only with union officers, for fear that they may adversely affect the strikers' morale. In some instances subterfuges have been employed by strikers or their wives in order to get out of the plant. Serious illness has been reported at home, or a birth in the family. Where too many such cases seemed to be reported a check was made, and the member immediately dropped. In some cases foremen have visited wives of sit-downers, making false reports of illness or hardships within the plant, in order to break down morale.

Except when trouble is feared, sit-downers are usually permitted to leave the plant for short intervals, under rules that they decide upon. In most cases they are required to return by a specified hour, and a check is made as they go and come. If an outside picket line is maintained as well, the strikers take turns staying within the plant. In one case a sit-downer who belonged to the National Guard was released for strike duty with the Guard.

Visitors are admitted only after a careful check of their credentials. Usually a pass signed by a responsible union officer is required. In many plants everyone who enters must submit to a search for weapons, and a similar search is made of all who leave. A communications system calls to the gate those who have visitors. A post office is sometimes set up to handle the mail, which may be censored. Gates and doors are often barricaded against a surprise attack, with guards on duty at all times. In Flint, sentries, in six-hour watches were on duty twenty-four hours a day, with an alarm system to warn quickly of impending danger. Sometimes metal strips are welded across doorways and windows, to make police entry more difficult, and to provide protection from gas bombs and bullets. In some plants pickets assigned to make the rounds have had to punch the time clock as they went on or off duty.

Heat, light, and water are important to the health and comfort of the strikers. Usually the companies have permitted these services to be maintained. The cutting off of these facilities has precipitated some of the most bitter battles yet fought by sit-downers. In some instances the employer has alternately turned the heat off and on.

Race relations may be another problem faced by sit-downers. In the Midland plant in Detroit both whites and negroes were employed. Workers of both races occupied the plant, and worked together in harmony throughout the strike.

In Flint an amusing episode occurred while the sit-downers were in possession of the plants. Chevrolet plant No. 4 had just been seized and considerable disorder had occurred. Following the seizure everything was peaceful, and the many camera men on the scene had little to do. They therefore engaged in a baseball game, with the still camera men playing the movie camera operators. The umpires were several hundred sit-downers on the roof of plant No. 4, and the spectators were the National Guardsmen on duty. One team, displeased with a decision, sat down on the ball field, and promptly won a reversal, amid cheers, from the union umpires. Several innings later the other team was similarly dissatisfied. Its tactics were to sing "Solidarity Forever;" and the umpires, after joining in the song, again reversed the decision.

Marching out of a plant when the strike has been won or a truce arranged offers opportunity for a colorful demonstration, as in Flint. The Bendix strikers marched out in military order, headed by their own drum and bugle corps, and paraded to the union hall. After the settlement proposals had been adopted, the strikers paraded through the business section of South Bend, headed by the effigy of the Bendix company union hanging on a long pole.

A Typical Set of Rules

Sit-downers must govern their community, and solve each problem as it arises. Fundamentally these problems are similar, though new situations will arise in each plant. The rules adopted by the sit-down strikers in the Standard Cotton Products Company in Flint, Michigan, may be taken as fairly typical. With fewer than a hundred strikers, they were able to transact business in a full meeting held at 10 o'clock each morning, without the more complex and elaborate organization that a large plant would require. A strike committee of five members was placed in charge. Other officers included a chairman, a secretary, a judge, a press agent, and three clerks. There was a patrol committee of two, a food committee of two, a clean-up committee of three, and an entertainment committee of one.

Posted on the wall of the mess hall were the following rules, which were added to from time to time by majority vote:

Rules and Regulations

Rule No. 1. Any man who disturbs anyone while sleeping without good reason will have to wash the dishes and mop floor for one day.

Rule No. 2. Any man found drinking or looking for arguments will wash dishes and mop floor for one day—1st offense.

Rule No. 3. Every man who leaves must get a pass from the committee and check with the clerk. Passes must be shown to the doorman when going in and out, and on returning must check with the clerk. The doorman must obey these rules very strictly.

Rule No. 4. Doormen answer the phone and if the call is important he calls a committee man. No long-distance calls shall be made. All local calls are allowed. No profane language used over phone.

Rule No. 5. When photographers or outsiders come in no one speaks to them but a committee man.

Rule No. 6. Everyone must line up single file before meals are served. Dishwashers will be appointed before each meal by the clean-up committee. Every man must serve his turn.

Rule No. 7. Anyone eating between meals must wash his own dishes.

Rule No. 8. Every man must attend meetings.

Rule No. 9. No standing on tables.

Rule No. 10. No passes will be issued after 12:00 P.M.—except emergency calls.

Rule No. 11. Judge's decision on all broken rules will be regarded as final.

Rule No. 12. No conversation about the strike to the management. Any information concerning the strike will be furnished by the committee.

Rule No. 13. No more than a two-hour grace period allowed on passes. No grace period on a 20-minute leave.

Rule No. 14. No women allowed in the plant at any time.

Rule No. 15. No passes issued during meals and not until the dishes are done unless it is business.

Rule No. 16. All committees must attend meetings and report their activities.

Rule No. 17. No card playing or walking around or any disturbance during meetings.

What of the Law?

Unquestionably most judges will hold the sit-down strike illegal, under the law of trespass. The fact that the law of trespass was developed in a different social situation will be of no avail. Yet labor need not be unduly disturbed, for most weapons used by it were first held illegal. That was true both of the strike and the boycott. Indeed strikes for certain purposes are still held illegal in many states, and the secondary boycott is also outlawed. Picketing is prohibited in many injunctions, including those issued by Judges Black and Gadola in Flint. The continued use of a logical weapon, backed by enough economic and political pressure, eventually results in its being held legal. If lobbying by labor does not force old-party legislators to declare the sit-down legal, the foundation of an independent party of labor will accomplish that end. Workers should concentrate on defeating the employer, and not be too much con cerned about a law that is framed largely in the interests of employers and owners.

Attacks upon the sit-down strike have already begun, and many more may be expected. Governor Hoffman of New Jersey, for example, has warned that the entire resources of the state, if necessary, would be used to eject sit-downers. In his view, workers have no more right to take possession of a factory than gangsters have to take possession of a bank. Early in 1937, legislation to outlaw the sit-down strike was being considered in Alabama and Vermont. New York City police at first refused to intervene against sit-downers. In February, 1937, however, more stringent rules were put in force, under which strikers will be ejected and arrested if a formal complaint is made by the owner of a plant. In the absence of such complaint the police will not interfere, so long as the strikers are orderly. Much more liberal is the attitude of Secretary of Labor Perkins, who has expressed doubt as to whether sit-downers violate any law.

Wyndham Mortimer, vice-president of the United Automobile Workers, has thus stated the case for the sit-down strike:

Is it wrong for a worker to stay at his job? The laws of the state and nation recognize, in a hundred ways, that the worker has a definite claim upon his job; more fundamentally, it is recognized that every workman has a moral right to continue on his job unless some definite misconduct justifies his discharge. These sit-down strikers are staying at their work-places; no one has a better right to be there than have these men themselves. No one else, certainly, has any right to those positions. But the sit-down strikers have performed valuable services in those factories; General Motors and the public alike have profited by those services. To call them trespassers now, and to deny their right as human beings to remain with their jobs, is logically unsound and is manifestly unjust.

The union asserts that the workers have a property right in their jobs which is superior to the company's right to the use of the property. This theory will be rejected by most judges today, but in time it may be accepted as good law. The legal concept of property rights has changed and developed with usage. In Flint the union also argued that General Motors was not entitled to an injunction on the ground that it had itself violated the laws relating to collective bargaining, and therefore did not come into court with clean hands. Judge Gadola rejected this theory, though other judges have applied this general principle of equity to labor injunction cases. Gadola did not justify General Motors' actions, but merely asked whether one wrong could be righted by another wrong. This attitude is contrary to the principles of equity.

The sit-down strike has served notice on society that mere ownership does not carry with it all possible rights with reference to a factory. Those who work in it, who make it produce with their labor and who depend upon it for their livelihood, should likewise have a voice in its control. Those who invest their lives in an industry have at least as much at stake as those who merely invest their money. The sit-down strike, brings these facts forcibly to public attention. It is interesting to note that, in the sit-down strike, workers are re-establishing the control over the tools of production that they lost with the Industrial Revolution.

The ethical case for the sit-down strike has well been presented by Rabbi Edward L. Israel, former chairman of the Social Justice Commission of the Central Conference of American Rabbis. The problem involved, Rabbi Israel asserts, is one of the comparative emphasis of human rights over against property rights. The entire struggle of the human race from bondage toward freedom, he points out, has been a constant battling against vested interests.

The ethical issue in the sit-down strike concerns itself with the right of an employee to his job. According to the average standard of wages in industry today, practically every working family is only a few days removed from starvation. We must therefore ask ourselves whether the right of hiring and firing, at a time when jobs are at a premium, can possibly be construed to be surrounded by such absolutistic and unassailable property prerogatives that it can literally place within the hands of an employer the power of life and death over the men who work for him.

No social conscience will grant any man such a right. By the same token, the worker has certain rights in his job. If he feels that collective bargaining through a national labor union is necessary for the preservation of those rights, he is definitely entitled to pursue such orderly methods as may force the employer to meet with his representatives in collective bargaining.

The argument that a worker has a property right in his job has thus been stated by Homer Martin, president of the automobile workers union:

What more sacred property right is there in the world than the right of a man in his job? This property right involves the right to support his family, feed his children and keep starvation away from the door. This property right is the very foundation stone of American homes. It is the most sacred, most fundamental property right in America. It means more to the stabilization of American life, morally, socially and economically, than any other property right.

Sit-down strikes, like other types of strikes, occur when long-standing grievances of workers have brought them to the breaking point. These employers who recognize unions and deal with them fairly need have little fear of sit-downs. If all employers recognized the right of workers to organize and bargain collectively, and obtain a fair share of the fruits of industry, few strikes would occur. If, when a strike occurred, the employer made no effort to operate with strike-breakers, there would be no need for a seizure of the plant. Employers will make more progress by removing the just grievances of workers than by attacking them on the basis of property laws framed in an earlier social situation, and designed for other purposes. The sit-down strike is here to stay. Of that workers are resolved. The law may change slowly, but change it must.

PART VII

Conscientious Objectors, World War II

21. Richard Gregg, *Pacifist Program in Time of War, Threatened War or Fascism*

The shadow of war that fell across America in the late 1930's raised again the old question about conscription, pacifism, and military service that for many had never been resolved. This time the debate took place with added intensity because Fascism as well as war seemed an imminent danger. In the following selection, Richard Gregg, friend of Gandhi and author of *The Power of Nonviolence*, presents a program which seeks to confront both war and Fascism.

Two Assumptions and a Definition of Pacifism

This discussion is based on two related assumptions. The first is that pacifism must be an effort to create by non-violent methods a new and better civilization. Pacifism is not just an attempt to postpone any threatened war, nor merely to create a permanent condition of non-war, leaving the rest of our insti-

Richard Gregg, *A Pacifist Program in Time of War, Threatened War or Fascism*, Pendle Hill Pamphlet No. 5 (Wallingford, Pa.: Pendle Hill, 1939), pp. 1–8, 16–23, 26–30, 57–60. Reprinted with the permission of Pendle Hill, Wallingford, Pa.

tutions and customs just as they are. We must build a new order. All of the ways and institutions of such a new order would be very different from what we are accustomed to. They would be different not merely because that new civilization would be free from war, its accompaniments and results, but because it would necessarily embody much more respect for personality, interest in people, justice, tolerance, freedom, and love than we now have.

Our second assumption is the reason for this enlarged task of pacifism. War is an important and necessary institution of our present civilization. War is not just an ugly excrescence, or superficial illness, or occasional maladjustment, or temporary personal mistake of a few leaders of an otherwise fair and healthy society; war is an inherent, inevitable, essential element of the kind of civilization in which we live. For that statement there is ample authority from statesmen, economists, sociologists, historians and philosophers of the Left, Right and Center. War is of the very tissue of our civilization, and the only way to do away with it is to change, non-violently and deeply, the motives, functions and structures of our civilization. Such change is required in order to meet successfully the vast changes of our environment during the past two hundred years. We must alter many habits and change many routines and expectancies. We cannot eliminate all conflicts, but we can reduce their number and use non-violent methods of settling them before they reach a violent stage. Our present order produces war. We must make a new civilization. This is a task to stir men's imaginations and energies.

If you say that such a task is too difficult, I reply in the terms of the old Sanskrit saying: "Magic powers do not come to a man because he does things that are hard, but because he does things with a pure heart." Miracles can be accomplished by singleness of purpose and utter devotion.

If you say that we pacifists are too few to do the work, and we must not be presumptuous and foolish, the answer is that every great human movement was begun by a very small group of people, and often when the clouds were dark. The decisive work of the government of all nations, in both the political and economic realms, is done by a few people. If society is in any sense an organism, the great changes produced in the bodies of animals by exceedingly small quantities of hormones may illustrate this point. In the realm of physics also we know that an integrated and delicately balanced system of forces, some of which may be very powerful, can be greatly altered by applying quite small forces at proper times and places.

Maybe you will say that such a task as remaking an entire civilization is too long, that we haven't time, that we must first stop the threatening war, and that only after that has been accomplished should we take up the larger problem. If you say that, you are simply denying one of our assumptions—that war is an integral element of our civilization. We cannot abolish an essential feature of a system, unless we alter the nature of the system. Concentrating all our efforts on postponing war would not leave energy for the deeper changes which are required if the causes are to be eliminated. The so-called normal forces in our present society are not strong enough to stabilize the situation during a breathing spell. Deep changes must begin now, before war comes to us, in order to get our better civilization later, whether war comes or not. My opinion is that if we direct all our energies toward making the deeper changes, we would probably escape war; but if we try to suppress or postpone the symptom, war, the pent-up forces will soon break out still more destructively. International diplomatic agreements do not alter civilizations. They are too superficial and fragile to meet the end.

Even with the acceleration of modern social processes it would probably, for psychological reasons, take at least three generations to remake a civilization. Yet that very acceleration, together with the delicacy of balance of modern economic and social forces, makes it possible in much shorter time to escape war, provided we work at its causes.

So sure am I that the real task of pacifists is to remake the entire civilization that I feel that the very word "pacifist" is so inadequate a description as to be practically a misnomer. The makers of peace will have to deal with far more concrete and detailed matters than an abstraction called peace.

If these assumptions be true, and if war or fascism should come or be imminent in a country which does not have universal compulsory military service in peace time, what ought a pacifist citizen of that country to do? I am not fitted by knowledge or experience to make suggestions to people of other nations, though possibly in this discussion there may be something that could be partly adapted for their use.

Program for the Pacifist

PLEDGE NOT TO FIGHT OR HELP WAR

Before war comes, absolute pacifists of eighteen years or over, men and women, ought first of all to sign a written pledge not to support or take part in any war, and file that pledge with some appropriate organization.

Such a pledge is more than a public gesture of refusal to do something on moral grounds. It is an affirmation that the human will is free, that a man can resist the slavery and dictatorship inherent in war. It is a step toward the renunciation of all domination, a step in support of a deeper freedom and democracy. Furthermore, such a written statement objectifies purpose, gets it outside. One can look at it and realize more fully and clearly its implications, relationships, and probable effects. Filing the pledge with a pacifist organization commits the signer to new relationships and new efforts, brings into play his sense of consistency, of honor, and of pride, starts new consistent friendships and gains strength from them. Modern war is so highly mechanized that more energy is needed for making and repairing machines than for fighting. Industrial conscription will be needed almost more than military conscription; women can do many industrial and farm jobs; so women as well as men will probably be conscripted. For all these reasons, women as well as men should sign such pledges.

Those who oppose such pledging of individuals perhaps forget that the governments of the United States, Great Britain, France, Germany, Japan, and many other countries took such a public pledge in the Briand-Kellogg Pact of Paris. That Pact states that "The High Contracting Parties solemnly declare in the names of their respective peoples that they condemn recourse to war for the solution of international controversies, and renounce it as an instrument of national policy in their relations with one another. The High Contracting Parties agree that the settlement or solution of all disputes or conflicts of whatever nature or of whatever origin they may be, which may arise among them, shall never be sought except by pacific means."

Each government that signed that Pact asked by implication all of its citizens to uphold it in so doing; that is, asked each citizen also to refuse to go to war. This is especially true in the United States where treaties of the Federal Government with other nations are considered a part of the law of the nation. And since each government that signed that Pact maintains courts to uphold and enforce the sanctity of contracts and of solemn public oaths, no government can with moral consistency demand that any one of its pacifist citizens who has given a public pledge renouncing war, should break that pledge. If you say that such a pledge is contrary to public policy and therefore invalid, I would say that by the Pact of Paris the governments explicitly stated what their public policy would be in this matter.

It is true that the Pact of Paris does not end the right of the signatory governments to self-defense, nor the right of certain European governments to go to war to fulfill certain prior treaties such as the pact of Locarno; nor does it prevent the British government from fighting in certain undefined areas of "interest." These exceptions were imposed by various governments as a condition of their signing the Pact, and were accepted by the United States Government. Nevertheless, until the signatory governments expressly repudiate the Pact, it must be regarded as at least a solemn aspiration, intended to prevail in every instance within the range of possible governmental action, and to be heartily supported by citizens in every instance possible to them. The exception of self-defense is no exception to absolute pacifists, for they believe that modern war has demonstrated its inability to defend anything of moral value, and further they believe that non-violent resistance is the most effective mode of self-defense. The other exceptions do not apply to the United States Government or its citizens.

If you cynically say that the Pact of Paris was only a hypocritical fraud which the nations never intended to keep, as proved by the fact that none of them disarmed after signing the Pact, it is also a fact that the governments of the United States and Great Britain both continually protested against the unilateral violation of treaties and said that such actions were one cause of war. That they are one cause is true. If governments have failed in regard to that Pact, there is all the more reason for the individual pacifist to keep his pledge. Private citizens therefore have weighty precedent and civic obligation in renouncing war, and strong political as well as moral sanction for keeping such a pledge.

Another objection is that no one should promise to do certain things without knowing what the circumstances will be at the time when the promise is to be fulfilled. It is argued that such promises would make one live not by faith or spontaneity but by mechanical rule. But everyone who marries—vowing to love, cherish and honor the partner till death do part—makes

a partly blind pledge, as does also everyone who signs a prom-
missory note. They do not know what the circumstances will be
in the future. Furthermore, although in some situations complete, uncommitted freedom of moral choice and action from
hour to hour and from day to day may be desirable, in the case
of war this is not so.

As has often been pointed out, before going to war all governments suppress many pertinent facts and fill the news with
so much distorted propaganda that it is impossible for any person, at the time he is conscripted, to know enough of the facts
to make a sound decision as to the rights and wrongs of the
particular defense or aggression. Also by that time, since he
does not live in a vacuum, he will have become influenced by
the prevailing war passions. That influence is not conducive to
sound judgment, nor at such a moment does he have time
enough to weigh the various considerations and think them
through carefully.

Those who object to advance pledges against war apparently
do so on the basis that certain wars may be justifiable. Wars,
they say, have been fought for such noble ends as saving
democracy, for religion, for "honor," for national independence,
for or against communism, for or against fascism, and so on.
They seem quite willing to overlook the fact that in modern
wars the alleged reason for fighting is very rarely the real
reason, and that it is practically impossible to ascertain the
facts at the time when the decision must be made. But even if
the alleged reasons were true, I believe that modern weapons
and methods of war, monstrously expensive, destructive, and
indiscriminate, have ended the possibility of war's saving or
promoting anything of real value. In war democracy van-
ishes; religion (for those who fight or support the fighting)
becomes a vast unreality, inconsistency, and deception; political independence, if outwardly retained, is rendered nuga-
tory by dependence upon financiers and upon militarists; revolution is made much more likely; fascism enters the moment

war is declared; and the terrible impoverishment and breakdown of social bonds at the end of the war makes even successful and true communism or fascism impossible. I wonder
whether even self-respect or honor will remain when people
survey the wreckage.

Those who do not believe all this will probably admit that
the people who would support wars if they considered them
morally defensible are in effect inviting the government to
frame up the story so that the entry into war "this time" looks
wholly justifiable. In such feats governments have had much
successful experience.

Sometimes people refuse to sign a pledge against war simply
because they are unwilling to face the issue, think the problem
through, and make a decision. Their reasons against pledging
are rationalizations of their unwillingness.[1]

---

[1] Let me note here one form of statement for signature which has
proved to be psychologically effective in persuading those who sign it to
face the problem squarely, abandon their previous ambiguity, and come
through to a clear, sure position. Though intended for church members,
it could be re-phrased for those whose grounds for pacifism are entirely intellectual or social.

"A Statement by members of the Broadway Tabernacle Church of New
York City on the relationship of the Christian way of life to the practice
of war, to be signed by such members of the Church as desire. This
statement is sponsored by the Young Men's Club.

'I have quietly considered what I would do, if my nation should again
be drawn into war.

'I am not taking a pledge because I do not know what I would do
when the heat of the war mood is upon the country. But in a mood of
calm consideration, I do today declare that I cannot reconcile the way of
Christ with the practice of war.

'I do therefore set down my name to be kept in the records of this
Church, so that it will be for me a reminder, if war should come; and
will be a solemn declaration to those who hold to this conviction in time
of war, that I believe them to be right; and I do desire with my whole
mind and heart that I shall be among those who keep to this belief.

'I set down my name to make concrete my present thought upon the
question of war, and declare my purpose to think and talk with others

A pledge not to go to war or support war is not merely a promise the fulfillment of which comes only at some time in the future. Because of the deeper meaning of pacifism, such a pledge is a present choice of a way of life, and action upon it commences as soon as the decision is reached. It is almost impossible to be peaceful in war time unless you have made up your mind in advance.

The written pledge is a necessary step, but only a slight advance. Carrying it out is harder and still more necessary. . . .

Refuse to Cooperate with War Preparations or Governmental "Alternative Service"

Numerous European governments are now introducing various schemes for the protection of citizens against bombing attacks by enemy airplanes. There is real danger, if war comes, of its beginning without any announcement other than a sudden rain of bombs from the air. Events in Spain, Ethiopia and China

---

about it that my beliefs in the way of Christ shall become operative in this and in other questions which now confuse our thought and action.

. . . .
       Date   Signature
Remarks

'We expect and would appreciate your personal comments upon this statement, in case you have reservations about it, or desire to enlarge upon the principle'."

The young men who are pacifists and members of this church work in pairs. A pair of them call on an older member of the church and say that if there is another war, they will be called to go. They ask the older person to think through with them what their position should be. They present him with a copy of the above statement and ask how he feels about it and whether he would be willing to sign it. Some of the older people wriggle, but they find it very hard to dodge the issue and to avoid the necessity of doing much thinking they never did before. A remarkably large proportion of this church are now conceived absolute pacifists.

have shown how extensively bombing from the air would be used, and its terrible results.

The protective schemes take various forms:—"blackouts" at night, especially in cities, underground shelters, gas masks for as many as possible, plans for moving children and old people out of cities, and the enlistment of a few persons in every small urban area to inform people of that area how to protect themselves against bomb attacks—whether gas, incendiary, or high explosive—also to keep up morale and prevent panic. Registration of all citizens is planned for the stated purpose of measuring and supplying them with gas masks.

In Great Britain it is widely believed that these measures are futile and that the reasons alleged for them are false. A committee of scientists has pointed out that the gas masks are utterly ineffective against vesicants like mustard gas; that no adequate protection is afforded for the mass of the population against high explosives; that high explosives would spoil any attempts to protect buildings against poison gas. A recent book by John Langdon-Davies explains a new method of silent approach that was used in bombing Barcelona in March, 1938. There the attacking planes rose to an altitude of over 20,000 feet and, with their engines stopped, glided for over fifty miles to their destination, thus evading detection by the sensitive sound detectors. They dropped high explosive bombs on the city and got away before the warning sirens could be sounded. Photographs illustrate the destruction.

On the basis of such evidence it is believed by many that the whole government effort in this matter is meant to frighten the citizenry enough beforehand so that they will be pliable and accept all sorts of repressive measures proposed under the guise of safety. It is claimed that the real purpose of the registration is to have a list which can be used for militaristic, industrial, and civic control by the government the instant war breaks out, or for a fascist coup. Government spokesmen have assured the public that these arrangements are solely for safety, but history shows that in time of war governments often do not abide by their promises and assurances. Those who give the assurances as to how laws are intended to be used and limited are usually in the legislature; but those who carry them out are in another branch of the government, with different traditions and often far away. The wording of laws is sometimes unduly broad and even ambiguous. The government is a huge, unwieldy organization, poorly coördinated. Those at the top who plan broad policies are often far-sighted, sensitive, and statesmanlike; but those who execute the laws in detail are sometimes short-sighted, petty, domineering, and callous, and have very different ideas as to the purposes and limitations of a law from those who framed it. In war time the pressure for results is tremendous, and mass excitement is intense. Judicial operations are always slow and expensive, and at such a time largely in abeyance. The military are in the saddle, and they are not noted for patience, democratic procedure, or political sagacity.

For these reasons I would advocate opposition to and refusal to join such governmental schemes for alleged safety in air raids. It will not do for pacifists to join in the hysterical herd fear. They can organize and operate first aid corps without being under government orders. Outside of government organization, they can feed, comfort, guide, reassure, and otherwise help terror-stricken people. They can carry out transport of food and supplies and otherwise keep the community life functioning independently of, or at least in effective supplement to, the government. They can do certain things to maintain community morale and prevent panic, such as organizing and working on sanitation squads, fire brigades, poison gas decontamination squads, squads for removal of wreckage, feeding such field squads, the care of children. And of course preparation of surgical bandages and dressings. Cheerful courage and fellowship can be expressed in singing together at work. From experience in Spain it seems that people subject to air raids need useful activity to relieve the anxiety and suspense between raids. That sort of strain can best be relieved by manual or physical work for one another in companionship. Governmental organization of such work is, in time of war, so full of compulsion and threats that it will not promote the kind of community that pacifists desire. Therefore they will want to do it independently, relying on human kindness rather than coercion.

If the government offers to the conscientious objector the chance to do ambulance work, nursing, or hospital work, may he or she accept it as legitimate alternative, non-combatant service? I believe not. Granted the compassionate motive for it, yet the compassion is being used by the government to make the wounded fit for further fighting, if possible, or at least to keep them and their families and friends loyal. Hospitals and nursing help to prolong the war. The wounded will be cared for even though the pacifists refuse such work. There will be no dearth of war-minded nurses, ambulance men, surgeons, physicians and hospital orderlies. If there were a real danger of such a shortage, it would mean that pacifism would be so widespread that there would be no danger of war.

I am assuming that the pacifist in refusing such service is not doing so out of cowardice. If he is afraid, he should either do some equally dangerous service independent of government and try to develop his courage or else join the army and fight.

If he has not chosen his own form of service to the community before war begins, and finds it necessary suddenly to choose an alternative service, let him insist on a job not subject to governmental control and orders, and serving civilians. Inasmuch as most civilians will be doing war work directly or indirectly, and war is now totalitarian, it may prove almost impossible to do any form of work which will not be warped and used by the government for war ends. But service to civilians can be done before war and after war, and therefore cannot be so completely bent to war uses as service to the fighting forces. Let him try to serve the community or society rather than the national state, for it is to the former that we owe most of our social and cultural heritage. Always there is work at housing, road making, farming, forestry, building flood control dams, civilian hospital work, subsistence gardens, drainage of swampy ground, racial reconciliation, promotion of friendship between people of different religions, helping the unemployed and very poor of every race or religious persuasion within reach, helping civil prisoners or orphans, helping refugees, interned enemy aliens and prisoners of war, educational and recreational work, and care of children, provided such jobs are wholly under civilian direction. If the government will not permit the pacifist to work free from its orders, then he is a candidate for jail.

Work with the Y. M. C. A., Y. W. C. A., Boy or Girl Scouts, Salvation Army, or any similar organization, if it is under military command, would be taboo for the pacifist. Nor would chaplaincy in the army or navy be right. But relief work under strictly civilian or pacifist church direction in or outside the war zone, or in neutral zones, may be regarded as consistent.

PAY TAXES

Should a pacifist refuse to pay taxes to the State at war? Of course refusal would not release him from paying indirectly a share of the expenses of war, at least as long as he stays out of jail. A fraction of the cost of everything that he uses or consumes goes toward taxes paid by the manufacturers and distributors of those goods, and is used in part for war purposes. The pacifist may refuse to pay a fine for non-payment of taxes, but he cannot prevent the government from seizing his property and using it or the cash proceeds from it for war.

The fact is that all money and property rights are created and maintained by the State. So far as the pacifist uses money and property he will have to "render unto Caesar the things that are Caesar's." As he has been using money and property, and helping others to pay taxes up till now, knowing that the government believes in war and has been preparing for war, he can hardly absolve himself from this measure of responsibility for war. The only way he can cease completely from helping economically to support war is by going to jail and staying there until his nation really abandons war as a method.

Indeed, where all of society is engaged in a system of which war is an integral part, it is impossible for any individual wholly to free himself from complicity, unless he cuts himself off entirely from society. Short of that, the question is—at what point will he make the wisest compromise? If he is trying only to save his own soul, there is some question as to the value of his martyrdom. If he sincerely believes that by going to jail for refusal to pay taxes or by paying a fine he is effectively arousing men's minds against the evil, he may be right. It is ironical to note, however, that through a fine the State secures about twice as much money from him as if he had paid his taxes.

Since modern war is so largely caused by the workings of our economic system, a thoroughgoing refusal to support war would have required pacifists to stop using that system long before they were fined or went to jail. Their economic action and their testimony to truth must go to a deeper level. Romantic, futile gestures will not do, no matter how conscientious. Pacifists should choose a different line. They should realize that in our pecuniary civilization a refusal to pay taxes is, like a general strike, an open and final challenge to the very existence of the State. This is not merely because the government could not function without money. It is a matter of administrative existence. If sincere pacifists were allowed to withhold payment of their taxes because the government spends money on preparing for war, sincere Christian Scientists must be given a similar privilege because the government supports hospitals and physicians. Vegetarians could refuse tax payments because the government inspects meat and subsidizes cattle farming. Wealthy and extreme conservatives could claim exemption because the government spends so much money on relief for unemployment. The same holds true of a refusal to pay a part of one's taxes proportional to what the government spends on war out of its total budget. A democratic government could not carry on its affairs if any individual taxpayer or minority group of taxpayers could dictate how tax funds should be allocated. I am not overlooking the fact that actually in most governments a minority of the taxpayers do secretly control much of government policy and administration, especially its foreign policy and military establishment. But that merely means that those governments are not truly democratic. A democratic government exists to administer certain activities for the whole body of citizens, and citizens may not interfere with its administration without penalty, except by due process through the legislative or executive branches. I am not saying that any of the ideals of any minorities are wrong. But to put them into effect in a democratic government they must get open control of the government by becoming a majority.

A refusal to pay taxes is a challenge to the existence of the government; against that challenge the State will do battle with all its resources. Pacifists who are consistent and practical, who agree with the initial assumptions of this pamphlet, should not refuse to pay taxes, at least until they have prepared themselves sufficiently to assure themselves a reasonable chance of success in such a struggle. Since our initial assumption is that the character of civilization itself must be altered, the preparation must be more than just a political struggle to win a majority of votes. That may be one of the steps, but the effort must go much deeper.

Pacifists should therefore continue to pay taxes until they have accomplished a considerable number of advances. Because desire for reform is apt to be intense, warm, and impatient, it usually does not estimate clearly and soundly either the obstacles, the changes, or the three-generation period required for non-violent adaptations to deep cultural alterations. Hence, at the risk of seeming fussy and prolix, I want to set forth in detail, as I see them, those required stages. Pacifists should continue to pay taxes until they (1) have worked out a plan of a better kind of State, (2) have worked out and tested a non-violent method of winning power and making changes, (3) have got into actual operation a number of the transitional organizations necessary, (4) have acquired skill and self-confidence in this non-violent method, (5) have in minor ways demonstrated to the public their executive capacity and responsibility, (6) in minor struggles have demonstrated to the public the effectiveness of the method and its actual non-violence, (7) have achieved an increase of social and political unity between formerly inharmonious groups in their nation, (8) have got into practical working some supplemental economic devices for helping to carry the most depressed part of the population during the stress of change and afterward. Not till all this has been done will the pacifists be prepared for a successful struggle with the State. Not till then can they hope that society will follow and trust them with the guidance of supreme political power. To refuse to pay taxes without thorough preparation of this sort would be poor strategy and be bound to fail. Obviously, here in the Occident, we pacifists have not yet made any such preparation. It will take a number of years, with attempts and failures as a part of learning, before we can win self-confidence and public trust.

In the meantime, to square his conscience and clarify his position, the pacifist may, of course, every time he pays his taxes, prior to war, protest to the government against the use of his tax money for war purposes.

The question naturally rises here, why should the pacifist refuse service in the army if he does not refuse to pay taxes? The answer is perhaps twofold. Wars are only occasional; the uses of the economic system are constant. It is feasible to refuse to take part in war, and yet be an active and useful citizen for most of one's life; but to refuse to use this economic system would almost completely cut a person off from modern society, or at least make his social contacts so tenuous and his existence so precarious as greatly to cut down his usefulness. Secondly, just as a victim of a swindle is not responsible for the use to which the swindler puts the stolen property or money, so the pacifist is morally not directly responsible for the use to which the State applies the tax money which it exacts from him by force of law. I do not mean that the State is a swindler, but the helplessness of the taxpayer is like that of the swindler's victim. For his own positive acts, however, for joining the army, and as a soldier killing and wounding enemies, the individual is morally responsible. I have answered elsewhere the argument that it is cowardly to help pay another person to do what one is unwilling to do oneself. . . .

AID THE STRUGGLE OF LABOR

What ought the pacifist to do in relation to the class struggle? I refer not only to the occasional violence that breaks out in strikes and lockouts, but also to the silent, covert violence of economic pressure and exploitation.

So far as possible the pacifist will try, by non-violent means, to alter our present social and economic system, and replace it by something better, as I have already indicated. Since that is slow work, there is much hardship and injustice along the way for him to ameliorate, just as a believer in violence might do ambulance work in war. As best he can, the pacifist will try to persuade labor unions to see that non-violent resistance is realistic and is, even under provocation and violence by employers, a much more effective method of struggle than violence. He should try to prevent open violence in any local industrial quarrel. Governor Murphy's work in the Detroit automobile strike of 1937 was a successful instance of this sort.

Pacifists will try to learn the truth about general industrial conditions in their locality and about any particular strike that may arise there, and will try to spread the truth abroad. And they will, when possible, promote specific proposals for conciliation or arbitration of conflicts.

If there should be continued violence in some strike, ought pacifists to act as stretcher bearers for the wounded—either strikers, police or others? If both sides are violent as a matter of policy, I would say no, as I would advise against pacifists being ambulance workers in international war. It merely helps prolong the violence. But if the labor union were really committed to non-violence, and yet some members break down under severe provocation, then I think pacifists may help take care of the wounded. During strikes pacifists can help the families of strikers in various ways.

Pacifists who are not union members may wonder in some strike whether they ought to help picket. Each case must depend on its own merits. If outsiders undertake a responsibility of that sort, it may be necessary to stay by it long after the strike is over. If a union is not strong enough to win a strike and enforce the terms of settlement, the withdrawal of outside help at once when the strike is over may result in such severe victimization of the strikers by the employer that the last state of the workers may be worse than the first. It does not do for outsiders to wade into an industrial conflict just out of emotional sympathy. Definite responsibility is involved and real understanding required.

REFUSE TO DEMONSTRATE WITH COMMUNISTS OR FASCISTS

In an industrial struggle should pacifists demonstrate together with Communists? Most Communists, being intelligent people, do not want to use violence, but they believe, quite rightly, that it is pretty sure to be used by the employer group and by the State in any big struggle, and Communists are willing in that event to use it in self-defense. Also their general attitude toward employers and financiers as a class and often toward them as individuals is not only one of distrust but ranges through contempt, anger, fear, hatred, and desire for revenge. Witness the adjectives of Communist leaders and the cartoons of Communist artists. Under severe stress such feelings inevitably find expression in physical violence. So if the police attack a crowd of demonstrators containing both pacifists and Communists, the latter are almost sure to fight back, and in the melée it is not easy to distinguish between pacifists and Communists. So the public will condemn the pacifists as severely as the Communists—indeed more so since their pacifism will seem to be mere hypocrisy. For these reasons I doubt whether, in justice to their beliefs and the desire to win converts, pacifists can afford to take part in public demonstrations with Communists. Since Fascists are committed to violence from the beginning, the same refusal applies to them. This is no "holier than thou" attitude, but a deep-seated conviction of the importance of method. And it involves a further conviction that no "popular front", no civil liberties, and no thorough democracy can nowadays be successful or enduring except on the basis of non-violence. Because modern violence is totalitarian, to it as a near-absolute one must oppose another near-absolute, pacifism without compromise.

BEHAVE WISELY IF IMPRISONED

On one further matter pacifists will want to be prepared. I refer to their conduct in prison, if they go there. What I suggest here is based chiefly on the advice of Gandhi to his followers.

Pacifists in jail are political prisoners, not ordinary criminals. They have courted imprisonment to prove the strength of their convictions, to testify to the truth as they see it, to try to win public opinion, and to try to persuade the government by their voluntary suffering. They are not trying at present to do away with jails.

Legal punishment is based, at least in theory, not on a desire for cruel revenge, but implies that the prisoner has a personality capable of change and growth, and therefore worthy of respect. A political prisoner has not, like the ordinary criminal, disobeyed the law for selfish reasons, but for the sake of ethical principles. Therefore he deserves more respect than an ordinary criminal. Certainly the pacifist has an unusual degree of respect for personality. But public hysteria in wartime is often cruel, and some prison superintendents and guards fail to act up to the highest standards of their occupation.

Pacifists in jail should work hard at the tasks set them, provided those tasks are regular prison work and not for military use. They should obey prison rules and regular discipline; should not object to inconveniences or mere hardships; should wear without objection prison clothing provided it is not military uniform; should not ask for or accept special privileges. They should be courteous and conform to all self-respecting, non-military gestures, modes of address or other signs of respect toward prison officials. They should be open and aboveboard, and not deceitful. They should not ask for any unnecessary conveniences.

But they are entitled to refuse to obey orders clearly intended to humiliate them or to insult or violate their beliefs, taking without protest any lawful punishment for their disobedience. They must use common sense and not be touchy or filled with false pride. If past history is repeated, there will probably be attempts by some prison officials to provide work which would get the conscientious objectors into an inconsistent position, thus undermining their resistance. If this happens, the conscientious objectors will be wise to refuse to do such work. Some of the prisons may be hastily arranged concentration camps without rules or facilities for work. In such case the prisoners can perhaps help the authorities develop kinds of work consistent with their position and good for the morale of all concerned, jailers as well as prisoners. Pacifist prisoners may protest against cruel treatment, against filth and insanitation of all kinds, or spoiled food. Any protests should be addressed at proper times to the duly constituted authorities. If, after adequate time has been allowed for consideration by the authorities, no answer or an utterly unsatisfactory answer is returned, the prisoners may refuse to work, taking as cheerfully as possible the legal penalties for such refusal. They should not resort to hunger strike unless the matter is of the gravest importance. It is usually countered by forcible feeding. Hunger strike is a two-edged weapon very dangerous to use— I mean morally dangerous—except on very rare occasions and by very clear-thinking, experienced persons who have a long record of orderly, responsible, well-balanced, and markedly unselfish conduct.

Perhaps the three hardest things about prison life are loneliness, weakening of initiative, and a temptation to resentment. To offset the first the prisoner will be wise to read as much as the prison permits, and when that is not possible, to develop as many ways of enriching and cultivating his inner life as possible. In this way he will also develop a field for initiative. If sooner or later he can get permission to have paper, pen and ink, he will find that recording his thoughts and then pondering on them will help him to solve many problems and develop a well-integrated personal philosophy that will give him poise and serenity. Or he may write stories, essays or poetry. The prisoner will find it a great help to set aside a regular time each day for silent meditation, even though it be very brief. If he is religious, he will use prayer as well as meditation, but meditation is advisable in all cases. It is not an escape from reality, but a way of making contact with underlying reality, principles and truths. It will enrich his inner world, do away with inner conflicts, and provide a field for initiative, spontaneity and freedom. Thus he may keep himself from being stunted and crippled by his punishment.

If prison officials are cruel, he can try to remember that it is probably due to frustrations, indignities, humiliations, or cruelties that they themselves suffered, perhaps when they were young, or perhaps to war hysteria. So it is a symptom of the evils of our civilization, and not all their personal fault.

In some situations it will be very difficult to decide what is the wisest way to act in prison. Many situations cannot be foreseen. The foregoing considerations will perhaps serve as a general guide. It will be helpful if pacifists, in advance of going to prison, can read accounts of the experiences of former conscientious objectors. . . .

Pacifist Program Under Fascism

Besides planning what he should do in case of war, the pacifist must consider what would be his duty in case of increasing domestic repression of liberties, of governmental violence turned not ostensibly against another nation, but against the majority of its own people, of what we call fascism or totalitarian dictatorship directed by any group. There are reasons for thinking that fascism in this and most countries is likely to come whether the present European and Far Eastern wars spread further or not.

External unification and economic centralization of the world are being brought about by swift modern communication and transport and the spread of literacy and the printing press. Along with these there is a decline of the present world economic system. These are taking place before self-restraint and self-control and moral foresight have developed sufficiently to meet the increased temptations and increased responsibilities. It is quite possible that these facts are creating new economic and political centralization and totalitarian control in all countries. Strong unexpected pressures demand swift decisions. The tempo of all economic and social processes has greatly speeded up. The old economic forces are probably not mobile enough to adapt themselves quickly to the rapid changes. Under the impact of inflation, unemployment, high tariffs, and more or less autarchy for military reasons, the working and the middle classes in all countries have suffered so severely that the demand for economic security is almost a mania. Many people are willing to yield up certain civil and political liberties in return for promises of security. Millions of unemployed and discouraged young people are naturally eager for a change which will provide activity and reasonable promise of the means of livelihood. Certain systems of political and economic ideas rationalize this situation.

It is also possible that the perfection of the airplane will, after the present war has spent its momentum, practically end large-scale warfare between industrialized European nations. Bombing from the air not only endangers statesmen, but makes probable the destruction of most of the industrial equipment of a nation in a big war. This would not only end the material supply for the fighting forces, but would make it impossible to profit by a victory because the victorious nation would not be able to manufacture for the newly won market. Modern war would also increase the likelihood of violent revolution. Hence the future leaders of Europe's industrialized nations will be likely to avoid war at whatever cost. If this proves true, the stresses and strains of modern society can be kept from smashing up most of our present institutions probably only by universal fascism and some civil wars after the manner of Spain. Because of the isolation afforded by the Atlantic and Pacific oceans the United States will, for a time, not be vitally affected by the danger from air attack. But the economic decline and other rapid changes operate here, and these may be sufficient to put fascism into control.

Even though the leaders of fascist movements begin as noble idealists, the power which they must assume in order to make a centralized economy work tends inevitably to grow. And presently the use and enjoyment of such immense power creates a permanent bureaucracy and poisons its members.

Such developments, especially their violence, will not prove effective, I think, to solve man's economic, political or social problems. After two or three generations the estimated rapid decrease in population of all industrialized countries may lighten the pressure toward centralization and dictatorships. Nevertheless, at present these tendencies increase, so what shall a pacifist wisely do about them?

Because fascism involves so much conflict and violence, it seems to me that if fascism comes, the pacifist's program should be practically the same as what I have already described in case of war. It should include great simplicity of living, training in small groups, perhaps no larger than three, refraining from adverse criticism of the government, silent non-violent work toward a better civilization (especially helping the unemployed and lowest paid workers of industry and agriculture toward self-help), taking a pledge against war and violence of any sort, refusal to join the military forces, maintaining contact with one another, working out plans for mutual aid, paying taxes, endeavoring to avoid indignation, resentment and bitterness, patient endurance of whatever suffering may come, promoting truth. As a fascist government would attempt to monopolize all public services, the pacifist would have to use ingenuity to discover interstices and be useful in them. The pledge not to go to war should include a pledge not to use violence in self-defense against fascist oppression. Such a program will require understanding of the power of non-violence. It will be furthered by a special interpretation of history from this point of view. Deep religious conviction will be needed in order to refrain entirely from bitterness in the face of prolonged violent repression and to keep up what the military men call morale. Assistance of the unemployed and poorest groups is expedient as well as just, because the more economic security they can have from sources other than the government, the less support they will give to a dictator's regime.

Christians will recall that Jesus lived in a period and coun-

try of brutal repression and restriction of liberty. In one sense
the Sermon on the Mount was, and still is, advice for living in
a dictatorship.

It should be remembered that we are all partly responsible
for our corporate failures to live up to our ideals of democracy,
justice, equality, and freedom. We are all involved in economic
and political mistakes. The changes in our economy are so
rapid as to come close to breakdown. The need for economic
security demands swift action to prevent starvation and suffering on a scale too great to be endured. It may be that all of us,
pacifists included, may have to yield up temporarily large
amounts of liberty of action and speech in order that the largest
possible numbers of people may live. In so doing we would be
paying part of the price for our own and our predecessors'
failures and mistakes. Such yielding would not be mere cring-
ing to an arbitrary and wholly personal tyrant. Yet personal
and bureaucratic tyranny creeps in soon. To resist that tyranny
non-violently and to suffer punishment voluntarily for our resistance will be another part of the price we must pay for past
errors. And the toil of building non-violent and better forms
and modes of human association will be yet another part of the
price we must pay. But we can have joy and deep satisfaction
in such work.

Some may say that the foregoing proposals are an abandonment of the method which Gandhi advocates and has used so
successfully against the imperial dictatorship he opposes. But
if they will study his writings and the record of his activities
more carefully, they will find that most of his time and energy
have been spent in constructive organization and propaganda
for reforms among his own people. The time he has devoted
to direct, open struggle against the Government in campaigns
of non-coöperation or civil disobedience has been relatively
small. Even during the times of open struggle, his criticisms of
the Government have been impersonal. He has not imputed
evil motives to any individuals in the Government, but has

always spoken of them as friends or as people he would like to be friendly with. He has clearly indicated that silence combined with constructive work is often the wisest policy.

22. Donald Benedict and Others, *Why We Refused to Register*

Unlike the legislation of World War I, the Burke-Wadsworth Bill of 1940 provided an alternative to military service for conscientious objectors in the form of Civilian Public Service camps.

Some objectors, however, felt that planting trees or fighting fires under government auspices was an inadequate testimony. In October 1940 eight students at Union Theological Seminary in New York City, who had been living in voluntary poverty in Harlem while pursuing their studies, refused even to register for the draft. The statement by some of this group to the court is the selection which follows.

It is impossible for us to think of the conscription law without at the same time thinking of the whole war system, because it is clear to us that conscription is definitely a part of the institution of war. . . .

"Excerpts from the Joint statement of Donald Benedict, Joseph J. Bevilacqua, Meredith Dallas, David Dellinger, George M. Houser, William H. Lovell, Howard E. Spragg and Richard J. Wichlei," *Why We Refused to Register,* published jointly by the Fellowship of Reconciliation, Keep America Out of War Congress, National Council for Prevention of War, Youth Committee Against War, Young Peoples Socialist League, and War Resisters League (New York, 1941[?]).

To us, the war system is an evil part of our social order, and we declare that we cannot cooperate with it in any way. War is an evil because it is in violation of the Way of Love as seen in God through Christ. It is a concentration and accentuation of all the evils of our society. War consists of mass murder, deliberate starvation, vandalism, and similar evils. Physical destruction and moral disintegration are the inevitable result. The war method perpetuates and compounds the evils it purports to overcome. It is impossible, as history reveals, to overcome evil with evil. The last World War is a notorious case of the failure of the war system, and there is no evidence to believe that this war will be any different. It is our positive proclamation as followers of Jesus Christ that we must overcome evil with good. We seek in our daily living to reconcile that separation of man from man and man from God which produces war.

We have also been led to our conclusion on the conscription law in the light of its totalitarian nature. It is a totalitarian move when our government insists that the manpower of the nation take a year of military training. It is a totalitarian move for the President of the nation to be able to conscript industry to produce certain materials which are deemed necessary for national defense without considering the actual physical needs of the people. We believe, therefore, that by opposing the Selective Service law, we will be striking at the heart of totalitarianism as well as war. . . .

We feel a deep bond of unity with those who decide to register as conscientious objectors, but our own decision must be different for the following reasons:

If we register under the act, even as conscientious objectors, we are becoming part of the act. The fact that we as conscientious objectors may gain personal exemption from the most crassly un-Christian requirements of the act does not compensate for the fact that we are complying with it and accepting its protection. If a policeman (or a group of vigilantes) stops us on the street, our possession of the government's card shows that we are "all right"—we have complied with the act for the militarization of America. If that does not hurt our Christian consciences, what will? If we try to rationalize on the theory that we must go along with the act in order to fight the fascism and militarism of which it is a part, it seems to us that we are doing that very thing which all pacifist Christians abhor: we are consciously employing bad means on the theory that to do so will contribute to a good end. . . .

In similar vein, it is urged that great concessions have been won for religious pacifists and that we endanger these by our refusal to accept them. Fascism, as it gradually supplanted democracy in Germany, was aided by the decision of Christians and leftists to accept a partial fascism rather than to endanger those democratic concessions which still remained. It is not alone for our own exemption from fighting that we work—it is for freedom of the American people from fascism and militarism.

Partial exemption of conscientious objectors has come about partly through the work of influential pacifists and partly through the open-mindedness of certain non-pacifists. But it has also been granted because of the fear of the government that, without such a provision, public opposition to war would be too great to handle. In particular, it seems to us that one of the reasons the government has granted exemption to ministers and theological students is to gain a religious sanction for its diabolical war. Where actual support could not be gained, it hoped to soothe their consciences so that they could provide no real opposition.

We do not contend that the American people maliciously choose the vicious instrument of war. In a very perplexing situation, they lack the imagination, the religious faith, and the precedents to respond in a different manner. This makes it all the more urgent to build in this country and throughout the world a group trained in the techniques of non-violent opposition to the encroachments of militarism and fascism. Until we build such a movement, it will be impossible to stall the war machine at home. When we do build such a movement, we will have forged the only weapon which can ever give effective answer to foreign invasion. Thus in learning to fight American Hitlerism we will show an increasing group of war-disillusioned Americans how to resist foreign Hitlers as well.

For these reasons we hereby register our refusal to comply in any way with the Selective Training and Service Act. We do not expect to stem the war forces today; but we are helping to build the movement that will conquer in the future.

23. Mulford Sibley and Asa Wardlaw,
Conscientious Objectors in Prison

This selection describes the dramatic techniques of civil disobedience employed to protest racial segregation and other objectionable aspects of prison life by some of those imprisoned as conscientious objectors. The demonstrations formed a bridge between the labor sit ins of the depression years and the use of nonviolence in the civil rights movement after the war ended.

Clearly the men who went to prison faced further problems of conscience inside the gates. Here, as outside, some felt impelled to resist the demands of authority. An absolutist objector might continue his non-cooperation with the system of

---

Mulford Sibley and Asa Wardlaw, *Conscientious Objectors In Prison 1940–1945* (Philadelphia: Pacifist Research Bureau, 1945), pp. 42–48. Reprinted by permission.

war and conscription in protest, not primarily against "abuses" of the prison system, but against the very idea of imprisoning objectors. Individual non-cooperation was climaxed in the course adopted by Corbett Bishop, who refused not only to eat but also to walk or carry out any order of the penal authorities. His action, or inaction, according to observers, was maintained without personal hostility or resentment. Other men, as a symbol of protest, refused on particular occasions to cooperate. One Socialist objector announced that he would refuse to work on May Day, 1944, "Because I wish to demonstrate loyalty to my fellow-workers and because I wish to protest the imprisonment of men of principle."

Non-cooperators sometimes expressed regret for the personal inconvenience they caused to prison officials, while justifying their course on principle. Although non-cooperators did not succeed invariably in keeping their attitudes on this high plane, the intention to do so is revealed in a number of personal records.

While complete non-cooperation was rare, protests and refusals at certain points in the prison routine were more common. Assignment to work obviously connected with the war brought individual refusals. Individual hunger strikes were undertaken, for varying reasons. James W. Ball, who was serving his second sentence, conducted a 30-day fast in July, 1943. The call to abstain from food came to him, according to his own statement, only after he had received his sentence, and he desired "to protest against the injustice which our government is doing in removing men from occupations to which they have been called by God." Several objectors refused to sign the power of attorney which would permit the prison censor to read their mail. As a result their correspondence privileges were denied.

To the Bureau of Prisons, those conscientious objectors who were active in the major prison strikes were primarily reformers "with a zeal for changing the social, political, economic, and cultural order." Some, according to the same source, were "bewildered and frustrated in their efforts to find a constructive answer to the complex problems of a world in conflict, and finding none, satisfy some inner need through protest and escape from reality." The Bureau held that the conscientious objector reformer's "motivation frequently stem from an over-protective home or a mother fixation, or from a revolt against authority as typified in the home and transferred to society at large. He is a problem child—whether at home, at school, or in prison." On the other hand, many pacifists looked upon prison strike leaders as among the most able, conscientious, and "normal" of all those men who had been attracted to the pacifist movement. Their fellow-prisoners, in so far as they were articulate, thought highly of the majority of strike leaders; and in a number of cases wardens and prison officials testified to their personal respect for the inmates who helped create so many perplexing problems.

The first strike at the Danbury Correctional Institution presumably arose because the warden had withdrawn his permission to a group of conscientious objectors to abstain from lunch on April 23, 1941, in order to hold a demonstration against war. When the sixteen, all of whom had been sentenced for refusal to register in the original draft, heard of the warden's action they refused to report for work the morning of April 23. They also refused to eat or observe any of the routine prescribed for inmates. Their punishment was solitary confinement for two days and confinement to cells for another thirty. There was one report that the strikers had previously made demands for abolition of racial segregation in the prison, and some maintained that they had planned to refuse work all along.

The second strike at Danbury involved the 82-day fast of Stanley Murphy and Louis Taylor . . .

A third strike began on August 11, 1943, when nineteen men

initiated a "work strike" in protest against the policy of racial segregation at meals. They were immediately confined to their cells and, with forty minutes a day for exercise and the official "monotonous" diet for food, remained there for 133 days, or until December 23, 1943. The visiting hour usually permitted each month was cut in half, and visits were held under the close scrutiny of guards. After the warden had promised to institute a cafeteria system for the dining room—a scheme which was to be introduced only gradually—the strikers returned to work in the hope that the policy of segregation in the dining room would be permanently eliminated.

Meanwhile, on May 13, 1943, a protest—variously called "work strike" and "hunger strike," but in reality neither—began at the Lewisburg Penitentiary as a demonstration against forced segregation of inmates on the basis of color. There had been some protest against segregation both at the main institution and at the prison farm. When a new group of Negroes came to the farm, making too many for the segregated table in the dining room, one was sent to the kitchen to eat, and even there required to sit at a separate table from the kitchen workers. Immediately, eight conscientious objectors in that section protested by declining to eat in the dining room. They either went without food or subsisted on what they could buy from the prison commissary.

After four days on such a limited diet—only certain types of food could be obtained at the commissary—the men felt too weak to work. Statement of this fact to the prison authorities was construed as refusal to work, for which they were sent to the "hole." There they accepted the usual "monotonous" diet. A little later they were placed together in one room, segregated from the remaining prison population, and their writing privileges limited to one letter a week.

In the meantime, five conscientious objectors from the main prison had gone on strike in sympathy with their fellows of the farm dormitory. They also were sent to the "hole" where they accepted the diet, and were then transferred to the segregation room with the other eight. For a few days the thirteen went on hunger strike after writing to Director Bennett and Attorney General Biddle, demanding abolition of racial segregation in prison.

By August 11, 1943, the so-called "work strike" of conscientious objectors had, for some of the participants, broadened out from protest of racial segregation into a strike against the prison system in general. The number of strikers had decreased to seven. On September 28, five of them (later six) focused upon a protest against prison censorship practices—through a real hunger strike. Paton Price, Jack Dixon, William Kuenning, Thomas Woodman, David Dellinger, and William Lovett thus strove to secure reform of what they termed the "cruel, unnecessary and discriminatory" system whereby prison officials denied inmates certain types of literature and arbitrarily censored their letters.

In a letter to James Bennett, Director of the Bureau of Prisons, the six fasters asked recognition of two "basic rights" for all prison inmates—not merely conscientious objectors. "The first," they said, "is the right of every prisoner to free correspondence with the outside world, at all times, regardless of his prison status. The second is the right of every prisoner to access to uncensored materials for reading and writing at all times, regardless of his prison status." The strikers agreed that it was legitimate for prison censors to open letters in order to detect plots and discover drug smuggling, as well as to exclude pornographic materials. They held that it was not legitimate for censors to exclude expressions of social or religious opinion or descriptions of conditions in prison.

Late in October, 1943, the hunger strikers had become so weakened as a result of their self-imposed discipline that officials began to feed them forcibly. Reports of the conflict attracted public interest. Pacifist and non-pacifist groups alike attempted to gain some settlement from the Bureau of Prisons.

Some pacifists, it may be noted, were highly critical of the methods of the strikers, and others expressed doubts, while still others commended their course.

In November Director Bennett, through the Warden of Lewisburg, suggested certain modifications in prison rules regarding censorship. After certain clarifications of these proposed changes, the strikers, on December 1, concluded their fast. The result of the strike, in retrospect, appears to have been a compromise. The Bureau of Prisons refused to promise that library, correspondence, and reading and writing privileges would be allowed to those in punishment status ("the hole" or other forms of restriction). Here wide administrative discretion was to be given to the warden. On the other hand, there was a definite promise that "inspection" of mail should not be interpreted to include the right of censorship of religious or political opinion. The strikers did *not* gain all they asked; but it seems equally clear that the prison authorities *did* modify inspection and literature regulations considerably.

In June, 1944, three conscientious objectors in Petersburg went on work strike, against racial segregation and the war-connected prison industry. They were placed in the "hole" on June 11, 1944. In the meantime, a large group in Danbury had begun a strike against the parole system—and one additional striker a week was, by agreement, to be added to the list. The prison authorities replied by transferring a number of the strikers from Danbury to Lewisburg, where seven of those transferred then began a hunger strike against being deprived of "good time" for failure to work. This continued to October 14, 1944, when one of the group was released, with the restoration of a part of the "good time" formerly denied, and another was reported paroled. Those remaining were joined by five others in a "rotation" strike, whereby five men would refuse to eat for a definite period, their places to be taken by another five for a similar (unannounced) term. Again the purpose was to secure definite promises from the Bureau of Prisons that men would not lose "good time" for refusal to work. A hunger strike of sympathy was begun in Danbury on October 4, 1944, and ended October 8, 1944.

In Ashland, a group began, in the fall of 1944, to protest racial segregation by a program of non-cooperation. This had been preceded by more than a year of effort to secure improvements gradually. The strike action brought little progress and the efforts of the men were somewhat relaxed until May 22, 1945, when a new group of objectors entered Ashland. On June 11, fifteen men refused to eat in the dining room and were placed in administrative segregation. Six were transferred to other prisons. In August, new difficulties at Lewisburg were precipitated by the reduction of "good time" of two non-objector inmates. Ten C.O.'s protested to the Warden and later refused to work, whereupon they also were deprived of thirty days "good time," and placed in segregation.

Meanwhile, both at Danbury and at Lewisburg a group of objectors, changing in numbers as some were released and others entered, followed a permanent policy of non-cooperation. At Milan also several men were carrying on simultaneously a program of non-cooperation, with varying individual reasons. Two were Negroes who refused to eat at racially segregated tables.

PART VIII

Direct Action for Peace,
Post-World War II

24. Maurice McCrackin,
"Pilgrimage of a Conscience"

In 1948 individuals inclined to radical direct action against nuclear war drew together in a group called Peacemakers. This organization revived Woolman's and Thoreau's practice of nonpayment of war taxes. Peacemakers also encouraged refusal to register for the draft. One of those Peacemakers who refused to pay income taxes was the Reverend Maurice McCrackin.

As a student, McCrackin was impressed by the stand of the Union Theological Seminary students who refused to register for the draft in 1940 (see Document 22). After the war McCrackin, pastor of a Presbyterian church in Cincinnati, began systematic nonpayment of income taxes. In 1958 he was arrested and served a six months' prison sentence. In May 1961 the Cincinnati Presbytery suspended McCrackin indefinitely from his position as pastor.

Maurice McCrackin, "Pilgrimage of a Conscience" (Cincinnati: 1961), mimeographed, pp. 9–11.

I decided that I would never again register for the draft nor would I consent to being conscripted by the government in any capacity. Nevertheless each year around March 15 without protest I sent my tax payments to the government. By giving my money I was helping the government do what I so vigorously declared was wrong. I would never give my money to support a house of prostitution or the liquor industry, a gambling house or for the purchase and distribution of pornographic literature. Yet year after year I had unquestionably been giving my money to an evil infinitely greater than all of these put together since it is from war's aftermath that nearly all social ills stem.

Income tax paid by the individual is essential to the continuance of the war machine. Over 50% of the military budget is paid for by individuals through their income tax payments and 75% to 80% of every dollar he pays via income tax goes for war purposes.

Again I examined what the principle of personal commitment to Jesus meant to me. Through the years I have tried to achieve a personal relationship with Jesus. This is the burden of the Christian gospel, that Jesus can be known personally and that he can bring a saving power into a man's life. For us as Christians to know Jesus personally has reality only as we try earnestly to grow more like him "unto the measure of the stature of His fullness." If we follow Jesus afar off, if we praise his life and teachings but conclude that neither apply to our daily living, what are we doing but denying and rejecting him? Jesus speaks with authority and with love to every individual, "Follow me. Take up your cross. Love one another as I have loved you." What would Jesus *want* me to do in relation to war? What *must* I do if I am his disciple? This was the conclusion I reached: If I can honestly say that Jesus would support conscription, throw a hand grenade, or with a flame thrower drive men out of caves, to become living torches—if I believe he would release the bomb over Hiroshima or Nagasaki, then I not only have the right to do these things as a Christian, I am even obligated to do them. But if, as a committed follower, I believe that Jesus would do none of these things, I have no choice but to refuse at whatever personal cost, to support war. This means that I will not serve in the armed forces nor will I voluntarily give my money to help make war possible.

Having had this awakening, I could no longer in good conscience continue full payment of my federal taxes. At the same time I did not want to withdraw my support from the civilian services which the government offers. For that reason I continued to pay the small percentage now allocated for civilian use. The amount which I had formerly given for war I now hoped to give to such causes as the American Friends Service Committee's program and to other works of mercy and reconciliation which help to remove the roots of war.

As time went on I realized, however, that this was not accomplishing its purpose because year after year the government ordered my bank to release money from my account to pay the tax I had held back. I then closed my checking account and by some method better known to the Internal Revenue Service than to me, it was discovered that I had money in a savings and loan company. Orders were given to this firm, under threat of prosecution, to surrender from my account the amount the government said I owed. I then realized suddenly how far government is now invading individual rights and privileges: money is given in trust to a firm to be kept in safety and the government coerces this firm's trustees into a violation of that trust. But even more evil than this invasion of rights is the violence done to the individual conscience in forcing him to give financial support to a thing he feels so deeply is wrong. I agree wholeheartedly with the affirmation of Presbytery made in February of 1958, that, "A Christian citizen is obligated to God to obey the law but when in conscience he finds the requirements of law to be in direct conflict with his obedience to God, he must obey God rather than man."

Disobedience to a civil law is an act against government, but obedience to a civil law that is evil is an act against God. At this point it came to me with complete clarity that by so much as filing tax returns I was giving to the Revenue Department assistance in the violation of my own conscience, because the very information I had been giving on my tax forms was being used in finally making the collection. So from this point on, or until there is a radical change for the better in government spending, I shall file no returns.

25. A. J. Muste,
Of Holy Disobedience

Abraham Johannes (A.J.) Muste was protesting against militarism long before the dropping of the atom bomb. The First World War led him to resign as pastor of a Dutch Reformed Church in Newtonville, Massachusetts, rather than keep silent about his pacifist convictions. Between the wars he threw himself into labor organization, first in the Lawrence, Massachusetts textile strike of 1919, then in the creation of the Brookwood Labor College, finally in the great organizational strikes in the rubber and automobile industries of the 1930's. Muste was one of the first to use the sit-down strike tactic, and stressed this method in the early struggles of the Congress Of Racial Equality. A. J. Muste has been a guiding spirit of the Fellowship of Reconciliation, the War Resisters League, the Committee for Nonviolent Action, Peacemakers, and the magazine *Liberation*, which he helped to found in 1956.

Of Holy Disobedience is Muste's reflective justification for total

A. J. Muste, *Of Holy Disobedience*, Pendle Hill Pamphlet No. 64 (Wallingford, Pa.: Pendle Hill, 1952), pp. 3–34. Reprinted with the permission of Pendle Hill, Wallingford, Pa.

non-co-operation with the state's preparations for war. Published in 1952, it can be viewed as helping to lay the intellectual groundwork for the dramatic activities of the Committee for Nonviolent Action in the following decade, in much the same way that Martin Luther King's *Stride Toward Freedom* set the stage for the student movement of 1960.

A book which the French writer, Georges Bernanos, wrote in Brazil—to which he had exiled himself because he would not remain in France under Nazi occupation—has just been published in this country. It is entitled *Tradition of Freedom* and is a hymn to freedom, an impassioned warning against obedience and conformity, especially obedience to the modern State engaged in mechanized, total war.

In the closing pages of this work, Bernanos writes:

I have thought for a long time now that if, some day, the increasing efficiency of the technique of destruction finally causes our species to disappear from the earth, it will not be cruelty that will be responsible for our extinction and still less, of course, the indignation that cruelty awakens and the reprisals and vengeance that it brings upon itself . . . but the docility, the lack of responsibility of the modern man, his base subservient acceptance of every common decree. The horrors which we have seen, the still greater horrors we shall presently see, are not signs that rebels, insubordinate, untameable men, are increasing in number throughout the world, but rather that there is a constant increase, a stupendously rapid increase, in the number of obedient, docile men.

It seems to me that this is a true and timely warning. It might serve as a text for a general appeal to American youth to adopt and practice the great and urgent virtues of Holy Disobedience, non-conformity, resistance toward Conscription, Regimentation and War. For the present I want to use Bernanos' words as an introduction to some observations on the discussion regarding the absolute and relative role of these "virtues" which goes on chiefly among pacifists, members of the Historic Peace Churches and other such groups. I think it will be readily apparent, however, that the principles set forth have a wider bearing and merit consideration by all who are concerned about the maintenance of freedom in our time and the abolition of war.

Most believers in democracy and all pacifists begin, of course, with an area of agreement as to the moral necessity, the validity and the possible social value of No-saying or Holy Disobedience. Pacifists and/or conscientious objectors all draw the line at engaging in military combat and most of us indeed at any kind of service in the armed forces. But immediately thereupon questions arise as to whether we should not emphasize "positive and constructive service" rather than the "negative" of refusal to fight or to register; or questions about the relative importance of "resistance" and "reconciliation," and so on. It is to this discussion that I wish to attempt a contribution. It may be that it will be most useful both to young men of draft age and to other readers if we concentrate largely on the quite concrete problem of whether the former should register, conform to other requirements of the Selective Service Act which apply to conscientious objectors and accept or submit to the alternative service required of them under the law as amended in June, 1951; or whether they shall refuse to register, or if they do register or are "automatically" registered by the authorities, shall refuse to conform at the next stage; and in any event refuse to render any alternative service under conscription. We deal, in other words, with the question whether young men who are eligible for it shall accept the IV-E classification or take the more "absolutist," non-registrant position. (For present purposes, consideration of the I-A-O position, the designation used for draftees who are willing to accept service in the armed forces provided this is non-combatant in character, may be omitted. The IV-E classification is the designation used for persons who are on grounds of religious training and belief opposed to participation in any war. Those who are given this classification are required to render alternative service, outside the armed forces and under civilian auspices, and designed to serve "the health, safety and interest of the United States.")

Two preliminary observations are probably necessary in order to avoid misunderstanding. In the first place, in every social movement there are varied trends or emphases, and methods of working. Those who hold to one approach are likely to be very critical of those who take another. Disagreements among those within the same movement may be more intense or even bitter than with those on the outside. I suppose it can hardly be denied that every movement has in it individuals whose contribution is negative, and that such individuals do not all come from within one wing of the movement. Objective evaluation also leads to the view that the cause is forwarded by various methods and through the agency of diverse individuals and groups. But this does not mean that discussion within the movement of trends and methods of work is not useful and essential. Even if it were true that each of several strategies was *equally* valid and useful, it would still be necessary that each be clearly and vigorously presented and implemented in order that the movement might develop its maximum impact.

Secondly, in what I shall have to say I am not passing moral judgment on individual draftees. But from the fact that a pacifist minister should not pass moral condemnation on the young man in his congregation who in obedience to his conscience enlists or submits to conscription, we do not deduce that this minister should abandon his pacifism or cease to witness to it. Similarly, the fact that in the pacifist movement we support various types of COs in following the lead of conscience does not rule out discussion as to the validity and usefulness of various strategies. It is one thing for a young and immature draftee to follow a course which amounts to "making the best of a bad business" and for others to give him sympathetic understanding and help. It is a very different thing for pacifist organizations or churches to advocate such a course or to rationalize it into something other than it really is.

As some of the readers of this statement are likely to be aware, the writer has advocated the non-registrant position. The majority in the pacifist movement probably believe that it is preferable for COs to accept or submit to the alternative civilian service which was required under the World War II Selective Service Act and is now again required under "peacetime conscription."

The varied considerations and arguments which currently enter into the discussion of this choice confronting the youth of draft age tend, as I see it, to fall into three categories, though there is a good deal of overlapping. One set of considerations may be said to center largely around the idea of Christian or human "vocation"; a second set has to do with the problem of "the immature 18-year-old"; the third with the relation of the pacifist and citizens generally to military conscription and the modern Power-State.

The argument for accepting alternative service, under the first category, has been stated somewhat as follows:

God calls us to love and serve our fellowmen. This is for Christians and other pacifists a matter of vocation. If, then, the government in war time, or under peace time conscription, requires some service of mercy or construction from us, which is not obviously and directly a part of war-making, we will raise no objection to undertaking such work. We may even seek, and shall certainly be grateful for the opportunity to demonstrate our desire to be good citizens and helpful members of society, and to show a reconciling spirit.

This question of the meaning and implications of Christian or human vocation in the context of military conscription clearly needs careful analysis.

Conscription and Vocation

The question of his vocation does not or should not arise suddenly for the Christian or any morally sensitive and responsible individual when Congress enacts a conscription law. The committed Christian has presumably been engaged in an occupation and a way of living which he believes to be in accord with the will of God. This need not be some unusual or spectacular occupation. A Christian farmer, factory worker, miner, teacher, raising a family and giving an example of unselfishness to his neighbors; his wife maintaining an unobtrusively wholesome Christian home; the children walking in the footsteps of such parents—all these may be following a true Christian vocation.

Then war or peace time conscription comes along. If these people are pacifists, they hold that direct participation in war or in combat training is inconsistent with a Christian profession and calling. They must, therefore, refuse such participation. At this point the government tells those of them who come under the draft that they must nevertheless render some civilian service within or under the conscription system. In most cases this will be something different from what they have been doing and will involve temporary removal from the home community.

It has for some time troubled me that a good many pacifists of draft age seem ready to acquiesce in this situation and that, furthermore, many who are not directly affected by the draft seem to feel that at such a time they must immediately find something else to do than that which they have been doing— something that is often referred to as "meaningful" or "sacrificial." Was what they were doing then so definitely not meaningful or sacrificial? Unfortunately, this is very likely the case in many instances. But it does not follow, as is seemingly often assumed, that this justifies going into some entirely new work, a "project," as we say, and perhaps preferably some relief work which has some connection with the war effort, something which society will regard as the "equivalent" of support of the war effort. Certainly the fact that a young man of draft age has not been following a meaningful or Christian vocation does not automatically or by itself constitute a warrant for submitting to conscription for so-called civilian service. It may well be that God calls him at this juncture to put meaning into the life he has been living and into the work he was supposed to be doing.

It is certainly incumbent on us to search our hearts as to whether this rush to get into other jobs and to go to distant places may be motivated by fear of men and of the authorities, by a desire to be thought well of, by a dread of the social displeasure or actual legal punishment which might fall upon us if we were to continue quietly at the work which we had been doing, living in the home town when war fever, if not outright hysteria, seizes the people. "If I were still pleasing men," said St. Paul, "I should not be the slave of Christ."

The Normal as Meaningful

I am convinced that our thinking in these matters is often distorted. What God calls men and women to, fundamentally, is to "be fruitful and multiply and replenish the earth and subdue it and have dominion" over the animal creation—to sow the grain, weave the cloth, build homes and temples to the Eternal. That is what most people should be doing most of the time. In fact, unless they did, even the armies would all soon have to stop in their tracks! War comes along and breaks into this normal life of human beings. That it does this is one of the gravest indictments of war. To resist this breaking up of orderly family and community life—not to yield to the subtle and insistent pressure to do something different under the tacit assumption that the normal cannot be meaningful—is one of the great services the people who believe in non-violence and reconciliation may render. "In returning and rest shall ye be saved, in quietness and in confidence shall be your strength."

To look at the matter from another angle, it is sometimes said that it is important that pacifists should make it clear that they can face hardship and danger and are ready to suffer, if need be, on behalf of their convictions. Granted that this is true, it by no means automatically follows that draft-age youths should submit to conscription or that other pacifists should on the advent of war or conscription leave what they are doing for other work. It may well be that the most challenging opportunity to display courage, hardihood and readiness to suffer will be found precisely in the community in which one has been living and in trying to do the ordinary things about which we have been speaking. There is reason to think that some Congressmen may have been influenced in supporting the "deferment," or virtual exemption, for COs under the original 1948 United States Selective Service Act because they were convinced that few who claim to be COs would have the nerve to stand up against the pressure to which one would be subjected as he tried to go his normal way in his home town or college, when others were being drafted and forced to leave home or college. Obviously, only a pacifist who was leading, not a self-indulgent but a disciplined life, who was ready to face danger and suffering and who deeply loved his fellows, could follow such a course. It is possible that some leave the home or college environment not because they wish to face hardship but because they yield to the temptation to try to avoid it.

Let us, after these preliminary observations, try to determine how—from the standpoint of the concept of Christian vocation —the pacifist may judge the action of a government which requires so-called alternative conscript service of him or of his children or fellow-pacifists. There are, so far as I can see, only three possible verdicts. One possibility is to say that the government is demanding that these conscripts shall at least temporarily *abandon* their Christian or true vocation for work to which they clearly are *not* "called." A second possibility is to say that the government is competent in these special circumstances to determine, and has correctly determined, that the alternative service to which it assigns COs constitutes their

Christian vocation for the time being. The third possibility is to reason that when the government thus forces a Christian into another occupation, it is performing an unwarranted and sinful act but that the Christian's duty in such a situation is to practice non-resistance. It, therefore, becomes his vocation to undertake the work which is imposed upon him, not because it is in itself somehow good but because non-resistance to evil constitutes Christian behavior.

The first case is easily disposed of. If the individual is convinced that he is being forced out of his Christian or human vocation into something which, therefore, requires him to disobey God or conscience, he has no alternative but to refuse to comply with the State's demand, perhaps resist it non-violently, and take the consequences. He will still probably be forced out of his accustomed place and work but his non-conformity or non-cooperation with the State's demand at this point becomes his true vocation.

The second possible attitude listed a moment ago is to hold that, in the context of conscription and provided it does not require service in the armed forces, the State may determine what one's Christian vocation is. Some of the Mennonite statements and those of some other pacifists seem to me to fall under this head. The position seems to me a very precarious one and I question whether Mennonites, for example, can maintain it as consistent with their own theology and Christian ethics.

The Role of Jehovah's Witnesses

In the first place, it is essential in the Christian concept of vocation that the "call" is from the Spirit speaking in the heart of the believer. And the believer must always remain in a position where he can be free to respond to the prompting of the Spirit. But how can this be under a conscription regime? The position of Jehovah's Witnesses that they cannot submit to conscription because they must always be free to "witness" to the faith, is in this respect surely a strong and impressive one. It has a bearing also, incidentally, on what we said some paragraphs earlier under general observations about Christian vocation. It seems to me that Christian pacifists need to give much more thought than they have done to the question whether in this particular respect the Witnesses, so far from being eccentric, are not taking the clear and consistent, centrally Christian, stand. The fact that the Witnesses can hardly be classified as pacifists in the usual sense of the term does not affect the relevance of this question for pacifists and indeed for Christians generally.

Furthermore in Mennonite thought, government, the State, though it is "an ordinance of God" to curb sin, is itself by definition also sinful, not Christian, not a part of "the order of redemption." Where, then, does the State get the competence, or the mandate to determine, of all things, the *Christian* vocation of a *believer?* And particularly the war-making arm or department of the State? If the war department or its adjunct, Selective Service, is qualified to determine Christian vocation as part of its conduct of, or preparation for, a war, then why should not the labor department in peace time tell Christians where to work?

There remains a third possible position, namely, that the State is undoubtedly doing an evil thing in taking the individual out of the work to which he feels God has called him but that the principle of non-resistance to evil then comes into operation and submission to this evil becomes the vocation of the persecuted Christian. Given certain premises, there is logic in this position, but it is nevertheless open to serious question. In the first place, non-resistance to an evil should not mean cooperation with it. "Depart from evil and do good," is the law. Pacifists in general, and Christian pacifists in particular, have to ask whether in conforming with any of the provisions of a draft law and especially in rendering conscript service regarded as of "national importance" by a war-making state, they are not helping conscription to run smoothly, helping thus to force conscription on millions of youth and thus in turn promoting war, since conscription is an integral part of an armaments race. The phenomenon of increased tension between nations when they lengthen the compulsory service period for youth is a familiar one. This, of course, raises the whole question of our evaluation of the meaning and role of military conscription, to which we shall return later.

In the meantime, one or two other comments need to be made on the phase of our problem under discussion. If what is really happening is that the war-making state is inflicting an evil on people, forcing them away from their vocation, subjecting them to a measure of persecution, then it seems we ought to keep this clearly in our own minds and ought not to let the government or public assume that we think otherwise. The expressions of "gratitude" which we have sometimes heard addressed to government for "permitting" pacifists to render alternative service seem inappropriate. We cannot have it both ways: accuse the State of the grave sin of invading the realm of Christian vocation and at the same time thank it for doing us a "favor" by making the invasion less than total. The State is not doing God or Christian people a favor in recognizing conscience, though that is what most United States Congressmen think they are doing in making some provision for COs. The pacifist who in any way encourages this notion is in danger of helping to give currency to the idea that conscience is a private whim which legislators may see fit to indulge for prudential reasons, as long as those who are afflicted with this peculiarity are very few in numbers. If non-resistant pacifists get off the high ground of patiently bowing the neck to Caesar's yoke, letting Caesar inflict the scourge of civilian conscript service upon them, they are immediately on the low ground of bargaining for indulgence for a small and, in that view, not too principled or brave a minority. Standing on that lower ground they have very little bargaining *power* and the results will reflect that fact—and pretty much did during World War II. On the other hand, both in Great Britain and in the United States the sufferings which the COs endured in World War I when there was virtually no legal or social recognition of them, were, according to all competent observers, largely responsible for the fact that fairly liberal provisions for COs were made in World War II. The Army did not want to "be bothered with these fellows again."

Two Miles or None

This does not, of course, mean that if the imposition of alternative service is accepted, it should be rendered grudgingly or that feelings of hostility toward government officials with whom one may deal are appropriate. Quite the contrary. If we decide to go with Caesar one mile, the Gospel enjoins us to go two! We have the choice of not going along at all or going two miles, but not a skimpy one mile.

I think it is now generally admitted that there was not a great deal of this glad, spontaneous "second miling" on the part of the conscript COs in World War II, though there was considerable talk about it among older folks. Civilian Public Service in large measure simply did not operate on the high spiritual plane that was originally hoped and is still sometimes implied or stated, but was for many making the best of a bad business, perhaps for lack of clear leading or the courage to follow another course.

It will be recalled that there were a considerable number of Civilian Public Service men who declared flatly that it was inconsistent, and indeed hypocritical, to talk of spontaneous service under conscription. "We are here," they said, "not because our desire to serve brought us here. We are here because the government as part of its war program passed a conscription law and under that law took us by the scruff of the neck and is forcing us to do this job. We have no choice but this or the army or jail. That fact is bound to color this whole experience, except perhaps for those who can shut their eyes to reality. Any one who denies this is a hypocrite."

It seems to me these COs placed the finger on an essential point. Compulsion does enter into "service" under a conscription law. It affects the whole picture. Therefore, the evaluation to be made of the IV-E position and of alternative service under it is not disposed of by asserting that "service is at least as real a part of Christian or pacifist life as witness or resistance." That statement is perfectly correct. Service of men, fellowship with them, on the one hand, and non-cooperation with evil, witness against injustice, non-violent resistance, on the other hand, are both essential in the pacifist way of life. There is some of each in every pacifist life. The most "reconciling" one refuses to use a gun or even, probably, to put on a uniform. Some of the most extreme "resisters" in prison were known for the thoughtful and gentle service they rendered to criminal fellow-inmates. A very discerning English pacifist observed: "For some their witness is their service, for others their service is their witness," or resistance. Each type needs to be on guard against the temptations peculiar to it, including the temptation to question the motives or underestimate the contribution of pacifists of the other type.

But the service which is the essence of pacifism is free, spontaneous, joyous, sacrificial, unbought. To magnify or glorify this is by no means automatically to magnify or glorify the IV-E position *under the draft*. Here, as we have pointed out, an element enters which is contradictory to pacifism, freedom and spontaneity—*the element of compulsion in a context of war and war preparation.*

It seems to me that it is important for pacifists to bear this in mind as we make plans to deal with the problem of alternative service under the amended 1948 Selective Service Act. No matter how "liberal" or "considerate" the conditions for administering alternative service may be in the estimation of government officials or the pacifist agencies, if alternative service is accepted or acquiesced in at all, it will inevitably pose grave problems from the standpoint of Christian vocation and it will not, I think, be possible to escape the contamination or corruption which "conscription" infuses into "service." At the moment it seems possible that Selective Service regulations will permit some individuals to remain at their accustomed occupations. We put aside for the time being certain questions to which we shall return as to what the act of registration itself implies in the context of conscription for atomic and biological war. Here we emphasize that once a man has appealed to the State to permit him to remain in his job and has been granted such permission, it is not exactly the same job as it was before. Others will not be given the same permission, and he should not evade the question whether he can acquiesce in and to a degree benefit from such discrimination. He will have to consider whether the consideration in his case arises from the fact that officials regard his work as in some way a contribution to the war effort, or from a desire to placate and silence an influential person. If he should conclude that he ought to change jobs, he would have to consult the authorities again, and what then?

In conferences with Selective Service officials efforts are being made to avoid some of the features of the war-time Civilian Public Service set-up which deeply troubled a good many Friends—such as the close supervision by military men allegedly functioning as civilians and the undesirable and frustrating character of much of the work to which IV-E men were assigned. Even if substantial concessions are obtained, it will be well for us to be on guard against idealizing the situation. It is hoped that a good many young men will be in effect furloughed to projects at home and abroad which will not be exclusively for COs of draft age and which will have real social value. It will not be the same as if these men had undertaken these jobs out of a sense of vocation and mission, apart from the context of conscription. We know that for the most part they did not volunteer until conscription came along. The same questions which the man who is permitted to remain in his own job faces, will confront these young men on projects. In addition, their term of service and rates of pay will be set by the government.

To sum up this first part of our analysis, it is my conclusion that the one consistent attitude toward conscript alternative service from the standpoint of Christian vocation—if one accepts such work at all—is that which regards submission or non-resistance to the evil which the State imposes upon him when it interferes with his normal occupation, as the vocation or duty of the Christian man. Any other attitude seems to me to involve a considerable measure of rationalization. The Mennonites came nearest to adopting this non-resistant position and the fact that the experience of Mennonite youths in Civilian Public Service was less frustrating and brought better results than was the case with others, save in exceptional instances, seems to me to bear out my analysis. As we have pointed out, those who non-resistantly take up their cross of conscription should bear it joyously and be ready to carry it the second mile.

The Immature Eighteen-Year-Old

We turn next to a brief consideration of the arguments for the IV-E as against the non-registrant position which center around the problem of "the immature 18-year-old youth." A number of 18-year-olds, it is pointed out, have a strong aversion to war and a leaning toward pacifism. They are, however, emotionally immature. If they have no choice but the army or jail all but a few will choose the army and are likely to be lost to the pacifist cause. They could be held and possibly even developed into a radical pacifist position, if they had a third choice, namely, civilian service. On the other hand, the youth who in the absence of such a third possibility, chooses prison rather than the army may suffer grave psychological injury.

I am sure no one will be disposed to be callous or "tough" in his attitude toward any youth faced with a problem such as we are discussing. Any one in the position of a counselor to an individual will want to avoid "psychological pressuring" to induce him to take this or that course, and will strive to help the young man to make his own decision, in accord with his own inner need and conviction, rather than to impose a decision upon him. But I conceive that it would be my duty as a Christian minister to have this same attitude in talking and praying with a young man who was going into the Army. I would have no right, nor do I think it would do any good, to "pressure" him against his conviction and inner need, to refuse service. But this would certainly not mean that I give up my own pacifist convictions, or refrain from doing all I can in general to spread them or from making this particular young man aware of my own thoughts and feelings. This in spite of the fact that if young men who had planned to submit to the draft are consequently won to the pacifist position, this may entail considerable suffering on their part, anguish for parents who disagree with them, and so on. It is fairly certain, incidentally, that in many typical Southern communities—and by no means exclusively in the South—a youth who chose the I-A-O (medical corps) position, not to mention IV-E, would have as tough a time as a non-registrant in many metropolitan centers. We cannot, then, escape the conclusion that as we have a responsibility to decide for the pacifist or non-pacifist position and to bear witness for pacifism, if that is the stand we take, so as pacifists we have a responsibility to decide whether complete non-cooperation with military conscription is the more consistent, committed and effective stand or not, and if we decide for the former, then to do what we can to make our stand and the reasons for it known.

I have the impression that even a great many, perhaps the majority, of pacifist ministers will work harder to keep a young pacifist parishioner from taking the "absolutist" position and going to jail rather than into civilian service, than they would work to get the run of the mill young parishioners to think seriously about not going into the army. They seem somehow to feel that a more awful thing is happening to the young CO who goes to jail than to the 18-year-old who goes into the army. It is my impression that this same feeling is an unconscious factor in the thinking of many lay pacifists when they react strongly against the idea of COs going to prison. This puzzles me greatly. Why should they have this reaction?

Army or Jail?

To my mind—even apart from the sufficiently appalling factor of being systematically trained for wholesale killing and subjected to the risk of being killed in brutal war—there are few if any more evil and perilous situations to put young men into than the armed forces. I should feel much deeper grief over having possibly had some part in getting some youth to go into the armed forces than over having some responsibility for bringing a young man to go to prison for conscience's sake. Are the qualms people feel about youthful COs going to prison in certain instances perhaps due to the fact that taking the non-registrant position is something very unusual and regarded with social disapproval, whereas becoming a soldier is extremely common and meets with the highest social approval? It may be, therefore, that there are some ministers and other older people who should examine themselves as to whether their feelings in the matter under discussion are due to the fact that they themselves might find life in the community or in the church very uncomfortable if they were suspected of having influenced a youth to take a radical anti-draft stand, whereas all men will speak well of them—or at least not too ill—if they have helped, or at least not hindered, young Christians in adjusting themselves to the idea of going into the army. Is it just possible that we older people are sometimes concerned with sparing ourselves when we think we are solely concerned about sparing teen-agers?

To return to the 18-year-old. There are young men who on physical and psychological grounds are exempted from army service. There may well be COs who should on similar grounds be exempted from any kind of service. If such a physically or mentally ill CO is refused exemption, he should perhaps be discouraged from undergoing the risks of prison experience if there is an alternative for him. This still leaves us with the problem of the majority of pacifist and non-pacifist youth who are not ill.

When we find ourselves concerned about what the teen-age religious CO who goes to prison must undergo and inclined to think that there is here an absolutely conclusive case for providing alternative service and urging most such COs to avail themselves of it, we might first take a look at two other categories of youth who are subject to the draft. One of them consists of those actually drafted into the armed services; the other of the so-called non-religious COs.

The great mass of teen-agers are going to be put through rigorous military training with all the hardships, the toughening and the temptations which this entails. They have to be ready to undergo actual battle experience. Many of them will actually experience modern war at the front. Is what the CO undergoes in prison vastly more terrible than this? Is it as terrible? It may be said that the soldier has social approbation whereas the pacifist, especially the "absolutist" meets social disapprobation and even ostracism. This is indeed a sore trial and many cannot endure it. Frankly, I am still left with more grief and pity in my heart for the teen-age soldier than for the teen-age "absolutist" CO. I am still left with a question whether we have a right to take any time and energy away from the struggle to lift the curse of conscription from the mass of youth and put it into an effort to secure alternative conscript service for COs.

There are, as we know, teen-age "absolutists" who feel the same way and who have demonstrated that they can endure whatever they may be called upon to endure. Nor is their lot without its compensations. They, also, "have their reward."

The So-Called Non-Religious CO

Religious COs who accept the IV-E classification and older pacifists who advocate this course have also to consider the non-religious CO. Under United States Law it is the so-called religious CO who is eligible for this classification; the so-called non-religious CO, though he may by unanimous consent be equally sincere, is not. The latter has no choice except the army or jail. The fact that he is only 18 years old does not alter that. Nothing in this entire field of pacifist policy and behavior is, frankly, harder for me to understand than how religious COs and many of the leaders of the peace churches and of the Fellowship of Reconciliation, can acquiesce in this situation and accept what is regarded as an advantage, a preferred position, under it. The white CO who accepted conscript alternative service when the Negro CO was automatically forced to choose the army or prison would be in an invidious position. So would the Gentile when his Jewish comrade was thus discriminated against. But in my mind the case is far more deplorable when it is the religious and the supposedly non-religious man who are involved. The white man or the Gentile might actually believe in discrimination or not regard it too seriously when the discrimination is in his favor. But for the religious man it should surely be a central and indispensable part of his faith that discrimination, most of all where two men acting in obedience to conscience are involved, is unthinkable and that if there is discrimination, he cannot be the beneficiary of it.

At any rate, the argument that there must be alternative service because *immature* 18-year-olds must by no means be subjected to prison experience seems to me to become completely impotent in the mouths of those religious pacifists who acquiesce in the arrangement under discussion and enable it to work—unless indeed they mean to contend that the average religious CO has less stamina than the non-religious CO and that, therefore, the former should be given gentler treatment.

Advocacy of alternative service for the teen-age CO is based on considerations relating to the future of the pacifist movement, as well as on the effect on the COs themselves. It is argued that if the only choice young pacifists have is the army or jail, there will be very few pacifists. This argument was not, however, first advanced when the draft age was lowered. It was often heard during World War II when most COs were older and more seasoned. It has always impressed me as a dubious argument and I wonder where it leads us. What, for example, is the relationship of this argument to the one which is also advanced—sometimes by the same person—that the IV-E position is very meaningful and perhaps to be preferred to the more "absolutist" one, because it is the IV-E man who gives a glorious demonstration of the spirit of selfless service which is the essence of pacifism at its best? These two concepts cannot very well be harnessed together as a team. We can hardly contend in one and the same breath that we want alternative service because most young pacifists are not ready to follow a stronger and more sacrificial course *and* that we want it because it is the strongest and most meaningful course pacifists can follow. It seems to me we have to decide whether our problem is to find shelter for COs or whether it is to find freedom and the opportunity for self-expression and service, even though the price be high.

To consider the matter for a moment from the tactical viewpoint, it seems quite certain that the number of 18-year-olds who take either the IV-E or the non-registrant position (perhaps even the I-A-O position might be included) will at least at the outset be small. The draft now gets the young man at the very age when it is most difficult for him to stand out in any way from the mass of his fellows. Even if he is intellectually pretty well convinced of the pacifist position, he is not emotionally mature enough to take it. It is a fair guess that the accessions to the pacifist movement, if military service and/or training becomes universal, will in the future come mainly from young people who have gone through the experience of life in the armed forces. In other words, the additional number of pacifists recruited because alternative service is provided may turn out to be very small. If so, the numerical advantage from the adoption of a less uncompromising pacifism is illusory.

There is one other factor which may be mentioned in this context, that we live in an age when the role of minorities is an increasingly difficult one. The pressures and the actual persecution to which they are subjected are severe. The trend is still partially obscured in the United States but if we pause to reflect that not a single bomb has as yet fallen on this country, we shall realize that this country is not an exception to the trend toward greater conformity and regimentation. As the New York *Times* editorialized some time ago in commenting on some features of the McCarran Act, if we are already resorting to such repressive measures, what will we do when a real crisis comes? In other words, while we spend a good deal of time arguing that COs should have some choice other than the army or jail, we are probably moving into a time when that will essentially be the only choice that members of minorities, including pacifists, have. It would seem then that our thought and energy should be devoted to two issues: whether and how this trend toward totalitarianism can be halted and how we

may prepare and discipline ourselves to meet the tests which
our fellow-pacifists in some other lands have already had to
meet?

The Nature of Conscription

This, however, leads to the third and last of the issues we
are trying to explore: the true nature of conscription, of
modern war, and of the conscripting, war-making State—and
the attitude which pacifists consequently should take toward
them.

Participation in alternative service is quite often defended
on the ground that our opposition is to war rather than conscription; except in the matter of war we are as ready to serve
the nation as anybody; therefore, as long as we are not drafted
for combat or forced against our will into the armed services,
we are ready to render whatever service of a civilian character
may be imposed upon us.

Is this a sound position? Let me emphasize that it is conscription for war under the conditions of the second half of
the twentieth century that we are talking about. The question
as to whether sometime and under some circumstances we
might accept conscription for some conceivable purpose not
related to war, is not here at stake. It is academic and irrelevant. The question with which we are dealing is that of conscripting youth in and for modern war.

As pacifists we are opposed to all war. Even if recruitment
were entirely on a voluntary basis, we would be opposed. It
seems to me we might infer from this that we should be *a
fortiori* opposed to military conscription, for here in addition to
the factor of war itself, the element of coercion by government
enters in, coercion which places young boys in a military
regime where they are deprived of freedom of choice in virtually all essential matters. They may not have the slightest
interest in the war, yet they are made to kill by order. This is

surely a fundamental violation of the human spirit which must cause the pacifist to shudder.

The reply is sometimes made that pacifists are *not* being conscripted for military purposes and therefore—presumably— *they* are not faced with the issue of the nature of military conscription. I shall later contend that it is not really possible to separate conscription and war, as I think this argument does. Here I wish to suggest that even if the question is the conscription of non-pacifist youth, it is a fundamental mistake for pacifists ever to relent in their opposition to this evil, ever to devote their energies primarily to securing provisions for COs in a draft law or to lapse into a feeling that conscription has somehow become more palatable if such provisions are made by the State. It is not our own children if we are pacifist parents, our fellow-pacifist Christians if we are churchmen, about whom we should be most deeply concerned. In the first place, that is a narrow and perhaps self-centered attitude. In the second place, pacifist youths have some inner resources for meeting the issue under discussion. The terrible thing which we should never lose sight of, to which we should never reconcile our spirits, is that the great mass of 18-year olds are drafted for war. They are given no choice. Few are at the stage of development where they are capable of making fully rational and responsible choice. Thus the fathers immolate the sons, the older generation immolates the younger, on the altar of Moloch. What God centuries ago forbade Abraham to do even to his own son—"Lay not thy hand upon the lad, neither do thou anything unto him"—this we do by decree to the entire youth of a nation.

We need to ask ourselves whether such conscription is in any real sense a lesser evil. As we have already said, the pacifist is opposed to war and we have all sensed the danger of arguing against conscription *on the ground that* the nation could raise all the troops it needed by voluntary enlistment. Nevertheless, there is a point to an impassioned argument which George Bernanos makes in the book we mentioned at the outset. He states that the man created by western or Christian civilization "disappeared in the day conscription became law . . . the principle is a totalitarian principle if ever there was one—so much so that you could deduce the whole system from it, as you can deduce the whole of geometry from the propositions of Euclid."

To the question as to whether France, the Fatherland, should not be defended if in peril, he has the Fatherland answer: "I very much doubt whether my salvation requires such monstrous behavior" as defense by modern war methods. If men wanted to die on behalf of the Fatherland, moreover, that would be one thing but "making a clean sweep, with one scoop of the hand, of an entire male population" is another matter altogether: "You tell me that, in saving me, they save themselves. Yes, if they can remain free; no, if they allow you to destroy, by this unheard of measure, the national covenant. For as soon as you have, by simple decree, created millions of French soldiers, it will be held as proven that you have sovereign rights over the persons and the goods of every Frenchman, that there are no rights higher than yours and where, then, will your usurpations stop? Won't you presently presume to decide what is just and what is unjust, what is Evil and what is Good?"

It is pretty certainly an oversimplification to suggest, as Bernanos here does, that the entire totalitarian, mechanized "system" under which men today live or into which they are increasingly drawn even in countries where a semblance of freedom and spontaneity remains, can be traced to its source in the military conscription which was instituted by the French Revolution in the eighteenth century. But what cannot, it seems to me, be successfully denied is that today totalitarianism, depersonalization, conscription, war, and the conscripting, war-making power-state are inextricably linked together. They constitute a whole, a "system." It is a disease, a creeping paralysis, which affects all nations, on both side of the global conflict. Revolution and counter-revolution, "peoples' democracies" and "western democracies," the "peace-loving" nations on both sides in the war, are cast in this mold of conformity, mechanization and violence. This is the Beast which, in the language of the Apocalypse, is seeking to usurp the place of the Lamb.

We know that "war will stop at nothing" and we are clear that as pacifists we can have nothing to do with it. But I do not think that it is possible to distinguish between war and conscription, to say that the former is and the latter is not an instrument or mark of the Beast.

Disobedience Becomes Imperative

Non-conformity, Holy Disobedience, becomes a virtue and indeed a necessary and indispensable measure of spiritual self-preservation, in a day when the impulse to conform, to acquiesce, to go along, is the instrument which is used to subject men to totalitarian rule and involve them in permanent war. To create the impression at least of outward unanimity, the impression that there is no "real" opposition, is something for which all dictators and military leaders strive assiduously. The more it seems that there is no opposition, the less worthwhile it seems to an ever larger number of people to cherish even the thought of opposition. Surely, in such a situation it is important not to place the pinch of incense before Caesar's image, not to make the gesture of conformity which is involved, let us say, in registering under a military conscription law. When the object is so plainly to create a situation where the individual no longer has a choice except total conformity or else the concentration camp or death; when reliable people tell us seriously that experiments are being conducted with drugs which will paralyze the wills of opponents within a nation or in an enemy country, it is surely neither right nor wise to wait until the "system" has driven us into a corner where we cannot retain a vestige of self-respect unless we say No. It does not seem wise or right to wait until this evil catches up with us, but rather to go out to meet it—to *resist*—before it has gone any further.

As Bernanos reminds us, "things are moving fast, dear reader, they are moving very fast." He recalls that he "lived at a time when passport formalities seemed to have vanished forever." A man could "travel around the world with nothing in his wallet but his visiting card." He recalls that "twenty years ago, Frenchmen of the middle class refused to have their fingerprints taken; fingerprints were the concern of convicts." But the word "criminal" has "swollen to such prodigious proportions that it now includes every citizen who dislikes the Regime, the System, the Party, or the man who represents them. . . . The moment, perhaps, is not far off when it will seem natural for us to leave the front-door key in the lock at night so that the police may enter at any hour of the day or night, *as it is to open our pocket-books to every official demand*. And when the State decides that it would be a practical measure . . . to put some outward sign on us, why should we hesitate to have ourselves branded on the cheek or on the buttock, with a hot iron, like cattle? The purges of 'wrong-thinkers,' so dear to the totalitarian regimes, would thus become infinitely easier."

To me it seems that submitting to conscription even for civilian service is permitting oneself thus to be branded by the State. It makes the work of the State in preparing for war and in securing the desired impression of unanimity much easier. It seems, therefore, that pacifists should refuse to be thus branded.

In the introductory chapter to Kay Boyle's volume of short stories about occupied Germany, *The Smoking Mountain*, there is an episode which seems to me to emphasize the need of Resistance and of not waiting until it is indeed too late. She tells about a woman, professor of philology in a Hessian university who said of the German experience with Nazism: "It was a gradual process." When the first *Jews Not Wanted* signs went up, "there was never any protest made about them, and, after a few months, not only we, but even the Jews who lived in that town, walked past without noticing any more that they were there. Does it seem impossible to you that this should have happened to civilized people anywhere?"

The philology professor went on to say that after a while she put up a picture of Hitler in her class-room. After twice refusing to take the oath of allegiance to Hitler, she was persuaded by her students to take it. "They argued that in taking this oath, which so many anti-Nazis had taken before me, *I was committing myself to nothing, and that I could exert more influence as a professor than as an outcast in the town.*"

She concluded by saying that she now had a picture of a Jew, Spinoza, where Hitler's picture used to hang, and added: "Perhaps you will think that I did this ten years too late, and perhaps you are right in thinking this. *Perhaps there was something else we could all of us have done, but we never seemed to find a way to do it, either as individuals or as a group, we never seemed to find a way.*" A decision by the pacifist movement in this country to break completely with conscription, to give up the idea that we can "exert more influence" if we conform in some measure, do not resist to the uttermost—this might awaken our countrymen to a realization of the precipice on the edge of which we stand. It might be the making of our movement.

The Reconciling Resistance

Thus to embrace Holy Disobedience is not to substitute Resistance for Reconciliation. It is to practice both Reconciliation and Resistance. In so far as we help to build up or smooth the way for American militarism and the regimentation which accompanies it, we are certainly not practising reconciliation toward the millions of people in the Communist bloc countries against whom American war preparations, including conscription, are directed. Nor are we practising reconciliation toward the millions of people in the Communist bloc countries against whom American war preparations, including conscription, are directed. Nor are we practising reconciliation towards the hundreds of millions in Asia and Africa whom we condemn to poverty and drive into the arms of Communism by our addiction to military "defense." Nor are we practising love toward our own fellow-citizens, including also the multitude of youths in the armed services, if against our deepest insight, we help to fasten the chains of conscription and war upon them.

Our works of mercy, healing and reconstruction will have a deeper and more genuinely reconciling effect when they are not entangled with conscript service for "the health, safety and interest" of the United States or any other war-making State. It is highly doubtful whether Christian mission boards can permit any of their projects in the Orient to be manned by men supposed to be working for "the health, safety and interest" of the United States. The Gospel of reconciliation will be preached with a new freedom and power when the preachers have broken decisively with American militarism. It can surely not be preached at all in Communist lands by those who have not made that break. It will be when we have gotten off the back of what someone has called the wild elephant of militarism and conscription on to the solid ground of freedom, and only then, that we shall be able to live and work constructively. Like Abraham we shall have to depart from the City-which-is in order that we may help to build the City-which-is-to-be, whose true builder and maker is God.

It is, of course, possible, perhaps even likely, that if we set ourselves apart as those who will have no dealings whatever with conscription, will not place the pinch of incense before Caesar's image, our fellow-citizens will stone us, as

Stephen was stoned when he reminded his people that it was they who had "received the law as it was ordained by angels, and kept it not." So may we be stoned for reminding our people of a tradition of freedom and peace which was also, in a real sense, "ordained by angels" and which we no longer keep. But, it will thus become possible for them, as for Paul, even amidst the search for new victims to persecute, suddenly to see again the face of Christ and the vision of a new Jerusalem.

Some one may at this point reflect that earlier in this paper I counseled against people too readily leaving the normal path of life and that I am now counseling a policy which is certain to create disturbance in individual lives, families and communities. That is so. But to depart from the common way in response or reaction to a conscription law, in the attempt to adapt oneself to an abnormal state of society, is one thing. To leave father, mother, wife, child, yea and one's own life also, at the behest of Christ or conscience is quite another. Our generation will not return to a condition under which every man may sit under his own vine and fig tree, with none to make him afraid, unless there are those who are willing to pay the high cost of redemption and deliverance from a regime of regimentation, terror and war.

Finally, it is of crucial importance that we should understand that for the individual to pit himself in Holy Disobedience against the war-making and conscripting State, wherever it or he be located, is not an act of despair or defeatism. Rather, I think we may say that precisely this individual refusal to "go along" is now the beginning and the core of any realistic and practical movement against war and for a more peaceful and brotherly world. For it becomes daily clearer that political and military leaders pay virtually no attention to protests against current foreign policy and pleas for peace when they know perfectly well that when it comes to a showdown, all but a handful of the millions of protesters will "go along" with the war to which the policy leads. All but a handful will submit to conscription. Few of the protesters will so much as risk their jobs in the cause of "peace." The failure of the policy-makers to change their course does not, save perhaps in very rare instances, mean that they are evil men who want war. They feel, as indeed they so often declare in crucial moments, that the issues are so complicated, the forces arrayed against them so strong, that they "have no choice" but to add another score of billions to the military budget, and so on and on. Why should they think there is any reality, hope or salvation in "peace advocates" who when the moment of decision comes also act on the assumption that they "have no choice" but to conform?

Precisely in a day when the individual appears to be utterly helpless, to "have no choice," when the aim of the "system" is to convince him that he is helpless as an individual and that the only way to meet regimentation is by regimentation, there is absolutely no hope save in going back to the beginning. The human being, the child of God, must assert his humanity and his sonship again. He must exercise the choice which he no longer has as something accorded him by society, which he "naked, weaponless, armourless, without shield or spear, but only with naked hands and open eyes" must create again. He must understand that this naked human being is the one *real* thing in the face of the mechanics and the mechanized institutions of our age. He, by the grace of God, is the seed of all the human life there will be on earth in the future, though he may have to die to make that harvest possible. As *Life* magazine stated in its unexpectedly profound and stirring editorial of August 20, 1945, its first issue after the atom bombing of Hiroshima: "Our sole safeguard against the very real danger of a reversion to barbarism is the kind of morality which compels the individual conscience, be the group right or wrong. The individual conscience against the atomic bomb? Yes. There is no other way."

26. Albert Bigelow,
"Why I am Sailing into
the Pacific Bomb-Test Area"

The Committee for Nonviolent Action (CNVA) was formed in 1957 with a dozen members. In 1958, CNVA promoted the voyage of a 30-foot sailing boat, *The Golden Rule,* into the forbidden nuclear testing area of the Western Pacific. In this document the boat's captain, former naval commander Albert Bigelow, describes the motives prompting the venture, which ended with the arrest and imprisonment of the crew in Honolulu.

My friend Bill Huntington and I are planning to sail a small vessel westward into the Pacific H-bomb test area. By April we expect to reach nuclear testing grounds at Eniwetok. We will remain there as long as the tests of H-bombs continue. With us will be two other volunteers.

Why? Because it is the way I can say to my government, to the British government, and to the Kremlin: "Stop! Stop this madness before it is too late. For God's sake, turn back!"

How have I come to this conviction? Why do I feel under compulsion, under moral orders, as it were, to do this?

The answer to such questions, at least in part, has to do with my experience as a Naval officer during World War II. The day after Pearl Harbor was attacked, I was at the Navy recruiting offices. I had had a lot of experience in navigating vessels. Life in the Navy would be a glamorous change from the dull mechanism of daily civilian living. My experience assured me of success. All this adventure ahead and the prospect of becoming a hero into the bargain.

Albert S. Bigelow, "Why I am Sailing into the Pacific Bomb-Test Area," *Liberation* (February 1958), 4–6.

I suppose, too, that I had an enormous latent desire to conform, to go along with the rest of my fellows. I was swayed by the age-old psychology of meeting force with force. It did not really occur to me to resist the drag of the institution of war, the pattern of organized violence, which had existed for so many centuries. This psychology prevailed even though I had already reflected on the fantastic wastefulness of war—the German *Bismarck* hunting the British *Hood* and sending it to the bottom of the sea, and the British Navy hunting the *Bismarck* and scuttling it.

I volunteered, but instead of being sent to sea, I was assigned to 90 Church Street in New York and worked in project "plot" establishing the whereabouts of all combat ships in the Atlantic. In a couple of months I escaped from this assignment and was transferred to the Naval Training Station at Northwestern University.

I had not been at Northwestern very long when I sensed that because of my past experience I would be made an instructor there and still not get to sea. So I deliberately flunked an examination in navigation and before long was assigned to a submarine chaser in the Atlantic.

The Turkey Shoot

From March to October of 1943 I was in command of a submarine chaser in the Solomon Islands, during the fighting. It was during this period that more than 100 Japanese planes were shot down in one day. This was called "the Turkey Shoot." The insensitivity which decent men must develop in such situations is appalling. I remember that the corpse of a Japanese airman who had been shot down was floating bolt upright in one of the coves, a position resulting from the structure of the Japanese life belts, which were different from our Mae Wests. Each day as we passed the cove we saw this figure, his face growing blacker under the terrific sun. We laughingly called him Smiling Jack. As a matter of fact, I think I gave him that name myself and felt rather proud of my wit.

Later in World War II, I was Captain of the destroyer escort *Dale W. Peterson*—DE 337—and I was on her bridge as we came into Pearl Harbor from San Francisco when the first news arrived of the explosion of an atomic bomb over Hiroshima. Although I had no way of understanding what an atom bomb was I was absolutely awestruck, as I suppose all men were for a moment. Intuitively it was then that I realized for the first time that morally war is impossible.

I don't suppose I had the same absolute realization with my whole being, so to speak, of the immorality and "impossibility" of nuclear war until the morning of August 7, 1957. On that day, I sat with a score of friends, before dawn, in the Nevada desert just outside the entrance to the Camp Mercury testing grounds. The day before, eleven of us, in protest against the summer-long tests, had tried to enter the restricted area. We had been arrested as we stepped one after another over the boundary line, and had been carried off to a ghost town which stands at the entrance to Death Valley. There we had been given a speedy trial under the charge of trespassing under the Nevada laws. Sentencing had been suspended for a year, and later in the afternoon we had returned to Camp Mercury to continue the Prayer and Conscience Vigil along with others who had remained there during our civil disobedience action.

In the early morning of August 7 an experimental bomb was exploded. We sat with our backs to the explosion site. But when the flash came I felt again the utterly impossible horror of this whole business, the same complete realization that nuclear war must go, that I had felt twelve years before on the bridge of U. S. S. *Dale W. Peterson,* off Pearl Harbor.

I think also that deep down somewhere in me, and in all men at all times, there is a realization that the pattern of violence meeting violence makes no sense, and that war violates something central in the human heart—"that of God," as we Quakers sometimes say. For example, when each of us at the trial the afternoon before had told why we were committing civil disobedience against nuclear tests, our attorney, Francis Heisler, said: "There isn't one of us in this court room who doesn't wish that he had walked into the testing grounds with these people this morning." Everybody, including the police and court officers, nodded assent.

Society of Friends

However, I am ahead of my story. At the close of the War, in spite of what I had felt on the bridge of that destroyer, I did not break away from my old life. For a time I was Housing Commissioner of Massachusetts. Like many other people who had been through the War, I was seeking some sort of unified life-philosophy or religion. I did a good deal of religious "window-shopping." I became impressed by the fact that in one way or another the saints, the wise men, those who seemed to me truly experienced, all pointed in one direction—toward nonviolence, truth, love, toward a way and a goal that could not be reconciled with war. For quite a while, to use a phrase of Alan Watts', I "sucked the finger instead of going where it pointed." But finally I realized that I did have to move in that direction, and in 1952 I resigned my commission in the Naval Reserve. It was promptly and courteously accepted. I felt a bit proud of doing it a month before I would have come into a pension. Such little things we pride ourselves on!

I came into contact with the Quakers, the Society of Friends. My wife, Sylvia, had already joined the Society in 1948. As late as 1955 I was still fighting off joining the Society, which seemed to me to involve a great, awesome commitment. I suppose I was like the man in one of Shaw's plays who wanted to be a Christian—but not yet.

The Hiroshima Maidens

Then came the experience of having in our home for some months two of the Hiroshima maidens who had been injured and disfigured in the bombing of August 6, 1945. Norman Cousins and other wonderful people brought them to this country for plastic surgery. There were two things about these girls that hit me very hard and forced me to see that I had no choice but to make the commitment to live, as best I could, a life of nonviolence and reconciliation. One was the fact that when they were bombed in 1945 the two girls in our home were nine and thirteen years old. What earthly thing could they have done to give some semblance of what we call justice to the ordeal inflicted upon them and hundreds like them? What possible good could come out of human action—war— which bore such fruits? Is it not utter blasphemy to think that there is anything moral or Christian about such behavior?

The other thing that struck me was that these young women found it difficult to believe that *we*, who were not members of their families, could love *them*. But *they* loved *us;* they har- bored no resentment against us or other Americans. How are you going to respond to that kind of attitude? The newly- elected president of the National Council of Churches, Edwin T. Dahlberg, said in his inaugural talk that instead of "massive retaliation" the business of Christians is to practice "massive reconciliation." Well, these Hiroshima girls practiced "massive reconciliation" on us, on me, who had laughed derisively at "Smiling Jack." What response can one make to this other than to give oneself utterly to destroying the evil, war, that dealt so shamefully with them and try to live in the spirit of sensitivity and reconciliation which they displayed?

As I have said, I think there is that in all men that abhors and rejects war and knows that force and violence can bring no good thing to pass. Yet men are bound by old patterns of feeling, thought and action. The organs of public opinions are almost completely shut against us. It seems practically impos- sible, moreover, for the ordinary person by ordinary means to speak to, and affect the action of, his government. I have had a recent experience of this which has strengthened my conviction that it is only by such acts as sailing a boat to Eniwetok and thus "speaking" to the government right in the testing area that we can expect to be heard.

Tell it to the Policeman

I was asked by the New England office of the American Friends Service Committee to take to the White House 17,411 signatures to a petition to cancel the Pacific tests. Ten thousand signatures had previously been sent in. I realize that even a President in good health cannot see personally everyone who has a message for him. Yet the right of petition exists—in theory—and is held to be a key factor in democratic process. And the President presumably has assistants to see to it that all serious petitions are somehow brought to his attention. For matters of this kind, there is Maxwell Rabb, secretary to the cabinet.

Twenty-seven thousand is quite a few people to have signed a somewhat unusual petition. The A. F. S. C. is widely known and recognized as a highly useful agency. I am known to Maxwell Rabb with whom I worked in Republican politics in Massachusetts. I was a precinct captain for Eisenhower in the 1952 primaries. Yet a couple of days work on the part of the staff of the Friends Committee on National Legislation failed to secure even an assurance that some time on Tuesday, December 31, the day I would be in Washington, Max Rabb would see me to receive the petitions. On that day I made five calls and talked with his secretary. Each time I was assured that she would call me back within ten minutes. Each time the return call failed to come and I tried again. The last time, early in the afternoon, I held on to the telephone for ten minutes, only to be told finally that the office was about to close for the day.

Each time I telephoned, including the last, I was told I could, of course, leave the petitions with the policeman at the gate. This I refused to do. It seems terrible to me that Americans can no longer speak to or be seen by their government. Has it become their master, not their servant? Can it not listen to their humble and reasonable pleas? This experience may in one sense be a small matter but I am sure it is symptomatic— among other things—of a sort of fear on the part of officials to listen to what in their hearts they feel is right but on which they cannot act without breaking with old patterns of thought. At any rate, the experience has strengthened in me the conviction that we must, at whatever cost, find ways to make our witness and protest heard.

I Am Going Because . . .

I am going because, as Shakespeare said, "Action is eloquence." Without some such direct action, ordinary citizens lack the power any longer to be seen or heard by their government.

I am going because it is time to *do something* about peace, not just *talk* about peace.

I am going because, like all men, in my heart I know that *all* nuclear explosions are monstrous, evil, unworthy of human beings.

I am going because war is no longer a feudal jousting match; it is an unthinkable catastrophe for all men.

I am going because it is now the little children, and, most of all, the as yet unborn who are the front line troops. It is my duty to stand between them and this horrible danger.

I am going because it is cowardly and degrading for me to stand by any longer, to consent, and thus to collaborate in atrocities.

I am going because I cannot say that the end justifies the means. A Quaker, William Penn, said, "A good end cannot sanctify evil means; nor must we ever do evil that good may come of it." A Communist, Milovan Djilas, says, "As soon as means which would ensure an end are shown to be evil, the end will show itself as unrealizable."

I am going because, as Gandhi said, "God sits in the man opposite me; therefore to injure him is to injure God himself."

I am going to witness to the deep inward truth we all know, "Force can subdue, but love gains."

I am going because however mistaken, unrighteous, and unrepentant governments may seem, I still believe all men are really good at heart, and that my act will speak to them.

I am going in the hope of helping change the hearts and minds of men in government. If necessary I am willing to give my life to help change a policy of fear, force and destruction to one of trust, kindness, and help.

I am going in order to say, "Quit this waste, this arms race. Turn instead to a disarmament race. Stop competing for evil, compete for good."

I am going because I have to—if I am to call myself a human being.

When you see something horrible happening, your instinct is to do something about it. You can freeze in fearful apathy or you can even talk yourself into saying that it isn't horrible. I can't do that. I have to act. This is too horrible. We know it. Let's all act.

27. Wilmer Young,
Visible Witness

In 1959 the Committee for Nonviolent Action organized a demonstration against land-launched missiles near Omaha, Nebraska. Among those arrested was Wilmer Young, an elderly Quaker, who tells of his experience in this document.

Wilmer J. Young, *Visible Witness: A Testimony for Radical Peace Action,* Pendle Hill Pamphlet No. 118 (Wallingford, Pa.: Pendle Hill, 1961), pp. 3–17. Reprinted with the permission of Pendle Hill, Wallingford, Pa.

On July 6, 1959, I found myself in jail in Omaha, Nebraska. Having lived for over seventy years without ever being in jail before, I have been asked to explain. Many men who, for one reason or another, have to beg for their daily bread have this experience often. But I, who had never been really hungry in my life and had lived by the accepted rules of society . . . !

Yet this did not just happen. It came after years of travail of spirit, and if I was foolish or unwise, it may be partly because, as a friend once said to me, "Thee is the most naïve person I have ever known." But it just might be for some better reason, and I'd like to see if I can explain it in a way that may make sense to some who are more sophisticated.

Just before going to Omaha, I had written to my three children that I was going out to help a group of people who were planning to protest the construction of a missile site. I said that I did not yet know what I myself would do there, but felt that I could probably be useful in some way, perhaps drive a car or help with the accounts.

I arrived at Omaha late Saturday night, June 19. The opening public meeting of the project called *Omaha Action* was scheduled to be held that night at the YMCA. I went directly there and found that the clerk at the desk knew nothing of the meeting. But, when I pressed him more, he did admit that he knew of one that was being held at a hotel not far away. His manner, together with the change of place, gave me my first evidence that things were not going to be entirely smooth.

At the hotel, where the meeting was already nearly over, there was an atmosphere of tension. In spite of considerable advertising, only about thirty people had come, and half of them were from our own group. The reporters who were there took pictures of the empty chairs and called special attention to the fact that very few Omaha people attended. It was clear that we were not being welcomed to Omaha. (Well, why should we be?)

A few days earlier, the one local paper had published a long editorial which attacked one of our members who had once been a Trotskyite, and failed to mention that this connection had been repudiated many years ago. Thus the stage was set for fear; no church in the city was found willing to hear any of us.

Sunday morning, some of our group of about fifteen went to hand out our *Omaha Action* leaflets on the streets; others attended church services. I went to the small Friends Meeting held in the YMCA, and found there some cousins who were sympathetic and did what they could to help us throughout our stay. In the afternoon, we met in an office that had been rented when the forerunners of the *Action* first arrived, and there made plans for the next few days. We divided into two groups, one group to go to Lincoln and walk the forty miles from there to the Mead Ordnance Base, the other to remain in Omaha overnight and, on Monday morning, start walking the thirty miles to the same spot.

Three days were allotted for this march. I was errand boy for the Omaha contingent, taking them food and their sleeping equipment at proper hours, and finding them places to sleep. This latter job proved to be another eye-opener for me. We were in open country, with many beautiful farms and farm homes, the kind of country where I grew up three hundred miles farther east, in Iowa. But to find a place where these walkers could get permission to sleep on somebody's ground required some looking around. Word had got around that we were coming, and nobody had any latchstrings out. For the first night, I found a wood where we were allowed to sleep. But the next night, I could not find any place where the owners would allow it, so the night was spent on a railway right-of-way. By this time, we had become somewhat apprehensive, but after getting the group settled, I returned the twenty-five miles to Omaha. Around midnight, two of us started back to call on both groups, to see if all was well. Everything was quiet and peaceful under the stars, and nothing more had happened than that a few epithets and firecrackers had been hurled their way.

On the third day, the groups converged and completed their march to the entrance of the Base nearest the missile site. They set up camp on a little bluff in some tall grass on the edge of a clover field. A round-the-clock vigil was then started which lasted over a week, and was continued in daytime until July 21, when the little camp was torn up at night by hostile youngsters.

The Mead Ordnance Base is twenty-six square miles in area, much of it leased for farming to people who formerly had their homes here but had been forced (in some cases) to sell to the Defense Department. This is near the headquarters of the Strategic Air Command. Our vigil site was just outside the entrance, where there was a very ordinary farm gate, and just inside, a little shelter for two guards was set up after we came. In normal times, the gate usually stood open and there were no guards.

I shall not soon forget a meeting held the next week, at which each person of our group gave his decision as to what part he would take in the actions of the following days. Fifteen persons (this perhaps counts a few who came later) said they planned to do some form of civil disobedience, as their part of the protest. When it came my turn, I found myself saying, somewhat to my surprise, that I too planned to offer civil disobedience. Having said it, I found I was quite calm about it and, what is even more surprising to me, I have never since regretted the decision, although it committed me to a form of action that was completely new to me. I shall try to explain this phenomenon later, in so far as I can.

As the vigil continued, we learned more about the situation. The construction of the missile site was still in a very early stage. Probably not over a hundred men were actually at work there, and they lived in the surrounding area of farms and small towns, some as far away as Omaha. Perhaps fifty cars and trucks went in and out of the Base each day. The men would hardly have dared stop and talk with us in the presence of the guards, or take our leaflets, even if they had wanted to. They could hardly fail to read our signs, but that was all. The signs were brief and easily read:

END MISSILE RACE

LET MANKIND LIVE

and

NON-VIOLENT PROTEST

AGAINST NUCLEAR MISSILE POLICY

It is significant that of all the newspaper pictures taken of us, so far as I saw them, only two showed the signs so that they could be read. Nor were they printed in the newspaper stories.

We were acutely conscious that, in this situation, we were only protesting. We could not find a way even to suggest that we did have a positive program in mind, calling for the strengthening of the United Nations, making use of the World Court, studying nonviolent resistance to evil and training for its use. We asked permission to address the workers at the Base during their lunch-hour or give them our literature. This was refused. We asked for their names, so that we might call on them in their homes. This too was refused. There seemed to be only one way in which we could present our positive program to anybody, and that was to hand out leaflets in Omaha and in the towns, and talk with individuals whenever we could. But you cannot present a whole theory on a four-page leaflet; and the channels we are used to using, such as the local newspaper, the churches, the radio, and TV, were all closed to us, as far as presenting any constructive program was concerned.

What could we do?

Let us remind ourselves for a moment that this condition

would be pretty much true in every town and city in America. We are not always aware of it, because we do not often make the attempt to challenge the thought patterns of our neighbors, and to get radical peace messages on the radio or into the papers. The only way we could see to get our message to the people was to dramatize our protest by getting arrested for illegal entry of the Base.

A few days after the meeting where the decisions for civil disobedience had been made, on July 1 at 10 a.m., we held a meeting for worship "after the manner of Friends" at the vigil site. This was a very solemn half hour for us, as it was the preliminary to three of us "going in" to the Base and thus breaking a law. None of us knew what the penalty incurred or even what the charge would be; nor did we know under what court the trial would come.

An 80-year-old man, extremely lively for that age, had come over the road in dramatic fashion, evidently expected by some of the onlookers. He carried a small American flag around our circle a couple of times, causing an occasional guffaw among our visitors, but he did not otherwise disturb our silent meeting. After the meeting, A. J. Muste came to the side of the road and preached a pacifist sermon to the people there. I have attended many meetings, and heard many sermons, but none I think more impressive. Facing him on the left, inside the fence, were perhaps thirty Air Force officers and the Federal Marshal. Opposite him across the road, stood some fifteen members of the American Legion who had come with placards of their own to picket us. There were possibly forty other people from nearby and from Omaha, including reporters and TV operators.

A. J. and the two others who were committed to offer civil disobedience that day then walked over to the gate, where Air Force officers and the Marshal were waiting for them. As is done in all such cases, we had given advance information to all officials likely to be involved.

It is difficult to describe the excitement for us in a simple first action of this kind. Later, these protests by disobedience of the law took on a quite routine character for us; but this time there were so many unknown factors of possibility. For instance, we had been holding the vigil on land next to that belonging to the Base. After considerable inquiry, we had found that this land belonged to another Federal Bureau, which had no office in Omaha and presumably no representative, so we had been using it without getting permission. Might not the Air Force, in cooperation with this Bureau, have us all arrested together for trespassing, or on some other charge, as soon as the first group of our people entered the Base? In case this were done, we thought it might be well for a couple of us to be away from the group and out on the highway, so as to go and notify our friends of what had happened. It had been decided, then, that as soon as A. J.'s sermon was finished, I was to leave immediately for a car parked some distance away, and another person was to keep away from the group but wait to find out what was done, and then come and join me. This now seems naïve—even to me!—but it seemed sensible at the time. We felt we were a long way from most of our friends.

A. J. Muste and the two others climbed over the gate, and were at once informed by the Air Force officers that the maximum penalty for entering was six months in prison and $500 fine. The officers then took them gently but firmly by the arm and led them out and shut the gate. Then the three again climbed over the gate and were immediately arrested by the Federal Marshal and taken to Omaha. This was termed "re-entry after warning" and the charge was "trespassing." They were put into the local jail in Omaha.

I had already volunteered, along with David Wyman, a young man from New York City, to do a similar action on July 6. We both wrote out statements, as did all the others later, of our reasons for offering civil disobedience, and presented them to the radio and press. For the most part, they were ignored.

After our usual meeting for worship at the vigil site, and before going into the Base, I read mine to the group instead of preaching a sermon as A. J. had done. About sixty persons were in the audience, including relatives of mine who had come from a Monthly Meeting of Friends in Iowa and, as before, a delegation of about eleven men from the nearby American Legion Post.

As we went up to the gate, the old man who had carried the little flag around our meeting on the first day came up and tried to stamp on my toes. He was very excited and failed to land on them, but his action disconcerted me a little and, as I crawled through the barbed wire fence, I put out one hand to shield myself. After getting through, I was surprised to see him lying flat on the ground. I realized at once that this incident would be used by the press; and, of course, not having any idea what had happened, I said the wrong thing, which was: "I'm sorry!" This of course seemed to imply that I had pushed him. The incident was thoroughly publicized by the Omaha paper, which said, under the headline PACIFIST WINS MEAD TUSSLE, that ". . . two elders with a combined age of 151 years brought violence to the non-violence demonstration of the Omaha Action pacifists;" and after describing the incident: " 'Sorry I pushed you,' said the septuagenarian to the octogenarian." This incident provoked the only notice the *New York Times* ever took of us, except when a congressman's son was sent to prison. It said: "What was supposed to be a non-violent demonstration produced a tussle between two elderly men." It was sometime afterward that we learned that the old gentleman had candidly told the paper published at Wahoo, Nebraska, that he had not been pushed—he had just lost his balance. It was a relief to have the error cleared up in the press—of Wahoo, Nebraska.

After David Wyman and I had gone through our formal entry and re-entry of the Base, we were taken promptly and put into a "tank" in the Omaha jail. It was designed for twelve men but we found there only our three predecessors, A. J. Muste, Ross Anderson, and Karl Meyer. We five spent two very stimulating days in conversation together there before being called before Federal Judge Robinson. By that time, two more of our comrades had joined us. A. J. presented our defense to the court. As had been previously decided, we pled "technically but not morally guilty" and of course were told that it had to be either "guilty" or "not guilty." We had also decided not to have a lawyer and not to give bail. I pled "guilty" to trespass.

The Judge's sentence was six months and $500 fine, with sentence suspended and one year on probation. I had not expected this and took some time to decide what to do. But Karl Meyer, a Catholic and the son of a congressman, knew at once what he would do. He told the probation officer that he could not accept probation, and probably would be out at the Base next day when two others of our group were planning to make their protest. True to his prediction, he went out the next day. The authorities were nervous about this, and they handcuffed him and obviously wanted to rough him up, but they did not. Apparently the Judge realized now for the first time that we were not the type of people that the press had tried to make out; he was quite angry with Karl and sent him to federal prison at once, warning the other members of *Omaha Action* at the same time that they need expect no leniency from that Court.

In the meantime, I had decided that I could not accept probation. Among several other stipulations, it meant monthly reports to a probation officer and staying away from all military installations for one year. So I addressed the Judge in a letter. After pointing out the direction that I believed our military policy is taking us, I said: "In view of these and other factors which I shall not go into here, what shall I do? I am an old man. I have had a happy life and found it interesting. That I should have my life ended now in a war is of small moment. But I have many young friends. I have three married children and eight lovely grandchildren. I'd like them all to have the opportunity for life as I have had. My one desire in this time is to make a maximum protest against the unnecessary descent of mankind into oblivion. I believe that, at the present time and under the circumstances of today, this protest requires me to spend this time in prison.—If I were an orator or a great writer or a diplomat, perhaps I would not need to do this. But for me, the processes of education, of speaking, of conferences, of writing, alone, seem likely to be 'too little and too late.' There come times in history when action is essential to break through the hard crust of inertia and custom. I believe this is one of those times.—It is in the tradition of my people, Quakers, to go to prison rather than take part in war. I believe the time has come for me, as a Quaker and a human being, to go to prison as a protest against preparation for war.

"You told me the other day that you were turning the prison key over to me. By my own act, in joining a vigil at the Mead Ordnance Plant, I propose to turn that key."

On July 21, therefore, I was arrested again at the Mead Base, this time for violation of the terms of probation. Before our meeting for worship began, the Chief Probation Officer simply asked me to come with him in his car. We had a very friendly talk on the 30-mile drive to Omaha. He said that if I didn't mind, he'd like to make some suggestions. Instead of stirring things up this way, why did we not do educational work in the usual way, write books and articles for magazines, give lectures, use the radio? This would not make people angry and excited, and they could think more clearly. I assured him that we had been trying to do these things for 25 years, and here he didn't even know it!—but I reminded him that one could not get the radio or any of the mass media to accept and use what we were offering. I told him that the very fact that he knew nothing about the writing and lecturing on peace that had been going on for years was a clear indication that other methods are needed.

He informed me that the Judge was away for a vacation and a conference, so that I would have to wait several days in jail. Later we learned that the Judge's conference was in order to get counsel about what his attitude toward *Omaha Action* ought to be.

My next six days with 34 other men in a "tank" designed for 32 was not as pleasant as the previous internment had been. A young man, Arthur Harvey, was with me this time. As we entered, carrying our mattresses, all eyes were upon us, and almost immediately a voice cried out, "Are you those pacifists?" Arthur replied "Yes!" with what seemed to me rather more gusto than the situation was likely to warrant. And sure enough, there was no gathering around to discuss our experiences. We were left to our own thoughts. The men would not look us in the eye if they could avoid it, nor greet us unless we spoke first.

The "tank" was about fifty feet long and sixteen wide, with two stories of nine cells each on one side, leaving a freeway of 8 x 50 feet on the main floor, for walking back and forth. There were benches to sit on along one side, and a narrow walkway and guard rail in front of the upper tier of cells. To get exercise one had to walk up and down past the cell doors in front of men who were sitting there reading or talking or smoking, or just sitting.

After a day or two, a man would now and then ask a question, and eventually some became rather friendly. The loneliness that one can feel in such a situation is very real. It was heightened one evening when three men asked about my sentence—this was a routine question—and after some discussion, one of the men said: "If I'd been the judge, I'd of given you twenty years." While the others talked, he kept shaking his head and muttering: "You mustn't let your country down."

After six days and nights, a few showed signs of seeing some light on pacifism, and many had become friendly, but I saw more clearly than ever how deep is the hold of the military mind in our country.

Getting letters was a tremendous help, but it made one feel all the more sympathy for many of the men who never got any letters at all; some of them had no contact with anyone outside. The many letters I got obviously caused considerable speculation among the men and really puzzled them. This particular "tank" was filled with men who were in for the more premeditated offences, such as forgery, robbery, sexual crimes and murder; there were few alcoholics. The men were relatively young, intelligent, and good-looking. This, as is almost inevitable in our prison system, was a fine school for teaching criminals to be more clever.

It was a county jail, reasonably well run as such jails go. I did not feel the urge, as some sincerely do, to protest the jail treatment, particularly to make things difficult for the jailers. There is a place for protest against the cruelties of prisons, but I wanted to make it as clear as possible that what I was protesting was the building of a missile base, and that I was trying to bear witness to a way of life that renounces war. The real cruelty of the prison system is that it is an arm of a larger system which protects the rich and powerful at the expense of the poor. A cardinal point in nonviolent resistance to evil is willingness to take on oneself the chief part of the suffering, and taking it cheerfully.

When I was called before the Judge again, a little farce was enacted. We both knew that I had been arrested the second time because I had appeared at the Base in violation of the terms of a probation I had stated I would not comply with, and that the Marshal had taken me away before the silent vigil began that morning. "Mr. Young," said the judge, "did you attend the vigil?" I smiled at him: "No, I was not allowed to do so." He then asked me if I had been in jail the last few days; and then he said, "Mr. Young, in view of the fact that you did not attend the vigil, I am going to continue you on probation." This, although it was clear that I had refused compliance with the terms of probation! A few days later we had another vigil at the entrance of the Base, and a number of Friends from the area joined us. Almost as soon as the meeting started, a man whom I did not know came up to me and said: "Mr. Young, the Attorney said to tell you that you will not be arrested."

It was now clear that if I were to reinforce my witness by serving a prison term at this time, I should have to repeat the entrance into the Ordnance Base, and thus force the hand of the Judge. Marjorie Swann, the mother of four children, and Arthur Harvey were in the same situation. We decided to spend ten days in making our decisions.

Several Friends from the Meeting at Paullina, Iowa, had come to visit us at various times and take part in the vigil. Most of them I had known for a long time, so I went there and we had a conference, in which I stated my dilemma and asked their advice. They were very sympathetic, but no one wanted to advise me to repeat my protest by civil disobedience. They thought that having made my position clear, I might now be satisfied. I also visited some other relatives, including our son Bill in Wyoming. He had spent three years in Civilian Public Service and later on had served a year and a day in a Federal prison for refusing to register for the military draft. After my visit, he wrote his mother: "I did not feel like discouraging Dad from going ahead." But in the end I refrained, largely because of my wife's strong feeling against a repetition of the illegal action in the circumstances. Marj Swann and Art Harvey did "go in" a second time and were sent to prison. The Judge was obviously very reluctant to put Marj or me into prison. The younger men, who were for the most part relatively free of responsibilities, he felt no particular compunction about, and in one or two cases said as much.

Looking back, I am inclined to feel that both Marj's decision and mine were right for ourselves. Her protest made far more impact than mine, and it may be pure rationalization on my part to think that what little impact mine made would not have been greatly augmented by my actually serving six months in prison. But in her case, the serving of the term while her husband took care of the children did make a great deal of difference and many hearts were deeply touched by their joint sacrifice.

28. Quebec-Washington-Guantanamo Walk for Peace, 1963–1964

In the early 1960's CNVA's main activity has been peace walks. In October 1961, after ten months of walking, thirty-one members of the San Francisco to Moscow Walk for Peace entered Red Square in Moscow. Then followed the 1962 walk from Nashville to Washington, and the 1963–1964 Quebec to Guantanamo Walk. The latter became involved in a dramatic contest with Laurie Pritchett, the police chief of Albany, Georgia. Forbidden to walk through the downtown business district lest it create a precedent for civil rights demonstrations, the peace marchers defied the city ordinance and were arrested two days before Christmas, 1963. In jail they fasted until their release on January 16, 1964. After negotiations with the city authorities once more proved unsuccessful, the walkers again entered the restricted area, were again arrested, and again fasted for about three weeks until, finally, a compromise was reached.

This document contains: (A) the statement of discipline which the Quebec-Washington-Guantanamo walkers adopted; (B) an explanation of the walkers' fasting, written by Bradford Lyttle, leader of this as of the earlier San Francisco to Moscow Walk; (C) a letter

---

"Discipline of Nonviolence for the Quebec-Washington-Guantanamo Walk for Peace" (New York: Committee for Nonviolent Action), mimeographed, n.d. [1963].

written while resting in Atlanta between two periods of imprisonment by Ray Robinson, a Negro member of the Walk; (D) a statement to the Recorder's Court of Albany by Barbara Deming, writer and Walk member; (E) a letter from prison, during the second period of imprisonment and fasting, by walker Katherine Havice, a young medical student.

A. *Discipline of Nonviolence**

1. Our attitude toward officials and others who may oppose us will be one of sympathetic understanding of the burdens and responsibilities they carry.

2. No matter what the circumstances or provocation, we will not respond with physical violence to acts directed against us.

3. We will not call names or make hostile remarks.

4. We will adhere as closely as we are able to the letter and spirit of truth in our spoken and written statements.

5. We will always try to speak to the best in all men, rather than seeking to exploit their weaknesses to what we may believe is our advantage.

6. We will always attempt to interpret as clearly as possible to anyone with whom we are in contact—and especially to those who may oppose us—the purpose and meaning of our actions.

B. *"The Peacewalkers' Struggle in Albany, Georgia"*

THE ISSUES:

The issues are twofold. There is a question of civil liberties over which the walkers have been arrested and imprisoned. Of far deeper significance is *the challenge which the walkers con-*

---

* Bradford Lyttle, "The Peacewalkers' Struggle in Albany, Georgia," New York, Committee for Nonviolent Action, mimeographed [January 22, 1964].

stitute for the system of oppression used to maintain institutions of racial segregation and other forms of social, political and economic inequality and injustice in "hard core" segregationist cities.

The civil liberties issue is simple and, on the surface, almost trifling. The authorities in Albany have designated a route through the city which they insist the walkers take. The route does not permit the Walk to pass through a number of commercial areas and along main thoroughfares where the walkers can distribute their leaflets and display their signs to considerable advantage. But it skirts the main, downtown shopping areas. The walkers have chosen a route that passes through these downtown areas. The authorities have arrested them and resisted a 24 day fast to deny them this route.

Why? No clear reason has ever been given. A parade permit issued by the authorities referred to traffic congestion due to an influx of Christmas shoppers in the downtown area. A reason commonly talked about by white people in Albany is that if the police let the walkers parade downtown they will have to allow other groups like the Nazis, Communists and Ku Klux Klan do so also. And many of these groups can become violent.

Almost certainly, the real and unexpressed reason is that if the walkers—a racially integrated group—are permitted to demonstrate downtown, the same right, heretofore grimly and desperately denied, will have to be granted to Albany's Negroes, to the Albany Movement. Albany Police Chief Laurie Pritchett stated it this way, "We will not have minority groups dictating policies to the city." And within the category of "minority groups" Negroes as well as peacewalkers certainly would be placed.

Intense segregationist feeling permeates Albany's history. Albany is an old slave trading center situated in the middle of the black belt. Over 42% of its population of 63,000 are

Negroes, and segregation has been so ruthlessly maintained that Dougherty County, whose seat is Albany, is one of the five Georgia counties with the highest number of lynchings. Negroes are denied all but traditional, menial jobs.

In 1961, Martin Luther King organized a mass integration movement in Albany that drew worldwide attention. More than 1200 Negroes poured into the city's jail, arrested in the course of parading and demonstrations of all kinds. But the segregationists resisted the Albany Movement, made no concessions, even refused to negotiate with or otherwise recognize the Negroes' militant leaders. King eventually withdrew, the Movement's swell broke, then ebbed and Albany became the symbol of hard core segregationist resistance to the mass demonstration technique.[1]

The Albany Movement was prevented from achieving its goal of integration by a system of police control that was able to blunt the overwhelming and disruptive effect of demonstrations. Working in close cooperation with the city's segregationist courts, the police arrested the Negro leadership, dispersed crowds with a minimum of violence. When the Movement tried to fill Albany's jails, hundreds of Negroes were farmed out to nearby county, state and city prisons. Soon the Movement lost its drive and ceased to be a threat. Later, the federal government instigated suits against several of the Movement's leaders. An all white jury in Macon has returned guilty-verdicts, which, if upheld, carry sentences of more than a year.

Creator of these successful tactics was Albany Police Chief Laurie Pritchett, whose fame as the man who had stopped the Negroes and King spread throughout the country.

Despite its severe setbacks and failure to achieve official recognition or any concrete success, the Albany Movement re-

---

[1] [See Document 30—Ed.]

mains, sustaining a partially successful boycott against down-town stores, holding weekly mass meetings and occasional small protest demonstrations.

The significance of our struggle in Albany lies in its relation to the system of police oppression described below—

THE SYSTEM OF POLICE OPPRESSION:

This has been carefully shaped to deal with Negro demonstrations. It is protected against every possible attack. At its foundation is the social and economic fabric of the city. Until 1940, Albany was controlled by fewer than half a dozen extremely wealthy families whose fortunes either antidated the Civil War or had been amassed early in the Century. Part of Albany constituted a "company town" for one giant textile industry. After the Second World War other businesses moved in and their owners began to have a voice in the city's affairs. Military influence grew. Turner Airforce Base, a SAC and MATS base, and the Marine Corps Supply Center, which serves the entire southeastern section of the United States, became the largest employers and economic element in the Albany area.

Politically, control of the city has always rested in the hands of rigid segregationists whose pride and financial security make them indifferent to international, national and even state criticisms of their unrelenting refusal of Negro demands for recognition and equal treatment. Albany has a Mayor and five City Commissioners who appoint a City Manager. He, in turn, appoints the Chief of Police. Although the Commissioners live in different districts of Albany, they are elected by the citizens at large. So effectively do they control the election apparatus that not one of the Commissioners is a Negro, although half of the population are.

The City Court with its judge appointed by the Commissioners assists the police force in repressing racial protests. The

Peacewalkers have been in Albany's court many times now and have seen and experienced legal processes so arbitrary as to be ludicrous if their effects weren't so painful and unjust. One receives the impression that sentences are determined by the Chief of Police and served before the trials take place. Probation documents are drawn up before evidence is heard, verdicts rendered. In one trial, our judge denied every objection of a Negro attorney, sustained all made by the City Attorney. Frequent whispered conferences took place between the Judge, City Attorney and Chief of Police. Local white attorneys, who might be in a position to object to these violations of due process, are unwilling publicly to comment upon matters which might embarrass the police and courts. "There's less justice in the Albany court than in Mississippi," was the astonished comment of a SNCC worker imprisoned with us.

This pattern of oppression is common enough to many cities in the Deep South. A difference in Albany, and one of its sources of even greater effectiveness, is the unusual policy of "nonviolence" which Chief Pritchett demands of his officers. Police brutality and violence to whites or Negroes, drunks, prostitutes, thiefs, demonstrators, peacewalkers, he condemns and seems to minimize in public and the jail. Negroes report cruel exceptions to the policy and believe Pritchett holds it, when he does, only to present a "good image" to the public and create the impression that he is a responsible, progressive law enforcement official. Chief Pritchett himself claims to believe in nonviolence in principle, "I'm a nonviolent man," he told me once, and as a tactic, "We know all about nonviolence in Albany. We beat Dr. King with it." He justifies the system he serves on the grounds that it maintains law and order. Without it, he claims, mob violence and police brutality would rule. He is a proud and complex person, at once a man who meticulously fashions his police and legal apparatus to hold the segregationist line and at the same time never calls a Negro "nigger." His wife, a Catholic, teaches in an integrated school.

THE NONVIOLENT WEAPON OF THE PEACEWALKERS:

One may ask, what possible chance does a small, racially integrated group of 20-30 peacewalkers have against such a system? Their pacifist, integrationist views and method of vigorous public demonstration strike abhorrence and fear in the hearts of Albany's rulers. No Albany judge recognizes their civil liberties, rights of free speech, as guaranteed by the 1st and 14th Amendments and sustained by innumerable Supreme Court decisions. Back in South Carolina, from where "northern agitators" come to Albany, a newspaper reporter smilingly told me, "You're not in Supreme Court country, son." Without blushing, Albany has endured waves of indignant protests from clergymen, liberals and others during Dr. King's integration protests. Gaining a bad reputation seems to mean little to the power structure. The daily newspaper is a kingpin in the segregation mechanism. So are the radio stations. All white Protestant churches are segregated, their ministers refrain from social action. A calm indifference and "stand offishness" pervades the white citizenry when even major racial and civil liberties conflicts develop. Georgia's Governor seems to have little influence over Albany's affairs.

Most of us in the Quebec-Washington-Guantanamo Walk for Peace believe we have only one powerful weapon with which we can battle for our civil liberties, our right to proclaim on the streets of Albany our vision of truth. That is the fast or hunger strike. If we are arrested we refuse to eat and within a period of time the authorities are faced with recognizing our rights and granting us our freedom or having on their hands people slowly dying of starvation, people who generate not only intense interest throughout the nation and even the world but stir the hearts of white citizens in Albany to doubt and misgivings. And it is expensive to hospitalize and force feed 20 people. Within a few days, thousands of dollars must be committed.

To be successful, the fast must be maintained steadily towards death by as many people as possible. They must be willing to endure emaciation, scurvy, extreme weakness, muscle deterioration, the pain of intravenous and tube feeding. They must be willing to risk fatal errors in judgment by police or doctors, or outbursts of violence from men driven to desperation by a protest that they cannot suppress.

The prolonged fast is our chief weapon. We have others. A number of walkers practice kinds of civil disobedience other than fasting. Some refuse to walk into their cells. They oppose the prison system in principle. Others will not walk to court. They cannot recognize an apparatus created in the name of justice for the purpose of denying justice. By these acts they offset, indeed annihilate and make ridiculous, the mantle of power and authority that the Albany court has gathered about itself.

Outside the jail and hospital we maintain an office and administrative center. We send news reports to the mass media, bulletins to hundreds of people, groups and organizations throughout the nation and world who sympathize with us. These friends respond by writing letters and sending telegrams on our behalf. In addition to interpreting the project to people outside of Albany, our staff does similar work within the city itself, visiting the newspaper editors, ministers and others, negotiating with officials, mustering local support wherever it can be found.

In Albany, a great source of strength and support comes from the Negro people who understand that the fight for our civil liberties is for theirs as well. They have provided a house for our office and living quarters. They help in many other ways and encourage us.

In our first engagement with the Albany power structure, 22 people were imprisoned. Nine fasted 24 days, three went to the hospital, two were fed intravenously, all the long term fasters eventually were given vitamin injections. It is our impression that the authorities were seriously worried by the protest and released us in the hope that we would depart. They have not, however, granted us the right to walk through the city's main shopping area. Recent conversations we have had with Chief Pritchett and City Manager S. A. Roos have convinced us that they deeply understand that our project and technique of fasting threaten their entire system—their power. They will go to great lengths to win. The struggle will be desperate.

IS IT WORTH IT?

Why risk your health and life to walk through downtown Albany? For those of us who probably will go to prison, the answer is that we believe we owe it to the struggle against racial injustice to do so. The horrible evil for which Albany has become a symbol is intolerable and must be ended even at great cost. If God, fate, or the science of nonviolence permits truth to win, we shall have shown that Albany's hitherto invincible system of oppression has a flaw: that a few people willing and able to couple prolonged, deliberately accepted suffering with an efficient medium of public communication and interpretation can generate enough sympathy in the hearts of their opponents and enough public support to make this carefully constructed machinery of oppression ineffective. The achievement of this in Albany would help the Negro people here—and the white too, by freeing them partly from the bonds of an inhuman system. But its larger implications may be even more important, for we will have created a technique of nonviolent struggle that can be used by others in other cities, North and South, even throughout the world. By this experiment, the science of nonviolence can be expanded, as it must rapidly be everywhere if our world is not to perish before the onslaught of weapons without which men believe they are naked before the power of cruelty and injustice. We write and talk about extending freedom and democratic institutions against totalitarianism by means of nonviolence. Albany, Georgia, has a totalitarian government. We should not skirt this challenge; we should make an experiment with the power of nonviolent action.

The struggle has a close relationship to our concern for American-Cuban relationships too, the main theme of the Walk. We will demonstrate unmistakably to the Cuban people and government where we stand in regard to racism and denials of free speech in the United States. We hope thereby to win their deep respect and increase the likelihood that we will be welcomed in Cuba even if we maintain a critical attitude towards some policies of the Cuban government. There is evidence that already this respect is being won, for on January 7 Radio Havana devoted a substantial part of a news broadcast to describing the Walk, its purpose, and its imprisonment and protest in Albany.

There are reasons why our battle for truth in Albany, Georgia, is important. We enter it in a spirit of the deepest comradeship, fully aware of each others weakness and strength, for behind us lie thousands of miles of walking in Canada and the United States, of cold, heat, dust and rain, fear of the unknown, the barren dirty walls of prisons in nine cities, a cattle prod in the hands of sadistic men, hurled eggs and rocks and countless threats and curses. Through all we have seen the power of nonviolence, of persistence, patience, entreaty, forgiveness, win out time and time again. Not one of us doubts that though our struggle here may carry us down to frightening depths, the eternal forces of truth that we are striving to release will in the end break forth and prevail at least in part.

We hope that you will stand with us in the terrible days that may lie ahead.

C. *Letter by Ray Robinson*

Jan 18, 1964
Atlanta, Ga.

Dear Staughton:

I have so much I want to tell you. Staughton I'm a very sick man, yes I about to go crazy, yes real crazy here in Atlanta. I have not been to sleep since God know when. I really afraid to close my eyes, I afraid I may not reopen them again, and I really scare. How long can I go on like this. I have not had good nights sleep down here in "Our" South. . . . I afraid they're going to "kill" my friends, I real honest the god friends, I will not idenify them by saying "whites". But I have been brought up so long believing that one had to idenify this way, Black & White, instead of just plain ol "humans". This idenifacation human is so easy. I don't want them being another Moore's. How many moore's has died? Not Physcail death, but mental death is so many hundred time worser. Let me died for my courragous White Brother. Hatred we not kill me. I got a Very Strong Weapon, Love just love until I can't love anymore, then "Welcome" death, I've done all I can do, but Please old God, Jesus, Gandhi, King Jr. Buddha anyone, Lewis, Some one else start cryin with me too, I mean real tears Walk talk honest feeling, I think We as of right now, if We believe in Peace, Freedoms any think in this field for the right of man, Things that is for him to enjoy, lets all get into the beautiful Struggle and try to help all men get free.

Ray Robinson

Letter from Ray Robinson to Staughton Lynd, original in files of Staughton Lynd.

D. *Statement to Recorder's Court,*

Albany, Georgia

I would like to appeal to this court—and through it, to the people of Albany—to try to imagine how it is that we see our actions, and to question your first impression of us.

That first impression, I'm afraid, is that we are outsiders, arrived in this city to get some publicity for ourselves, feeling no respect or concern for the people of this city, and happy enough to cause them trouble.

But, I would plead, we have taken the actions we have moved not by a feeling of contempt for the people of Albany but by a feeling of kinship with you. What brought us here was a desire to *talk* with you—at the very deepest level possible. It troubles us very much to be called "outsiders" so often— because we feel very strongly that a time in history has arrived when men can no longer afford to think of other men as outsiders. We believe that it always has been so, that men were meant to recognize each other as brothers—members of one human family.

This is certainly the message of Jesus—and of all the great spiritual teachers. We believe beyond this, that a new age has arrived that makes it absolutely necessary that we recognize our close kinship with each other—with all men—because unless we do, we may well destroy mankind.

We now have the power to do this, for the first time in history—because of a revolution in science. Because of the same revolution, we also have the power at last to feed, to clothe, to give shelter to every living man—to live as members of the human family should, showing care for every member in it. We believe that in this new age it has become absolutely

---

Barbara Deming, statement read in Recorder's Court, Albany, Georgia, February 5, 1964, published under the title ". . . Our Terribly Real Kinship," *Liberation* (March 1964), p. 8.

necessary for us to begin to live with this care for one another
—not only for those close to us but for all those we have been
used to think of as outsiders. We believe that we must learn
to struggle with each other, when we have differences, only as
those in a true family do—by persuasion, by example, by refusing to cooperate with actions of which we disapprove, but
never with violence, always unwilling to destroy each other,
either in body or spirit. We are simply too bound to one
another now—all of us. The actions of a group of people anywhere in the world can drastically affect the lives of other people anywhere else in the world. How can one speak of outsiders any longer in the old sense?

Because one cannot, we believe it is necessary, as it never
was before in history, for people to learn to speak with one
another—especially people with differences; and for them to
be *free* to do this; and for all barriers to this freedom to fall.

My plea, then, is that you recognize that we seek our freedom to speak here—that we struggle with you for it—not out
of contempt for you, but out of a sharp sense of urgency, and
out of a sense of our terribly real kinship with you.

BARBARA DEMING

E. *Letter by Katherine Havice*

Albany City Jail
12:30 a.m., Feb. 16, 1964

Dear Art,

Many thoughts run through my head tonight. It is a more
or less typical Saturday night here, with its usual attendant un-
dercurrent of noise. A small world of suffering seems concentrated here. Last night a young man beat up a middle aged

---

Letter to a personal friend by Katherine Havice, mimeographed by
the Committee for Nonviolent Action, New York, 1964.

one and sent him to the hospital. Tonight there are the many usual drunks howling "mother fucker" at the jailers for imprisoning them, and a man with many psychologically caused medical difficulties, such as fainting spells, trouble breathing, wishing to be free, and general howling. The latter, probably a poor guy who may even come to jail to get some sort of concern and attention. A few cases of D.T.'s. A Negro youngster of about 15 crying in the background while a cop goes about his business whistling a cheerful tune. Then later a Negro woman who as best as I can gather was being dragged and molested by a man, when a cop shot him through the head and brought her down for questioning. She was terrified because she felt she would be charged with it and somehow it was all connected with a robbery. I find myself starting to dissociate myself from it the way one does in a hospital, but here it all seems far worse because no one is being helped or cured, just suffering.

It feels good to me to be here still and because of the hopeful turn of events to be still involved with whatever suffering we share in a meaningful way. My wish to get out was a weakness based on the feeling of irrelevancy and impotence of our witness to the Albany issue. It is far better for my inner peace to be involved again for however long it takes.

Ah, Art, the problem is not how to survive the suffering by dissociating from it. The problem is somehow to stay vitally concerned. Otherwise we manage to live good sterile lives ensconced in our apartments in Denver or Stanford. The problem it seems is far more to keep a small edge of ourselves rubbed raw and smarting so we can somehow understand, with our lives, all lives. The first sonnet struck me with this like a blow:

> And yet, some [T]hing that moves among the stars,
> And holds the cosmos in a web of law,
> Moves too in me: a hunger, a quick thaw
> Of soul that liquefies the ancient bars,

> As I, a member of creation, sing
> The burning oneness binding everything.[1]

I have always seen it as a 3 year old, a 3 year old with the face of every child, unhappy, or wondering with a sort of bewilderment how it happened what is happening. And somehow I know that as long as there is this child before me I can't stop caring and I hope trying to create a world where he/she can live without always this look. Or at least in a world where he or she can hope to grow up and know love. And all this wars in me with the wish for an apartment, peace and quiet, good music, a "respectable" life, a bath, pizza, a walk in the forest. Not always wars because I believe there are combinations that can bring answers to both. (I hope.)

Another of my frequent thoughts—Hiroshima was bombed when I was very close to being that above child—when I was 5. And while this would seem to absolve me because I was too young, it really doesn't at all. You see it was bombed so children like myself could grow up in a world "safe for democracy". It was bombed with me as its justification. And somehow—somehow—I've got to tell the world never to do it again —at least not for me.

But then one is again faced with the question: what does one do to somehow balance the suffering and joy within one's life so it is viable. Peace-walking or projects such as this are no long term answer because one can not live at such a pitch year after year. But then how to be incorporated within the peace movement without simply being reduced to an office machine or an AFSC educational director? (both of which seem very sterile to me.) If one decides to work in the integration movement much can be said for simply moving to the area and taking up a witness within a profession and the Movement—such as your thought of practicing in the South. But a

---

[1] [Kenneth Boulding, *There is a Spirit; The Nayler Sonnets* (Nyack, N.Y.: Fellowship Publications, 1945), p. 1, lines 9-14. Reprinted with the permission of The Fellowship of Reconciliation, Ed.]

way to work in the peace movement on a comparable personal level seems harder to find. I have thought of the value of continuing to interrelate the two movements through establishing a nonviolent action group keyed to both in the South. I still have the hunch that the most good can be done for the peace movement by attempting to broaden the relevance of the nonviolent ethic with the Negro people down here who are already beginning to understand. Have you been to a church service yet where nonviolence was preached? It can be one of the most heartening experiences I know.

Speaking of kids earlier—I wanted to tell you of two of the most wonderful times I've had on the walk. One was in Salisbury, North Carolina when a number of little Negro kids came running around where I was working on the Bulletin. They stood around shyly for awhile, then one little girl hesitatingly and very fearfully reached out and touched my hair because it was so different from her own. Soon they were all stroking it. It was an act of trust towards me that they would be allowed to do this, that reached across innumerable barriers.

And the most wonderful to me—we were walking along the road at the very end of a long hard day and the Walk passed some little kids aged 5-7 hauling and struggling with huge buckets and gallon jugs of water the half mile to their shack up the road. Dave Dellinger, big man that he is, caught up and overtook the first little boy. He reached down with his free hand that wasn't carrying his sign and took the bucket to carry it. Barbara Deming came up behind the littlest and took the gallon jug from him and walked on. The kids were startled at first but soon were skipping along beside their buckets and jugs at the side of the line of walkers, looking up every few steps and grinning at us. The walk stopped for the day just a little way short of their house and the kids carefully took their buckets back and walked on home with their parents out in front watching what to them must have been a truly miraculous sight—the grown white people helping the Negro kids haul the water. It somehow symbolized to me all that we are possibly hoping to do and say. And yet as we moved on we knew we will always have been simply an isolated miracle in these kids' lives. Nothing will have changed, and for the rest of their childhood they will haul the water that long half mile while the whites have running water and the white people will curse them and call them "boy".

The wonder of it all is not that the Albany people have not joined us sooner but that they have come to trust us at all. C. B. and Slater King speak with real wonder when they saw a Negro taxicab driver spontaneously wave to two white walkers walking downtown. There is so much that has happened and that is happening that if we do not actually do—we still allow to happen. Our concern has to reach out.

I went to a Baptist church on December 21 with Carl, and was the only white person there. A man got up and castigated the whites for their impossibilities as I tried to sink into my seat; but he ended by pointing to me and saying in ringing tones: "But there is a miracle—a living divine miracle in your presence! Listen to her, do what she says!" *That* simply because I went to a church. (And me an atheist.) It makes one feel very inadequate. I must close this—it is very good to have you out there. Life is very good.

Very much love,
Kit

29. Declaration of Conscience Against the War in Vietnam

In 1960, one hundred twenty-one French intellectuals, including Jean-Paul Sartre, Simone de Beauvoir, and Andre Breton, signed a manifesto supporting civil disobedience against the attempt of

Declaration Of Conscience Against The War In Vietnam (New York: published jointly by the Catholic Worker, the Committee for Nonviolent Action, the Student Peace Union, and the War Resisters League, 1965).

France to suppress the independence movement in its colony, Algeria. "We respect and we justify the refusal to take arms against the Algerian people," they wrote. "We respect and we justify the conduct of Frenchmen who believe it their duty to bring aid and protection to oppressed Algerians in the name of the people of France."

In 1965 an even larger group of Americans signed a similar declaration pledging "conscientious refusal to cooperate with the United States government in the prosecution of the war in Vietnam." In late Spring 1965, the statement was broadened to include "refusal to cooperate with U.S. military intervention in the Dominican Republic, or the affairs of any other nation." By the summer some six thousand signatures were on the Declaration.

The signers included such veterans of the nonviolent movement as David Dellinger, Dorothy Day, Ammon Hennacy, Bradford Lyttle, A. J. Muste, and Robert Swann; well known leaders of the civil rights movement such as James Bevel, John Lewis, Robert [Moses] Parris, A. Phillip Randolph, and Bayard Rustin; and a number of clergymen, academics, and intellectuals among them Kenneth Boulding, W. H. Ferry, Erich Fromm, Paul Goodman, Nobel Prize-winning Linus Pauling, and the editor of this volume. Like the Quebec-to-Guantanamo Walk, the Declaration of Conscience signified a tendency of peace and civil right activists to join in supporting each other's causes.

Because the use of the military resources of the United States in Vietnam and elsewhere suppresses the aspirations of the people for political independence and economic freedom;

Because inhuman torture and senseless killing are being carried out by forces armed, uniformed, trained and financed by the United States;

Because we believe that all peoples of the earth, including both Americans and non-Americans, have an inalienable right to life, liberty, and the peaceful pursuit of happiness in their own way; and

Because we think that positive steps must be taken to put an end to the threat of nuclear catastrophe and death by chemical or biological warfare, whether these result from accident or escalation—

We hereby declare our conscientious refusal to cooperate with the United States government in the prosecution of the war in Vietnam.

We encourage those who can conscientiously do so to refuse to serve in the armed forces and to ask for discharge if they are already in.

Those of us who are subject to the draft ourselves declare our own intention to refuse to serve.

We urge others to refuse and refuse ourselves to take part in the manufacture or transportation of military equipment, or to work in the fields of military research and weapons development.

We shall encourage the development of other nonviolent acts, including acts which involve civil disobedience, in order to stop the flow of American soldiers and munitions to Vietnam.

NOTE: *Signing or distributing this Declaration of Conscience might be construed as a violation of the Universal Military Training and Service Act, which prohibits advising persons facing the draft to refuse service. Penalties of up to 5 years imprisonment, and/or a fine of $5,000 are provided. While prosecutions under this provision of the law almost never occur, persons signing or distributing this declaration should face the possibility of serious consequences.*

PART IX

Direct Action for Civil Rights, Post-World War II

30. Martin Luther King, Jr., "Pilgrimage to Nonviolence"

Martin Luther King, Jr. was born in Atlanta in 1929. He graduated from Morehouse College in 1948, received the B.D. from Crozer Theological Seminary in 1951 and the Ph.D. in 1955 from Boston University, in the field of systematic theology. Just before graduation Reverend King was appointed pastor at the Dexter Avenue Baptist Church in Montgomery, Alabama, where he was catapulted into national prominence as leader of the 1955–1956 Montgomery bus boycott.

"Pilgrimage to Nonviolence" deals not so much with the Montgomery boycott as with the intellectual and spiritual evolution which led King, its leader, to a commitment to nonviolence. Particularly significant are (1) the distinction between varieties of love (*eros*, *philia*, and *agape*), and (2) the emphasis upon creating and restoring "community" as the purpose of nonviolent action. Elsewhere in his writings, King speaks of creating the "blessed community," a phrase which has become widely current.

Martin Luther King, Jr., "Pilgrimage to Nonviolence," *Stride Toward Freedom* (New York: Harper & Bros., 1958), pp. 90–107. *Stride Toward Freedom: The Montgomery Story* by Martin Luther King, Jr. Copyright © by Martin Luther King. Reprinted by permission of Harper & Row, Publishers, Incorporated.

Often the question has arisen concerning my own intellectual pilgrimage to nonviolence. In order to get at this question it is necessary to go back to my early teens in Atlanta. I had grown up abhorring not only segregation but also the oppressive and barbarous acts that grew out of it. I had passed spots where Negroes had been savagely lynched, and had watched the Ku Klux Klan on its rides at night. I had seen police brutality with my own eyes, and watched Negroes receive the most tragic injustice in the courts. All of these things had done something to my growing personality. I had come perilously close to resenting all white people.

I had also learned that the inseparable twin of racial injustice was economic injustice. Although I came from a home of economic security and relative comfort, I could never get out of my mind the economic insecurity of many of my playmates and the tragic poverty of those living around me. During my late teens I worked two summers, against my father's wishes— he never wanted my brother and me to work around white people because of the oppressive conditions—in a plant that hired both Negroes and whites. Here I saw economic injustice first-hand, and realized that the poor white was exploited just as much as the Negro. Through these early experiences I grew up deeply conscious of the varieties of injustice in our society.

So when I went to Atlanta's Morehouse College as a freshman in 1944 my concern for racial and economic justice was already substantial. During my student days at Morehouse I read Thoreau's *Essay on Civil Disobedience* for the first time. Fascinated by the idea of refusing to coöperate with an evil system, I was so deeply moved that I reread the work several times. This was my first intellectual contact with the theory of nonviolent resistance.

Not until I entered Crozer Theological Seminary in 1948, however, did I begin a serious intellectual quest for a method to eliminate social evil. Although my major interest was in the fields of theology and philosophy, I spent a great deal of time reading the works of the great social philosophers. I came early to Walter Rauschenbusch's *Christianity and the Social Crisis,* which left an indelible imprint on my thinking by giving me a theological basis for the social concern which had already grown up in me as a result of my early experiences. Of course there were points at which I differed with Rauschenbusch. I felt that he had fallen victim to the nineteenth-century "cult of inevitable progress" which led him to a superficial optimism concerning man's nature. Moreover, he came perilously close to identifying the Kingdom of God with a particular social and economic system—a tendency which should never befall the Church. But in spite of these shortcomings Rauschenbusch had done a great service for the Christian Church by insisting that the gospel deals with the whole man, not only his soul but his body; not only his spiritual well-being but his material well-being. It has been my conviction ever since reading Rauschenbusch that any religion which professes to be concerned about the souls of men and is not concerned about the social and economic conditions that scar the soul, is a spiritually moribund religion only waiting for the day to be buried. It well has been said: "A religion that ends with the individual, ends."

After reading Rauschenbusch, I turned to a serious study of the social and ethical theories of the great philosophers, from Plato and Aristotle down to Rousseau, Hobbes, Bentham, Mill, and Locke. All of these masters stimulated my thinking—such as it was—and, while finding things to question in each of them, I nevertheless learned a great deal from their study.

During the Christmas holidays of 1949 I decided to spend my spare time reading Karl Marx to try to understand the appeal of communism for many people. For the first time I carefully scrutinized *Das Kapital* and *The Communist Manifesto.* I also read some interpretive works on the thinking of Marx and Lenin. In reading such Communist writings I drew certain conclusions that have remained with me as convictions to this day.

First I rejected their materialistic interpretation of history. Communism, avowedly secularistic and materialistic, has no place for God. This I could never accept, for as a Christian I believe that there is a creative personal power in this universe who is the ground and essence of all reality—a power that cannot be explained in materialistic terms. History is ultimately guided by spirit, not matter. Second, I strongly disagreed with communism's ethical relativism. Since for the Communist there is no divine government, no absolute moral order, there are no fixed, immutable principles; consequently almost anything—force, violence, murder, lying—is a justifiable means to the "millennial" end. This type of relativism was abhorrent to me. Constructive ends can never give absolute moral justification to destructive means, because in the final analysis the end is preëxistent in the mean. Third, I opposed communism's political totalitarianism. In communism the individual ends up in subjection to the state. True, the Marxist would argue that the state is an "interim" reality which is to be eliminated when the classless society emerges; but the state is the end while it lasts, and man only a means to that end. And if any man's so-called rights or liberties stand in the way of that end, they are simply swept aside. His liberties of expression, his freedom to vote, his freedom to listen to what news he likes or to choose his books are all restricted. Man becomes hardly more, in communism, than a depersonalized cog in the turning wheel of the state.

This deprecation of individual freedom was objectionable to me. I am convinced now, as I was then, that man is an end because he is a child of God. Man is not made for the state; the state is made for man. To deprive man of freedom is to relegate him to the status of a thing, rather than elevate him to the status of a person. Man must never be treated as a means to the end of the state, but always as an end within himself.

Yet, in spite of the fact that my response to communism was and is negative, and I considered it basically evil, there were points at which I found it challenging. The late Archbishop of Canterbury, William Temple, referred to communism as a Christian heresy. By this he meant that communism had laid hold of certain truths which are essential parts of the Christian view of things, but that it had bound up with them concepts and practices which no Christian could ever accept or profess. Communism challenged the late Archbishop and it should challenge every Christian—as it challenged me—to a growing concern about social justice. With all of its false assumptions and evil methods, communism grew as a protest against the hardships of the underprivileged. Communism in theory emphasized a classless society, and a concern for social justice, though the world knows from sad experience that in practice it created new classes and a new lexicon of injustice. The Christian ought always to be challenged by any protest against unfair treatment of the poor, for Christianity is itself such a protest, nowhere expressed more eloquently than in Jesus' words: "The Spirit of the Lord is upon me, because he hath anointed me to preach the gospel to the poor; he hath sent me to heal the brokenhearted, to preach deliverance to the captives, and recovering of sight to the blind, to set at liberty them that are bruised, to preach the acceptable year of the Lord."

I also sought systematic answers to Marx's critique of modern bourgeois culture. He presented capitalism as essentially a struggle between the owners of the productive resources and the workers, whom Marx regarded as the real producers. Marx interpreted economic forces as the dialectical process by which society moved from feudalism through capitalism to socialism, with the primary mechanism of this historical movement being the struggle between economic classes whose interests were irreconcilable. Obviously this theory left out of account the numerous and significant complexities—political, economic, moral, religious, and psychological—which played a vital role in shaping the constellation of institutions and ideas known today as Western civilization. Moreover, it was dated in the sense that the capitalism Marx wrote about bore only a partial resemblance to the capitalism we know in this country today. But in spite of the shortcomings of his analysis, Marx had raised some basic questions. I was deeply concerned from my early teen days about the gulf between superfluous wealth and abject poverty, and my reading of Marx made me ever more conscious of this gulf. Although modern American capitalism had greatly reduced the gap through social reforms, there was still need for a better distribution of wealth. Moreover, Marx had revealed the danger of the profit motive as the sole basis of an economic system: capitalism is always in danger of inspiring men to be more concerned about making a living than making a life. We are prone to judge success by the index of our salaries or the size of our automobiles, rather than by the quality of our service and relationship to humanity—thus capitalism can lead to a practical materialism that is as pernicious as the materialism taught by communism.

In short, I read Marx as I read all of the influential historical thinkers—from a dialectical point of view, combining a partial yes and a partial no. In so far as Marx posited a metaphysical materialism, an ethical relativism, and a strangulating totalitarianism, I responded with an unambiguous "no"; but in so far as he pointed to weaknesses of traditional capitalism, contributed to the growth of a definite self-consciousness in the masses, and challenged the social conscience of the Christian churches, I responded with a definite "yes."

My reading of Marx also convinced me that truth is found neither in Marxism nor in traditional capitalism. Each represents a partial truth. Historically capitalism failed to see the truth in collective enterprise and Marxism failed to see the truth in individual enterprise. Nineteenth-century capitalism failed to see that life is social and Marxism failed and still fails to see that life is individual and personal. The Kingdom of God is neither the thesis of individual enterprise nor the antithesis of collective enterprise, but a synthesis which reconciles the truths of both.

During my stay at Crozer, I was also exposed for the first time to the pacifist position in a lecture by Dr. A. J. Muste. I was deeply moved by Dr. Muste's talk, but far from convinced of the practicability of his position. Like most of the students of Crozer, I felt that while war could never be a positive or absolute good, it could serve as a negative good in the sense of preventing the spread and growth of an evil force. War, horrible as it is, might be preferable to surrender to a totalitarian system—Nazi, Fascist, or Communist.

During this period I had about despaired of the power of love in solving social problems. Perhaps my faith in love was temporarily shaken by the philosophy of Nietzsche. I had been reading parts of *The Genealogy of Morals* and the whole of *The Will to Power*. Nietzsche's glorification of power—in his theory all life expressed the will to power—was an outgrowth of his contempt for ordinary morals. He attacked the whole of the Hebraic-Christian morality—with its virtues of piety and humility, its other-worldliness and its attitude toward suffering—as the glorification of weakness, as making virtues out of necessity and impotence. He looked to the development of a superman who would surpass man as man surpassed the ape.

Then one Sunday afternoon I traveled to Philadelphia to hear a sermon by Dr. Mordecai Johnson, president of Howard University. He was there to preach for the Fellowship House of Philadelphia. Dr. Johnson had just returned from a trip to India, and to my great interest, he spoke of the life and teachings of Mahatma Gandhi. His message was so profound and electrifying that I left the meeting and bought a half-dozen books on Gandhi's life and works.

Like most people, I had heard of Gandhi, but I had never studied him seriously. As I read I became deeply fascinated by his campaigns of nonviolent resistance. I was particularly moved by the Salt March to the Sea and his numerous fasts. The whole concept of "Satyagraha" (*Satya* is truth which

equals love, and *agraha* is force; "Satyagraha," therefore, means
truth-force or love force) was profoundly significant to me. As
I delved deeper into the philosophy of Gandhi my skepticism
concerning the power of love gradually diminished, and I came
to see for the first time its potency in the area of social reform.
Prior to reading Gandhi, I had about concluded that the ethics
of Jesus were only effective in individual relationship. The
"turn the other cheek" philosophy and the "love your enemies"
philosophy were only valid, I felt, when individuals were in
conflict with other individuals; when racial groups and nations
were in conflict a more realistic approach seemed necessary.
But after reading Gandhi, I saw how utterly mistaken I was.

Gandhi was probably the first person in history to lift the
love ethic of Jesus above mere interaction between individuals
to a powerful and effective social force on a large scale. Love
for Gandhi was a potent instrument for social and collective
transformation. It was in this Gandhian emphasis on love and
nonviolence that I discovered the method for social reform that
I had been seeking for so many months. The intellectual and
moral satisfaction that I failed to gain from the utilitarianism
of Bentham and Mill, the revolutionary methods of Marx and
Lenin, the social-contracts theory of Hobbes, the "back to nature" optimism of Rousseau, and the superman philosophy of
Nietzsche, I found in the nonviolent resistance philosophy of
Gandhi. I came to feel that this was the only morally and
practically sound method open to oppressed people in their
struggle for freedom.

But my intellectual odyssey to nonviolence did not end here.
During my last year in theological school, I began to read the
works of Reinhold Niebuhr. The prophetic and realistic elements in Niebuhr's passionate style and profound thought were
appealing to me, and I became so enamored of his social ethics
that I almost fell into the trap of accepting uncritically everything he wrote.

About this time I read Niebuhr's critique of the pacifist position. Niebuhr had himself once been a member of the pacifist ranks. For several years, he had been national chairman of the Fellowship of Reconciliation. His break with pacifism came in the early thirties, and the first full statement of his criticism of pacifism was in *Moral Man and Immoral Society*. Here he argued that there was no intrinsic moral difference between violent and non-violent resistance. The social consequences of the two methods were different, he contended, but the differences were in degree rather than kind. Later Niebuhr began emphasizing the irresponsibility of relying on nonviolent resistance when there was no ground for believing that it would be successful in preventing the spread of totalitarian tyranny. It could only be successful, he argued, if the groups against whom the resistance was taking place had some degree of moral conscience, as was the case in Gandhi's struggle against the British. Niebuhr's ultimate rejection of pacifism was based primarily on the doctrine of man. He argued that pacifism failed to do justice to the reformation doctrine of justification by faith, substituting for it a sectarian perfectionism which believes "that divine grace actually lifts men out of the sinful contradictions of history and establishes him above the sins of the world."

At first, Niebuhr's critique of pacifism left me in a state of confusion. As I continued to read, however, I came to see more and more the shortcomings of his position. For instance, many of his statements revealed that he interpreted pacifism as a sort of passive nonresistance to evil expressing naïve trust in the power of love. But this was a serious distortion. My study of Gandhi convinced me that true pacifism is not nonresistance to evil, but nonviolent resistance to evil. Between the two positions, there is a world of difference. Gandhi resisted evil with as much vigor and power as the violent resister, but he resisted with love instead of hate. True pacifism is not unrealistic submission to evil power, as Niebuhr contends. It is rather a cour-

ageous confrontation of evil by the power of love, in the faith
that it is better to be the recipient of violence than the in-
flicter of it, since the latter only multiplies the existence of
violence and bitterness in the universe, while the former may
develop a sense of shame in the opponent, and thereby bring
about a transformation and change of heart.

In spite of the fact that I found many things to be desired
in Niebuhr's philosophy, there were several points at which he
constructively influenced my thinking. Niebuhr's great contribution to contemporary theology is that he has refuted the false
optimism characteristic of a great segment of Protestant liberalism, without falling into the anti-rationalism of the continental
theologian Karl Barth, or the semi-fundamentalism of other
dialectical theologians. Moreover, Niebuhr has extraordinary
insight into human nature, especially the behavior of nations
and social groups. He is keenly aware of the complexity of human motives and of the relation between morality and power.
His theology is a persistent reminder of the reality of sin on
every level of man's existence. These elements in Niebuhr's
thinking helped me to recognize the illusions of a superficial
optimism concerning human nature and the dangers of a false
idealism. While I still believed in man's potential for good,
Niebuhr made me realize his potential for evil as well. Moreover, Niebuhr helped me to recognize the complexity of man's
social involvement and the glaring reality of collective evil.

Many pacifists, I felt, failed to see this. All too many had an
unwarranted optimism concerning man and leaned unconsciously toward self-righteousness. It was my revolt against
these attitudes under the influence of Niebuhr that accounts for
the fact that in spite of my strong leaning toward pacifism, I
never joined a pacifist organization. After reading Niebuhr, I
tried to arrive at a realistic pacifism. In other words, I came to
see the pacifist position not as sinless but as the lesser evil in
the circumstances. I felt then, and I feel now, that the pacifist
would have a greater appeal if he did not claim to be free

from the moral dilemmas that the Christian nonpacifist confronts.

The next stage of my intellectual pilgrimage to nonviolence came during my doctoral studies at Boston University. Here I had the opportunity to talk to many exponents of nonviolence, both students and visitors to the campus. Boston University School of Theology, under the influence of Dean Walter Muelder and Professor Allen Knight Chalmers, had a deep sympathy for pacifism. Both Dean Muelder and Dr. Chalmers had a passion for social justice that stemmed, not from a superficial optimism, but from a deep faith in the possibilities of human beings when they allowed themselves to become coworkers with God. It was at Boston University that I came to see that Niebuhr had over-emphasized the corruption of human nature. His pessimism concerning human nature was not balanced by an optimism concerning divine nature. He was so involved in diagnosing man's sickness of sin that he overlooked the cure of grace.

I studied philosophy and theology at Boston University under Edgar S. Brightman and L. Harold DeWolf. Both men greatly stimulated my thinking. It was mainly under these teachers that I studied personalistic philosophy—the theory that the clue to the meaning of ultimate reality is found in personality. This personal idealism remains today my basic philosophical position. Personalism's insistence that only personality—finite and infinite—is ultimately real strengthened me in two convictions: it gave me metaphysical and philosophical grounding for the idea of a personal God, and it gave me a metaphysical basis for the dignity and worth of all human personality.

Just before Dr. Brightman's death, I began studying the philosophy of Hegel with him. Although the course was mainly a study of Hegel's monumental work, *Phenomenology of Mind*, I spent my spare time reading his *Philosophy of History* and *Philosophy of Right*. There were points in Hegel's philosophy that I strongly disagreed with. For instance, his absolute idealism was rationally unsound to me because it tended to swallow up the many in the one. But there were other aspects of his thinking that I found stimulating. His contention that "truth is the whole" led me to a philosophical method of rational coherence. His analysis of the dialectical process, in spite of its shortcomings, helped me to see that growth comes through struggle.

In 1954 I ended my formal training with all of these relatively divergent intellectual forces converging into a positive social philosophy. One of the main tenets of this philosophy was the conviction that nonviolent resistance was one of the most potent weapons available to oppressed people in their quest for social justice. At this time, however, I had merely an intellectual understanding and appreciation of the position, with no firm determination to organize it in a socially effective situation.

When I went to Montgomery as a pastor, I had not the slightest idea that I would later become involved in a crisis in which nonviolent resistance would be applicable. I neither started the protest nor suggested it. I simply responded to the call of the people for a spokesman. When the protest began, my mind, consciously or unconsciously, was driven back to the Sermon on the Mount, with its sublime teachings on love, and the Gandhian method of nonviolent resistance. As the days unfolded, I came to see the power of nonviolence more and more. Living through the actual experience of the protest, nonviolence became more than a method to which I gave intellectual assent; it became a commitment to a way of life. Many of the things that I had not cleared up intellectually concerning nonviolence were now solved in the sphere of practical action.

Since the philosophy of nonviolence played such a positive role in the Montgomery Movement, it may be wise to turn to a brief discussion of some basic aspects of this philosophy.

First, it must be emphasized that nonviolent resistance is not a method for cowards; it does resist. If one uses this method because he is afraid or merely because he lacks the instruments of violence, he is not truly nonviolent. This is why Gandhi often said that if cowardice is the only alternative to violence, it is better to fight. He made this statement conscious of the fact that there is always another alternative: no individual or group need submit to any wrong, nor need they use violence to right the wrong; there is the way of nonviolent resistance. This is ultimately the way of the strong man. It is not a method of stagnant passivity. The phrase "passive resistance" often gives the false impression that this is a sort of "do-nothing method" in which the resister quietly and passively accepts evil. But nothing is further from the truth. For while the nonviolent resister is passive in the sense that he is not physically aggressive toward his opponent, his mind and emotions are always active, constantly seeking to persuade his opponent that he is wrong. The method is passive physically, but strongly active spiritually. It is not passive nonresistance to evil, it is active nonviolent resistance to evil.

A second basic fact that characterizes nonviolence is that it does not seek to defeat or humiliate the opponent, but to win his friendship and understanding. The nonviolent resister must often express his protest through noncoöperation or boycotts, but he realizes that these are not ends themselves; they are merely means to awaken a sense of moral shame in the opponent. The end is redemption and reconciliation. The aftermath of nonviolence is the creation of the beloved community, while the aftermath of violence is tragic bitterness.

A third characteristic of this method is that the attack is directed against forces of evil rather than against persons who happen to be doing the evil. It is evil that the nonviolent resister seeks to defeat, not the persons victimized by evil. If he is opposing racial injustice, the nonviolent resister has the vision to see that the basic tension is not between races. As I like to say to the people in Montgomery: "The tension in this city is not between white people and Negro people. The tension is, at bottom, between justice and injustice, between the forces of light and the forces of darkness. And if there is a victory, it will be a victory not merely for fifty thousand Negroes, but a victory for justice and the forces of light. We are out to defeat injustice and not white persons who may be unjust."

A fourth point that characterizes nonviolent resistance is a willingness to accept suffering without retaliation, to accept blows from the opponent without striking back. "Rivers of blood may have to flow before we gain our freedom, but it must be our blood," Gandhi said to his countrymen. The nonviolent resister is willing to accept violence if necessary, but never to inflict it. He does not seek to dodge jail. If going to jail is necessary he enters it "as a bridegroom enters the bride's chamber."

One may well ask: "What is the nonviolent resister's justification for this ordeal to which he invites men, for this mass political application of the ancient doctrine of turning the other cheek?" The answer is found in the realization that unearned suffering is redemptive. Suffering, the nonviolent resister realizes, has tremendous educational and transforming possibilities. "Things of fundamental importance to people are not secured by reason alone, but have to be purchased with their suffering," said Gandhi. He continues: "Suffering is infinitely more powerful than the law of the jungle for converting the opponent and opening his ears which are otherwise shut to the voice of reason."

A fifth point concerning nonviolent resistance is that it avoids not only external physical violence but also internal violence of spirit. The nonviolent resister not only refuses to shoot his opponent but he also refuses to hate him. At the center of nonviolence stands the principle of love. The nonviolent resister would contend that in the struggle for human dignity, the oppressed people of the world must not succumb to the temptation of becoming bitter or indulging in hate campaigns. To retaliate in kind would do nothing but intensify the existence of hate in the universe. Along the way of life, someone must have sense enough and morality enough to cut off the chain of hate. This can only be done by projecting the ethic of love to the center of our lives.

In speaking of love at this point, we are not referring to some sentimental or affectionate emotion. It would be nonsense to urge men to love their oppressors in an affectionate sense. Love in this connection means understanding, redemptive good will. Here the Greek language comes to our aid. There are three words for love in the Greek New Testament. First, there is *eros*. In Platonic philosophy *eros* meant the yearning of the soul for the realm of the divine. It has come now to mean a sort of aesthetic or romantic love. Second, there is *philia* which means intimate affection between personal friends. *Philia* denotes a sort of reciprocal love; the person loves because he is loved. When we speak of loving those who oppose us, we refer to neither *eros* nor *philia;* we speak of a love which is expressed in the Greek word *agape. Agape* means understanding, redeeming good will for all men. It is an overflowing love which is purely spontaneous, unmotivated, groundless, and creative. It is not set in motion by any quality or function of its object. It is the love of God operating in the human heart.

Agape is disinterested love. It is a love in which the individual seeks not his own good, but the good of his neighbor (I Cor. 10:24). *Agape* does not begin by discriminating between worthy and unworthy people, or any qualities people possess. It begins by loving others *for their sakes.* It is an entirely "neighbor-regarding concern for others," which discovers the neighbor in every man it meets. Therefore, *agape* makes no distinction between friend and enemy; it is directed toward both. If one loves an individual merely on account of his friendliness, he loves him for the sake of the benefits to be gained from the friendship, rather than for the friend's own sake. Consequently, the best way to assure oneself that Love is disinterested is to have love for the enemy-neighbor from whom you can expect no good in return, but only hostility and persecution.

Another basic point about *agape* is that it springs from the *need* of the other person—his need for belonging to the best in the human family. The Samaritan who helped the Jew on the Jericho Road was "good" because he responded to the human need that he was presented with. God's love is eternal and fails not because man needs his love. St. Paul assures us that the loving act of redemption was done "while we were yet sinners"—that is, at the point of our greatest need for love. Since the white man's personality is greatly distorted by segregation, and his soul is greatly scarred, he needs the love of the Negro. The Negro must love the white man, because the white man needs his love to remove his tensions, insecurities, and fears.

Agape is not a weak, passive love. It is love in action. *Agape* is love seeking to preserve and create community. It is insistence on community even when one seeks to break it. *Agape* is a willingness to sacrifice in the interest of mutuality. *Agape* is a willingness to go to any length to restore community. It doesn't stop at the first mile, but it goes the second mile to restore community. It is a willingness to forgive, not seven times, but seventy times seven to restore community. The cross is the eternal expression of the length to which God will go in order to restore broken community. The resurrection is a symbol of God's triumph over all the forces that seek to block community. The Holy Spirit is the continuing community creating reality that moves through history. He who works against community is working against the whole of creation. Therefore, if I respond to hate with a reciprocal hate I do nothing but intensify the cleavage in broken community. I can only close the gap in broken community by meeting hate with love. If I meet hate with hate, I become depersonalized, because creation is so designed that my personality can only be fulfilled in the context of community. Booker T. Washington was right: "Let no man pull you so low as to make you hate him." When he pulls you that low he brings you to the point of working against community; he drags you to the point of defying creation, and thereby becoming depersonalized.

In the final analysis, *agape* means a recognition of the fact that all life is interrelated. All humanity is involved in a single process, and all men are brothers. To the degree that I harm my brother, no matter what he is doing to me, to that extent I am harming myself. For example, white men often refuse federal aid to education in order to avoid giving the Negro his rights; but because all men are brothers they cannot deny Negro children without harming their own. They end, all efforts to the contrary, by hurting themselves. Why is this? Because men are brothers. If you harm me, you harm yourself.

Love, *agape*, is the only cement that can hold this broken community together. When I am commanded to love, I am commanded to restore community, to resist injustice, and to meet the needs of my brothers.

A sixth basic fact about nonviolent resistance is that it is based on the conviction that the universe is on the side of justice. Consequently, the believer in nonviolence has deep faith in the future. This faith is another reason why the nonviolent resister can accept suffering without retaliation. For he knows that in his struggle for justice he has cosmic companionship. It is true that there are devout believers in nonviolence who find it difficult to believe in a personal God. But even these persons believe in the existence of some creative force that works for universal wholeness. Whether we call it an unconscious process, an impersonal Brahman, or a Personal Being of matchless power and infinite love, there is a creative force in this universe that works to bring the disconnected aspects of reality into a harmonious whole.

31. CORE and SNCC, Statements of Principle

The use of mass nonviolence in Montgomery fanned into flame a spark which had been kept alive for more than a decade by members of the Congress Of Racial Equality (CORE). In February 1942 James Farmer, then race relations secretary of the Fellowship of Reconciliation, proposed the formation of a group composed of both pacifists and nonpacifists to take nonviolent action against racial discrimination. That same year the Chicago Committee of Racial Equality began to use against segregated facilities the sit-in techniques devised by labor organizers during the depression. In 1943 the Congress Of Racial Equality (a name reminiscent of the Congress of Industrial Organizations) was formed.

CORE's organizing procedures were strongly influenced by its philosophy of nonviolence (see Document 31A). The same spirit was evident in the statement of purpose of the Student Nonviolent Coordinating Committee (SNCC), formed in 1960 to coordinate the activities of thousands of students using the sit-in, "kneel-in," "jail-in," and cognate nonviolent techniques to integrate public accommodations facilities (see Document 31B).

Congress Of Racial Equality, "CORE Rules for Action," flier (New York: n.d. [1963]). Reprinted with the permission of the Congress Of Racial Equality.

A. CORE Rules for Action

GUARANTEES OF THE INDIVIDUAL TO THE GROUP

1. A CORE member will investigate the facts carefully before determining whether or not racial injustice exists in a given situation.

2. A CORE member will seek at all times to understand both the attitude of the person responsible for a policy of racial discrimination, and the social situation which engendered the attitude. The CORE member will be flexible and creative, showing a willingness to participate in experiments which seem constructive, but being careful not to compromise CORE principles.

3. A CORE member will make a sincere effort to avoid malice and hatred toward any group or individual.

4. A CORE member will never use malicious slogans or labels to discredit any opponent.

5. A CORE member will be willing to admit mistakes.

6. He will meet the anger of any individual or group in the spirit of good will and creative reconciliation: he will submit to assault and will not retaliate in kind either by act or word.

7. A member will never engage in any action in the name of the group except when authorized by the group or one of its action units.

8. When in an action project a CORE member will obey the orders issued by the authorized leader or spokesman of the project, whether these orders please him or not. If he does not approve of such orders, he shall later refer the criticism back to the group or to the committee which was the source of the project plan.

9. No member, after once accepting the discipline of the group for a particular action project, shall have the right of withdrawing. However, should a participant feel that under further pressure he will no longer be able to adhere to the

Rules for Action, he shall then withdraw from the project and leave the scene immediately after notifying the project leader.

10. Only a person who is a recognized member of the group or a participant accepted by the group leader in a particular project shall be permitted to take part in that group action.

GUARANTEES FROM THE LOCAL GROUP TO THE INDIVIDUAL

11. Each member has the right to dissent from any group decision and, if dissenting, need not participate in the specific action planned.

12. Each member shall understand that all decisions on general policy shall be arrived at only through democratic group discussion.

13. A CORE member shall receive the uncompromising support of his CORE group as he faces any difficulties resulting from his authorized CORE activities.

B. Student Nonviolent Coordinating Committee, Statement of Purpose

We affirm the philosophical or religious ideal of nonviolence as the foundation of our purpose, the presupposition of our faith, and the manner of our action. Nonviolence as it grows from the Judaeo-Christian tradition seeks a social order of justice permeated by love. Integration of human endeavor represents the crucial first step towards such a society.

Through nonviolence, courage displaces fear; love transforms hate. Acceptance dissipates prejudice; hope ends despair. Peace dominates war; faith reconciles doubt. Mutual regard

---

The Student Nonviolent Coordinating Committee, *Constitution* (as revised in Conference, April 29, 1962 [originally adopted Raleigh, N.C., April 1960]). Mimeographed, n.d., on file at SNCC office, Atlanta, Georgia.

cancels emnity. Justice for all overcomes injustice. The redemptive community supercedes systems of gross social immorality.

Love is the central motif of nonviolence. Love is the force by which God binds man to himself and man to man. Such love goes to the extreme; it remains loving and forgiving even in the midst of hostility. It matches the capacity of evil to inflict suffering with an even more enduring capacity to absorb evil, all the while persisting in love.

By appealing to conscience and standing on the moral nature of human existence, nonviolence nurtures the atmosphere in which reconciliation and justice become actual possibilities.

32. Thomas Gaither,
Jailed-In

The first national CORE project was a Journey of Reconciliation in which twenty-five persons spent two weeks testing bus segregation in the upper South. This was in 1947. CORE workers, such as the Reverend James Lawson of Nashville, were also prominent in the lunch-counter sit-ins of 1960. The sit-ins began as the spontaneous action of three students at North Carolina A. and T. College in Greensboro, North Carolina on February 1, 1960. By September 1960 the sit-ins had involved 70,000 students, 3,600 of whom were arrested. A number of these demonstrators, such as Thomas Gaither, elected not only to commit civil disobedience but to refuse bail when arrested. This technique became known as "jail-in," or "jail no bail."

Thomas Gaither, *Jailed-In* (New York: League for Industrial Democracy, 1961). Reprinted with the permission of the Congress Of Racial Equality.

Eight Friendship Junior College students and I served 30 days on the York County road gang for the "crime" of sitting-in at McCrory's lunch counter in Rock Hill, South Carolina. While hundreds of students have been jailed since the start of the sit-in movement, we were the first to be committed to a road gang, which is the present-day version of the dreaded southern chain gang.

We could have paid $100 fines, or we could have posted $200 bail each and gone out pending appeal. Instead, we chose to be jailed-in. All nine of us felt that this would strengthen the impact of our protest. Furthermore, instead of the city being $900 richer for the injustice it had committed, it would have to pay the expense of boarding and feeding us for 30 days.

What Happened Before

The story behind our case opens on Lincoln's Birthday, 1960. This was the date of the first sit-ins at Rock Hill, which were also the first in the state of South Carolina. Immediately following the original sit-in at Greensboro, North Carolina, on February 1, students at Friendship Junior College in Rock Hill expressed interest in joining the south-wide protest movement. Under the very able leadership of Abe Plummer and Arthur Hamm, they sought advice from Rev. C. A. Ivory and other local civil rights leaders. CORE Field Secretary James T. McCain, who has worked for civil rights in South Carolina for most of his life, was dispatched to Rock Hill to help train the students in sit-ins and other nonviolent techniques. A Student Civic Committee was established for the purpose of planning and coordination. By Lincoln's Birthday, preparations for the first sit-in were complete.

On that date groups of students entered the Woolworth and McCrory stores and sat down at the lunch counters. A gang of whites rapidly gathered, some of them armed with homemade ammonia bombs, which were hurled at the sit-inners. A counterman kept wiping the surfaces with an ammonia-soaked rag. The students remained quietly in their seats.

Violence by whites continued in the days that ensued. Negro adults, who were not involved in sit-ins in any way, were assaulted on the streets. Rev. Ivory received repeated threatening phone calls.

On March 15, Friendship Junior College students joined a mass protest demonstration in Orangeburg in which 350 were arrested and herded into an open-air stockade. Being a student at Claflin College, I was among those jailed on that day. It was on this occasion that Governor Hollings asserted that no such demonstrations would be tolerated, adding: "*They think they can violate any law, especially if they have a Bible in their hands.*"

In Rock Hill, sit-ins and picketing continued throughout the school year. After the college students left for summer vacation, a number of high school students became involved. Arthur Hamm, one of the college student leaders, remained in town to give them direction. On June 7, Hamm was arrested while sitting-in at McCrory's. Arrested with him was Rev. Ivory, who had the courage to engage in this type of action even though he is crippled and confined to a wheelchair. The gross indignity of arresting a crippled minister in a wheelchair gave this incident nationwide publicity. Wheeling Rev. Ivory out the rear entrance and across the street to the jail, was an awkward task for Police Captain Honeysucker. Shaking-down the minister in his wheelchair for concealed weapons and taking him downstairs for fingerprinting also presented a problem. Finally, after going through all the procedures of being booked, Rev. Ivory was rolled into a cell where he stayed until his attorney got him out on bail. Hamm, too, was released. Next day he was back at his sit-ins and picketing with a group of high school students. Before the end of June, Hamm had to leave Rock Hill for a summer job with the American Friends Service Committee.

During July and August the campaign slowed down. But with September and the reopening of college, sit-ins were resumed. At about this same time, I went to work as a CORE field secretary and one of the first places to which I was dispatched was Rock Hill.

The Town of Rock Hill

This textile manufacturing town of 33,000 people was not new to me. Both my father and mother had attended Friendship Junior College. As a child, I used to come into town often. I even recall visiting the McCrory and Woolworth stores, now the focal points of the struggle for lunch counter integration in Rock Hill. I never bought more than a bag of popcorn or some cashews but it occurred to me even then to wonder why we couldn't ever sit down and get something to eat at the counter. Of course, I didn't realize why.

By the time of the memorable Montgomery bus boycott, I was 17 and I well remember the sympathy action taken by Negroes in Rock Hill. Following the lead of Montgomery, they too decided to stop riding the buses until they were free to sit where they chose. Within a few months the bus company went out of business. The job of furnishing transportation for Negroes was undertaken by a special committee, initiated by Rev. Ivory. The committee eventually bought two buses, one of which is still running today.

As I walked up the street upon arrival in Rock Hill last fall, a little Negro boy suddenly rushed out in front of me. He was dirty, ragged and suffering from a severe cold. We got to talking. His mother is a domestic worker who in addition brings home wash. His father has worked for years in the bleachery. He has never been promoted and never will be. His wage scale is low: unions have somehow not been able to make inroads at Rock Hill. The total weekly income of both he and his wife is less than $45. I describe this family because it seems to me so typical of the Negro's lot in a town like Rock Hill.

It is a town of many churches, but the worship of God is on a strictly segregated basis. Rock Hill's first kneel-ins occurred only recently, on the Sunday of the big supporting demonstration on our behalf when we were on the road gang. The Negro kneel-inners were admitted at three of the white churches but barred at two others. Even the Christian so-called liberals in Rock Hill feel that Negroes should be satisfied with second class citizenship. One exception is the Catholic school in town, which desegregated without incident—and without any outcry from the segregationists. In addition to Friendship, the town has another small Negro church-run college, Clinton, and a state-operated white girls' college, Winthrop. The heads of the two Negro colleges were at first fairly neutral in regard to the local sit-ins. They did not come out in public support, but neither did they pressure students against participation, as was the case in Baton Rouge and in some other Negro college communities. However, as the situation developed, James Goudlock, president of Friendship College took a strong position in support of the sit-ins.

As for the public officials, they have been blatantly pro-segregation and opposed to any compromise. Rock Hill's mayor has flatly refused to set up a bi-racial committee of the type which has been established in some southern communities as an outcome of the student protests. Much of the ill-will evidenced by whites when the Rock Hill sit-ins started, was brought on by the segregationist agitation of local and state political leaders.

My familiarity with Rock Hill, coupled with my experience in the student movement in South Carolina, were factors in CORE's dispatching me there soon after I took the field secretary's job. Upon arrival, it didn't take me long to conclude that the most urgent need was for training student leaders. The

Friendship students who had become involved in sit-ins and picketing at the start of the 1960-61 school year were mostly freshmen. I suggested that CORE hold an action workshop. This took place on the weekend of Dec. 9-11 at the college from which I had graduated the previous year: Claflin, in Orangeburg. One outcome was a full understanding by the students of the effectiveness of jail-ins, as opposed to accepting bail or paying fines. Immediately after the workshop a really intensified program of sit-ins and picketing got under way in Rock Hill.

As Robert McCullough, one of our jail-inners, later told the press regarding the month of January preceding our arrest: *"City officials pointed out that we had staged 19 demonstrations during January and suddenly we felt sort of ashamed of ourselves that we hadn't staged 31. After all, there are 31 days in January, so what had we been doing the other 12 days?"*

Hour of Decision

The 26th day of January had been selected as the date for the sit-in, which inevitably would lead to the jail-in. Rev. Diggs, the college chaplain had suggested that the students involved should first register for the spring term to make sure of being able to return to classes following release from jail. To facilitate this the sit-in date was changed to the 31st. From Sumter, where I had been working with students at Morris College, I returned to Rock Hill on January 25.

On the 29th we held a meeting in an attempt to enroll more students in the action. Two members of the basketball team, Mack Workman and David "Scoop" Williamson signed up. The way some of the original members of our group felt was summarized by John Gaines when he said: *"I will go to jail and stay there, even if no one else does."*

Making a decision to go to jail for the first time was not easy.

In some cases, it meant leaving a girl friend; in others, antagonizing parents who had little understanding of nonviolent action and much fear for their children's safety. There was also the danger that parents might be fired from their jobs as a result of their children's action.

On the night before the scheduled sit-in . . . in fact at about one in the morning . . . Clarence Graham, who had been considering the matter for some days, reached his final decision and got out of bed to write a letter of explanation to his mother and father.

"Try to understand that what I'm doing is right," the letter said. *"It isn't like going to jail for a crime like stealing or killing, but we are going for the betterment of all Negroes."*

Came January 31, the nine of us committed to be jailed-in and one who was to come out on appeal as a legal test, assembled in the college lounge. Willie McCleod was prepared to the extent of carrying his toothbrush in his pocket. Surprised to see Willy Massey, a student with a goatee and dressed like a typical cool cat, I asked why he had come to the meeting. *"Man, I'm going to jail!"* was his reply. An atmosphere of parting sorrow filled the room. Girlfriends were there to say goodbye and, in some cases, to ask their boyfriends to reconsider.

At the end of the meeting we headed uptown for McCrory's and Woolworth's. Woolworth's lunch counter had been discontinued in the course of the month-long intensive campaign and had been replaced with a flower counter, but picketing continued. McCrory's lunch counter was still open. It closed down the day after our demonstration. As we walked uptown, some of us wondered whether any of our group would change his decision on the way and withdraw. None did.

As we approached the stores we were stopped briefly by Police Captain Honeysucker and an official of the South Carolina Law Enforcement Division, who advised us to return to the campus, and avoid *"getting in trouble."* Instead, we established picket lines at the two stores. Fifteen minutes later, our group entered McCrory's and took seats at the lunch counter.

Arrest and Trial

The manager, who was perspiring and obviously jittery, told us *"We can't serve you here."* Hardly were the words out of his mouth when city and state police who were standing by roughly pushed us off our stools and hauled us out the back door onto a parking lot area and across the street to jail. We were first searched and then locked in cells. We started singing freedom songs and spirituals. An hour or so later we were joined by another Negro prisoner named NuNu, who had been picked up for being drunk. At 5:30 we were fed a piece of cold barbecued chicken and cold coffee without sugar. Then we received a visit from Rev. Ivory and Rev. Diggs. We slept on bare steel bunks, which bruised our bones but not our morale. At dawn we were awakened by a prisoner on the white side asking for a cigaret. He kept yelling and banging on the walls.

It was February 1 and, as I noted mentally, the first anniversary of the south-wide sit-in movement. We were taken into the courtroom for trial. The charge was trespassing.

On direct examination, Lieutenant Thomas admitted that he had given us only between 3 and 15 *seconds* to leave the store. However, he changed this to between 3 and 15 *minutes* when cross-examined by our attorney, Ernest A. Finney, Jr. So confused did the lieutenant become with his two stories, that he requested and obtained permission to rest a little before proceeding. Finally, even Judge Billy Hayes stated that according to the evidence, we had not been given sufficient time to leave the store, even if we had wanted to take the opportunity of doing so. Police Captain Honeysucker, who was seated to the judge's right, looked dejected. An atmosphere of indecision prevailed. Were we finally going to win a legal case in a lower court in the deep south? We were called upon to enter our pleas. We pleaded not guilty. Hardly were the words out of our mouths, when the judge pronounced us guilty and sentenced us to 30 days hard labor on the road gang or $100 fines. Surprise and shock filled the courtroom when it became known that we had chosen to be jailed-in. The only thing they had to beat us over the head with was a threat of sending us to jail. So we disarmed them by using the only weapon we had left . . . jail without bail. It was the only practical thing we could do. It upset them considerably.

"You're on the Chain Gang Now"

From the courtroom we were taken to the York County road gang stockade. We got there about four in the afternoon. It consisted of two large dormitories, one for whites the other for Negroes. It was like a barracks except for the bars and mesh-wire which made it unmistakably like a jail.

First, we were taken to the clothing room to get our prison clothes. In charge was Captain Dagler, who, as we learned later, was one of the toughest guards in the camp. *"Boy, cut that thing from under your chin and pull off that jitterbug hat,"* he said to Willy Massey. *"You're on the chain gang now!"* Meanwhile, "Scoop" Williamson was trying to scoop a pair of shoes out of the huge pile on the middle of the floor. He finally found a pair that fitted.

Inside the prison, our initial feeling was one of uncertainty. As we entered the Negro dormitory, we were met with curious stares from the other prisoners. Some already knew, via the grapevine, why we were there; others didn't.

"The Stuff is On"

One prisoner commented *"The stuff is on, now!"* Others echoed the slogan. By the *"stuff"* they meant anti-Negro hatred. They explained that the *"stuff"* had been *"on"* only recently in the white dormitory, following the much-publicized marriage of the Negro singer-actor, Sammy Davis, Jr. and the white screen star, May Britt. *"If anybody bothers you, let us know; we can handle them,"* volunteered one of the prisoners in talking to James Wells. The latter explained that all in our group believe in nonviolence. Our would-be protector seemed surprised.

As it turned out, the Negro prisoners' fears regarding our effect on the white prisoners, proved unfounded. Most of us worked in integrated gangs (until after we were put in solitary) without incident. In fact, when we were in solitary, a white prisoner took the initiative of writing the FBI that he considered this unjust. Another white prisoner volunteered to assert that it was wrong to single-out Negro prisoners only— including us students—to go out on Lincoln's Birthday, a Sunday, and erect a barbed wire fence in anticipation of the crowds expected to visit us on that occasion. By the end of our stretch, some of the white prisoners would actually request us to sing one of the freedom hymns which we had sung at our morning devotional services.

The only *"stuff"* which did occur was a single incident in which a white prisoner serving life, upon coming in from work one day, started cursing at Clarence Graham and Robert McCullough and finally drew a knife on them. The two simply looked at him and walked on. When the Negro prisoners heard about it, some of them were ready to fight. Again, we had to try to explain our adherence to nonviolence.

"A Prison—Not a Damned School"

As to the Negro prisoners, they held us in high esteem. We were called upon repeatedly to serve as final authorities in arguments. Our presence prompted frequent discussions of world problems. We conducted classes in English and Current Events.

But we were barred from keeping up with our studies. On our sixth day in jail, Captain Dagler ordered me to gather up all the college textbooks which the students had brought along and carry them up-front. He said th. the books were being taken away from us because the prison did not want to be responsible for them. I assured him that each of us was willing to assume responsibility for his own books. He retorted that he was simply carrying out orders. I then inquired who had given the orders, to which he answered:

"Quit asking questions. This is a prison—not a damned school. If this was a school, we'd have teachers here."

Obviously, it was a prison. We got up at 5:30 in the morning, ate a breakfast of grits, fatback with flour gravy and black coffee. Then, we went out for the day's labor. On our first day, the temperature was 24°.

My first job was loading sand onto a truck. There was one white prisoner on my gang; the rest were Negroes. Among them was NuNu, who had been thrown into our cell at the city jail the day we were arrested. NuNu was always the center of attention. He had apparently been involved in numerous petty difficulties with the law.

The guards' attitudes toward us ranged from indifference to hostility. Captain Jim, the guard bossing my work gang was a fat, jovial type who seemed to me surprisingly broad-minded. I discovered he had been raised among Negroes. He frequently recalled how, when he was a youth, he used to play baseball with Negro kids on Sundays and whenever there was spare time. He usually referred to Negroes as "darkies," not seeming to realize that the term is derogatory.

On February 7 we were joined by a student from Charlotte, North Carolina and one from Petersburg, Virginia. Along with two female students from Nashville and Atlanta, Diane Nash and Ruby Smith, they had sat-in at a Rock Hill lunch counter. Like us, all four had been sentenced to 30 days and had refused to pay fines. There being no road gang for women, the two girls were confined to the women's county jail.

With the addition of the two new students—Charles Jones and Charles Sherrod—the jail-inners on our road gang totaled 11. Our original group included John Gaines, Clarence Graham, Willie McCleod, Robert McCullough, Willy Massey, James Wells, David Williamson, Mack Workman and myself.

Solitary

February 7 was memorable for us because we spent the entire morning in solitary confinement. The periodic shouting, cursing and other loud noises which emanated from the prisoners' quarters apparently did not bother the officials. However, for several days they had objected to our singing hymns at the morning devotional services which we had initiated.

One line that particularly irritated them was *"Before I'll be a slave, I'll be buried in my grave."* No sooner would we start to sing, than a guard would order us to *"cut out that damned fuss!"* Of course, we refused and simply kept on singing. When this happened on February 7, Captain Maloney, the prison superintendent, put us in solitary.

He accused us of *"trying to run the prison."* I tried to explain that we were simply exercising our right of religious freedom. He replied: *"If y'all are that religious, why ain't y'all preachers?"* I explained that two of us were actually studying for the ministry.

At this point, Charles Jones, as a goodwill gesture, stepped forward and presented the prison superintendent with a box of chocolates which he had received as a present. Maloney slammed it down on a table outside the solitary cell door and proceeded to lock us in.

We found ourselves in a 12-by-12 foot, dark room furnished with a commode, a small sink and one lone drinking cup. Obscuring the window was a metal sheet and steel bars. Lights went on at mealtimes only and meals consisted of bread and water.

But on this occasion we never got a chance to taste this

sumptuous food. Shortly after noon, Captain Maloney unlocked our door and asked if we were ready to go back to work. He fully realized that we had no intention of ceasing our morning hymn-singing, but in order to save face, he did not raise the issue.

We were given a meal of beans, cornbread, milk and a peach, and were driven under heavy guard to the city dump, where the county maintains a topsoil pit. We eleven students were now on a separate work gang. It soon became clear that in putting us back to work, rather than keeping us in solitary, the prison officials' strategy was to *"work-the-hell"* out of us. By quiting time we had shoveled 14 loads of topsoil onto the 7-ton dump trucks. It was backbreaking work.

Visiting

The parents' difficulty at grasping what we were trying to accomplish did not deter them from coming to the camp on visiting days. I mentioned earlier how Clarence Graham, had been so worried about his parents' reactions, that he drafted an explanatory letter to them at 1 a.m. of the day we were to be arrested. Both his father and mother came to visit. So did John Gaines's 95-year-old great-grandmother, who is in a wheelchair. She brought $200 cash just in case John should want to change his mind and accept bail.

"I don't think I ever got it explained completely to my great-grandmother," Gaines explained. *"She was afraid they'd work me too hard and that I couldn't stand it. She was still puzzled when I told her that it was a privilege for a Negro to go to jail for his rights."*

Regarding his grandmother, who is a cook at the college, Gaines said: *"She told me I was disobedient when I said I had to go to jail. But once I got locked up, she was quite changed. She came to jail and asked me if I was all right or needed anything."*

Gaines's grandmother's attitude was typical of many of the

parents who came to visit. In addition to relatives, friends and supporters came from many parts of the country. This gave us great encouragement. On our first Sunday, a caravan of 60 cars and a bus brought more than 300 Negro and white visitors to the isolated road camp.

The following Sunday, Lincoln's Birthday, over 1,000 local citizens and students from other states participated in a pilgrimage to Rock Hill on behalf of our cause. It was early that morning that we were ordered to erect a barbed-wire fence around the compound. From the dormitory window, I could see an endless line of highway patrol cars. Some residents in the vicinity had posted their property in such a way that if Negroes should step on it, they could be accused of trespassing. A few white hoodlums speeded their cars up and down the road in an attempt at intimidation. But the pilgrimage was not deterred. Guards, posted between us and our visitors, started to take notes on what was being said. They failed to dampen our enthusiasm over this significant demonstration of support for our efforts. We were additionally encouraged to learn that since our arrest, the jail-ins had spread to Atlanta and Lynchburg bringing the total number of students involved—including us—to almost 100.

Speed-up

As the days went by, following our return to work from solitary, it became increasingly clear that we were the victims of a speed-up. Starting the second day, we were expected to load 36 trucks of topsoil, or double the workload of other prisoners. I was cited by the captain as an experienced chain gang man— possibly because I was the oldest in the group—and singled-out to lead the pace. In a kidding vein, Massey kept yelling at me to shovel faster. *"Come on Moses!"* he would say.

We decided to refuse to go along with the speedup. Two of our gang, Jones and Sherrod had gotten sick, the former with an injured shoulder muscle. On February 13 our work output decreased considerably. The following morning, the prison superintendent warned us that unless we worked faster we would be transferred to the state penitentiary. When we reached the topsoil pit, we found an additional truck had been dispatched for us to load. We worked at a moderate pace and after about an hour and a half, a group of prison officials arrived to inspect us. As they departed, John Gaines waved to them in a joking manner. His wave was misinterpreted as a threatening gesture, and Gaines was ordered into the officials' car.

The rest of us stopped work and planted our shovels in the topsoil. We started toward the officials to inquire where they were taking Gaines. They told us to resume work—or join Gaines. We chose the latter, as a move of solidarity. We were then loaded onto one of the dump trucks, and driven back to camp.

Back Into Solitary

Upon arrival at the stockade, we found ourselves back in solitary confinement for a second time. But before locking us in, a guard came and took Gaines away. Our attempts to inquire where he was being taken proved fruitless. Aware of what might happen to a lone Negro "agitator" in the hands of white southern prison guards, we feared for Gaines's safety. We decided to go on a hunger strike until we learned his whereabouts. This did not constitute too much of a sacrifice, since the only food in solitary was bread—three times a day. But it was at least some demonstration of our concern.

Furthermore it had an impact on the guards. They seemed quite disturbed at the end of the first day to discover there were 24 pieces of corn bread to be removed from our cell. Lying on the floor in this cramped space, with only our jackets on or under us—and with Mack Workman's snoring—we didn't get too much sleep during our first night in solitary. The lack of sleep added to the gnawing of the hunger strike on our stomachs made us feel miserable on the second day. Some of us had stomach aches; others felt as if our bellies had shrunk. Graham described it as *"a turbulent dispute between my backbone and my stomach."* We kidded ourselves with graphic descriptions of our favorite things to eat.

In the course of the third day, we were finally told what had happened to Gaines. He had been transferred to the county jail and was unharmed. Upon learning this, we decided to end our hunger strike. The superintendent and the guards had become so worried over the hunger strike that when we resumed eating, they were happier than we were. They brought us seconds on everything. We were ordered back to work.

Jail Term Ends—Struggle Goes On

The labor was not easy, but the speed-up plan prescribed for us earlier was no longer in evidence. During our last few days on the road gang, we worked laying drainage pipes under rural roads. Prison officials were anxious to avoid any publicity or supporting demonstrations on the day of our release. Captain Dagler made this known to us on our final day, March 2. After only half a day's work, he took us back to the stockade. We were given lunch, ordered to change into our regular clothes and loaded aboard a caged truck. The prison superintendent and his assistant escorted us to the Rock Hill city limits.

There we were set free and walked in a group to the Friendship campus. Our 30 days on the road gang were over, but not our struggle to end lunch counter discrimination in Rock Hill.

As Clarence Graham expressed it at our first major press conference after getting out: *"If requesting first class citizenship in the south is to be regarded as a crime, then I will gladly go back to jail again."*

One of our group, Willy Massey, *was* back in jail again less than two weeks later. He and four other students were arrested

March 14 while picketing a drug store with a segregated lunch counter. Like our group, they refused to pay fines. The day before, two other members of our group—John Gaines and Robert McCullough—were assaulted on the picket line by white hoodlums. Gaines was clubbed unconscious and taken to York County hospital. Two hours later, he and McCullough resumed picketing accompanied with three others of our group —Clarence Graham, James Wells and me.

These students are determined to carry on the nonviolent action campaign until Rock Hill's lunch counters desegregate. Our jail-in has strengthened—not weakened—that determination. Unfortunately, I cannot stay with them. CORE field secretaries have to cover considerable territory and I will be dispatched elsewhere. For me, Rock Hill was my second jail-in. My first was in Miami, Florida, in August when seven of us at CORE's Interracial Action Institute remained 10 days in jail rather than accept bail. The Rock Hill experience has fortified my conviction in the effectiveness of jail-ins in cases of unjust arrests.

33. William Mahoney,
"In Pursuit of Freedom"

In 1961 CORE initiated the Freedom Rides, modeled on the earlier Journey of Reconciliation. This time the riders ventured into the Deep South, meeting mob violence at Anniston, Birmingham and Montgomery, Alabama. A number of riders were arrested in Jackson, Mississippi and imprisoned in the state penitentiary at Parchman. In this document, William Mahoney, leader of the Washington, D. C. Nonviolent Action Group, recounts his experience.

William Mahoney, "In Pursuit of Freedom," *Liberation* (September 1961), 7–11. Reprinted with the permission of *Liberation* magazine.

In early May I heard from fellow Howard University students that the Congress on Racial Equality was looking for volunteers to ride from Washington, D.C. to New Orleans by bus to determine whether bus station facilities were integrated in compliance with Supreme Court rulings. I was sympathetic to the idea, but approaching final examinations and a 34-hour-a-week job made my participation at that time out of the question.

I forgot about the CORE-sponsored trip, known as the Freedom Ride, until Monday, May 15th, when the morning papers were delivered to the dormitory desk at which I was working and I saw pictures of a fellow Howard student with whom I had participated the past year and a half in the Non-Violent Action Group (N.A.G.) of Washington, leaving a flaming bus on the outskirts of Anniston, Alabama. The caption said that the student, whose name is Henry Thomas, had been struck on the head as he left the bus. I was infuriated.

In protest against the savagery displayed by segregationist mobs at Anniston, Birmingham, and Montgomery, I joined N.A.G. in picketing the White House and also spent a few hours on a CORE picket line at Trailways bus terminal. Pedestrians didn't coldly pass by our signs as they usually do, but stopped and stared, deep in thought.

Late one evening, two members of N.A.G., Paul Detriecht and John Moody, called at my room to say goodbye before leaving for Montgomery. Paul and John joined the Freedom Riders in time to attend the meeting, at the Montgomery First Baptist Church, which became the target of an angry mob. The National Guard was called out and the Freedom Riders went into hiding to avoid possible arrest and segregationist fury. While in hiding, Paul called N.A.G. and pleaded for as many as possible from the District to come down to Montgomery. The project seemed to be at its most trying stage and my brothers in the South needed every person they could possibly muster, so I decided to go. I could quit the 60-cent-an-hour job and either take exams early or have them put off until I returned.

The next few days were a sleepless scramble to have exam dates changed, find some place to leave my clothes and books, resign from my job, constantly debate my reasons for going, and continue my regular studies. I knew that my parents would oppose my decision, so I wrote them a letter of explanation (which I mailed while already on the way to Alabama). I consoled myself with the thought that all revolutions have created such conflicts within families: even Gandhi and Tolstoy had to further the nonviolent movement against the wishes of their families.

At 11 p.m. on Friday, May 26th, Frank Hunt, also a N.A.G. member, and I boarded a Greyhound bus in Washington with tickets for Montgomery. Frank is a recent graduate of the University of Maryland and was on the Freedom Ride during a vacation from his job as an *Afro-American News* reporter.

At our first stop in Virginia Frank and I were confronted with what the Southern white has called "separate but equal." A modern rest station with gleaming counters and picture windows was labelled "White," and a small wooden shack beside it was tagged "Colored." The colored waiting room was filthy, in need of repair, and overcrowded. When we entered the white waiting room Frank was promptly but courteously, in the Southern manner, asked to leave. Because I am a fair-skinned Negro I was waited upon. I walked back to the bus through the cool night trembling and perspiring. This was the pattern at all rest stations from Washington to Jackson, Mississippi.

During our one-day journey Frank and I discussed race problems and eavesdropped on other passengers' conversations. An Air Force man just back from overseas sat in front of us talking to three other white passengers about the Freedom Riders. The consensus was that the integrationists should be hung from the nearest tree. At this point Frank pulled his straw hat over his face and sank down in his seat, and I resumed work on a take-home mathematics exam. At one point a woman spoke loudly about the hardship she was suffering as a Negro, saying that she was the last hired at a job, the worst paid and the first fired. She complained about the high rents one had to pay even to live in a slum. The whites in the front showed no reaction to the woman's loud tale of despair. It was as though the bus riders were from two different worlds, the inhabitants of each being invisible to those of the other.

The Montgomery bus station was surrounded by Army jeeps, trucks, and the National Guard in battle gear. Some of the soldiers, who could be seen as they moved from the shadows into the light of the station, had fierce looking beards, which had been grown for the coming Civil War Centennial celebration. We found the people from the Christian Leadership Council who had been sent to meet us and drove away cautiously, realizing that the least traffic violation would be an excuse for our arrest. We eluded the detectives following us and, winding our way through the city, went to Reverend and Mrs. Abernathy's house, where we met seven other people with whom we were to continue. The house was protected by the National Guard. We didn't meet Reverend Abernathy, for he had been taken to jail with other leaders.

Arrival and Arrest

At 7:00 Sunday morning, we entered the Montgomery bus station amidst a confusion of photographers, reporters, National Guardsmen and bus passengers. The white lunch counter was closed before we arrived and when we entered the colored waiting room, its lunch counter was quickly shut down.

With two rifle-carrying Guardsmen in the front seat and jeeps leading and following the bus we sped to the border. Waiting rooms at all stops along the way were closed. At the state line the commanding officer of the Guard boarded the bus and in a pleasant voice wished us luck, saying that we could expect a long stay in Mississippi.

Once across the state line we passed a couple of police cars, which began to follow us. At our first stop the station was cordoned off a block in every direction. A police officer jumped on the bus and forbade anyone to move. One woman, who was a regular passenger, frantically tried to convince the police that she was not involved with us. After checking her ticket the police let her get off.

As we rolled toward Jackson, every blocked-off street, every back road taken, every change in speed caused our hearts to leap. Our arrival and speedy arrest in the white bus station in Jackson, when we refused to obey a policeman's order to move on, was a relief. A paddy wagon rushed us down the street to the police station.

While being interrogated I asked the detective if he knew that legally and by the moral standards America professes to the world we had a right to act as we did and that his actions were helping to tear down any respect the world might have had for our country. He said that this might be so but that the South had certain traditions which must be respected.

While waiting in line to be fingerprinted and photographed we were watched by huge policemen who repeatedly inspected their pistols. As a Negro inmate walked past on an errand an officer stamped his foot, which sent the fellow scurrying away like a whipped puppy. The giant men with stars on their chest roared with laughter, having displayed the brand of Southern hospitality we might expect.

At 2 p.m. on May 29th, after spending the night in a barracks-like room of which I can only remember, with trepidation, a one-foot-high sign written on the wall in blood, "I love Sylvia," our group joined nine other Freedom Riders in court. The others were from Tennessee and were among those who had been attacked in Birmingham and Montgomery. In the court's opening exercises Judge Spencer repeated frequently that, "This is a regular Monday afternoon court."

We were charged with a breach of the peace and then the tall, wiry state prosecutor examined Police Chief Wray, the only witness called to the stand. Chief Wray said that we had been orderly but had refused to move on when ordered to do so by his men. Mr. Young, our lawyer, asked if he would have required us to move on if we had entered the colored waiting room. Chief Wray said no. Mr. Young concluded that we must have been arrested for integrating the white waiting room. Chief Wray's face turned from its usual dirty white to a rose red.

The judge picked up a piece of paper and *read* the verdict: "Guilty as charged . . . two-hundred dollar fine or work it off in jail at three dollars a day." We refused to pay Mississippi a continental.

Reunion in Jackson

On Tuesday, we were taken across the street to the county jail and locked up with the first group to have been arrested in Jackson. I had finally caught up with Henry Thomas, John Moody, and other friends. Paul Detriech was held in the city jail with other white Freedom Riders. Henry told me that a couple of days earlier they had been taken to the county penal farm. While there several of them, including a young lady, had been beaten with blackjacks for not replying "yes, sir" to the warden's queries. When the F.B.I. learned of the incident, the Riders were returned to the county jail, and the warden brought before a prison board. The warden justified his actions by saying that he had struck all of them, including the frail woman, in self-defense. The board acquitted him.

The thirty or more of us occupied five cells and a dining hall on the top floor. At night we slept on lumpy bags of cotton and were locked in small, dirty, blood-spattered, roach-infested cells. Days were passed in the hot, overcrowded dining room playing cards, reading, praying and, as was almost inevitable, fighting among ourselves over the most petty things. The sermons offered during our self-imposed devotional period by such men as the Reverends Lawson, Vivien and Dunn were refreshing. But I guess any invocation of freedom and equality sounds excellent to a man behind bars. In the evening one of the prisoners in the cell block below ours sang Negro spirituals with the voice of a lonely, wild animal. At every rift one could feel the pain that must have inspired it.

Time crawled painfully, 15 days becoming 45 meals, 360 hours, 100 card games or 3 letters from home. The killing of a roach or the taking of a shower became major events, the subjects of lengthy debate. But morale remained high; insults and brutality became the subject of jokes and skits. The jailers' initial hostility was broken down by responding to it with respect and with good humor. Mr. Young later informed us that the treatment of all prisoners in Jackson jails improved after our matriculation.

On June 12th, a man named Leon Horne was put in with us, and was readily accepted. The next day, after spending the night sleeping in his clothes on an unmade bed in my cell, he was taken away by the turnkey. We never saw him again until we managed to smuggle a newspaper into the jail and found his picture on the front page. In a press conference he had called us everything from Communists to embezzlers of publicly solicited funds. We learned later from our lawyer that Horne had formed the first N.A.A.C.P. chapter in Jackson and run off with its funds. The authorities continued to hold him and one day two of our fellows were placed in a cell close enough to talk with him. He told them that he had been forced into making the statements. This is believable, for the authorities put pressure on two others to make similar statements. In one case, a Negro woman was intimidated by a white woman prisoner who beat her with a shoe, while the authorities pressed her, but she failed to yield.

The police were more successful in their tactics with Reverend Gleason. They took him out, brought him cokes, candy and a meal at a local restaurant and the good Reverend told the Southern newspapers just about anything they wanted to hear. When he got to his home in Chicago he denied all that he had said in Jackson.

The jails began to bulge as even Mississippi Negroes, who according to Southern whites are happy, began to join in the protest. To relieve the crowding, about fifty of us were piled into trucks at 2 a.m. June 15th and sped off into the night. It was rumored that in spite of a law against putting persons convicted of misdemeanors into a penitentiary, we were going to the state penitentiary.

Parchman Penitentiary

In the light before sunrise a small caravan of trucks led by a police car sped north on Highway 49 over the flat Mississippi land. Two Negro children walking through a field of young cotton were silhouetted against an orange and blue horizon as they stopped and knowingly pointed to the swiftly moving prison trucks. The procession turned on to the grounds of Parchman Penitentiary, stopped briefly at the main gate, and then moved directly to a restricted area of the sprawling plantation.

One of the larger vehicles, containing twenty-six of the political prisoners, had broken down and was being towed the last few miles to the prison by a pick-up truck which carried luggage. The little pick-up towed its monstrous burden past an observation tower, through a barbed-wire-fence gate, and came to rest in a muddy yard by the front door of a squat, modern red-brick building.

The barked commands of a law officer sent all except two

of the Freedom Riders scurrying from the truck into a double line at the front of the building. Surrounded by a group of gun brandishing hecklers, tired unshaven men helplessly listened as sun-reddened faces, sagging from age and dissipation, spat vile remarks at them.

Torture

Terry Sullivan and Felix Singer, the two white men who remained in the truck, were refusing to cooperate with their captors. So far their limp bodies had been carefully handled. Hearing a commotion behind them, the men in line turned around in time to see Terry and Felix being thrown from the van onto the wet sand-and-gravel drive. They were then dragged through wet grass, mud puddles, and across a rough cement walk to the rear of the group. There was both pain and conviction in their faces. One of their tormentors laughed:

"Ain't no newspapermen out here, what you actin' like that for?"

Terry replied. "We refuse to cooperate because we have been unjustly imprisoned."

As they were pulled down the walk and into the building, a fat red-faced man wearing cowboy boots ran after them, stamping on the corrugated bottom of Felix's canvas shoes and yelling, "Pull them by the feet, pull them by the feet."

A guard with a serious face under his Stetson hat, examining a long black, rubber-handled tube, walked through the gate, past the smiling guards and police, and the curious, worried prisoners, and into the building.

The black tube was a cattle-shocker, which delivers a powerful charge of electricity when applied to the flesh. After the two passive resisters refused to obey a command to undress, the instrument was applied to their bodies. When they realized that the men squirming in pain on the cement floor were not going to yield to the torture, the official ripped the clothes from their bodies and threw them into a cell. All of this even though the law forbids corporal or any unusual punishment of recalcitrant prisoners.

The group outside was brought into the hallway, asked to undress, and then herded, two per cell, into the little six-by-ten compartments they were to occupy for the next month or more. The cells were segregated but the cell blocks were not.

A six-foot, three inch, two-hundred-fifty-pound brute stuffed shorts and tee-shirts through the bars to them. These were the only garments they were to wear while inmates of the maximum-security unit of Parchman Penitentiary.

The guard that handed out the uniforms brought the noon meal and sometimes engaged in heated debates about the philosophy of nonviolence and related issues. He was lovingly named Spike. One of our fellows gave him two stamps. One had a picture of Gandhi on it and the other a picture of Robert E. Lee. He said: "Here are two men. One led his nation to freedom through nonviolence, the other left his nation in ruin through the use of violence." From the thick lips of Spike's grizzled baby face came the profound reply: "If your movement would get rid of trash like you it might have a chance of succeeding." The next day Spike elaborated upon his criticism of the movement. He asked either Abraham Bassford or Price Chatham (it was hard to tell who was talking for we couldn't see each other) why he had come to the South stirring up trouble. The reply was: "Thoreau says in his *Essay on Civil Disobedience*, that under a government which imprisons any unjustly the true place for a just man is also a prison."

Spike rebutted: "If you all wouldn't read so many comic books and look at so much television you wouldn't be in the trouble you are now," and marched down the hall pushing a rattling cart of dishes, another intellectual triumph under his belt.

Processing of the prisoners continued with fingerprinting and photographing. They came for Terry and Felix last.

Their naked bodies were pulled down the row of cells by a

Negro inmate in prison stripes to a room at the end of the cell block. There mere muffled sounds of furious motion and a frightening scream which reverberated down the steel-and-cement corridor, leaving indelible marks upon the minds of all who heard it. Then came more cries above the snickering of the guards.

"They're breaking my arm, they're breaking my arm."

"They're beating my head against the cement."

On Saturday, June 24th the guards decided that the Freedom Riders' singing was too loud and took their mattresses away as punishment. At first this was taken as a joke and songs were made up about the incident, but after three days of sleeping on a cement floor or steel shelf with an air-conditioning system on full blast the cell block became silent and gloomy. Another time when the Riders sang too loud for the guards, six of them were dragged down the hall with wrist-breakers (clamps tightened upon the wrists) and thrown into dark six-by-six boxes for a couple of days. As the spunky fellows were being taken to solitary they sang, "I'm Going to Tell God How You Treat Me."

When fellow prisoner Jim Farmer, national director of CORE, went before the superintendent to protest the treatment he was told that if we didn't cooperate conditions would deteriorate. A request was made for a written statement of rules to define what was meant by cooperation, but none was ever issued. Consequently the imprisoned men drew up their own code of minimum standards for they felt that although they were obligated to respect the authorities, the authorities had an obligation to treat them as human beings. The code was:

Having, after due consideration, chosen to follow without reservation the principles of nonviolence, we resolve while in any prison:

to practice nonviolence of speech and thought as well as action
to treat even those who may be our captors as brothers
to engage in a continual process of cleansing of the mind and
body in rededication to our wholesome cause

to intensify our search for orderly living even when in the midst of seeming chaos.

Most felt that the search for order and meaning in life could best be carried out in group devotion, where sermons could be delivered and group singing take place. Phrases pertaining to the Freedom Rides were put to the tune of Negro spirituals, work songs, and union songs. When Henry Thomas finished with Harry Belafonte's "Day Oh," it became:

> Freedom, Freedom
> Freedom come and I gonna go home.
> I took a trip down Mississippi way (Hey)
> Freedom come and I gonna go home.
> Met much violence on Mother's Day[1] (Hey)
> Freedom come and I gonna go home. . . .

Protest and Purification

Cleansing of the mind and body included fasting for some. Fasts were also engaged in as protest. The purpose and extent of these acts of dedication were misrepresented to the public. For example the press reported that Price Chatham lost three pounds. Actually he lost about thirty-five pounds.

Some prisoners refused to fast and flaunted the fact in front of others who were fasting, perhaps in order to compensate for their guilt. Others gave in to their hunger after a few days and soon became boisterous eaters. A few fasted until there was a thin veil between them and death.

Questions have been raised as to the character of people who willingly withstand such punishment. Are they publicity seekers? Are they Communists?

In cell 14 was a middle-aged art dealer from Minneapolis who had three dollars to his name and had come on the Freedom Ride "because it is one way of fighting a system which

---

[1] The attacks at Anniston and Birmingham occurred on Mother's Day.

not only hurts the Negro but is a threat to world peace and prosperity. Some of the same men in whose interest it is to have segregation, so it is for them to have war industries, to recklessly speculate in other countries and in general to meticulously exploit masses of peoples. I also came because I wanted to see for myself what is happening in the South."

My cellmate, a Negro worker, came because he had been chased home by white toughs once too often, because his sister was determined to come, and because a friend of his, William Barbee, had been almost killed by a mob while on a Freedom Ride. He admits that his behavior is not ordinarily disciplined, but he readily accepted any restrictions required of him by the movement. He had sung professionally and took the lead in many of our group songs.

On my right, in cell 12, was the son of a well-to-do business man who had come because it was his moral duty. His aim was to "change the hearts of my persecutors through the sympathy and understanding to be gained by nonviolent resistance." He spoke proudly of his father who had fought hard and "made it," and was constantly defending North America's economic and political system from the attacks made upon it by myself and the art dealer. We never changed each other's views but the arguments passed time and gave us mental exercise.

These three philosophies—political, emotional, and moralist—represent the three major viewpoints I found while spending forty days in various Mississippi prisons.

The name of Gandhi was constantly on the minds and lips of most of the imprisoned Riders. Anything Gandhi had said or done was interpreted and reinterpreted to be applied to the situation in Mississippi. As with all religious movements, from Christianity to Marxism, factions arose which read their prophet's teaching as best suited them. Those who went on long fasts justified this by Gandhi's remark that at times he had to fast in spite of his followers' refusals to join him; others, who would fast only when there were numbers large enough to be politically effective, said that they took this stand in accord with Gandhi's practice of only making *meaningful* sacrifices.

At 5 p.m. on July 7th those remaining of the first and second groups were released on appeal bonds after 40 days in jail. When we left, the number of Freedom Riders in jail was close to a hundred. We were taken back to the city jail to sign our bonds in a little pick-up led by a police car.

Colored workers were leaving the fields as we sped down the highway. The women were clad in gay-colored prints, making me think of pictures the old people used to paint in my mind of slave days. How my heart hurt every time we passed a car driven by a Negro, for he would, upon hearing our police escort's siren, come to a stop in the grass by the side of the road, whereas a white driver would only move to the edge of the road and reduce his speed.

Before parting for our various destinations we stood in a circle, grasped hands and sang a song called "We Will Meet Again." As I looked round the circle into my companions' serious faces and saw the furrowed brows of the 19- and 20-year-old men and women, I knew that we *would* meet again.

34. Voter Registration, Southwest Mississippi, 1961

The Student Nonviolent Coordinating Committee (SNCC), formed in 1960 to coordinate sit-in activities, decided in 1961 to concentrate on voter registration. The areas selected for registration drives were rural regions with Negro majorities: southwestern Georgia and the state of Mississippi.

The persistence and self-sacrifice of SNCC workers in these "hardcore" areas of the South called forth an answering courage from local Negro communities. In Pike, Walthall, and Amite counties of southwestern Mississippi, voter registration was begun in the late summer of 1961 by a handful of students, such as John Hardy (see Document 34A). White Mississippians responded with violence, including the pistol-beating of John Hardy and the murder of Reverend Herbert Lee, local leader of the registration drive.

Meantime two students, Brenda Travis and Isaac Lewis, at the Burgland High School in McComb, Mississippi, had been expelled for attempting to integrate the Greyhound bus station; their expulsion led to a boycott of the school by their fellow-students and strong support from parents (see Documents 34 B–E). SNCC workers Robert Moses, Charles McDew, and Dion Diamond taught mathematics, science and history to the expelled and boycotting students at "Nonviolent High," the first Mississippi "freedom school," in a room above a McComb grocery store. Late in October the entire SNCC staff in Pike County was imprisoned; unable to pay bail, their spirit remained defiant (see Document 34F).

A. *John Hardy, Walthall County Report*

John Hardy is a Negro, 21 years old, who was born and raised in Nashville and lived for four years in Memphis. His father works as a porter in the Methodist Publishing House and Parthenon Press. His mother works as a dormitory maid at David Libscom College. He attended the 15th Avenue Baptist Church in Nashville, where he was a member of the Junior choir, chairman of the Junior Deacon Board, and treasurer of the Youth Church. He is not married. He has completed two years of college at Tennessee Agricultural and Industrial State College, where he studied speech, drama, and political science. He is presently working with the Student Nonviolent Coordinating Committee as a voting registration instructor.

This organization is currently sponsoring a voter registration project in Walthall, Amite, and Pike Counties, Mississippi.

John Hardy, "Walthall County Report," n.d. [September 1961], on file at the Atlanta office of the Student Nonviolent Coordinating Committee.

John came from Nashville to Pike County in the latter part of July or early part of August along with other college students who were helping in the voter registration school in McComb, Mississippi. They discussed the possibility of setting up a voter registration school in Walthall County, and John consented to setting up such a school there. During the week some other students came in to help John conduct the registration school in Pike County. Three of these students, Jimmy Travis, MacArthur Cotton, and George Love, volunteered to go with them to set up the school in Walthall County. Jimmy Travis and George Love are from Jackson, Mississippi, and MacArthur Cotton is from Kosciusko, Mississippi. Love and Cotton are entering their sophomore years at Tugaloo College, and Travis begins as a freshman there this year.

The four of them went to Walthall County on August 18, 1961, and went to the Mt. Merian Baptist Church that morning. This was where they were to set up the school. They conducted classes that day and helped to instruct about thirty people.

They held their classes in the church in the main room of the church. They worked all day their first day from about 10:00 in the morning until about 5:00 that night. After that they conducted their classes from Monday through Friday at 9:30 to 12:00 noon in the morning, from 2:00 until 4:30 in the afternoon and from 6:30 until 9:00 in the evening. They kept this schedule for the first week they were there. The second week they held their classes from 4:30 until 9:00 in the evening. The attendance was better the second week because the people in the community became more interested, and the hours were better for those who worked.

The material they used in the class was a facsimile of the registration form, a copy of the constitution of the State of Mississippi and a personal excuse sheet on which the person could state why he had not previously attempted to register and to vote. They talked with each individual and explained to them how to fill out the facsimile of the registration form. The purpose of this was to show the person how to fill out the form and to show them what would be expected of them. They gave them a section of the constitution to copy and asked them to tell what it meant. They would answer questions. They would go over the form. John gave each person a copy of some of the sections of the constitution and told everyone to study, because the registrar could ask about any provision of the constitution. This is the procedure they used in all of the classes they conducted. Twice they had some singing and prayers to encourage the people to attend the classes. One time they took an offering to help pay for expenses of the project such as gas, oil, pencils, paper, and other things.

The first time any Negroes attempted to register after the registration school was started was on August 30, 1961, around 9:00 a.m. Ruby Magee, Sidney Ellsey, Easley Walker, Ira Ryan, and John Turner went down to the Registrar's office. All of these persons except Mr. Walker attended registration classes which John had given. He went with them. They all went into the Registrar's office. When they got to the outer office outside the Registrar's office, Miss Magee said she had to put some money in the parking meter where her car was parked. John told her he would put the money in for her since he was not trying to register. When he returned all of the people were in the Registrar's inner office. Miss Magee and Mr. Ellsey were seated at the Registrar's desk. Mr. Ellsey was seated in front of the desk and was not filling out any form. Miss Magee was seated at the end of the desk at Mr. Wood's (the registrar) left and was filling out a form. Mr. Turner and Mr. Ryan were standing in the inner office, and Mr. Walker was standing just outside the door to the inner office. John sat in a chair in the outer office and later stood in the outer office by the door to the registrar's office. Miss Magee finished the forms, but about the time she began to define the section of the constitution Mr. Walker, Mr. Ryan, and Mr. Turner left. They said there was too little time for them to complete an application before the office closed at noon for the day. When Miss Magee finished, the registrar took the form, looked it over several times for about three or four minutes, and then laid it on the side of his desk. Two white women entered his office and talked to him. John didn't hear their conversation. Mr. Wood then went to the outer office with the women and transacted some business with them at the desk in the outer office. This took about five minutes. When they finished Mr. Wood returned to the inner office and took Miss Magee's form and looked it over again. Then he wrote on it (It seemed to John as though he wrote on the line required for signature of the registrar.) and put it in a stamping machine—looked at it again and placed it in a file. Next he asked Mr. Ellsey what he wanted. Mr. Ellsey said he wanted to register. Mr. Wood turned to Miss Magee and asked her what Mr. Ellsey said. She told Mr. Wood that he wanted to register, so Mr. Wood gave him a form. Mr. Ellsey started to fill out the form, and John started to walk out of the inner office. The sheriff and another white man were in the outer office, and he called to John. He told him to "come here". He asked him personal questions pertaining to his name and whether or not he had a driver's license. John told him he didn't have a driver's license, and he asked why. He said he didn't drive. Then he asked John about the school and whether or not he was conducting the registration classes. The other white man was taking notes on a pad at this time, and after the sheriff stopped talking this man introduced himself to John. Although his name has been forgotten, John later learned he was the editor of the *Tylertown Times,* Mr. Paul Pittman. He interviewed John at this time after the sheriff left. John told him about the voter's registration school project, its purpose, who was sponsoring it, where it was being held and other information pertaining to the project. In the August 31st *Tylertown Times* an article related to this interview was published on the front page of the paper.

John continued to conduct the voter registration school at

Mt. Meriah. On the following Monday, September 4th, a meeting was held at the Mt. Meriah Church. There were about 70 to 80 persons there. At this meeting John encouraged those who wanted to attempt to register to go down and try. He told them that those who were interested in becoming first-class citizens should exercise this right to vote, and that in order for them to vote they had to become registered. He asked those who were willing to go down to give their names to him and the date they would go. About [10] said they would go.

Classes were also held on Tuesday and Wednesday, and each night the students tried to encourage the people to go down and attempt to register. Mrs. Peters and Mr. Wilson were in a class on Wednesday night and said they were willing to go down to register. John told them he would go with them. The next morning they stopped by for him between 8:30 and 9:00 a.m. Mr. Wilson, Mrs. Peters, MacArthur Cotton and John drove in to town together in a pick-up truck. They parked in the street down by the fish market, and John went with Mr. Peters and Mr. Wilson to the Courthouse. They went into the Courthouse, and Mrs. Peters and Mr. Wilson went into the registration office. John stood just outside the door to the inner office, about four to five feet away from the registrar's desk.

The registrar asked what they wanted. Mrs. Peters stated they had come to register to vote. Mr. Wood said he wasn't registering anyone since he was already involved in a court suit, and that he didn't want to have anything to do with them. When this happened John stepped into the doorway to the inner office and looked at Mrs. Peters and asked her what the trouble was. He told Mr. Wood his name was John Hardy. He then said to him, "I have been wanting to see you" and said some words to him. John remembers the statement, "What right do you have coming down here messing in these people's business, and why don't you go back where you came from." While he was saying this he arose from his desk and walked past John into the outer office. John just turned and took a step into the outer office. Mr. Wood took about two or three steps into the outer office and reached behind a desk. He opened the upper left hand drawer and pulled a gun from the drawer. He turned to John, pointed to the door with his left arm, and said, "I want you to get the hell out of this office and never come back." He had the gun in his hand and held it in a gripping fashion. John doesn't remember where he had the gun pointed; he didn't say anything; he was frightened and turned and started to walk out of the office. As Mr. Wood ordered him out he raised the gun to about the level of his head. When John was very near the doorway to the hallway he felt a blow to his head. He can only remember being very dazed, and the next thing he knew Mr. Wilson and Mrs. Peters were helping him across the street and up an alleyway. He felt something running down his head and saw blood dripping off from himself. . . .

B. *Mississippi Violence vs Human Rights*

CHRONOLOGY OF VIOLENCE AND INTIMIDATION IN MISSISSIPPI

1961

. . . AUGUST 15, AMITE COUNTY: Robert Moses, Student Non-Violent Coordinating Committee (SNCC) registration worker, and three Negroes who had tried unsuccessfully to register in Liberty, were driving toward McComb when a county officer stopped them. He asked if Moses was the man ". . . who's been trying to register our niggers." All were taken to court and Moses was arrested for "impeding an officer in the discharge of his duties," fined $50 and spent two days in jail.

AUGUST 22, AMITE COUNTY: Robert Moses went to Liberty with three Negroes, who made an unsuccessful attempt to register. A block from the courthouse, Moses was attacked and beaten by Billy Jack Caston, the sheriff's first cousin. Eight stitches were required to close a wound in Moses' head. Caston

---

Committee For The Distribution of the Mississippi Story, *Mississippi Violence vs Human Rights* [Atlanta: 1963].

was acquitted of assault charges by an all-white jury before a justice of the peace.

AUGUST 26, MC COMB, PIKE COUNTY: Hollis Watkins, 20, and Elmer Hayes, 20, SNCC workers, were arrested while staging a sit-in at the F. W. Woolworth store and charged with breach of the peace. They spent 36 days in jail.

AUGUST 27 and 29, MC COMB, PIKE COUNTY: Five Negro students from a local high school were convicted of breach of the peace following a sit-in at a variety store and bus terminal. They were sentenced to a $400 fine each and eight months in jail. One of these students, a girl of 15, was turned over to juvenile authorities, released, subsequently rearrested, and sentenced to 12 months in a state school for delinquents.

AUGUST 29, MC COMB, PIKE COUNTY: Two Negro leaders were arrested in McComb as an aftermath of the sit-in protest march on city hall, charged with contributing to the delinquency of minors. They were Curtis C. Bryant of McComb, an official of the NAACP, and Cordelle Reagan, of SNCC. Each arrest was made on an affidavit signed by Police Chief George Guy, who said he had information that the two ". . . were behind some of this racial trouble."

AUGUST 30, MC COMB, PIKE COUNTY: SNCC workers Brenda Travis, 16, Robert Talbert, 19, and Isaac Lewis, 20, staged a sit-in in the McComb terminal of the Greyhound bus lines. They were arrested on charges of breach of the peace and failure to obey a policeman's order to move on. They spent 30 days in jail.

SEPTEMBER 5, LIBERTY, AMITE COUNTY: Travis Britt, SNCC registration worker, was attacked and beaten by whites on the courthouse lawn. Britt was accompanied at the time by Robert Moses. Britt said one man hit him more than 20 times. The attackers drove away in a truck.

SEPTEMBER 7, TYLERTOWN, WALTHALL COUNTY: John Hardy, SNCC registration worker, took two Negroes to the county courthouse to register. The registrar told them he ". . . wasn't registering voters" that day. When the three turned to leave,

Registrar John Q. Wood took a pistol from his desk and struck Hardy over the head from behind. Hardy was arrested and charged with disturbing the peace.

SEPTEMBER 13, JACKSON, HINDS COUNTY: Fifteen Episcopal ministers (among them three Negroes) were arrested for asking to be served at the lunch counter of the Greyhound bus terminal. They were charged with inviting a breach of the peace. They were found not guilty of the charge on May 21, 1962, by County Judge Russell Moore.

SEPTEMBER 25, LIBERTY, AMITE COUNTY: Herbert Lee, a Negro who had been active in voter registration, was shot and killed by white state representative E. H. Hurst in downtown Liberty. No prosecution was undertaken, the authorities explaining that the representative had shot in self-defense.

OCTOBER 4, MCCOMB, PIKE COUNTY: The five students who were arrested as a result of the August 29 sit-in in McComb returned to school, but were refused admittance. At that, 116 students walked out and paraded downtown to the city hall in protest. Police arrested the entire crowd, but later released all but 19, all of whom were 18 years old or older. They were charged with breach of the peace and contributing to the delinquency of minors and allowed to go free on bail totalling $3,700. At the trial on October 31, Judge Brumfield, finding the students guilty, and sentencing each to a $500 fine and six months in jail, said: "Some of you are local residents, some of you are outsiders. Those of you who are local residents are like sheep being led to the slaughter. If you continue to follow the advise of outside agitators, you will be like sheep and be slaughtered."

C. A Statement from the Burgland High School Students

We the Negro youth of Pike County feel that Brenda Travis and Isaac Lewis should not be barred from an education for

Students of Burgland High School, "A Statement from the Burgland High School Students," McComb, Mississippi, October 4, 1961. On file at the Atlanta office of the Student Nonviolent Coordinating Committee.

protesting against injustice. We feel that as a member of Burgland High School they have fought this battle for us. To prove that we appreciate them for doing this, we will suffer whatever punishment they have to take with them.

In school we are taught democracy, but the rights that democracy has to offer have been denied to us by our oppressor: we have not had the right to vote; we have not had a balanced school system; we have not had an opportunity to participate in any of the branches of our local, state and federal government.

However, we are children of God, who makes the sun shine on the just and unjust. So we petition all our fellowmen to love rather than hate, to build rather than tear down, to bind our nation with love and justice without regard to race, color or creed.

D. P.T.A. Requests Readmittance of Students

P.T.A. Board
Burgland H.S.
McComb, Miss.
October 14, 1961

Mr. R. S. Simpson
Mr. C. C. Higgins
Members of the Board of Education
McComb, Mississippi

Dear Sirs:

We parents feel the time has come for everyone, white and black, to recognize that we are all children in the family of man, twigs and branches stemming from the same tree of

---

Burgland High School P. T. A. Board, "P.T.A. Requests Readmittance of Students," McComb, Mississippi, October 14, 1961, mimeographed. On file at the Atlanta office of the Student Nonviolent Coordinating Committee.

life. We feel everyone should recognize that if the tree catches fire all its branches will be scorched. To prevent such a scorching, it will be necessary for each race to select representatives to assemble for the purpose of proposing firm, constructive and just solutions to community problems.

To select the matter immediately before us, Mr. Higgins, Mr. Simpson, the members of the Board of Education, and the parents of the students at Burgland High School should meet in an effort to achieve a good solid understanding of each other's position. We feel that our principle, Mr. Higgins, is a victim of circumstances beyond his control, that the fight is with the Board of Education and the Superintendent, Mr. Simpson. We are sure that they will hear our plea. We want our children back in school without their being placed under undue pressure and strain.

We know that the Board has the right to expell and suspend students, but why should the children have to sign slips to be readmitted to their school? Such slips can have no legal status, in fact, they are only a form of coercion. This requirement merely puts the parents on the spot.

We are asking Mr. Simpson to request the authorities who are responsible for placing Brenda Travis in reform school to obtain her immediate release so that she may resume her studies, along with Isaac Lewis, at the Burgland High School. We feel she has been done a gross injustice.

We are very much concerned about our "walk-out" students and we want them in our school, the Burgland High School. If we all would read our Bibles we would see that the time is far spent for man to do all the carrying on; the Supreme Man is taking over now, our Heavenly Father. We all saw that the students, when they were marching with the entire police force behind them, were fearing no evil.

Read the twenty-third Psalm: . . . He leadeth me beside the still waters. He restoreth my soul: he leadeth me in the paths of righteousness for his name's sake.

Yea, though I walk through the valley of the shadow of death, I will fear no evil: for thou art with me; thy rod and thy staff they comfort me.

In conclusion we would like to repeat our feeling that both white and colored must reach an understanding of these issues; if we don't it will be something to bring damage to the State of Mississippi and the entire Nation.

> *Respectfully yours,*
> *Burgland High School*
> *P.T.A.*

E. *Statement by a High-School Student*

> Suzette Miller
> Subject: English
> Instructor: C. McDew

Why I walked out of Bur[g]land High School:

I am Suzette Miller a student of the present Freshman class. I don't have much to lose, but I do have a lot to gain, That is my equal rights.

Brenda Travis is a female that made a protest in McComb Bus Station. She was also a student at Burgland Hi, but is now an ex-student.

I was in the walk out because I am A student at Burgland just like Brenda. Because she wasn't allowed back in school I don't feel that I should allow myself to go back.

I walked out and to be readmitted I have to sign a paper saying that if I walk out any more I will be expelled, and if I didn't sign the paper asking for readmittance back in school.

[McComb, Mississippi, 1961. Ed.]

Now I am expelled for the remainder of the school year. But I will keep protesting until the battle is won.

I am now a student of The Nonviolent High school. In my heart I believe where there is a will there is a way.

Now is the time to put God first and to let him lead us.

Our white brothers and sisters think that we want war. War is not needed now in Mississippi, If we ever needed any thing we need God. He is the way and the light.

If we would stop and think we could see what we need and what are we doing to try to get it.

We as a race come to face with our enemies kind and willing to have them as brother and sisters. We would have better families, homes, churches, towns, and states.

May God forever bless us all over land and contry. "Oh God show us the right way".

F. Robert Moses, *Message from Jail*

We are smuggling this note from the drunk tank of the county jail in Magnolia, Mississippi. Twelve of us are here, sprawled out along the concrete bunker; Curtis Hayes, Hollis Watkins, Ike Lewis and Robert Talbert, four veterans of the bunker, are sitting up talking—mostly about girls; Charles McDew ("Tell the story") is curled into the concrete and the wall; Harold Robinson, Stephen Ashley, James Wells, Lee Chester Vick, Leotus Eubanks, and Ivory Diggs lay cramped on the cold bunker; I'm sitting with smuggled pen and paper, thinking a little, writing a little; Myrtis Bennett and Janie Campbell are across the way wedded to a different icy cubicle.

Later on, Hollis will lead out with a clear tenor into a freedom song, Talbert and Lewis will supply jokes, and McDew will discourse on the history of the black man and the Jew.

Robert Moses, Magnolia, Mississippi [November 1961]. On file at the Atlanta office of the Student Nonviolent Coordinating Committee.

McDew—a black by birth, a Jew by choice, and a revolutionary by necessity—has taken on the deep hates and deep loves which America and the world reserve for those who dare to stand in a strong sun and cast a sharp shadow. . . .

This is Mississippi, the middle of the iceberg. Hollis is leading off with this tenor, "Michael row the boat ashore, Alleluia; Christian brothers don't be slow, Alleluia; Mississippi's next to go, Alleluia." This is a tremor in the middle of the iceberg—from a stone that the builders rejected.

35. Voter Registration, Southwest Georgia, 1961 1963

SNCC's southwest Georgia project led to the Albany, Georgia, demonstrations of 1961–1962, in which local police made more than 1,000 arrests. The demonstrations began early in November 1961 when Albany State College students tested the Interstate Commerce Commission ruling requiring integration of facilities for interstate travel. When they were arrested, they were supported by adults and high-school students (see Documents 35 A and B) who organized mass protest marches. After the great wave of marches in 1961–1962, the heroic everyday routine of voter registration continued (see Document 35C). On August 8, 1963, two white registration workers (Ralph Allen and John Perdew) and one Negro (Don Harris) were arrested in nearby Americus, charged with insurrection—a capital crime in Georgia—and held without bail until their release almost three months later. While in prison they corresponded surreptitiously with a member of the Americus movement, Gloria Wise (see Document 35D).

A. *Handbill, Albany Nonviolent Movement*

THE ALBANY NONVIOLENT MOVEMENT
MEETS
THURSDAY 7 pm NOVEMBER 9th

MACEDONIA BAPTIST CHURCH

CORNER JEFFERSON & CHERRY

REV. L.W. WHITE

To those who love the Lord and Freedom:

COME; LISTEN; LEARN; LOVE!

"We believe in the Fatherhood of God and the brotherhood of man. We believe that God made of one blood all nations for to dwell on all the face of the earth".

Our beliefs have consequences.

If we are of one blood, children of one common Father, brothers in the household of God, then we must be of equal worth in His family, entitled to equal opportunity in the society of men. That "all men are created equal, that they are endowed by their creator with certain unalienable rights, that among these are life, liberty and the pursuit of happiness", we hold to be self evident.

Moreover, if there is the seed of God in every man, then every man has, by reason of that fact alone, worth and dignity. It follows that no man may, with impunity, discriminate against or exploit another. And if the nature of man is such as we affirmed, then nothing less than its full recognition, nothing less than the dignity and respect due him simply because he is a man, can ever satisfy him.

Our faith leads us one step further. Like responds to like

[Albany, Georgia, November 9, 1961] mimeographed. On file at the Atlanta office of the Student Nonviolent Coordinating Committee.

for the most part. If there is in every man a measure of goodness and truth, this quality will respond when it meets its kind and truth and goodness have no color. We are called upon, therefore, to love our fellow men, all of them, with all the risks that that implies and all the privileges that it promises.

Our faith is incurably optimistic and unyieldingly realistic. It teaches us that we live in an ordered universe in which the moral law of cause and effect, of means and ends, is as un changeable as any physical law. *Violence corrupts* and destroys both the user and the victim; *the power of Love and Nonviolence is creative and redeems both.*

In such a faith we look forward with confidence to a new day when man will be measured by what he is and not by his race, creed, color, or nationality. That day can be near if we go forward with energy, faith, and knowledge. It can be very far away if we respond with fear and ignorance. In that day each man will be free to contribute to his fullest capacity for the good of all men; his opportunity to develope will not be curtailed. Segregation and second-class citizenship will take their places with slavery as evils of the past. No two men will be alike; but no two will be different in value to society because of race, color, religion, or nationality. Just as we now know that all are hurt by injury to any one, so in that tomorrow all will benefit by the achievement of each. As prejudice feeds on prejudice, so brotherhood will feed on brotherhood.

SUPPORT THE STUDENTS

COME

MACEDONIA BAPTIST CHURCH

"We Shall Overcome"

B. *Statement by a High-School Student*

My name is Roychester Patterson, II. My age is seventeen (17), and I am a high school senior. I live at 601 First Avenue,

S.E. I went to Carver High School. I was an honor student for ten (10) years. My mother's name is Mrs. Carolyn Daniels. My father's name is Mr. Roychester Patterson.

The school I attended was unequiped and incapable of furnishing a qualified education for students who plan to go out to college. It is incapable of giving students the necessary knowledge with which to compete with other students from better schools. Our school needs typewriters, science equipment, library books, text books, home economics equipment, more buses, maps, and math facilities. We also need an auditorium and gymnasium. These are the things that three other students and I went to the principal, E. E. Sykes, and asked for. He told us, there was nothing he could do, so we went to the Supt. Frank Christie, who said that he did something for the colored schools every year. We then mentioned the funds that the State Department of Education sends to every County to supply the school needs. He then told us there was nothing he could do. So the next day we criticized the administration for its inefficiency. The day after that, the Supt. Christie came to the school and called me in a conference and threatened me, "Patterson if you don't change your attitude, you'll have to leave Terrell County. You're sitting on a keg of dynamite whether you know it or not."

A few weeks later P.T.A. meeting was coming up, so we went around and got the parents to come out to P.T.A., we tried to explain to them what the school needed, but the Principal, E. E. Sykes, exploaded and wouldn't let us finish, so we made a house to house campaign.

We later told the State Department about these lack of necessary facilities and they threatened to send in the Fact Finding Committee and the Supt. ordered thousands of dollars worth of facilities for our school.

Then SNCC came into Terrell for Voter Registration and asked for our help, so we gave him our support, we tried to

"Roychester Patterson, II" [1962], on file at the Atlanta office of the Student Nonviolent Coordinating Committee.

get all of the students who were eligible to register and vote. I made a speech to this affect to an assemblage of students trying to get the students to register, I made the speech to a group of students during lunch hour on the basketball court when the principal came out and tried to break-up the meeting, but the students refused to go to class unless they be given the priviledge to listen to my speech. So he allowed me to finish, meanwhile he called the cops, four of them came. The sheriff, L. T. Matthews, the deputy, Mathis, the chief of Police, Cherry, and the Revenue, Hancock. They came to the school and threatened us with vulgar language. Later that day I went to Albany, while the demonstrations were going strong. Upon seeing several of friends in the line I immediately joined the march, because I felt very close; I had been a student at Monroe High during my junior year.

I spent two days in jail, on Friday I went to school only to find that I had been expelled from school. Because the students thought that they had me in Dawson's jail, they boycotted the lunchroom, wouldn't go to class, and wouldn't participate in school activities.

So I dropped out of school and went to work for SNCC on Voter Registration and no violence had erupted until on Saturday, February 3, 1962. A friend and I took a lady up to register and a white brother decided as long as no one did anything to me, I would be an obstacle in the way of their racket.

All of this happened because almost everybody said, to crack Terrell County was impossible and I've always wanted to do the impossible. I did what I did because I have a conviction that each man should be judged by his personal worth and not for the color of his skin. I admire men like M. L. King, Roy Wilkins and Thurgood Marshall.

I did this because I am deeply attached to my peeple and I want them to know freedom and enjoy rights as human beings.

All of this happened between September 7, 1961 and February 3, 1962.

C. [Jack] Chatfield, Lee County Report

TO: SNCC
           Atlanta, Ga.

FROM: Chatfield
           Leesburg, Ga.

SUBJECT: Lee County Report

Tuesday, April 16
Chico and I went to Lee County. We were joined by a local Albany lad, James Crawford . . . Crawford had just gotten out of jail after a three week stay; he was jailed, ostensibly, for "investigation" (72 hours is the law). He told us he had been expelled from school because he had missed so many days; I told him he could come to Lee County; he came.

Wednesday, April 17
Chico, Crawford and I went to Terrell County; we have arranged that everybody goes to Terrell on Wednesday, which is Terrell tent-meeting day. We went to Bronwood, spoke to people there.
Went to Terrell Meeting that night, in tent in Sasser.

Friday, April 19
We canvassed in Leesburg; asked one lady who owns well-known (only) cafe-service station-grocery store whether or not we could put a poster up on her wall. She said, no, that would not be practical, what with the situation in the South today, and whatall. Later on we talked to her son, who showed more hope.

Leesburg, Georgia [1963], on file at the Atlanta office of the Student Nonviolent Coordinating Committee.

Saturday, April 20

The four Lee County girls—Brenda Hurd, Gloria Hawkins, Jackie Shinault, Katie Mae James—plus one older girl, Claritha Coven, and the three of us went to downtown Leesburg. . . . The four girls were wearing something they had made in home economics class: "Freedom" headbands or "Freedom sashes"; two of them wore sashes with Freedom written on them; two wore headbands with same. All four had occasion to walk into the registrar's office when he left at 11:15 instead of 12:00.

They went into the office and were told that the deputy registrar was an old man and that he had to leave early all the time.

We were able to get two young boys to go into the courthouse, knowing full well that Mr. Yeoman wasn't there. Soon we will have to protest Mr. Yeoman's absence, and have to have a reason. The boys entered ostensibly to register; but in reality to build a case. They will go next Saturday, they say.

We chalked up more promises than we had had in a long time. There were no incidents. I went for a short time to the home of Willie Frank Bell (who stays with the Durney family) to ask him whether he would sign an affidavit saying he went to the courthouse and was told that the deputy registrar would not be in except for Fridays and Saturdays. He said he would have to ask his parents, who were not home. He said he would attempt to register again shortly.

Monday, April 22

Chico, James Crawford and I carried two Smithville people down to the courthouse. . . .

We heard from Willie Frank Bell that he and one other boy had gone to the courthouse that morning, but that 8 or 10 white men had stepped out into the hall as they entered; the two boys left, apparently they thought the white men might make a bit of trouble.

Thursday, April 25

We picked up one lady in Smithville and headed to Leesburg. James and Eddie went into the courthouse with Mrs. Geraldine Johnson, while I sat in the car.

According to James Crawford, this is what happened:

The three walked into courthouse. James said, "This lady wants to register."

White lady (sheriff's wife) said, "Have a seat outside."

James and Mrs. Johnson went outside (Eddie Moore was in corridor). The lady started to sit down but James told her not to sit down, because there were seats inside the office. Just then Sol Yeoman, deputy registrar came out of office across the hall:

"What do you want?" he asked.

James said: "I brung this lady down to register."

Yeoman told them to come inside. He handed the lady a card, instructed her to fill out the front, sign her name on the back. He told her to go outside into the hall, which the lady did.

Yeoman said to James: "Why did you bring this lady down here?"

James said: "Because she wants to be a first class citizen like y'all."

Yeoman said, "Where are you from?"

James: "Albany."

Yeoman: "Who do you work for?"

James: "SNCC."

Yeoman: "What is that?"

James: "Student Non-Violent Coordinating Committee."

Yeoman: asked if he and the lady were kinfolk; James told him they were not. Then Yeoman asked him why he had brought her down here.

James: "I brung her down to register and vote."

Yeoman: "Who are you to bring people down to register?"

James: "It's my job to bring people down to register."

Yeoman asked him whether or not he had heard about the boy in Mississippi who was shot in the head. James told him he had not.

Yeoman: "Suppose you get two bullets in your head right now?"

James: "I got to die anyhow."

Yeoman: "If I don't do it I can get somebody else to do it."

Yeoman again: "Are you scared?"

James: "No."

Yeoman: "Suppose somebody came in that door and shoot you in the back of the head right now. What would you do?"

James: "I couldn't do nothing. If they shoot me in the back of the head there are people coming from all over the world."

Yeoman: "What people?"

James: "The people I work for."

The lady was trembling and had put "Sumter County" where she should have "Smithville". James told her to write Smithville in the slot. Yeoman got angry, said, "Now you're through" to the lady. He told her to put her name on the back of the card. As they left the courthouse, James turned back and said, "I'll be back, I'll be back Saturday. That's what I'm here for—to die or live."

We then took the lady back to Smithville. From Smithville we went to Koinonia Farm, where I was supposed to pick up Don Harris and take him to Albany. When we got there we heard about Ralph's getting beaten and started into Albany.

Our car broke down on the way to Smithville. The white man who owned the land where the car had stopped said for us to move down the road, off his property. We rolled the car down, locked it, and hitched a ride into Smithville on the back of a truck. We went straight to the Burney's house because they had a phone. We called Albany and told them what the story was.

About fifteen minutes after we arrived, two white men in a

two-tone 1955 Chevrolet pulled up in front and asked for Robert Burney, the owner of the house. He was not at home. The men left. I was told that the same men (who are Field Smith and Williard Smith) had come yesterday and had told Robert Burney that we ("that white boy") had better not come back; they had told Mr. Burney that it was no good that their boys play basketball with "that white boy".

Shortly thereafter, a second car with four men in it pulled up. It was black 1953 Ford. James Crawford says he was sure that the men had guns. I got on the telephone to Albany.

The Ford came back down the second time, after having driven around the block. Mr. Robert Burney, in the meantime, had come home after having gone to the store up the street and been told that we had better get out of his house.

A third car, a 1954 two-tone Oldsmobile, pulled up. We had been told that Sherrod was on the way. Willie Frank Bell had loaded his shotgun. Gracie Bell, age 13 or 14, was in the living room watching TV.

"Do you mind being shot at?" I asked her.

"No," she said. "Not if it's for our country."

Finally Sherrod arrived. Just before this Mr. Burney, tears in his eyes, had told us to leave the house. We had started out across a field (it was dark) when we saw Sherrod and the other car pulling up. We ran back across the field and got in.

As we were going through Smithville we saw the 1954 Oldsmobile parked and a group of people near it. They saw us, got into the car, and someone shouted something. Then they moved behind us again, picked up a bit of speed, and rammed us from behind. Marion Gaines was crying in my arms, hysterically (we were sitting facing the car behind us, in the back section of the Rambler, so that we could see the car behind us moving toward us and hit us).

They followed us a few minutes longer and left. A nice evening. Six people had applied for registration.

D. *Letters from Sumter County Jail*

I

Dear Gloria,
   Why, why do you say:
         "White boy, only a fool
         Would leave his 'heaven
         On earth' just to fight
         For undeserving Negroes."?[1]
I do not understand, Gloria. It's no heaven on earth I left.
I can remember thinking to myself before I left school to return to work for SNCC (I went back for 1st semester last
year)—I can remember thinking that it wouldn't matter very
much to me if I did find myself in a position where I might
be killed because there wasn't really very much to return to.
That's your "heaven on earth" Gloria. And it's only since I've

---

Letters by Ralph Allen, Donald Harris, and John Perdew to Gloria
Wise, Sumter County Jail, Americus, Georgia, 1963. Original in possession of Gloria Wise, copies in the files of Staughton Lynd.

---

[1] In a letter opening this correspondence Gloria Wise sent Ralph
Allen the following poem:
         White boy, white boy
         You got no business here
         Don't you know how
         hard it is down here
         With us black folk
         who are afraid and
         those who are not.
         White boy, only a fool
         would leave his "heaven
         on earth" just to fight
         for undeserving Negroes.
         We are black!, white boy.
         You have no reason
         to be here because you
         are white, white boy.

been back down here that I've begun to be afraid of dying again—I mean in the abstract, for we are always afraid of the pain of dying.

Another thing about "heaven on earth." Depends on what you mean by heaven. If you mean a place where everyone has so much money they have no sensitivity—no love, no sympathy, and no hopes beyond their own narrow little worlds—if this is heaven then it would stack up. But to me the conceited, loud, self-centered all-American free white and 21 college boy stinks. I know, I was one. But something happened to make me human, something that I don't yet understand and which is only now beginning to piece itself together in my mind. And I am happy to be human. I am happy that I am here, in the Sumter County Jail rather than sitting in a plush chair in the ADΦ living room drinking beer to keep from having to think and to feel anything real outside of the fraternity house. (I quit ADΦ 2 years ago—before I ever even came down here.) But what I'm driving at is that something has to be made to happen to all those blissful ignorant idiots. I used to think that maybe by appealing to their consciences we might be able to make them decent and instill in them some human feelings. I used to think that maybe if I talked with them and tried to lay their stupidity out before them they might be struck by humanity. Nay, Gloria. Nay, nein, non, nada, nothing. They are very thick in their heads, and they are surrounded by great fortresses of money. And they make me sick when they ask "Would you marry a Negro?"

I think that the only answer is that they must suffer in order to become human. Do you realize, Gloria, that white Americans are the only folk in the world who have never been touched by large scale disaster—defeat in war, famine, fall of economic markets etc.? That is what makes so many of them so inhuman and conceited. And it is no wonder that U.S. foreign policy is so inhuman and undemocratic—viz. aid to Haitian, Spanish, and Portugese dictatorships, and lack of aid to countries labelled "Communist"—no wonder this is so when we see what happens to anybody who doesn't fit the white American mold. For instance, blacks. James Baldwin keeps making the point over and over that however much any man oppresses another, by that much also he diminish his own humanity. The free white and 21's may seem to have a lot, but they are really very shallow and inhuman.

There's a poem by E. E. Cummings which reads:

> "What if a much of a which of a wind
> Should give the truth to a summer's lie,
> Bloodies with dizzying leaves the sun"[2]
> . . . I don't recall more . . .

The poem asks the question, what if a change of season should come over the blissful placidity of the average life—the life of free-white-twenty-one? What if the fall of the year should come with winds blowing and leaves falling? Well, Gloria, that's what I hope we can do. I hope we can upset people enough to make them human, and, mostly I hope we can get things straight here for ourselves—"with freedom and justice for *all all all*."

One last thing. I love 4 people, my mother, a girl in New York named K.C., another named M.T., and a minister named Charles Sherrod. K., M., and Sherrod are all black. If I did not have my friends, I would be very much alone. And I don't want to eat in anyone's restaurant alone, to go to nobody's movie alone, to swim in nobody's pool alone. . . You dig? Don't thank me again please Gloria, it makes me wince. I guess I started it all by thanking you first, but let's call it even and forget it.

We are very happy in here.

Sincerely,
Ralph [*Allen*]

---

[2] e. e. cummings, "what if a much of a which of a wind," *1 x 1* (New York: Henry Holt and Co., 1944), Poem XX:
what if a much of a which of a wind
gives the truth to summer's lie;
bloodies with dizzying leaves the sun

II

8-30-63

Dear Gloria,

Thank you for seeing about my car—it's not your fault they took it, and it probably can be repaired (I hope!).

If you haven't done so already, I wonder if you'd mail a couple of letter that are in my briefcase, one to Harvard and one to the National Merit Scholarship Corp. I wrote them the day before I was arrested to tell them I wouldn't be going to college this year. (Now I couldn't if I wanted to!)

Looks like the big Washington March was pretty impressive. This shows that we won't be violent unless the police start something. I hope, though, that no one came away with the feeling that we can now relax and wait for a handout from Capitol Hill. Even if the bill is passed we'll still have to put pressure on store owners, theater managers, restaurants, factories, etc. to force them to obey the law of the land which they have so consistently defied. We've also got to work on the Negro community to unify it and get people in the habit of expecting respect and equal treatment.

Any news on when our trial is? [It] seems to be unclear now, although [we had thought] it would be Sept. 3.

The idea of picketing the school is tremendous! This is a way of spreading the effect of the Movement farther among students, who now form the backbone of the action workers. And it also carries the message that those on the outside, as much as those in jail, consider themselves unfree, unsuited for education until the prisoners are released. Good show.

Any more news from Americus or Albany?

Sincerely yours,
John [*Perdew*]

III

Gloria—

. . . One of my main concerns has been those who will be tried on Tuesday. I hope their needs and their families' needs have been taken care of as well as we have. After all, this is part of my job. SNCC workers walk around 24 hours per day half-way expecting to be arrested any minute.

I cannot, Gloria, in any way, shape or form tell you what to do or even suggest anything. I don't know the situation, how *people feel*, what *needs* to be done, etc. [The school boycott] sounds *fine*, but I can't say yes or no from here. (Make sure a *high* percentage is "ready" in anything involving schools, expelling 5 or 10 people is not difficult, but expelling 250 or 300 is).

Well, just have confidence in yourselves—believe in each other. You know what to do and pretty much how to do it. You know you always have the support (and as much help as possible) from SNCC. . . .

. . . Say hello and thanks to your parents. I know what needs to be done will be done—that's why I'm quiet, confident and very relaxed.

> "The enemy is only great
> Because we are on our knees:
> Let us rise."

D[onald] [Harris]

Saturday, 11 AM

I just reread this. Excuse it and remember it was written in the wee, small hours of the morning.

Take *good care* of the others in jail—don't worry about us. Remember the Movement is *not* dependent on Ralph, John or Don, but on the confidence Negro citizens of Americus and Sumter County have in *each other* as well as *themselves*.

IV

Dear Gloria,

Aye, yes yes yes yes—your letter . . . and the tuna fish sandwiches . . . and your letter.

I have been reading Nietzsche. Ever read Nietzsche? He's one of us blasphemers. A very inspiring writer at once bitterly destructive and thrillingly creative. He destroys all the time worn conceptions of God, of good and evil, of sympathy and values. It is as if he were speaking to the white citizenry of Americus and thrashing them with bitter words for the stupidity of their segregated lives—as if he just went through all the things that they held to be worth segregating and tore them down; and then as if out of the rubble and destruction arose a small black boy and a small white girl walking hand-holdingly happy patty cakingly playful through it all. It is only through destruction that we will create, says Nietzsche. Of course, he deals mostly with the concept of God and of the values of society, but it's all applicable to the situation. Nietzsche says that God is dead, that people have killed him by formalizing a ritual around him.

Nietzsche also says that one who would be the friend of a man must also be his enemy. That is, that one who would be a man's friend must not be afraid to tell him the truth about himself.

We heard today . . . that the kids refused to go to school and that about 75 demonstrated in a school. Gloria in excelsis Deo! John and I went wild for approximately 4 minutes, and we could hear Don shrieking from down the corridor when he got the news.

Also, thanks very much for the Bible. . . .

> *Sincerely,*
> *Ralph* [*Allen*]

V

Friend, Gloria—

The summer has been many things:—happy, sad, frightening, tense, educational, etc. The adjectives could stretch for miles. At the same time it has changed things, this is to say that it has caused people to change "things." ("Things" do not change of their own accord.) Some people here changed— behavior, attitudes and ideas. Some people are now more gregarious in nature—both socially (among other people) and intellectually. Others, of course, have turned introvert. Is there though, some singular occurrence or event that we can point to or denote as evidence and say, "This is what we have done"?

More than any other, I must agree with a comment made in June by an NAACP officer when Medgar Evers was shot and killed in Mississippi. He prophesied, "The summer will be very long and very hot." With this, I can agree.

I'll not continue with the interrogatives of "the summer." We are both of the same "meat" in the same oven being roasted by the intense blaze of social injustice. I think it will suffice to say that you, or your portion (of the meat) is more tender, more sensitive than mine. This is, of course, your home. You know, first hand, the people: how they *(you)* feel, what they *(you)* want—I do not. You, no doubt, have thought of, and probably answered, many of the questions I have posed. Hopefully, when you have time or when we meet again you will help me answer, for myself, those questions I asked of you. We must fill the gap you see—my looking from outside in, your looking from inside out. The heat from the fire of this summer was too hot to bear again. It must be extinguished.

As you may be able to discern by my writing my mind is ulcerating and my sanity is silently ebbing. I'm told though, that all the worldly philosophers—the great ones anyway—

began with frenzied scribblings in a jail cell. By this, I am comforted.

Since the hour is well past 4 AM, I think I'd better start looking to my heart rather than my head. (You understand, I am sure, that great philosophers, dangerous political prisoners and the like *do not* have hearts, for you however, I take exception.) . . .

. . . Stay well, friend—

"*. . . Until we've all been freed . . .*"

Don [*Harris*]

c/o Sheriff
Sumter County
Georgia

36. Birmingham Manifesto, 1963

1963 was a climactic year for the American nonviolent movement. As a Quebec-to-Guantanamo peace march proceeded down the East Coast, President John Kennedy negotiated a ban on atmospheric nuclear tests with the Soviet Union. The eloquent Birmingham Manifesto, released on April 3, 1963, launched turbulent demonstrations that shocked America more than any previous racial incident. Although this crisis produced little change in Birmingham, it precipitated the peaceful "March on Washington" of August, 1963, and the subsequent struggle in Congress for sweeping civil rights legislation.

F. L. Shuttlesworth and N. H. Smith, "The Birmingham Manifesto." Reprinted with permission from *Freedomways* magazine (Winter 1964), pp. 20–21.

The patience of an oppressed people cannot endure forever. The Negro citizens of Birmingham for the last several years have hoped in vain for some evidence of good faith resolution of our just grievances.

Birmingham is part of the United States and we are *bona fide* citizens. Yet the history of Birmingham reveals that very little of the democratic process touches the life of the Negro in Birmingham. We have been segregated racially, exploited economically, and dominated politically. Under the leadership of the Alabama Christian Movement for Human Rights, we sought relief by petition for the repeal of city ordinances requiring segregation and the institution of a merit hiring policy in city employment. We were rebuffed. We then turned to the system of the courts. We weathered set-back after set-back, with all of its costliness, finally winning the terminal, bus, parks and airport cases. The bus decision has been implemented begrudgingly and the parks decision prompted the closing of all municipally-owned recreational facilities with the exception of the zoo and Legion Field. The airport case has been a slightly better experience with the experience of hotel accommodations and the subtle discrimination that continues in the limousine service.

We have always been a peaceful people, bearing our oppression with super-human effort. Yet we have been the victims of repeated violence, not only that inflicted by the hoodlum element but also that inflicted by the blatant misuse of police power. Our memories are seared with painful mob experience of Mother's Day 1961 during the Freedom Rides. For years, while our homes and churches were being bombed, we heard nothing but the rantings and ravings of racist city officials.

The Negro protest for equality and justice has been a voice crying in the wilderness. Most of Birmingham has remained silent, probably out of fear. In the meanwhile, our city has acquired the dubious reputation of being the worst big city in race relations in the United States. Last fall, for a flickering moment, it appeared that sincere community leaders from religion, business and industry discerned the inevitable confrontation in race relations approaching. Their concern for the city's image and commonweal of all its citizens did not run deep enough. Solemn promises were made, pending a postponement of direct action, that we would be joined in a suit seeking the relief of segregation ordinances. Some merchants agreed to desegregate their rest-rooms as a good-faith start, some actually complying, only to retreat shortly thereafter. We hold in our hands now, broken faith and broken promises.

We believe in the American Dream of democracy, in the Jeffersonian doctrine that "all men are created equal and are endowed by their Creator with certain inalienable rights, among these being life, liberty and the pursuit of happiness."

Twice since September we have deferred our direct action thrust in order that a change in city government would not be made in the hysteria of community crisis. We act today in full concert with our Hebraic-Christian tradition, the law of morality and the Constitution of our nation. The absence of justice and progress in Birmingham demands that we make a moral witness to give our community a chance to survive. We demonstrate our faith that we believe that The Beloved Community can come to Birmingham.

We appeal to the citizenry of Birmingham, Negro and white, to join us in this witness for decency, morality, self-respect and human dignity. Your individual and corporate support can hasten the day of "liberty and justice for all." This is Birmingham's moment of truth in which every citizen can play his part in her larger destiny. The Alabama Christian Movement for Human Rights, in behalf of the Negro community of Birmingham.

F. L. SHUTTLESWORTH, President
N. H. SMITH, Secretary

37. Martin Luther King, Jr.,
Letter from Birmingham City Jail

There was an ominous aspect to the Birmingham victory. Birmingham touched the nation's conscience because it was so violent: day after day Negro school children faced dogs and fire hoses, and on more than one occasion Reverend Martin Luther King, Jr. and local civil rights leaders lost control of the demonstrators. King's "Letter from Birmingham City Jail" responded sharply to a communication from eight Alabama religious leaders which said: "When rights are consistently denied, a cause should be pressed in the courts and in negotiations among local leaders, and not in the streets." King's letter expressed disillusion with white moderates, and asserted that, while individuals could always be redeemed, "history is the long and tragic story of the fact that privileged groups seldom give up their privileges voluntarily."

MARTIN LUTHER KING, JR.
Birmingham City Jail
April 16, 1963

Bishop C. C. J. CARPENTER
Bishop JOSEPH A. DURICK
Rabbi MILTON L. GRAFMAN
Bishop PAUL HARDIN
Bishop NOLAN B. HARMON
The Rev. GEORGE M. MURRAY
The Rev. EDWARD V. RAMAGE
The Rev. EARL STALLINGS

My dear Fellow Clergymen,
    While confined here in the Birmingham City Jail, I came across your recent statement calling our present activities "un-

---

Martin Luther King, Jr., *Letter from Birmingham City Jail* (Philadelphia: American Friends Service Committee, 1963), pp. 3–14. Reprinted with the permission of Martin Luther King, Jr.

wise and untimely." Seldom, if ever, do I pause to answer criticism of my work and ideas. If I sought to answer all of the criticisms that cross my desk, my secretaries would be engaged in little else in the course of the day and I would have no time for constructive work. But since I feel that you are men of genuine goodwill and your criticisms are sincerely set forth, I would like to answer your statement in what I hope will be patient and reasonable terms.

I think I should give the reason for my being in Birmingham, since you have been influenced by the argument of "outsiders coming in." I have the honor of serving as president of the Southern Christian Leadership Conference, an organization operating in every Southern state with headquarters in Atlanta, Georgia. We have some eighty-five affiliate organizations all across the South—one being the Alabama Christian Movement for Human Rights. Whenever necessary and possible we share staff, educational, and financial resources with our affiliates. Several months ago our local affiliate here in Birmingham invited us to be on call to engage in a nonviolent direct action program if such were deemed necessary. We readily consented and when the hour came we lived up to our promises. So I am here, along with several members of my staff, because we were invited here. I am here because I have basic organizational ties here. Beyond this, I am in Birmingham because injustice is here. Just as the eighth century prophets left their little villages and carried their "thus saith the Lord" far beyond the boundaries of their home town, and just as the Apostle Paul left his little village of Tarsus and carried the gospel of Jesus Christ to practically every hamlet and city of the Graeco-Roman world, I too am compelled to carry the gospel of freedom beyond my particular home town. Like Paul, I must constantly respond to the Macedonian call for aid.

Moreover, I am cognizant of the interrelatedness of all communities and states. I cannot sit idly by in Atlanta and not be concerned about what happens in Birmingham. Injustice anywhere is a threat to justice everywhere. We are caught in an inescapable network of mutuality tied in a single garment of destiny. Whatever affects one directly affects all indirectly. Never again can we afford to live with the narrow, provincial "outside agitator" idea. Anyone who lives inside the United States can never be considered an outsider anywhere in this country.

You deplore the demonstrations that are presently taking place in Birmingham. But I am sorry that your statement did not express a similar concern for the conditions that brought the demonstrations into being. I am sure that each of you would want to go beyond the superficial social analyst who looks merely at effects, and does not grapple with underlying causes. I would not hesitate to say that it is unfortunate that so-called demonstrations are taking place in Birmingham at this time, but I would say in more emphatic terms that it is even more unfortunate that the white power structure of this city left the Negro community with no other alternative.

In any nonviolent campaign there are four basic steps: (1) collection of the facts to determine whether injustices are alive, (2) negotiation; (3) self-purification; and (4) direct action. We have gone through all of these steps in Birmingham. There can be no gainsaying of the fact that racial injustice engulfs this community. Birmingham is probably the most thoroughly segregated city in the United States. Its ugly record of police brutality is known in every section of this country. Its unjust treatment of Negroes in the courts is a notorious reality. There have been more unsolved bombings of Negro homes and churches in Birmingham than any city in this nation. These are the hard, brutal, and unbelievable facts. On the basis of these conditions Negro leaders sought to negotiate with the city fathers. But the political leaders consistently refused to engage in good faith negotiation.

Then came the opportunity last September to talk with some of the leaders of the economic community. In these negotiating sessions certain promises were made by the merchants—such as the promise to remove the humiliating racial signs from the stores. On the basis of these promises Rev. Shuttlesworth and the leaders of the Alabama Christian Movement for Human Rights agreed to call a moratorium on any type of demonstrations. As the weeks and months unfolded we realized that we were the victims of a broken promise. The signs remained. As in so many experiences of the past we were confronted with blasted hopes, and the dark shadow of a deep disappointment settled upon us. So we had no alternative except that of preparing for direct action, whereby we would present our very bodies as a means of laying our case before the conscience of the local and national community. We were not unmindful of the difficulties involved. So we decided to go through a process of self-purification. We started having workshops on non-violence and repeatedly asked ourselves the questions, "Are you able to accept blows without retaliating?" Are you able to endure the ordeals of jail?"

We decided to set our direct action program around the Easter season, realizing that with the exception of Christmas, this was the largest shopping period of the year. Knowing that a strong economic withdrawal program would be the by-product of direct action, we felt that this was the best time to bring pressure on the merchants for the needed changes. Then it occurred to us that the March election was ahead, and so we speedily decided to postpone action until after election day. When we discovered that Mr. Connor was in the run-off, we decided again to postpone action so that the demonstrations could not be used to cloud the issues. At this time we agreed to begin our nonviolent witness the day after the run-off.

This reveals that we did not move irresponsibly into direct action. We too wanted to see Mr. Connor defeated; so we went through postponement after postponement to aid in this community need. After this we felt that direct action could be delayed no longer.

You may well ask, "Why direct action? Why sit-ins, marches, etc.? Isn't negotiation a better path?" You are exactly right in your call for negotiation. Indeed, this is the purpose of direct action. Nonviolent direct action seeks to create such a crisis and establish such creative tension that a community that has constantly refused to negotiate is forced to confront the issue. It seeks so to dramatize the issue that it can no longer be ignored. I just referred to the creation of tension as a part of the work of the nonviolent resister. This may sound rather shocking. But I must confess that I am not afraid of the word tension. I have earnestly worked and preached against violent tension, and there is a type of constructive nonviolent tension that is necessary for growth. Just as Socrates felt that it was necessary to create a tension in the mind so that individuals could rise from the bondage of myths and half-truths to the unfettered realm of creative analysis and objective appraisal, we must see the need of having nonviolent gadflies to create the kind of tension in society that will help men rise from the dark depths of prejudice and racism to the majestic heights of understanding and brotherhood. So the purpose of the direct action is to create a situation so crisis-packed that it will inevitably open the door to negotiation. We, therefore, concur with you in your call for negotiation. Too long has our beloved Southland been bogged down in the tragic attempt to live in monologue rather than dialogue.

One of the basic points in your statement is that our acts are untimely. Some have asked, "Why didn't you give the new administration time to act?" The only answer that I can give to this inquiry is that the new administration must be prodded about as much as the outgoing one before it acts. We will be sadly mistaken if we feel that the election of Mr. Boutwell will bring the millennium to Birmingham. While Mr. Boutwell is much more articulate and gentle than Mr. Connor, they are both segregationists dedicated to the task of maintaining the status quo. The hope I see in Mr. Boutwell is that he will be reasonable enough to see the futility of massive resistance to desegregation. But he will not see this without pressure from the devotees of civil rights. My friends, I must say to you that we have not made a single gain in civil rights without determined legal and nonviolent pressure. History is the long and tragic story of the fact that privileged groups seldom give up their privileges voluntarily. Individuals may see the moral light and voluntarily give up their unjust posture; but as Reinhold Niebuhr has reminded us, groups are more immoral than individuals.

We know through painful experience that freedom is never voluntarily given by the oppressor; it must be demanded by the oppressed. Frankly I have never yet engaged in a direct action movement that was "well timed," according to the timetable of those who have not suffered unduly from the disease of segregation. For years now I have heard the word "Wait!" It rings in the ear of every Negro with a piercing familiarity. This "wait" has almost always meant "never." It has been a tranquilizing thalidomide, relieving the emotional stress for a moment, only to give birth to an ill-formed infant of frustration. We must come to see with the disinguished jurist of yesterday that "justice too long delayed is justice denied." We have waited for more than three hundred and forty years for our constitutional and God-given rights. The nations of Asia and Africa are moving with jet-like speed toward the goal of political independence, and we still creep at horse and buggy pace toward the gaining of a cup of coffee at a lunch counter.

I guess it is easy for those who have never felt the stinging darts of segregation to say wait. But when you have seen vicious mobs lynch your mothers and fathers at will and drown your sisters and brothers at whim; when you have seen hate filled policeman curse, kick, brutalize, and even kill your black brothers and sisters with impunity; when you see the vast majority of your twenty million Negro brothers smothering in an air-tight cage of poverty in the midst of an affluent society;

when you suddenly find your tongue twisted and your speech stammering as you seek to explain to your six-year-old daughter why she can't go to the public amusement park that has just been advertised on television, and see tears welling up in her little eyes when she is told that Funtown is closed to colored children, and see the depressing clouds of inferiority begin to form in her little mental sky, and see her begin to distort her little personality by unconsciously developing a bitterness toward white people; when you have to concoct an answer for a five-year-old son asking in agonizing pathos: "Daddy, why do white people treat colored people so mean?"; when you take a cross country drive and find it necessary to sleep night after night in the uncomfortable corners of your automobile because no motel will accept you; when you are humiliated day in and day out by nagging signs reading "white" men and "colored"; when your first name becomes "nigger" and your middle name becomes "boy" (however old you are) and your last name becomes "John," and when your wife and mother are never given the respected title "Mrs."; when you are harried by day and haunted by night by the fact that you are a Negro, living constantly at tip-toe stance never quite knowing what to expect next, and plagued with inner fears and outer resentments; when you are forever fighting a degenerating sense of "nobodiness";—then you will understand why we find it difficult to wait. There comes a time when the cup of endurance runs over, and men are no longer willing to be plunged into an abyss of injustice where they experience the bleakness of corroding despair. I hope, sirs, you can understand our legitimate and unavoidable impatience.

You express a great deal of anxiety over our willingness to break laws. This is certainly a legitimate concern. Since we so diligently urge people to obey the Supreme Court's decision of 1954 outlawing segregation in the public schools, it is rather strange and paradoxical to find us consciously breaking laws. One may well ask, "How can you advocate breaking some laws and obeying others?" The answer is found in the fact that there are two types of laws; There are *just* laws and there are *unjust* laws. I would be the first to advocate obeying just laws. One has not only a legal but moral responsibility to obey just laws. Conversely, one has a moral responsibility to disobey unjust laws. I would agree with Saint Augustine that "An unjust law is no law at all."

Now what is the difference between the two? How does one determine when a law is just or unjust? A just law is a man-made code that squares with the moral law or the law of God. An unjust law is a code that is out of harmony with the moral law. To put it in the terms of Saint Thomas Aquinas, an unjust law is a human law that is not rooted in eternal and natural law. Any law that uplifts human personality is just. Any law that degrades human personality is unjust. All segregation statutes are unjust because segregation distorts the soul and damages the personality. It gives the segregator a false sense of superiority and the segregated a false sense of inferiority. To use the words of Martin Buber, the great Jewish philosopher, segregation substitutes an "I-it" relationship for the "I-thou" relationship, and ends up relegating persons to the status of things. So segregation is not only politically, economically, and sociologically unsound, but it is morally wrong and sinful. Paul Tillich has said that sin is separation. Isn't segregation an existential expression of man's tragic separation, an expression of his awful estrangement, his terrible sinfulness? So I can urge men to obey the 1954 decision of the Supreme Court because it is morally right, and I can urge them to disobey segregation ordinances because they are morally wrong.

Let us turn to a more concrete example of just and unjust laws. An unjust law is a code that a majority inflicts on a minority that is not binding on itself. This is *difference* made legal. On the other hand a just law is a code that a majority compels a minority to follow that it is willing to follow itself. This is *sameness* made legal.

Let me give another explanation. An unjust law is a code inflicted upon a minority which that minority had no part in enacting or creating because they did not have the unhampered right to vote. Who can say the legislature of Alabama which set up the segregation laws was democratically elected? Throughout the state of Alabama all types of conniving methods are used to prevent Negroes from becoming registered voters and there are some counties without a single Negro registered to vote despite the fact that the Negro constitutes a majority of the population. Can any law set up in such a state be considered democratically structured?

These are just a few examples of unjust and just laws. There are some instances when a law is just on its face but unjust in its application. For instance, I was arrested Friday on a charge of parading without a permit. Now there is nothing wrong with an ordinance which requires a permit for a parade, but when the ordinance is used to preserve segregation and to deny citizens the First Amendment privilege of peaceful assembly and peaceful protest, then it becomes unjust.

I hope you can see the distinction I am trying to point out. In no sense do I advocate evading or defying the law as the rabid segregationist would do. This would lead to anarchy. One who breaks an unjust law must do it *openly, lovingly* (not hatefully as the white mothers did in New Orleans when they were seen on television screaming "nigger, nigger, nigger") and with a willingness to accept the penalty. I submit that an individual who breaks a law that conscience tells him is unjust, and willingly accepts the penalty by staying in jail to arouse the conscience of the community over its injustice, is in reality expressing the very highest respect for law.

Of course there is nothing new about this kind of civil disobedience. It was seen sublimely in the refusal of Shadrach, Meshach, and Abednego to obey the laws of Nebuchadnezzar because a higher moral law was involved. It was practiced superbly by the early Christians who were willing to face

hungry lions and the excruciating pain of chopping blocks, be-
fore submitting to certain unjust laws of the Roman Empire.
To a degree academic freedom is a reality today because
Socrates practiced civil disobedience.

We can never forget that everything Hitler did in Germany
was "legal" and everything the Hungarian freedom fighters did
in Hungary was "illegal." It was "illegal" to aid and comfort a
Jew in Hitler's Germany. But I am sure that, if I had lived in
Germany during that time, I would have aided and comforted
my Jewish brothers even though it was illegal. If I lived in a
communist country today where certain principles dear to the
Christian faith are suppressed, I believe I would openly advocate disobeying these anti-religious laws.

I must make two honest confessions to you, my Christian
and Jewish brothers. First I must confess that over the last few
years I have been gravely disappointed with the white moderate. I have almost reached the regrettable conclusion that the
Negroes' great stumbling block in the stride toward freedom is
not the White Citizens' "Counciler" or the Ku Klux Klanner,
but the white moderate who is more devoted to "order" than to
justice; who prefers a negative peace which is the absence
of tension to a positive peace which is the presence of justice;
who constantly says "I agree with you in the goal you seek, but
I can't agree with your methods of direct action"; who paternal-
istically feels that he can set the time-table for another man's
freedom; who lives by the myth of time and who constantly
advises the Negro to wait until a "more convenient season."
Shallow understanding from people of good will is more frustrating than absolute misunderstanding from people of ill will.
Lukewarm acceptance is much more bewildering than outright
rejection.

I had hoped that the white moderate would understand that
law and order exist for the purpose of establishing justice,
and that when they fail to do this they become the dangerously
structured dams that block the flow of social progress. I had

hoped that the white moderate would understand that the present tension in the South is merely a necessary phase of the transition from an obnoxious negative peace, where the Negro passively accepted his unjust plight, to a substance-filled positive peace, where all men will respect the dignity and worth of human personality. Actually, we who engage in nonviolent direct action are not the creators of tension. We merely bring to the surface the hidden tension that is already alive. We bring it out in the open where it can be seen and dealt with. Like a boil that can never be cured as long as it is covered up but must be opened with all its pusflowing ugliness to the natural medicines of air and light, injustice must likewise be exposed, with all of the tension its exposing creates, to the light of human conscience and the air of national opinion before it can be cured.

In your statement you asserted that our actions, even though peaceful, must be condemned because they precipitate violence. But can this assertion be logically made? Isn't this like condemning the robbed man because his possession of money precipitated the evil act of robbery? Isn't this like condemning Socrates because his unswerving commitment to truth and his philosophical delvings precipitated the misguided popular mind to make him drink the hemlock? Isn't this like condemning Jesus because His unique God consciousness and neverceasing devotion to His will precipitated the evil act of crucifixion? We must come to see, as federal courts have consistently affirmed, that it is immoral to urge an individual to withdraw his efforts to gain his basic constitutional rights because the quest precipitates violence. Society must protect the robbed and punish the robber.

I had also hoped that the white moderate would reject the myth of time. I received a letter this morning from a white brother in Texas which said: "All Christians know that the colored people will receive equal rights eventually, but is it possible that you are in too great of a religious hurry? It has taken Christianity almost 2000 years to accomplish what it has. The teachings of Christ take time to come to earth." All that is said here grows out of a tragic misconception of time. It is the strangely irrational notion that there is something in the very flow of time that will inevitably cure all ills. Actually time is neutral. It can be used either destructively or constructively. I am coming to feel that the people of ill will have used time much more effectively than the people of good will. We will have to repent in this generation not merely for the vitriolic words and actions of the bad people, but for the appalling silence of the good people. We must come to see that human progress never rolls in on wheels of inevitability. It comes through the tireless efforts and persistent work of men willing to be co-workers with God, and without this hard work time itself becomes an ally of the forces of social stagnation.

We must use time creatively, and forever realize that the time is always ripe to do right. Now is the time to make real the promise of democracy, and transform our pending national elegy into a creative psalm of brotherhood. Now is the time to lift our national policy from the quicksand of racial injustice to the solid rock of human dignity.

You spoke of our activity in Birmingham as extreme. At first I was rather disappointed that fellow clergymen would see my nonviolent efforts as those of the extremist. I started thinking about the fact that I stand in the middle of two opposing forces in the Negro community. One is a force of complacency made up of Negroes who, as a result of long years of oppression, have been so completely drained of self-respect and a sense of "somebodiness" that they have adjusted to segregation, and of a few Negroes in the middle class who, because of a degree of academic and economic security, and because at points they profit by segregation, have unconsciously become insensitive to the problems of the masses. The other force is one of bitterness and hatred and comes perilously close to advocating violence. It is expressed in the various black nationalist groups that are springing up over the nation, the largest and best known being Elijah Muhammad's Muslim movement. This movement is nourished by the contemporary frustration over the continued existence of racial discrimination. It is made up of people who have lost faith in America, who have absolutely repudiated Christianity, and who have concluded that the white man is an incurable "devil." I have tried to stand between these two forces saying that we need not follow the "do-nothingism" of the complacent or the hatred and despair of the black nationalist. There is the more excellent way of love and nonviolent protest. I'm grateful to God that, through the Negro church, the dimension of nonviolence entered our struggle. If this philosophy had not emerged I am convinced that by now many streets of the South would be flowing with floods of blood. And I am further convinced that if our white brothers dismiss us as "rabble rousers" and "outside agitators"—those of us who are working through the channels of nonviolent direct action —and refuse to support our nonviolent efforts, millions of Negroes, out of frustration and despair, will seek solace and security in black nationalist ideologies, a development that will lead inevitably to a frightening racial nightmare.

Oppressed people cannot remain oppressed forever. The urge for freedom will eventually come. This is what has happened to the American Negro. Something within has reminded him of his birthright of freedom; something without has reminded him that he can gain it. Consciously and unconsciously, he has been swept in by what the Germans call the *Zeitgeist,* and with his black brothers of Africa, and his brown and yellow brothers of Asia, South America, and the Caribbean, he is moving with a sense of cosmic urgency toward the promised land of racial justice. Recognizing this vital urge that has engulfed the Negro community, one should readily understand public demonstrations. The Negro has many pent-up resentments and latent frustrations. He has to get them out. So let him march sometime; let him have his prayer pilgrimages to the city hall; understand why he must have sit-ins and freedom rides. If his repressed emotions do not come out in these non-violent ways, they will come out in ominous expressions of violence. This is not a threat; it is a fact of history. So I have not said to my people, "Get rid of your discontent." But I have tried to say that this normal and healthy discontent can be channeled through the creative outlet of nonviolent direct action. Now this approach is being dismissed as extremist. I must admit that I was initially disappointed in being so categorized.

But as I continued to think about the matter I gradually gained a bit of satisfaction from being considered an extremist. Was not Jesus an extremist in love? "Love your enemies, bless them that curse you, pray for them that despitefully use you." Was not Amos an extremist for justice—"Let justice roll down like waters and righteousness like a mighty stream." Was not Paul an extremist for the gospel of Jesus Christ—"I bear in my body the marks of the Lord Jesus." Was not Martin Luther an extremist—"Here I stand; I can do none other so help me God." Was not John Bunyan an extremist—"I will stay in jail to the end of my days before I make a butchery of my conscience." Was not Abraham Lincoln an extremist—"This nation cannot survive half slave and half free." Was not Thomas Jefferson an extremist—"We hold these truths to be self evident that all men are created equal." So the question is not whether we will be extremist but what kind of extremist will we be. Will we be extremists for hate or will we be extremists for love? Will we be extremists for the preservation of injustice —or will we be extremists for the cause of justice? In that dramatic scene on Calvary's hill three men were crucified. We must never forget that all three were crucified for the same crime—the crime of extremism. Two were extremists for immorality, and thus fell below their environment. The other, Jesus Christ, was an extremist for love, truth, and goodness, and thereby rose above His environment. So, after all, maybe the South, the nation, and the world are in dire need of creative extremists.

I had hoped that the white moderate would see this. Maybe I was too optimistic. Maybe I expected too much. I guess I should have realized that few members of a race that has oppressed another race can understand or appreciate the deep groans and passionate yearnings of those that have been oppressed, and still fewer have the vision to see that injustice must be rooted out by strong, persistent, and determined action. I am thankful, however, that some of our white brothers have grasped the meaning of this social revolution and committed themselves to it. They are still all too small in quantity, but they are big in quality. Some like Ralph McGill, Lillian Smith, Harry Golden, and James Dabbs have written about our struggle in eloquent, prophetic, and understanding terms. Others have marched with us down nameless streets of the South. They have languished in filthy, roach-infested jails, suffering the abuse and brutality of angry policemen who see them as "dirty nigger lovers." They, unlike so many of their moderate brothers and sisters, have recognized the urgency of the moment and sensed the need for powerful "action" antidotes to combat the disease of segregation.

Let me rush on to mention my other disappointment. I have been so greatly disappointed with the white Church and its leadership. Of course there are some notable exceptions. I am not unmindful of the fact that each of you has taken some significant stands on this issue. I commend you, Rev. Stallings, for your Christian stand on this past Sunday, in welcoming Negroes to your worship service on a non-segregated basis. I commend the Catholic leaders of this state for integrating Springhill College several years ago.

But despite these notable exceptions I must honestly reiterate that I have been disappointed with the Church. I do not say that as one of those negative critics who can always find something wrong with the Church. I say it as a minister of the gospel, who loves the Church; who was nurtured in its bosom; who has been sustained by its spiritual blessings and who will remain true to it as long as the cord of life shall lengthen.

I had the strange feeling when I was suddenly catapulted into the leadership of the bus protest in Montgomery several years ago that we would have the support of the white Church. I felt that the white ministers, priests, and rabbis of the South would be some of our strongest allies. Instead, some have been outright opponents, refusing to understand the freedom movement and misrepresenting its leaders; all too many others have been more cautious than courageous and have remained silent behind the anesthetizing security of stained glass windows.

In spite of my shattered dreams of the past, I came to Birmingham with the hope that the white religious leadership of this community would see the justice of our cause and, with deep moral concern, serve as the channel through which our just grievances could get to the power structure. I had hoped that each of you would understand. But again I have been disappointed.

I have heard numerous religious leaders of the South call upon their worshippers to comply with a desegregation decision because it is the law, but I have longed to hear white ministers say follow this decree because integration is morally right and the Negro is your brother. In the midst of blatant injustices inflicted upon the Negro, I have watched white churches stand on the sideline and merely mouth pious irrelevancies and sanctimonious trivialities. In the midst of a mighty struggle to rid our nation of racial and economic injustice, I have heard so many ministers say, "Those are social issues with which the Gospel has no real concern," and I have watched so many churches commit themselves to a completely other-worldly religion which made a strange distinction between body and soul, the sacred and the secular.

So here we are moving toward the exit of the twentieth century with a religious community largely adjusted to the status quo, standing as a tail light behind other community agencies rather than a headlight leading men to higher levels of justice.

I have travelled the length and breadth of Alabama, Mississippi, and all the other Southern states. On sweltering summer days and crisp autumn mornings I have looked at her beautiful churches with their spires pointing heavenward. I have beheld the impressive outlay of her massive religious education buildings. Over and over again I have found myself asking: "Who worships here? Who is their God? Where were their voices when the lips of Governor Barnett dripped with words of interposition and nullification? Where were they when Governor Wallace gave the clarion call for defiance and hatred? Where were their voices of support when tired, bruised, and weary Negro men and women decided to rise from the dark dungeons of complacency to the bright hills of creative protest?"

Yes, these questions are still in my mind. In deep disappointment, I have wept over the laxity of the Church. But be assured that my tears have been tears of love. There can be no deep disappointment where there is not deep love. Yes, I love the Church; I love her sacred walls. How could I do otherwise? I am in the rather unique position of being the son, the grandson, and the great grandson of preachers. Yes, I see the Church as the body of Christ. But, oh! How we have blemished and scarred that body through social neglect and fear of being nonconformist.

There was a time when the Church was very powerful. It was during that period when the early Christians rejoiced when they were deemed worthy to suffer for what they believed. In those days the Church was not merely a thermometer that recorded the ideas and principles of popular opinion; it was a thermostat that transformed the mores of society. Wherever the early Christians entered a town the power structure got disturbed and immediately sought to convict them for being "disturbers of the peace" and "outside agitators." But they went on with the conviction that they were a "colony of heaven" and had to obey God rather than man. They were small in number but big in commitment. They were too God-intoxicated to be "astronomically intimidated." They brought an end to such ancient evils as infanticide and gladiatorial contest.

Things are different now. The contemporary Church is so often a weak, ineffectual voice with an uncertain sound. It is so often the arch-supporter of the status quo. Far from being disturbed by the presence of the Church, the power structure of the average community is consoled by the Church's silent and often vocal sanction of things as they are.

But the judgment of God is upon the Church as never before. If the Church of today does not recapture the sacrificial spirit of the early Church, it will lose its authentic ring, forfeit the loyalty of millions, and be dismissed as an irrelevant social club with no meaning for the twentieth century. I am meeting young people every day whose disappointment with the Church has risen to outright disgust.

Maybe again I have been too optimistic. Is organized religion too inextricably bound to the status quo to save our nation and the world? Maybe I must turn my faith to the inner spiritual Church, the church within the Church, as the true *ecclesia* and the hope of the world. But again I am thankful to God that some noble souls from the ranks of organized religion have broken loose from the paralyzing chains of conformity and joined us as active partners in the struggle for freedom. They have left their secure congregations and walked the streets of Albany, Georgia, with us. They have gone through the highways of the South on torturous rides for freedom. Yes, they have gone to jail with us. Some have been kicked out of their churches and lost the support of their bishops and fellow ministers. But they have gone with the faith that right defeated is stronger than evil triumphant. These men have been the leaven in the lump of the race. Their witness has been the spiritual salt that has preserved the true meaning of the Gospel in these troubled times. They have carved a tunnel of hope through the dark mountain of disappointment.

I hope the Church as a whole will meet the challenge of this decisive hour. But even if the Church does not come to the aid of justice, I have no despair about the future. I have no fear about the outcome of our struggle in Birmingham, even if our motives are presently misunderstood. We will reach the goal of freedom in Birmingham and all over the nation, because the goal of America is freedom. Abused and scorned though we may be, our destiny is tied up with the destiny of America. Before the pilgrims landed at Plymouth, we were here. Before the pen of Jefferson etched across the pages of history the majestic words of the Declaration of Independence, we were here. For more than two centuries our foreparents labored in this country without wages; they made cotton "king"; and they built the homes of their masters in the midst of brutal injustice and shameful humiliation—and yet out of a bottomless vitality they continued to thrive and develop. If the inexpressible cruelties of slavery could not stop us, the opposition we now face will surely fail. We will win our freedom because the sacred heritage of our nation and the eternal will of God are embodied in our echoing demands.

I must close now. But before closing I am impelled to mention one other point in your statement that troubled me profoundly. You warmly commended the Birmingham police force for keeping "order" and "preventing violence." I don't believe you would have so warmly commended the police force if you had seen its angry violent dogs literally biting six unarmed, nonviolent Negroes. I don't believe you would so quickly commend the policemen if you would observe their ugly and inhuman treatment of Negroes here in the city jail; if you would watch them push and curse old Negro women and young Negro girls; if you would see them slap and kick old Negro men and young Negro boys; if you will observe them, as they did on two occasions, refuse to give us food because we wanted to sing our grace together. I'm sorry that I can't join you in your praise for the police department. It is true that they have been rather disciplined in their public handling of the demonstrators. In this sense they have been rather publicly "nonviolent." But for what purpose? To preserve the evil system of segregation. Over the last few years I have consistently preached that nonviolence demands that the means we use must be as pure as the ends we seek. So I have tried to make it clear that it is wrong to use immoral means to attain moral ends. But now I must affirm that it is just as wrong, or even moreso, to use moral means to preserve immoral ends. Maybe Mr. Connor and his policemen have been rather publicly nonviolent, as Chief Pritchett was in Albany, Georgia, but they have used the moral means of nonviolence to maintain the immoral end of flagrant racial injustice. T. S. Eliot has said that there is no greater treason than to do the right deed for the wrong reason.

I wish you had commended the Negro sit-inners and demonstrators of Birmingham for their sublime courage, their willingness to suffer, and their amazing discipline in the midst of the most inhuman provocation. One day the South will recognize its real heroes. They will be the James Merediths, courageously and with a majestic sense of purpose, facing jeering and hostile mobs and the agonizing loneliness that characterizes the life of the pioneer. They will be old, oppressed, battered Negro women, symbolized in a seventy-two year old woman of Montgomery, Alabama, who rose up with a sense of dignity and with her people decided not to ride the segregated buses, and responded to one who inquired about her tiredness with ungrammatical profundity: "My feets is tired, but my soul is rested." They will be young high school and college students, young ministers of the gospel and a host of the elders, courageously and nonviolently sitting in at lunch counters and willingly going to jail for conscience sake. One day the South will know that when these disinherited children of God sat down at lunch counters they were in reality standing up for the best in the American dream and the most sacred values in our Judeo-Christian heritage, and thus carrying our whole nation back to great wells of democracy which were dug deep by the founding fathers in the formulation of the Constitution and the Declaration of Independence.

Never before have I written a letter this long (or should I say a book?). I'm afraid that it is much too long to take your precious time. I can assure you that it would have been much shorter if I had been writing from a comfortable desk, but what else is there to do when you are alone for days in the dull monotony of a narrow jail cell other than write long letters, think strange thoughts, and pray long prayers?

If I have said anything in this letter that is an overstatement of the truth and is indicative of an unreasonable impatience, I beg you to forgive me. If I have said anything in this letter that is an understatement of the truth and is indicative of my having a patience that makes me patient with anything less than brotherhood, I beg God to forgive me.

I hope this letter finds you strong in the faith. I also hope that circumstances will soon make it possible for me to meet each of you, not as an integrationist or a civil rights leader, but as a fellow clergyman and a Christian brother. Let us all hope that the dark clouds of racial prejudice will soon pass away and the deep fog of misunderstanding will be lifted from our fear-drenched communities and in some not too distant tomorrow the radiant stars of love and brotherhood will shine over our great nation with all of their scintillating beauty.

Yours for the cause of
Peace and Brotherhood
MARTIN LUTHER KING, JR.

38. John Lewis,
Speech at March on Washington, 1963

The March on Washington of August 28, 1963 was a peaceful demonstration of over 200,000 people on behalf of federal legislation for "jobs and freedom." It reflected the cumulating impatience of Negro Americans a decade after the Supreme Court declared segregated schools unconstitutional. A speech by John Lewis, SNCC national chairman, (delivered in an abridged version, but presented here as originally drafted) called for a nonviolent invasion of the South.

We march today for jobs and freedom, but we have nothing to be proud of. For hundreds and thousands of our brothers are not here. They have no money for their transportation, for they are receiving starvation wages . . . or no wages, at all.

In good conscience, we cannot support, wholeheartedly, the administration's civil rights bill, for it is too little, and too late. There's not one thing in the bill that will protect our people from police brutality.

This bill will not protect young children and old women from police dogs and fire hoses, for engaging in peaceful demonstrations. This bill will not protect the citizens in Danville, Virginia, who must live in constant fear in a police state. This bill will not protect the hundreds of people who have been arrested on trumped-up charges. What about the three young men in Americus, Georgia, who face the death penalty for engaging in peaceful protest?

John Lewis, "Text of Speech to be delivered at Lincoln Memorial: Original," August 28, 1963 (Atlanta: Student Nonviolent Coordinating Committee), mimeographed.

The voting section of this bill will not help thousands of black citizens who want to vote. It will not help the citizens of Mississippi, of Alabama, and Georgia, who are qualified to vote, but lack a 6th Grade education. "One man, one vote," is the African cry. It is ours, too. (It must be ours.)

People have been forced to leave their homes because they dared to exercise their right to register to vote. What is in the bill that will protect the homeless and starving people of this nation? What is there in this bill to insure the equality of a maid who earns $5 a week in the home of a family whose income is $100,000 a year?

For the first time in 100 years this nation is being awakened to the fact that segregation is evil and that it must be destroyed in all forms. Your presence today proves that you have been aroused to the point of action.

We are now involved in a serious revolution. This nation is still a place of cheap political leaders who build their careers on immoral compromises and ally themselves with open forms of political, economic and social exploitation. What political leader here can stand up and say "My party is the party of principles"? The party of Kennedy is also the party of Eastland. The party of Javits is also the party of Goldwater. Where is *our* party?

In some parts of the South we work in the fields from sun-up to sun-down for $12 a week. In Albany, Georgia, nine of our leaders have been indicated not by Dixiecrats but by the Federal Government for peaceful protest. But what did the Federal Government do when Albany's Deputy Sheriff beat Attorney C. B. King and left him half-dead? What did the Federal Government do when local police officials kicked and assaulted the pregnant wife of Slater King, and she lost her baby?

It seems to me that the Albany indictment is part of a conspiracy on the part of the Federal Government and local politicians in the interest of expediency.

I want to know, which side is the Federal Government on? The revolution is at hand, and we must free ourselves of the chains of political and economic slavery. The non-violent revolution is saying, "We will not wait for the courts to act, for we have been waiting for hundreds of years. We will not wait for the President, the Justice Department, nor Congress, but we will take matters into our own hands and create a source of power, outside of any national structure that could and would assure us a victory." To those who have said, "Be Patient and Wait", we must say that, "Patience is a dirty and nasty word." We cannot be patient, we do not want to be free gradually, we want our freedom, and we want it now. We cannot depend on any political party, for both the Democrats and the Republicans have betrayed the basic principles of the Declaration of Independence.

We all recognize the fact that if any radical social, political and economic changes are to take place in our society, the people, the masses, must bring them about. In the struggle we must seek more than more civil rights; we must work for the community of love, peace and true brotherhood. Our minds, souls, and hearts cannot rest until freedom and justice exist for *all the people.*

The revolution is a serious one. Mr. Kennedy is trying to take the revolution out of the street and put it into the courts. Listen, Mr. Kennedy, Listen Mr. Congressman, listen fellow citizens, the black masses are on the march for jobs and freedom, and we must say to the politicians that there won't be a "cooling-off" period.

All of us must get in the revolution. Get in and stay in the streets of every city, every village and every hamlet of this nation, until true Freedom comes, until the revolution is complete. In the Delta of Mississippi, in southwest Georgia, in Alabama, Harlem, Chicago, Detroit, Philadelphia and all over this nation. The black masses are on the march!

We won't stop now. All of the forces of Eastland, Barnett,

Wallace and Thurmond won't stop this revolution. The time
will come when we will not confine our marching to Washington. We will march through the South through the Heart of
Dixie, the way Sherman did. We shall pursue our own
"scorched earth" policy and burn Jim Crow to the ground—
non-violently. We shall fragment the South into a thousand
pieces and put them back together in the image of democracy.
We will make the action of the past few months look petty.
And I say to you, WAKE UP AMERICA!!!

39. Bayard Rustin,
Nonviolence on Trial

Bayard Rustin, organizer of the March on Washington but equally
active in direct action for peace, is a symbol both of the profound
interdependence of the postwar peace and civil rights movements,
and of the increasingly revolutionary temper of American nonviolence in the 1960's. In the spring and summer of 1964, Rustin
explored the meaning of nonviolence in a speech to the national
council of the Fellowship of Reconciliation (see Document 39A)
and in an eye-witness' reflection on rioting in Harlem (see Document 39B). Rustin argued that nonviolence would have to become
revolutionary if it wished to remain the dominant strategy of the
civil rights' movement; he added, however, that while in that process
the nature of nonviolence might change, the distinction between
nonviolence and violence remained clear and essential.

Bayard Rustin, "Nonviolence on Trial," *Fellowship* (July 1964),
5–8. Reprinted with the permission of the publisher, The Fellowship of
Reconciliation.

A. *Speech to the Fellowship of Reconciliation, 1964*

. . . For the American Negro, the 1954 Supreme Court Decision for which the NAACP spent millions of dollars and 50 years of its work in achieving, was a kind of declaration of independence for Negroes. They felt that this principalled decision, which was going to affect every act the rest of their life, meant that something truly significant was happening and that it would happen quickly. But the fact of the matter is that, ten years after the Supreme Court Decision (and I do not choose at this moment to go into the reasons for this—they are not all due to segregation and discrimination) the objective reality is that there are now more Negroes in segregated schools than in 1954, there are more Negroes without work than in 1954, and there is more segregated housing in the United States than in 1954. In fact, any one who is familiar with the pattern of housing in the South, will know that we never had, prior to 1964, the rigid kind of ghettoization that we now have in the North. More recently the pattern of putting Negroes into ghettos in the southern cities has been developing.

Now the move toward violence is not a move from one spiritual platform to another. It is the move which always occurs in a situation where the tactics that have been advocated and used are inadequate for dealing with the objective needs. In this particular revolutionary situation, after ten years of vigorous activity, when in no southern city is there a break through, despite the thousands and thousands who have gone to jail, despite bombings of churches and people, despite the millions of dollars tied up in bail and the millions paid in fines —when all of this activity has gone into a situation—when no breakthrough has occurred in the South and in the North Negroes are being increasingly pushed to the wall—always the rank and file raise two fundamental questions: One, what about the leadership over these ten years, with the implication that there must be something wrong with it if conditions can get worse and worse as we work harder and harder. And the second question is, what about the basic method, nonviolence. Obviously if things get worse and worse, there must be something wrong with that method. So Malcolm Xism, the violence which is appearing in most of these civil rights organizations and to some extent in its leadership, springs from an evaluation of the past ten years and the frustration which is inevitably coming to the fore in such cases.

THE NEGRO CAST AS A REVOLUTIONARY

The second factor in the crisis: the American Negro, who has thought, up to this point, that the problem was fighting segregation and discrimination, now discovers that it is not only segregation and discrimination he must fight, but that he must fight basic assumptions and institutions of this entire society. Now this is most frustrating for a minority, because any minority tends to want to become a part of the society as it exists. (And let no one be taken in by James Baldwin's essays about how the great masses of Negroes are alienated. That is not true. Baldwin and a few others are alienated.)

But the average Negro wants to become a part of these decaying institutions as they now exist. He wants his part of the gate, consciously. Subconsciously, however, any movement on the part of Negroes must be revolutionary, although the Negro may not know it, precisely because too many basic assumptions and institutions of the society have been built on his second-class position.

And therefore if the structure is built on him and he stands up and shakes himself, he is automatically shaking those institutions which have been constructed upon him. For example: if and when Negroes get the right to vote, Negroes want the right to vote in Mississippi on fundamentally one thing. They are just like all other Americans who do not really vote on foreign policy, or war, but most Negroes want the right to vote about the thing in Mississippi that disturbs them most, which is—fundamentally—who will be sheriff.

And it is for that reason that Negroes were often advised to bolt the Democratic party in the South to vote Republican. They are no more longminded than white people. They know there's not going to be a Negro sheriff. And therefore when they vote, they're going to vote for the less dangerous sheriff, who has to be a Democrat.

So far, so good. However, if and when the Negro ever does get the right to vote, he will disrupt automatically certain assumptions held about the political structures of this country. No longer can there be a one-party system in the South, because acting in his own fundamental interest, the Negro will send up forces which will splinter and re-align.

No longer can Eastland and his ilk be in the United States Senate and thereby frustrate for millions of white people every imaginable bit of social legislation, including the right of white people over sixty-five to get any medical assistance, the need for federal aid to education, etc.

MOOD OF REVOLT CAUGHT ON SLOWLY

So that the Negro Movement, while being revolutionary in character, is not, in idea, revolutionary. Now this is important because, so far, the Negro revolt, which we now all think of as such a magnificent thing, was in many respects a very fragile and insignificant thing if one looks at it, not in its spiritual aspect, but in terms of its results. For example, if I were to ask you to name the four or five outstanding examples of Negro revolt, you would have to name the revolt over public accommodations. When Martin Luther King attracted the attention of the American people to the rights of Negroes to sit down in their home-town bus, he then influenced the sit-in movement, which was about the right to sit down and eat with dignity in your own home town. Then came the freedom rides which had to do with the right to sit down and eat and travel with dignity outside your home town.

With the exception of very, very minor school integration, which was token and which only emotionally attracted the attention of the Negro people because of the violence—Authorine Lucy here, James Meredith here, five children there —in reality the movement did not affect the people's thought about school; it had to do with parks, and swimming pools, and libraries and with public accommodations.

Now I want to be understood here. In reality CORE, five times as strong as it was when it was in the FOR, could have achieved most of that if there had been five hundred Negroes willing to go to jail over and over again and not one white person was needed. Is it good to have them? Spiritually it is a profound thing to have them, but they were not needed. I am talking about social reality.

For any fifty Negroes who are prepared to sit down on their backsides over and over again and go to jail can in fact make a breakthrough in public accommodations.

But when Martin King and Fred Shuttlesworth opened up the Birmingham struggle, they opened up a Pandora's box, because they came up with two ideas which completely revolutionized the nature of the civil rights struggle. The first is what I would call the package deal. We are no longer going to have everybody brutalized in Birmingham about transporta tion. Or schools. We want the schools integrated; we want so many jobs; we want so many decent houses; we want the ghettos broken up; we want everything; we want it now and we want it everywhere.

Now of course a good bit of this was sloganism and they knew it. After all, they're like labor leaders. If you want ten cents an hour more, you ask for fifty, and then you settle for something like seven.

But they did something else which I think they did not know they were doing; and that is that they moved the center of gravity from that which was achievable within the economic and political strength of the Negro people from public accommodations to three profound things which cannot be had for either white people or Negro people.

First, Capitalism as usual—without some profound social and economic change. When a Negro came up against decent housing, when he came up asking for a job in the face of automation, when he came up asking that the schools be really integrated, he was asking not first of all, for integrated schools, but he was asking for quality schools which cannot be had without billions and billions of dollars being poured into them.

He was asking for the revolutionizing of an entire school system of this country, for there cannot be any integration without it. For no white people are ever going to bus their white children into the ghettos of Harlem or Bedford-Styvesant, or Southside Chicago. Q.e.d., the only way you can ever get white and Negro students into the same schools is to make schools which are so vastly superior to schools as we now know them, that the question of bussing will not be a question. Nobody fights about going to Harlem—the middle of Harlem—to the High School of Music and Art. They fight, lie, cheat and study hard to get in there—precisely because it is a superior school. In fact, the white people running to the suburbs and into private schools have all but destroyed the American school system in the ghetto and in our large cities.

If you talk about jobs, Mr. Young, my dear friend, again comes up with some ridiculous statements about preferential treatment for Negroes. Now what in the name of God, with fifty million poor in this country, eight million statistically unemployed, does preferential treatment for Negroes mean?— except with Pitney-Bowes and I.B.M. who have such difficulty getting any skilled workers that they're willing to take Negroes.

What does it mean? It means that ultimately you are saying: white man move over and give me a job because for three hundred years I have been mistreated. He will say, move where? With automation taking jobs away from white workers as they are and with Negroes even faster, he has nowhere to move.

NO JOBS, BLACK OR WHITE

And therefore the civil rights movement cannot demand black jobs and this is a profound frustration for the movement. The movement has to say, white brother, working or not working, and black brother, working or not working, come together, create a political movement (by which I do not mean a political party) for putting all men back to work under the slogan that if the private sector of the economy cannot put men back to work, then you the government must do it. You demand that all men be put back to work, that all men be trained by government, and you cannot talk about training in a vacuum. For if you pick up fifty Negroes and fifty whites in the streets of New York and say you are going to train them now to be medical technicians because they are not prepared to be anything else, a year from now medical technicians will be automated. Then you'll have to pick them all up again and say now we'll train them for something else. This is what makes President Johnson's program an absolute fiasco, except that some of us with some imagination can work under his slogan of the revolution about the poor, to demand what is right. But nobody, but nobody can tell you what to train people for unless it is done within a planned economy, in which you know where automation is to take place, at what rate, and what industries it is going to touch.

Now the second reason that the Negro is profoundly frustrated is that because the fundamental problem which affects his daily life, he cannot solve without massive allies from the churches, the unions and other segments of society. But he is trebly frustrated because, if you say this to him, he says to you, none of these so-called allies are prepared to move. Therein lies the reason why you will get more and more desperate, more and more gimmicky, more and more extremist, more and more irresponsible activity out of the Negro community. Now that irresponsibility and activity is the result of the failure of any other segment of society to come to stand by the side of the Negro in motion from an effort to deal with the problem. The white poor are the most demoralized in the country; you can't organize them; it's not their fault. In 1929 the reason you got unemployment leagues in the early thirties was that there were men who only yesterday were working; there was a crash and tomorrow they were without jobs. This thing has been going on here so insidiously and slowly that these people have forgotten they ever worked or what work means to them spiritually, as long as they have underneath them these pillows of various forms of public assistance which are inadequate to make men of them but are adequate enough to prevent any sense of movement and rebellion.

SOCIETY BUILT ON NEGROES' BACK

My third point: It is, however, only because the Negro continues to move, no matter how erratically, that anybody else can move. Now I would like to say to most of you since you're church people, that the most significant work being done on the civil rights bill now—everyone recognizes this, even the NAACP—is being done by Protestants, Catholics and Jews. If we get that civil rights bill, it will fundamentally be the churches of this country and the work they are doing in Congress and the field that makes that bill possible. . . .

. . . Another illustration. I'm trying to explain why Negroes are going to be climbing cranes, lying down in front of things, tying up bridges and all sorts of things that seem absolutely senseless. It is out of the frustration that they know that if they do not move, nothing else can. It was the Negro sit-in movement which destroyed McCarthyism on our campuses. Nothing else. McCarthyism would still be there if it weren't for the sit-in movement. The sit-in movement's greatest contribution was not that Negroes got the right to eat in some restaurants, but that they restored political debate to the campuses of this country.

And there are many illustrations in which the trade union movement only moved under the pressure of Phillip Randolph and the Negro American Labor Council. Therefore we are advising Negroes vigorously to continue action on the one hand wherever they can, while on the other hand we are getting them to see the great need for allies. But it is their movement that will create these allies if they can be created and nothing less.

LOVE IN RETURN FOR HATE NOT A PRESENT OPTION

In the case for nonviolence, now I happen to believe (and I have so written Martin King) that the Negro community is no longer taking Martin Luther King's brand of nonviolence. That is not to say that anything you or I believe is not true. Love conquers all, if it can be conquered. But no Negro leader if he wants to be listened to is going to tell any Negroes that they should love white people. Furthermore I won't do it because I won't encourage that kind of psychological dishonesty. They don't love them, they have no need to love them, no basis on which they can love them. Who can love people who do these things to people?

Furthermore, the commandment, treat one as you would be treated—I am not a theologian—but I think it needs reexamination, because I think that's exactly what people do. I think all we can say to Negroes now is, to love yourself; have dignity, yourself; be honest with yourself; love justice, yourself; and because you love yourself and your children, first of all, little

black children who are being bombed, our churches which
have been bombed, you thereby use tactics which are com-
mensurate with getting dignity, and that means strategic
nonviolence.

Now to the degree that moral elements are involved, they
have to emerge not out of what you will to be, because you
are not an individual in these matters, but you are a fraction
between what you will to be and what society impresses upon
you. And therefore what is needed at this period is a thorough
dedication to loving yourself. Now if, in the process, the non-
injury means that you are not hurting white people, all well
and good, but that concept following the emergence of Malcolm X and the other elements in the Negro community, can
never be put in the old terms which we put it before in the
30's, in the 40's and 50's, I can tell you that.

DO WE ABANDON THE VIOLENT?

Secondly, we who believe in nonviolence have got to make it
very very clear that while we resist and hate violence, we are
able to understand how much man can take and therefore any
Negro who resorts to violence will get our moral support, financial support and support in the courts, because it is wrong to
turn one's back on people who have been so demoralized and
trampled on that they literally have no choice except to fight
back, and then turn to them and say that was naughty. We
have got to make that clear or we have no ability to sell what
we truly mean when we say love.

Further, in social terms, my friends, most of the conflicts
which I've been in, the people didn't accept nonviolence in
our terms anyhow. That came afterwards. The fall in the crime
rate in Montgomery was the significant thing, not whether people said they loved white people, but that they stopped cutting
up themselves on Saturday night. For truly no man is capable
of loving his neighbor who does not love himself—that any

psychiatrist will quickly tell you. It is self-hate which is the basis of many of our problems and once we begin to love ourselves, only then are we truly capable of loving others and very clearly the Negro has to work through that.

B. *"The Harlem Riot and Nonviolence"*

From dusk till dawn for four nights during the tragic event called the Harlem Riot, I walked the streets with a team of 75 boys and men. We took the injured to CORE's first aid station or to the hospital. We dispersed crowds. We did what we could to protect women and children and had some minor success in urging police who had arrested innocent people to free them—especially when doing so contributed to crowd dispersal.

The experiences of those four terrible nights has deepened my faith in nonviolence and I should like to share with you some of my thoughts ten days later.

ENDS AND MEANS

We pacifists maintain that the law of ends and means does, in fact, operate. Never was this more clearly illustrated. Most of the people who engaged in disorder were youths between 18 and 25. They are the unemployed, the forgotten, the poorest of the poor—without hope and with no faith in a society which has doomed them to utter despair. It is they who are forced to live by their wits, seeking out a living by gambling, selling numbers or dope, and sometimes selling themselves.

They revolted in the only way left to them. They would make society listen. Like a child in an attention-seeking tantrum, they resorted to violence in a loud outcry of despair.

Bayard Rustin, "The Harlem Riot & Nonviolence," *WRL News* [War Resisters League], (July-August 1964), p. 3.

We pacifists claim that social progress must spring from social justice. In their ugly way, these youths were expressing what we, by nonviolent resistance, believe. If society will not remove the slums and give them work and dignity, they will cry out again.

VIOLENCE DEGRADES

We pacifists assert that violence degrades all who become involved in it. How true! I know many police officers in Harlem by name and many more by sight and reputation. One of the saddest aspects of those nights was the fact that many police officers who are among the better-behaved, reacted with the greatest fear and consequently with the most brutal conduct. I saw a white officer who had once turned over to me a 15-year-old thief on pledge that I take him home and report his behavior to his father—beat a woman to the ground mercilessly. When I urged him to stop, he turned on me.

On the other hand, I saw a Negro churchwoman help to blockade a street to stop a white taxi driver. After her sons had beaten him almost to unconsciousness, she helped them to rob him, leaving him in great agony on the street. Thus on those nights I saw violence degrade on every side. I heard men who usually talk reasonably, demand that youth be given guns to shoot "police and uncle toms."

FORCE STEMS PROGRESS

We pacifists urge nonviolence because if change toward justice is to take place, it must be in an atmosphere where creative conflict and debate are possible. Wherever great force is used— and I am certain from what I saw that the force used by police was far more than necessary to maintain order—it is used to support the status quo and not to encourage real debate and creative conflict.

The riot has not encouraged real debate: it has given

strength to the supporters of reaction. It has brought an injunction against certain groups. It has led to the police commissioner's temporarily prohibiting rallies in the name of law and order. It has brought division of leadership where unity was needed if nonviolent campaigns for justice are to be pursued. It has confused many young people. It has left the powers-that-be in a position to call for "law and order" for protection of white people—a very false position since the riot was economic rather than basically racial.

NONVIOLENCE IN A VIOLENT SITUATION

Perhaps the most important lesson I learned from this experience is that nonviolence is relevant to a degree—even when fear, brutality and violence rage. On the second afternoon of the riot, I spoke at a big Harlem church. Several speakers preceded me, calling upon youth to use violence. One speaker called for a Mau Mau, another for armed resistance to police. Another said: "I want 100 men to leave this church with me for guerrilla warfare."

Then I spoke and urged nonviolence. I was booed, applauded and then booed again. I appealed for 100 men to join me in the streets and work nonviolently "to end the brutality toward all men." When the meeting ended, I rose to leave the church and was surrounded by a hostile group intent on beating me. From the audience came 75 men who moved-in to protect me without violence. The hostile group scattered.

That night and for three succeeding nights, those 75 men walked in danger through the streets and were responsible for helping many persons and saving many lives. Some were beaten, as I was, for advocating nonviolence but only one deserted.

And so, reliving those four nights of terror and ugliness, I become more dedicated to nonviolence, for I see clearly how resort to violence dehumanizes all who are caught-up in its whirlpool.

PART X

Nonviolent Revolution

40. Reinhold Niebuhr,
"The Preservation of Moral Values
in Politics"

As a young pastor in Detroit during the 1920's, Reinhold Niebuhr
was inclined toward both socialism and pacifism. *Moral Man and
Immoral Society,* published in 1932, marked the transition from this
early phase of Niebuhr's thought to his later and better-known emphasis on the innate evil of man and the impossibility of a Kingdom
of God on earth. Niebuhr maintained that there was no intrinsic
moral distinction between violent and nonviolent resistance. But
Moral Man and Immoral Society retained to some degree Niebuhr's
early concern with the Social Gospel as well as anticipating his
later justification of war. In this chapter from the book, Niebuhr
demanded that Christians recognize the reality of class conflict and
the way in which nonviolence can be used to justify oppression

Any political philosophy which assumes that natural impulses,
that is, greed, the will-to-power and other forms of self-assertion, can never be completely controlled or sublimated by

reason, is under the necessity of countenancing political policies which attempt the control of nature in human history by setting the forces of nature against the impulses of nature. If coercion, self-assertion and conflict are regarded as permissible and necessary instruments of social redemption, how are perpetual conflict and perennial tyranny to be avoided? What is to prevent the instruments of today's redemption from becoming the chain of tomorrow's enslavement? A too consistent political realism would seem to consign society to perpetual warfare. If social cohesion is impossible without coercion, and coercion is impossible without the creation of social injustice, and the destruction of injustice is impossible without the use of further coercion, are we not in an endless cycle of social conflict? If self-interest cannot be checked without the assertion of conflicting self-interests how are the counter-claims to be prevented from becoming inordinate? And if power is needed to destroy power, how is this new power to be made ethical? If the mistrust of political realism in the potency of rational and moral factors in society is carried far enough, an uneasy balance of power would seem to become the highest goal to which society could aspire. If such an uneasy equilibrium of conflicting social forces should result in a tentative social peace or armistice it would be fairly certain that some fortuitous dislocation of the proportions of power would ultimately destroy it. Even if such dislocations should not take place, it would probably be destroyed in the long run by the social animosities which a balance of power creates and accentuates.

The last three decades of world history would seem to be a perfect and tragic symbol of the consequences of this kind of realism, with its abortive efforts to resolve conflict by conflict. The peace before the War was an armistice maintained by the balance of power. It was destroyed by the spontaneous combustion of the mutual fears and animosities which it created. The new peace is no less a coerced peace; only the equilibrium of social and political forces is less balanced than it was before

the War. The nations which pretended to fight against the
principle of militarism have increased their military power,
and the momentary peace which their power maintains is certain to be destroyed by the resentments which their power
creates.

This unhappy consequence of a too consistent political realism would seem to justify the interposition of the counsels of
the moralist. He seeks peace by the extension of reason and
conscience. He affirms that the only lasting peace is one which
proceeds from a rational and voluntary adjustment of interest to
interest and right to right. He believes that such an adjustment
is possible only through a rational check upon self-interest and
a rational comprehension of the interests of others. He points to
the fact that conflict generates animosities which prevent the
mutual adjustment of interests, and that coercion can be used
as easily to perpetuate injustice as to eliminate it. He believes,
therefore, that nothing but an extension of social intelligence
and an increase in moral goodwill can offer society a permanent solution for its social problems. Yet the moralist may be
as dangerous a guide as the political realist. He usually fails to
recognise the elements of injustice and coercion which are
present in any contemporary social peace. The coercive elements are covert, because dominant groups are able to avail
themselves of the use of economic power, propaganda, the
traditional processes of government, and other types of nonviolent power. By failing to recognise the real character of these
forms of coercion, the moralist places an unjustified moral onus
upon advancing groups which use violent methods to disturb a
peace maintained by subtler types of coercion. Nor is he likely
to understand the desire to break the peace, because he does
not fully recognise the injustices which it hides. They are not
easily recognised, because they consist in inequalities, which
history sanctifies and tradition justifies. Even the most rational
moralist underestimates them, if he does not actually suffer
from them. A too uncritical glorification of co-operation and

mutuality therefore results in the acceptance of traditional injustices and the preference of the subtler types of coercion to
the more overt types.

An adequate political morality must do justice to the insights
of both moralists and political realists. It will recognise that
human society will probably never escape social conflict, even
though it extends the areas of social co-operation. It will try to
save society from being involved in endless cycles of futile conflict, not by an effort to abolish coercion in the life of collective man, but by reducing it to a minimum, by counselling
the use of such types of coercion as are most compatible with
the moral and rational factors in human society and by discriminating between the purposes and ends for which coercion
is used.

A rational society will probably place a greater emphasis
upon the ends and purposes for which coercion is used than
upon the elimination of coercion and conflict. It will justify
coercion if it is obviously in the service of a rationally acceptable social end, and condemn its use when it is in the service
of momentary passions. The conclusion which has been forced
upon us again and again in these pages is that equality, or to
be a little more qualified, that equal justice is the most rational
ultimate objective for society. If this conclusion is correct, a
social conflict which aims at greater equality has a moral justification which must be denied to efforts which aim at the
perpetuation of privilege. A war for the emancipation of a
nation, a ,race or a class is thus placed in a different moral
category from the use of power for the perpetuation of imperial
rule or class dominance. The oppressed, whether they be the
Indians in the British Empire, or the Negroes in our own
country or the industrial workers in every nation, have a higher
moral right to challenge their oppressors than these have to
maintain their rule by force. Violent conflict may not be the
best means to attain freedom or equality, but that is a question
which must be deferred for a moment. It is important to insist,

first of all, that equality is a higher social goal than peace. It may never be completely attainable, but it is the symbol for the ideal of a just peace, from the perspective of which every contemporary peace means only an armistice within the existing disproportions of power. It stands for the elimination of the inequalities of power and privilege which are frozen into every contemporary peaceful situation. If social conflict in the past has been futile that has not been due altogether to the methods of violence which were used in it. Violence may tend to perpetuate injustice, even when its aim is justice; but it is important to note that the violence of international wars has usually not aimed at the elimination of an unjust economic system. It has dealt with the real or fancied grievances of nations which were uniformly involved in social injustice. A social conflict which aims at the elimination of these injustices is in a different category from one which is carried on without reference to the problem of justice. In this respect Marxian philosophy is more true than pacifism. If it may seem to pacifists that the proletarian is perverse in condemning international conflict and asserting the class struggle, the latter has good reason to insist that the elimination of coercion is a futile ideal but that the rational use of coercion is a possible achievement which may save society. It is of course dangerous to accept the principle, that the end justifies the means which are used in its attainment. The danger arises from the ease with which any social group, engaged in social conflict, may justify itself by professing to be fighting for freedom and equality. Society has no absolutely impartial tribunal which could judge such claims. Nevertheless it is the business of reason, though always involved in prejudice and subject to partial perspectives, to aspire to the impartiality by which such claims and pretensions could be analysed and assessed. Though it will fail in instances where disputes are involved and complex, it is not impossible to discover at least the most obvious cases of social disinheritance. Wherever a social group is obviously defrauded of its rights, it is natural to give the assertion of its rights a special measure of moral approbation. Indeed this is what is invariably and instinctively done by any portion of the human community which has achieved a degree of impartiality. Oppressed nationalities, Armenians fighting against Turkey, Indians against England, Filipinos against America, Cubans against Spain, and Koreans against Japan have always elicited a special measure of sympathy and moral approbation from the neutral communities. Unfortunately the working classes in every nation are denied the same measure of sympathy, because there is no neutral community which is as impartial with reference to their claims as with reference to the claims of oppressed nationalities. In the case of the latter there is always some group of nations, not immediately involved in the struggle, which can achieve and afford the luxury of impartiality. Thus Europeans express their sympathy for our disinherited Negroes and Americans have a special degree of interest in the struggle for the emancipation of India.

In spite of the partiality and prejudice which beclouds practically every social issue, it is probably true that there is a general tendency of increasing social intelligence to withdraw its support from the claims of social privilege and to give it to the disinherited. In this sense reason itself tends to establish a more even balance of power. All social power is partially derived from the actual possession of physical instruments of coercion, economic or martial. But it also depends to a large degree upon its ability to secure unreasoned and unreasonable obedience, respect and reverence. Inasfar as reason tends to destroy this source of its power, it makes for the diminution of the strength of the strong and adds to the power of the weak. The expropriators are expropriated in another sense beside the one which Marx analysed. Reason divests them of some of their moral conceit, as well as of some measure of the social and moral approbation of their fellows. They are not so certain of the approval of either their own conscience or that of the impartial community. Divested of either or both, they are like Samson with his locks shorn. A considerable degree of power has gone from them. The forces of reason in society are not strong enough to guarantee that this development will ever result in a complete equality of power; but it works to that end. The very fact that rational men are inclined increasingly to condemn the futility of international wars and yet to justify the struggles of oppressed nationalities and classes, proves how inevitably reason must make a distinction between the ultimate ends of social policies and how it must regard the end of equal social justice as the most rational one.

We have previously insisted that if the purpose of a social policy is morally and rationally approved, the choice of means in fulfilling the purpose raises pragmatic issues which are more political than they are ethical. This does not mean that the issues lack moral significance or that moral reason must not guard against the abuse of dangerous political instruments, even when they are used for morally approved ends. Conflict and coercion are manifestly such dangerous instruments. They are so fruitful of the very evils from which society must be saved that an intelligent society will not countenance their indiscriminate use. If reason is to make coercion a tool of the moral ideal it must not only enlist it in the service of the highest causes but it must choose those types of coercion which are most compatible with, and least dangerous to, the rational and moral forces of society. Moral reason must learn how to make coercion its ally without running the risk of a Pyrrhic victory in which the ally exploits and negates the triumph.

The most obvious rational check which can be placed upon the use of coercion is to submit it to the control of an impartial tribunal which will not be tempted to use it for selfish ends. Thus society claims the right to use coercion but denies the same right to individuals. The police power of nations is a universally approved function of government. The supposition is that the government is impartial with reference to any disputes arising between citizens, and will therefore be able to use its power for moral ends. When it uses the same power against other nations in international disputes, it lacks the impartial perspective to guarantee its moral use. The same power of coercion may therefore represent the impartiality of society, when used in intra-national disputes, and a threat against the interests of the larger community of mankind when used in international disputes. Thus the effort is made to organise a society of nations with sufficient power to bring the power of individual nations under international control. This distinction between the impartial and the partial use of social and political coercion is a legitimate one, but it has definite limits. The limits are given by the impossibility of achieving the kind of impartiality which the theory assumes. Government is never completely under the control of a total community. There is always some class, whether economic overlords or political bureaucrats, who may use the organs of government for their special advantages. This is true of both nations and the community of nations. Powerful classes dominate the administration of justice in the one, and powerful nations in the other. Even if this were not the case there is in every community as such, an instinctive avoidance of social conflict and such a superficiality in dealing with the roots of social disaffection, that there is always the possibility of the unjust use of the police power of the state against individuals and groups who break its peace, no matter how justified their grievance. A community may be impartial in using coercion against two disputants, whose dispute offers no peril to the life and prestige of the community. But wherever such a dispute affects the order or the prestige of the community, its impartiality evaporates. The prejudice and passion with which a staid, genteel and highly cultured New England community conducted itself in the Sacco-Vanzetti case is a vivid example. For these reasons it is impossible to draw too sharp a moral distinction between the use of force and coercion under the control of impartial tribunals and its use by individuals and groups who make it a frank instrument of their own interests.

The chief distinction in the problem of coercion, usually made by moralists, is that between violent and non violent coercion. The impossibility of making this distinction absolute has been previously considered. It is nevertheless important to make a more careful analysis of the issues involved in the choice of methods of coercion in the social process. The distinguishing marks of violent coercion and conflict are usually held to be its intent to destroy either life or property. This distinction is correct if consequences are not confused with intent. Non-violent conflict and coercion may also result in the destruction of life or property and they usually do. The difference is that destruction is not the intended but the inevitable consequence of non-violent coercion. The chief difference between violence and non-violence is not in the degree of destruction which they cause, though the difference is usually considerable, but in the aggressive character of the one and the negative character of the other. Non-violence is essentially non co-operation. It expresses itself in the refusal to participate in the ordinary processes of society. It may mean the refusal to pay taxes to the government (civil disobedience), or to trade with the social group which is to be coerced (boycott) or to render customary services (strike). While it represents a passive and negative form of resistance, its consequences may be very positive. It certainly places restraints upon the freedom of the objects of its discipline and prevents them from doing what they desire to do. Furthermore it destroys property values, and it may destroy life; though it is not generally as destructive of life as violence. Yet a boycott may rob a whole community of its livelihood and, if maintained long enough, it will certainly destroy life. A strike may destroy the property values inherent in the industrial process which it brings to a halt, and it may imperil the life of a whole community which depends upon some vital service with which the strike interferes. Nor

can it be maintained that it isolates the guilty from the innocent more successfully than violent coercion. The innocent are
involved with the guilty in conflicts between groups, not because of any particular type of coercion used in the conflict but
by the very group character of the conflict. No community can
be disciplined without affecting all its members who are dependent upon, even though they are not responsible for, its
policies. The cotton spinners of Lancashire are impoverished
by Gandhi's boycott of English cotton, though they can hardly
be regarded as the authors of British imperialism. If the
League of Nations should use economic sanctions against
Japan, or any other nation, workmen who have the least to do
with Japanese imperialism would be bound to suffer most from
such a discipline.

Non-co-operation, in other words, results in social consequences not totally dissimilar from those of violence. The differences are very important; but before considering them it is
necessary to emphasise the similarities and to insist that nonviolence does coerce and destroy. The more intricate and inter-
dependent a social process in which non-co-operation is used,
the more certainly is this the case. This insistence is important
because non-resistance is so frequently confused with nonviolent resistance. Mr. Gandhi, the greatest modern exponent
of nonviolence, has himself contributed to that confusion. He
frequently speaks of his method as the use of "soul-force" or
"truth-force." He regards it as spiritual in distinction to the
physical character of violence. Very early in his development of
the technique of non-violence in South Africa he declared:
"Passive resistance is a misnomer. . . . The idea is more completely expressed by the term 'soul-force.' Active resistance is
better expressed by the term 'body-force.'" A negative form of
resistance does not achieve spirituality simply because it is
negative. As long as it enters the field of social and physical
relations and places physical restraints upon the desires and
activities of others, it is a form of physical coercion. The con-

fusion in Mr. Gandhi's mind is interesting, because it seems to arise from his unwillingness, or perhaps his inability, to recognise the qualifying influences of his political responsibilities upon the purity of his original ethical and religious ideals of non-resistance. Beginning with the idea that social injustice could be resisted by purely ethical, rational and emotional forces (truth-force and soul-force in the narrower sense of the term), he came finally to realise the necessity of some type of physical coercion upon the foes of his people's freedom, as every political leader must. "In my humble opinion," he declared, "the ordinary methods of agitation by way of petitions, deputations, and the like is no longer a remedy for moving to repentance a government so hopelessly indifferent to the welfare of its charge as the Government of India has proved to be," an indictment and an observation which could probably be made with equal validity against and about any imperial government of history. In spite of his use of various forms of negative physical resistance, civil-disobedience, boycotts and strikes, he seems to persist in giving them a connotation which really belongs to pure non-resistance. "Jesus Christ, Daniel and Socrates represent the purest form of passive resistance or soul-force," he declares in a passage in which he explains the meaning of what is most undeniably non-violent resistance rather than non-resistance. All this is a pardonable confusion in the soul of a man who is trying to harmonise the insights of a saint with the necessities of statecraft, a very difficult achievement. But it is nevertheless a confusion.

In justice to Mr. Gandhi it must be said that while he confuses the moral connotations of non-resistance and non-violent resistance, he never commits himself to pure non-resistance. He is politically too realistic to believe in its efficacy. He justified his support of the British Government during the War: "So long as I live," he said, "under a system of government based upon force and voluntarily partook of the many facilities and privileges it created for me, I was bound to help that govern-

ment to the extent of my ability when it was engaged in war.
. . . My position regarding that government is totally different
today and hence I should not voluntarily participate in its
wars." Here the important point is that the violent character of
government is recognised and the change of policy is explained
in terms of a change in national allegiance and not in terms of
pacifist principles. His controversy with his friend C. F.
Andrews over his policy of permitting the burning of foreign
cloth and his debate with the poet Rabindranath Tagore about
the moral implication of the first non-violent resistance campaign in 1919–21, prove that in him political realism qualified
religious idealism, in a way which naturally bewildered his
friends who carried less or no political responsibility. The first
non-co-operation campaign was called off by him because it
issued in violence. The second campaign also resulted in
inevitable by-products of violence, but it was not called off for
that reason. Gandhi is not less sincere or morally less admirable
because considerations of political efficacy partly determine his
policies and qualify the purity of the doctrine of "ahimsa" to
which he is committed. The responsible leader of a political
community is forced to use coercion to gain his ends. He may,
as Mr. Gandhi, make every effort to keep his instrument under
the dominion of his spiritual ideal; but he must use it, and it
may be necessary at times to sacrifice a degree of moral purity
for political effectiveness.

The use of truth-force or soul-force, in the purer and more
exact meaning of those words, means an appeal to the reason
and goodwill of an opponent in a social struggle. This may be
regarded as a type of resistance, but it is not physical coercion.
It belongs in the realm of education. It places no external restraints upon the object of its discipline. It may avail itself of a
very vivid and dramatic method of education. It may dramatise
the suffering of the oppressed, as for instance Mr. Gandhi's
encouragement to his followers to endure the penalties of their
civil disobedience "long enough to appeal to the sympathetic

cord in the governors and the lawmakers." But it is still education and not coercion.

It must be recognised, of course, that education may contain
coercive elements. It may degenerate into propaganda. Nor can
it be denied that there is an element of propaganda in all education. Even the most honest educator tries consciously or unconsciously to impress a particular viewpoint upon his disciples.
Whenever the educational process is accompanied by a dis-
honest suppression of facts and truths, relevant to the point at
issue, it becomes pure propaganda. But even without such dis-
honest intentions there is, in all exchange of ideas, a certain
degree of unconscious suppression of facts or inability to see
all the facts. That is the very reason the educational process
alone cannot be trusted to resolve a social controversy. Since
reason is never pure, education is a tool of controversy as well
as a method of transcending it. The coercive elements in education do not become moral merely because they operate in
the realm of mind and emotion, and apply no physical restraints. They also must be judged in terms of the purposes
which they serve. A distinction must be made, and is naturally
made, between the propaganda which a privileged group uses
to maintain its privileges and the agitation for freedom and
equality carried on by a disinherited group. It may be true that
there is a difference in degree of coercive power between
psychological and physical types of coercion, as there is between violent and non-violent types. But such differences
would establish intrinsic moral distinctions, only if it could be
assumed that the least coercive type of influence is naturally
the best. This would be true only if freedom could be regarded
as an absolute value. This is generally believed by modern
educators but it betrays the influence of certain social and economic circumstances to a larger measure than they would be
willing to admit. Freedom is a high value, because reason cannot function truly if it is under any restraints, physical or
psychic. But absolute intellectual freedom is achieved by only

a few minds. The average mind, which is molded by a so-called free educational process, merely accepts contemporary assumptions and viewpoints rather than the viewpoints which might be inculcated by an older or a newer political or religious idealism. The very education of the "democratic" educators is filled with assumptions and rationally unverifiable prejudices, taken from a rapidly disintegrating nineteenth-century liberalism. Psychic coercion is dangerous, as all coercion is. Its ultimate value depends upon the social purpose for which it is enlisted.

Mr. Gandhi's designation of non-violence and non-co-operation as "soul-force" is less confusing and more justified when this emphasis upon non-violence of spirit is considered. Nonviolence, for him, has really become a term by which he expresses the ideal of love, the spirit of moral goodwill. This involves for him freedom from personal resentments and a moral purpose, free of selfish ambition. It is the temper and spirit in which a political policy is conducted, which he is really designating, rather than a particular political technique. Thus, while justifying his support of England during the War, he declared: "Non-violence works in a most mysterious manner. Often a man's actions defy analysis in terms of nonviolence; equally often his actions may bear the appearance of violence when he is absolutely non-violent in the highest sense of the term, and is subsequently found to be so. All I can claim for my conduct is that I was, in that instance cited, actuated in the interest of non-violence. There was no thought of sordid national or other interests." What Mr. Gandhi is really saying in these words is that even violence is justified if it proceeds from perfect moral goodwill. But he is equally insistent that non-violence is usually the better method of expressing goodwill. He is probably right on both counts. The advantage of non-violence as a method of expressing moral goodwill lies in the fact, that it protects the agent against the resentments which violent conflict always creates in both parties to a conflict, and that it proves this freedom of resentment and ill-will to the contending party in the dispute by enduring more suffering than it causes. If non-violent resistance causes pain and suffering to the opposition, it mitigates the resentment, which such suffering usually creates, by enduring more pain than it inflicts. Speaking of the non-violent resistance which Gandhi organised in South Africa he declared: "Their resistance consisted of disobedience to the orders of government, even to the extent of suffering death at their hands. Ahimsa requires deliberate self-suffering, not a deliberate injuring of the supposed wrong-doer. In its positive form, Ahimsa means the largest love, the greatest charity." Speaking before the judge who was to sentence him to prison during his first civil disobedience campaign in India he said: "Non-violence requires voluntary submission to the penalty for non co-operation with evil. I am therefore to invite and submit cheerfully to the highest penalty which can be inflicted upon me for what in law is a deliberate crime." The social and moral effects of these very vivid proofs of moral goodwill are tremendous. In every social conflict each party is so obsessed with the wrongs which the other party commits against it, that it is unable to see its own wrongdoing. A non-violent temper reduces these animosities to a minimum and therefore preserves a certain objectivity in analysing the issues of the dispute. The kindly spirit with which Mr. Gandhi was received during the course of the second Round-table Conference by the cotton spinners of Lancashire, whom his boycott had impoverished, is proof of the social and moral efficacy of this spiritual non-violence. It was one of the great triumphs of his method.

One of the most important results of a spiritual discipline against resentment in a social dispute is that it leads to an effort to discriminate between the evils of a social system and situation and the individuals who are involved in it. Individuals are never as immoral as the social situations in which they are involved and which they symbolise. If opposition to a system leads to personal insults of its representatives, it is always felt as an unjust accusation. William Lloyd Garrison solidified the south in support of slavery by the vehemence of his attacks against slave-owners. Many of them were, within the terms of their inherited prejudices and traditions, good men; and the violence of Mr. Garrison's attack upon them was felt by many to be an evidence of moral perversity in him. Mr. Gandhi never tires of making a distinction between individual Englishmen and the system of imperialism which they maintain. "An Englishman in office," he declares, "is different from an Englishman outside. Similarly an Englishman in India is different from an Englishman in England. Here in India you belong to a system that is vile beyond description. It is possible, therefore, for me to condemn the system in the strongest terms, without considering you to be bad and without imputing bad motives to every Englishman." It is impossible completely to disassociate an evil social system from the personal moral responsibilities of the individuals who maintain it. An impartial teacher of morals would be compelled to insist on the principle of personal responsibility for social guilt. But it is morally and politically wise for an opponent not to do so. Any benefit of the doubt which he is able to give his opponent is certain to reduce animosities and preserve rational objectivity in assessing the issues under dispute.

The value of reducing resentments to a minimum in social disputes does not mean that resentment is valueless and wholly evil. Resentment is, as Professor Ross observed, merely the egoistic side of the sense of injustice. Its complete absence simply means lack of social intelligence or moral vigor. A Negro who resents the injustice done his race makes a larger contribution to its ultimate emancipation than one who suffers injustice without any emotional reactions. But the more the egoistic element can be purged from resentment, the purer a vehicle of justice it becomes. The egoistic element in it may be objectively justified, but, from the perspective of an opponent in a social dispute, it never seems justified and merely arouses his own egotism.

Both the temper and the method of non-violence yield another very important advantage in social conflict. They rob the opponent of the moral conceit by which he identifies his interests with the peace and order of society. This is the most important of all the imponderables in a social struggle. It is the one which gives an entrenched and dominant group the clearest and the least justified advantage over those who are attacking the *status quo*. The latter are placed in the category of enemies of public order, of criminals and inciters to violence and the neutral community is invariably arrayed against them. The temper and the method of non-violence destroys the plausibility of this moral conceit of the entrenched interests. If the non-violent campaign actually threatens and imperils existing arrangements the charge of treason and violence will be made against it none-the-less. But it will not confuse the neutral elements in a community so easily. While there is a great deal of resentment in Britain against the Indian challenge of its imperial dominion, and the usual insistence upon "law and order" and the danger of rebellion by British imperialists, it does not have quite the plausible moral unction which such pretensions usually achieve.

Non-violent coercion and resistance, in short, is a type of coercion which offers the largest opportunities for a harmonious relationship with the moral and rational factors in social life. It does not destroy the process of a moral and rational adjustment of interest to interest completely during the course of resistance. Resistance to self-assertion easily makes self-assertion more stubborn, and conflict arouses dormant passions which completely obscure the real issues of a conflict. Non-violence reduces these dangers to a minimum. It preserves moral, rational and co-operative attitudes within an area of conflict and thus augments the moral forces without destroying them. The conference and final agreement between Mr. Gandhi and the Viceroy Lord Irwin, after the first Round-table Conference, was a perfect example of the moral possibilities of a non-violent social dispute. The moral resources and spiritual calibre of the two men contributed to its success. But it would have been unthinkable in a dispute of similar dimensions carried on in terms of violence. It was a telling example of the possibility of preserving co-operative and mutual attitudes within an area of conflict, when the conflict is conducted with a minimum of violence in method and spirit.

The differences between violent and non-violent methods of coercion and resistance are not so absolute that it would be possible to regard violence as a morally impossible instrument of social change. It may on occasion, as Mr. Gandhi suggests, be the servant of moral goodwill. And non-violent methods are not perfect proofs of a loving temper. During the War one sect of the pacifist Doukhobors petitioned the Canadian Government to withdraw the privileges of conscientious objectors from another sect which had disassociated themselves from it, "for no reason other than to satisfy the feeling of illwill towards their brothers." The advantages of non-violent methods are very great but they must be pragmatically considered in the light of circumstances. Even Mr. Gandhi introduces the note of expediency again and again, and suggests that they are peculiarly adapted to the needs and limitations of a group which has more power arrayed against it than it is able to command. The implication is that violence could be used as the instrument of moral goodwill, if there was any possibility of a triumph quick enough to obviate the dangers of incessant wars. This means that non-violence is a particularly strategic instrument for an oppressed group which is hopelessly in the minority and has no possibility of developing sufficient power to set against its oppressors.

The emancipation of the Negro race in America probably waits upon the adequate development of this kind of social and political strategy. It is hopeless for the Negro to expect complete emancipation from the menial social and economic position into which the white man has forced him, merely by trusting in the moral sense of the white race. It is equally hopeless to attempt emancipation through violent rebellion.

There are moral and rational forces at work for the improvement of relations between whites and Negroes. The educational advantages which have endowed Negro leaders to conduct the battle for the freedom of their race have come largely from schools established by philanthropic white people. The various inter-race commissions have performed a commendable service in eliminating misunderstanding between the races and in interpreting the one to the other. But these educational and conciliatory enterprises have the limitations which all such purely rational and moral efforts reveal. They operate within a given system of injustice. The Negro schools, conducted under the auspices of white philanthropy, encourage individual Negroes to higher forms of self-realisation; but they do not make a frontal attack upon the social injustices from which the Negro suffers. The race commissions try to win greater social and political rights for the Negro without arousing the antagonisms of the whites. They try to enlarge, but they operate nevertheless within the limits of, the "zones of agreement." This means that they secure minimum rights for the Negro such as better sanitation, police protection and more adequate schools. But they do not touch his political disfranchisement or his economic disinheritance. They hope to do so in the long run, because they have the usual faith in the power of education and moral suasion to soften the heart of the white man. This faith is filled with as many illusions as such expectations always are. However large the number of individual white men who do and who will identify themselves completely with the Negro cause, the white race in America will not admit the Negro to equal rights if it is not forced to do so. Upon that point one may speak with a dogmatism which all history justifies.

On the other hand, any effort at violent revolution on the

part of the Negro will accentuate the animosities and prejudices of his oppressors. Since they outnumber him hopelessly,
any appeal to arms must inevitably result in a terrible social
catastrophe. Social ignorance and economic interest are arrayed
against him. If the social ignorance is challenged by ordinary
coercive weapons it will bring forth the most violent passions
of which ignorant men are capable. Even if there were more
social intelligence, economic interest would offer stubborn
resistance to his claims.

The technique of non-violence will not eliminate all these
perils. But it will reduce them. It will, if persisted in with the
same patience and discipline attained by Mr. Gandhi and his
followers, achieve a degree of justice which neither pure moral
suasion nor violence could gain. Boycotts against banks which
discriminate against Negroes in granting credit, against stores
which refuse to employ Negroes while serving Negro trade,
and against public service corporations which practice racial
discrimination, would undoubtedly be crowned with some
measure of success. Non-payment of taxes against states which
spend on the education of Negro children only a fraction of
the amount spent on white children, might be an equally
efficacious weapon. One waits for such a campaign with all
the more reason and hope because the peculiar spiritual gifts
of the Negro endow him with the capacity to conduct it successfully. He would need only to fuse the aggressiveness of the
new and young Negro with the patience and forbearance of
the old Negro, to rob the former of its vindictiveness and the
latter of its lethargy.

There is no problem of political life to which religious imagination can make a larger contribution than this problem of
developing non-violent resistance. The discovery of elements of
common human frailty in the foe and, concomitantly, the appreciation of all human life as possessing transcendent worth,
creates attitudes which transcend social conflict and thus mitigate its cruelties. It binds human beings together by reminding

them of the common roots and similar character of both their vices and their virtues. These attitudes of repentance which recognise that the evil in the foe is also in the self, and these impulses of love which claim kinship with all men in spite of social conflict, are the peculiar gifts of religion to the human spirit. Secular imagination is not capable of producing them; for they require a sublime madness which disregards immediate appearances and emphasises profound and ultimate unities. It is no accident of history that the spirit of non-violence has been introduced into contemporary politics by a religious leader of the orient. The occident may be incapable of this kind of non-violent social conflict, because the white man is a fiercer beast of prey than the oriental. What is even more tragic, his religious inheritance has been dissipated by the mechanical character of his civilisation. The insights of the Christian religion have become the almost exclusive possession of the more comfortable and privileged classes. These have sentimentalised them to such a degree, that the disinherited, who ought to avail themselves of their resources, have become so conscious of the moral confusions which are associated with them, that the insights are not immediately available for the social struggle in the Western world. If they are not made available, Western civilisation, whether it drifts toward catastrophe or gradually brings its economic life under social control, will suffer from cruelties and be harassed by animosities which destroy the beauty of human life. Even if justice should be achieved by social conflicts which lack the spiritual elements of non-violence, something will be lacking in the character of the society so constructed. There are both spiritual and brutal elements in human life. The perennial tragedy of human history is that those who cultivate the spiritual elements usually do so by divorcing themselves from or misunderstanding the problems of collective man, where the brutal elements are most obvious. These problems therefore remain unsolved, and force clashes with force, with nothing to mitigate the brutalities or eliminate the futilities of the social struggle. The history of human life will always be the projection of the world of nature. To the end of history the peace of the world, as Augustine observed, must be gained by strife. It will therefore not be a perfect peace. But it can be more perfect than it is. If the mind and the spirit of man does not attempt the impossible, if it does not seek to conquer or to eliminate nature but tries only to make the forces of nature the servants of the human spirit and the instruments of the moral ideal, a progressively higher justice and more stable peace can be achieved.

41. David Dellinger, "The Future of Nonviolence"

In a final selection, David Dellinger directly confronts the relation of revolution and nonviolence. One of those who refused to cooperate with the draft law of 1940, Dellinger was imprisoned throughout the war. On one occasion he fasted sixty days to protest prison segregation. After the war, Dellinger founded a cooperative community, worked in Peacemakers and CNVA, and helped to edit *Liberation* magazine. He twice visited Cuba after its 1959 revolution. The impact of that experience is evident in Dellinger's contention that a violent revolution against injustice may in time become nonviolent, but nonviolence can never be used to protect injustice and exploitation.

David Dellinger, "The Future of Nonviolence," *Studies on the Left* (Winter 1965), pp. 90–96.

The theory and practice of active nonviolence are roughly at the stage of development today as those of electricity in the early days of Marconi and Edison. A new source of power has been discovered and crudely utilized in certain specialized situations, but our experience is so limited and our knowledge so primitive that there is legitimate dispute about its applicability to a wide range of complicated and critical tasks. One often hears it said that nonviolent resistance was powerful enough to drive the British out of India but would have been suicidal against the Nazis. Or that Negroes can desegregate a restaurant or bus by nonviolence but can hardly solve the problem of jobs or getting rid of the Northern ghettos, since both of these attempts require major assaults on the very structure of society and run head on into the opposition of entrenched interests in the fields of business, finance, and public information. Finally, most of those who urge nonviolent methods on the Negro hesitate to claim that the United States should do away with its entire military force and prepare to defend itself in the jungle of international politics by nonviolent methods.

I

There is no doubt in my mind that nonviolence is currently incapable of resolving some of the problems that must be solved if the human race is to survive—let alone create a society in which all persons have a realistic opportunity to achieve material fulfillment and personal dignity. Those who are convinced that nonviolence can be used in *all* conflict situations have a responsibility to devise concrete methods by which it can be made effective. For example, can we urge the Negroes of Harlem or the *obreros* and *campesinos* (workers and peasants) of Latin America to refrain from violence if we offer them no positive method of breaking out of the slums, poverty, and cultural privation that blight their lives and condemn their children to a similar fate? It is contrary to the best tradition of nonviolence to do so. Gandhi often made the point that it is better to resist injustice by violent methods than not to resist at all. He staked his own life on his theory that nonviolent resistance was the superior method, but he never counselled appeasement or passive non-resistance.

The major advances in nonviolence have not come from people who have approached nonviolence as an end in itself, but from persons who were passionately striving to free themselves from social injustice. Gandhi discovered the method almost by accident when he went to South Africa as a young, British-trained lawyer in search of a career, but was "sidetracked" by the shock of experiencing galling racial segregation. Back in India, the humiliations of foreign rule turned him again to nonviolence, not as an act of religious withdrawal and personal perfectionism, but in line with his South African experience, as the most practical method Indians could use in fighting for their independence. During World War I, not yet convinced that the method of nonviolence could be used successfully in such a large-scale international conflict, he actually helped recruit Indians for the British Army. By contrast, during World War II, after twenty more years of experimentation with nonviolence, he counselled nonviolent resistance to the Nazis and actually evolved a plan for nonviolent opposition to the Japanese should they invade and occupy India.

In 1956 the Negroes of Montgomery, Alabama catapulted nonviolence into the limelight in the United States, not out of conversion to pacifism or love for their oppressors, but because they had reached a point where they could no longer tolerate certain racial injustices. Martin Luther King, who later became a pacifist, employed an armed defense guard to protect his home and family during one stage of the Montgomery conflict. In 1963, one of the leaders of the mass demonstrations in Birmingham said to me: "You might as well say that we never heard of Gandhi or nonviolence, but we were determined to get

our freedom, and in the course of struggling for it we came
upon nonviolence like gold in the ground."

There is not much point in preaching the virtues of non
violence to a Negro in Harlem or Mississippi except as a
method for winning his freedom. For one thing, the built-in
institutional violence imposed on him every day of his life
looms too large. He can rightly say that he wants no part of a
nonviolence that condemns his spasmodic rock-throwing or
desperate and often knowingly unrealistic talk of armed self-
defense, but mounts no alternative campaign. It is all too easy
for those with jobs, adequate educational opportunities, and
decent housing to insist that Negroes remain nonviolent—to
rally to the defense of "law and order." "Law and order is the
Negro's best friend," Mayor Robert Wagner announced in the
midst of the 1964 riots in Harlem. But nonviolence and a repressive law and order have nothing in common. The most destructive violence in Harlem is not the bottle-throwing, looting, or
muggings of frustrated and demoralized Negroes. Nor is it the
frequent shootings of juvenile delinquents and suspected criminals by white policemen, who often reflect both the racial
prejudices of society and the personal propensity to violence
that led them to choose a job whose tools are the club and the
revolver. The basic violence in Harlem is the vast, impersonal
violation of bodies and souls by an unemployment rate four
times that of white New Yorkers, a median family income between half and two thirds that of white families, an infant
mortality rate of 45.3 per thousand compared to 26.3 for New
York as a whole, and inhuman crowding into subhuman housing. (It has been estimated that if the entire population of the
United States were forced to live in equally congested conditions, it would fit into three of New York City's five boroughs.)
Many white Americans are thrilled by the emotional catharsis
of a law-abiding March on Washington (or even a fling at
civil disobedience), in which they work off their guilt feelings,
conscious and unconscious, by "identifying" for a day with the

black victims of society. But when the project is over the whites do not return home anxious to know whether any of their children have been bitten by a rat, shot by a cop, or victimized by a pimp or dope peddler.

Commitment to nonviolence must not be based on patient acquiescence in intolerable conditions. Rather, it stems from a deeper knowledge of the self-defeating, self-corrupting effect of lapses into violence. On the one hand, Gandhi did not ally himself with those who profit from injustice and conveniently condemn others who violently fight oppression. On the other hand, he temporarily suspended several of his own nonviolent campaigns because some of his followers had succumbed to the temptations of violent reprisal. In perfecting methods of nonviolence, he gradually crystallized certain attitudes toward the nature of man (even oppressive, exploitative, foreign-invader man), which he formulated in the terminology of his native religion and which he considered indispensable for true nonviolence. Just as his basic insights have been translated by religious Western pacifists (including Martin Luther King) from their original language to that of Christianity, so they can be clothed without loss in the secular humanist terminology which is more natural to large numbers of Northern Negroes and white civil rights activists.

The key attitudes stem from a feeling for the solidarity of all human beings, even those who find themselves in deep conflict. George Meredith once said that a truly cultivated man is one who realizes that the things which seem to separate him from his fellows are as nothing compared with those which unite him with all humanity. Nonviolence may start, as it did with the young Gandhi and has with many an American Negro, as a technique for wresting gains from an unloved and unlovely oppressor. But somewhere along the line, if a nonviolent movement is to cope with deep-seated fears and privileges, its strategy must flow from a sense of the underlying unity of all human beings. So must the crucial, semi-spontaneous, inventive actions that emerge (for good or ill) in the midst of crisis.

This does not mean that Negroes, for example, must "love" in a sentimental or emotional way those who are imprisoning, shooting, beating, or impoverishing them. Nor need they feel personal affection for complacent white liberals. But it is not enough to abandon the use of fists, clubs, Molotov cocktails, and guns. Real nonviolence requires an awareness that white oppressors and black victims are mutually entrapped in a set of relationships that violate the submerged better instincts of everyone. A way has to be found to release the trap and free both sets of victims. Appeals to reasons or decency have little effect (except in isolated instances) unless they are accompanied by tangible pressures—on the pocketbook, for example —or the inconveniences associated with sit-ins, move-ins, strikes, boycotts or nonviolent obstructionism. But for any lasting gain to take place the struggle must appeal to the whole man, including his encrusted sense of decency and solidarity, his yearnings to recapture the lost innocence when human beings were persons to be loved, not objects to rule, obey, or exploit.

This reaching out to the oppressor has nothing to do with tokenism, which tends to creep into any movement, including a nonviolent one. In fact, tokenism is a double violation of the attitude of solidarity, because it permits the oppressor to make, and the oppressed to accept, a gesture which leaves intact the institutional barriers that separate them. One can gain a token victory or make a political deal without needing to have any invigorating personal contact with the "enemy," certainly without bothering to imagine oneself in his place so as to understand his needs, fears and aspirations. But the more revolutionary a movement's demands, the more imperative it is to understand what is necessary for the legitimate fulfillment of the persons who make up the opposition.

"We're going to win our freedom," a Negro leader said at a mass meeting in Birmingham last year, "and as we do it we're going to set our white brothers free." A short while later, when the Negroes faced a barricade of police dogs, clubs and fire hoses, they "became spiritually intoxicated," as another leader described it. "This was sensed by the police and firemen and it began to have an effect on them. . . . I don't know what happened to me. I got up from my knees and said to the cops: 'We're not turning back. We haven't done anything wrong. All we want is our freedom. How do you feel doing these things?' " The Negroes started advancing and Bull Connor shouted: "Turn on the water!" But the firemen did not respond. Again he gave the order and nothing happened. Some observers claim they saw firemen crying. Whatever happened, the Negroes went through the lines. The next day, Bull Connor was reported by the press to have said: "I didn't want to mess their Sunday clothes, all those people from church." Until now this mood of outgoing empathetic nonviolence has been rarely achieved in this country. It was only part of the story in Birmingham, where in the end a more cautious tokenism gripped the top leaders. But it is the clue to the potential power of nonviolence.

Vinoba Bhave indicates something of the same sort on the level of international conflict when he says: "Russia says America has dangerous ideas so she has to increase her armaments. America says exactly the same thing about Russia. . . . The image in the mirror is your own image; the sword in its hand is your own sword. And when we grasp our own sword in fear of what we see, the image in the mirror does the same. What we see in front of us is nothing but a reflection of ourselves. If India could find courage to reduce her army to the minimum, it would demonstrate to the world her moral strength. But we are cowards and cowards have no imagination."

II

The potential uses of nonviolent power are tremendous and as yet virtually unrealized. But it is important to understand that nonviolence can never be "developed" in such a way as to carry out some of the tasks assigned to it by its more naive converts—any more than God (or the greatest scientist) could draw a square circle. It would be impossible, for instance, to defend the United States of America, as we know it, nonviolently. This is not because of any inherent defect in the nonviolent method but because of a very important strength: nonviolence cannot be used successfully to protect special privileges that have been won by violence. The British could not have continued to rule India by taking a leaf out of Gandhi's book and becoming "nonviolent." Nor would the United States be able to maintain its dominant position in Latin America if it got rid of its armies, navies, "special forces," C.I.A.-guerrillas, etc. Does anyone think that a majority of the natives work for a few cents a day, live in rural or urban slums, and allow forty-four per cent of their children to die before the age of five because they love us? Or that they are content to have American business drain away five hundred million dollars a year in interest and dividends, on the theory that the shareholders of United Fruit Company or the Chase Manhattan Bank are more needy or deserving than themselves?

It follows that advocates of nonviolence are overly optimistic when they argue from the unthinkability of nuclear war and the partially proven power of nonviolence (in India and the civil rights struggle) to the position that simple common sense will lead the United States (the richest, most powerful nation in the world, on whose business investments and armed forces the sun never sets) to substitute nonviolent for violent national defense. In recent years a number of well-intentioned peace groups have tried to convince the government and members of the power elite that the Pentagon should sponsor studies with this end in view. But nonviolent defense requires not only willingness to risk one's life (as any good soldier, rich or poor, will do). It requires renunciation of all claims to special privileges and power at the expense of other people. In our society most people find it more difficult to face economic loss while alive than death itself. Surrender of special privilege is certainly foreign to the psychology of those who supply, command, and rely on the military. Nonviolence is supremely the weapon of the dispossessed, the underprivileged, and the egalitarian, not of those who are still addicted to private profit, commercial values, and great wealth.

Nonviolence simply cannot defend property rights over human rights. The primacy of human rights would have to be established within the United States and in all of its dealings with other peoples before nonviolence could defend this country successfully. Nonviolence could defend what is worth defending in the United States, but a badly needed social revolution would have to take place in the process. Guerrilla warfare cannot be carried on successfully without the active support and cooperation of the surrounding population, which must identify justice (or at least its own welfare) with the triumph of the guerrillas. Nonviolence must rely even more heavily than guerrilla warfare on the justice of its cause. It has no chance of succeeding unless it can win supporters from previously hostile or neutral sections of the populace. It must do this by the fairness of its goals. Its objectives and methods are intimately interrelated and must be equally nonviolent.

The followers of Gandhi were imprisoned, beaten and, on more than one occasion, shot by the British during the Indian independence campaign. Today, some Americans consider the death of a nonviolent campaigner as conclusive evidence that "nonviolence won't work" and call for substitution of a violent campaign—in which people will also be killed and the original aims tend to be lost in an orgy of violence. But instead of allowing the British in effect to arm them, thereby giving the British the choice of weapons, the Gandhians kept right on fighting nonviolently and in the end succeeded in "disarming" the British. A number of times the first row of advancing Indians was shot, but a second and a third row kept on moving forward until the British soldiers became psychologically incapable of

killing any more, even risking death at the hands of their
superiors by disobeying orders to keep on firing. Eventually it
became politically impossible for the commanders and the
Prime Ministers to issue such orders. Need I add that if the
Indians had been shot while trying to invade England and
carry off its wealth, it would not have mattered how courageously nonviolent they had been, they could not have aroused
this response.

If a Medgar Evers or a Goodman, Schwerner, or Cheney is
killed fighting for a cause that is considered unjust, he is
quickly dismissed as a fanatic. Indeed, at this stage of the
struggle that is exactly what many white Southerners have
done. But if the nonviolent warriors freely risk death in devotion to a cause that people recognize, even against their wills,
as legitimate, the act has a tremendous effect. Willingness to
sacrifice by undergoing imprisonment, physical punishment or,
if need be, death itself, without retaliation, will not always
dislodge deeply engrained prejudice or fear, but its general effect is always to work in that direction. By contrast, infliction of
such penalties at best intimidates the opposition and at worst
strengthens resistance, but in any case does not encourage
psychological openness to a creative resolution of the underlying conflict of views or values.

Perhaps we can paraphrase Von Clausewitz's well known observation that war is but the continuation of the politics of
peace by other means, and say that the social attitudes of nonviolent defense must be a continuation of the social attitudes of
the society it is defending. A little thought should convince us
of the impossibility of keeping Negroes and colonial peoples
in their present positions of inferiority once privileged white
America is unable to rely on overt or covert violence. Secondly,
it is ludicrous to expect such persons to join their oppressors
in the uncoerced defense of the society that has treated them so
poorly. (Even with the power of the draft at its disposal—
backed by the threat of imprisonment and ultimately the firing

squad—the United States found it necessary to make unprecedented concessions and promises to Negroes during World War II in order to keep up black morale.) Finally, there is the crucial question of how we can expect to treat our enemies nonviolently if we do not treat our friends and allies so.

On the crudest level, as long as we are willing to condemn two out of five children in Latin America to early death, in order to increase our material comforts and prosperity, by what newly found awareness of human brotherhood will we be able to resist the temptation to wipe out two out of five, three out of five, or even five out of five of the children of China in overt warfare if it is dinned into us that this is necessary to preserve our freedom, or the lives of ourselves and our own children? If we cannot respect our neighbors more than to keep large numbers of them penned up in rat-infested slum ghettos, how will we develop the sense of human solidarity with our opponents, without which nonviolence becomes an empty technicality and loses its power to undermine and sap enemy hostility and aggressiveness? How will we reach across the propaganda-induced barriers of hate, fear, and self-righteousness (belief in the superiority of one's country, race or system) to disarm ourselves and our enemies?

Index

THE AMERICAN HERITAGE SERIES

THE COLONIAL PERIOD

Adams, John   *The Political Writings of John Adams: Representative Selections*   AHS 8   George A. Peek, Jr.
The English Libertarian Heritage: From the Writings of John Trenchard and Thomas Gordon in The Independent Whig *and* Cato's Letters   AHS 32   David L. Jacobson
The Great Awakening   AHS 34   Alan Heimert, Perry Miller
Puritan Political Thought   AHS 33   Edmund S. Morgan

THE REVOLUTIONARY ERA

The American Revolution as a Democratic Movement   AHS 36   Alfred Young
The Antifederalists   AHS 38   Cecelia Kenyon
Early American Libertarian Thought: Freedom of the Press from Zenger to Jefferson   AHS 41   Leonard W. Levy
Franklin, Benjamin   *The Political Thought of Benjamin Franklin*   AHS 64   Ralph Ketcham
Paine, Thomas   *Common Sense and Other Political Writings*   AHS 5   Nelson F. Adkins

THE YOUNG NATION

Calhoun, John C.   *Disquisition on Government and Selections from the* Discourse   AHS 10   C. Gordon Post
Channing, William Ellery   *Unitarian Christianity and Other Essays*   AHS 21   Irving H. Bartlett
Democracy, Liberty, and Property: The State Constitutional Conventions of the 1820's   AHS 43   Merrill D. Peterson

The Library of Liberal Arts

Below is a representative selection from The Library of Liberal Arts. This partial listing—taken from the more than 200 scholarly editions of the world's finest literature and philosophy—indicates the scope, nature, and concept of this distinguished series.